MW01284935

THE SWORD AND THE CLAYMORE

A HISTORY OF THE BRITISH ISLES

First Edition

John Priestley

October 2011

Published by Lulu Books

www.lulu.com

© Copyright 2011

Lulu ID

ISBN 978-1-4478-6649-7

Author's email:
jrp_consultancy@yahoo.co.uk

ACKNOWLEDGEMENT

I would like to thank Dr Richard Walsh, former historian and librarian of Hull and Leeds Universities and of the BBC, for reviewing this book for me.

CONTENTS

By the same author and also published by Lulu Books:

Tyke on a Bike – the canals of northern Britain, as viewed by a Yorkshireman
Upward Road – first volume of autobiography
Get Rich Slow – second volume of autobiography

Chapter 1 – The Stone and Bronze Ages

In many respects, this is a standard history of the British Isles up until the end of the First World War in 1919. However, in one matter it does differ from similar histories, in that more weight is given to the period of prehistory and history up to the Norman Conquest than is usual. This is because, in the view of the author, this period, though remote, is one of the most important epochs in our history. The ancestors of most of the current population arrived in the country during this time. Some of the most important ancient monuments in northern Europe (such as Stonehenge and Hadrian's Wall) were built. The English language also arrived here, though not in a form which would be understood today. Also from these times come the foundations of the law, the English counties, the structure of society, most of the place names and river names, and even the national character. These are not remote considerations, because all any observer needs to do is to look at the physical characteristics of the people he passes in the street. If he is in Glasgow, the people will not look the same as they do in say York. The natives of Cornwall do not resemble the natives of Northumberland. Their histories are different, and it shows to this day.

In geological terms, until very recently most of the British Isles was covered in ice. At the ice maximum, England was connected to the continent, the Thames was a tributary of the Rhine and the North Sea was a mass of fens and islets. Scotland was connected to Ulster, and the Isle of Man and Anglesey were not islands. The ice did not even begin to melt until about 15,000 years ago, but once it began to recede, it did so quickly, in chaotic conditions of flood and torrent. By 9500 BC the ice had gone and continuous habitation of these islands could begin. Mankind had lived here before, to be sure, in the interglacial periods, when he at times shared the land with such exotic creatures as hippos, lions and hyenas. However during the peak of the ice ages man retreated like a sensible fellow to the south of France, where as Cro-Magnon man he drew cave paintings 30,000 years ago.

The country to which the people returned did not look quite the way it does today. In general, the south-east sank into the sea and the north rose out of it by isostatic recovery from the weight of the ice. The coastline took on an approximation to the one we see today, but with important differences. There has been much erosion in East Yorkshire and East Anglia since those times and indeed the important East Anglian medieval town of Dunwich now lies on the sea bed. The Humber Spit and the Romney Marshes in Kent did not exist. More importantly, the fenlands inland from the Wash were totally undrained and in practice stretched right up to where Stamford and Huntingdon now stand. The extensive marshes in Somerset were also unsuitable for much habitation at this time, and large parts of Staffordshire and Lancashire were unusable bogs. Large forests in the Weald, Gloucestershire (the Forest of Dean) and much of the midlands (including Sherwood Forest) presented a barrier to settlement into Norman times. The Pennines were virtually uninhabited in areas today where the valleys are crammed with towns. By way of contrast, some areas such as Dartmoor which are only moorland now were farmed in prehistoric times, and still carry old field boundaries.

However, some things have not changed, because the two-fold division into upland and lowland Britain continues to this day. A line drawn roughly from the mouth of the Tees to the mouth of the Exe marks the axis about which much of the history of the country has turned. North of this line are the older, harder rock formations out of which are carved Dartmoor, the Welsh mountains, the Pennines, the Cheviots and the Highlands and Islands of Scotland. South of it are the younger and softer limestones, chalk, sandstones and clays which have always been the main seat of agriculture and, until the Industrial Revolution, of the wealth of the country. The Industrial Revolution was also a geographical revolution in which upland Britain became for the first time, if temporarily, the economic heartland of Britain.

It used to be thought that this great north-south divide governed invasions of the country, the idea being that waves of invaders would arrive in Kent or Sussex and conquer lowland Britain. Their strength would then be dissipated in the hills of upland Britain, where old cultures and languages could survive for centuries afterwards. This did happen in the case of the Romans and William the Conqueror, both of whom took over the English population more or less unaltered with armies of only a few thousand men. The Anglo-Saxons, however, who migrated en masse as a people, spread from east to west. In the case of the Danes and Vikings, the boundary of the Danelaw was at right-angles to the Tees-Exe line, in a wavy line from Chester to London, through the heavily settled midlands.

The first people to arrive back in Britain could have walked here, because the land bridge to the continent still existed. After that became inundated, people would have arrived in dugout canoes and other small craft, finding their way up the rivers and getting onto high and dry ground as soon as possible. The first arrivals took place while the Middle Stone age or Mesolithic period was in progress. The characteristic tools of the period were microliths, small and finely shaped flints which were mounted using resin in wood or bone. These are found at many sites. One such is Star Carr, near Scarborough. Here they occur amongst the bones of dozens of animals, mainly red and roe deer, cracked open to extract the marrow.

The period of the Mesolithic was relatively short in Britain because starting from about 4,000 BC, agriculture arrived and the New Stone Age or Neolithic period had begun. Farming spread slowly at first as the land had to be cleared of forests. Not until about 1500 BC is there a dramatic increase in the pollens of grass and cereals, and a corresponding fall-off in those of oak and aspen. Until that time it is likely that a form of "slash and burn" agriculture was practised, where the woodland was cut down and burnt and the land was farmed for a few years until its fertility dropped. The farmers then moved on to clear more land. Settled agriculture on the same land, where the trees are uprooted and steps are taken to maintain fertility, would have been established later. The main farming tools were the mattock and the ard, a primitive wooden plough which could score a furrow in the earth, but which could not turn the sod.

So who were these Neolithic farmers? Agriculture was first established in the "Fertile Crescent" of the Middle East, especially in the valleys of the Tigris and the Euphrates (which stretch back into modern Turkey). Genetic evidence shows that there was some movement of farming people along the principal trade routes and valleys of Europe, but these new genes fall away north-westwards from Turkey. It seems that the local hunter-gathers largely changed their way of living, and learnt how to farm the land. However, tradition records that the first farmers in Ireland were "Partholon's people". Arriving at about 2000 BC, they are said to have come to Ireland from southern Italy and Sicily. Nevertheless, there is evidence of agriculture in Ireland before this time.

The characteristic tool of the Neolithic is the polished axe. Flint was the ideal material for this, and its uneven distribution across the country soon created its own infrastructure. In places where it was abundant it was actually mined. The remains of mines excavated in the thousand years after 2800 BC can be found at Grimes Graves in Norfolk. Some of these mines are forty feet deep and fifty feet wide at the surface. In places where there was no flint, fine-grained igneous rocks could be polished up and given a fine cutting edge. Centres of axe production of this type were located in the Lake District, Wales, Northern Ireland and Cornwall. Axes of both types are widely distributed across the country.

It is a fact that archaeology is the study mainly of stone and bone, and there is nothing likely to excite an archaeologist more than a good grave. In Ireland and northern Scotland are found passage graves. These are circular stone mounds containing a single burial chamber, accessed by a passage. The passage graves near Sligo in north-western Ireland have been reliably dated to approximately 4400 BC and are therefore the oldest man-made structures in the British Isles, and indeed some of the oldest in the world. Graves of this type are also found in Spain, Brittany and as far north as Sweden, so the culture which produced them spread very widely. It is not known whether these graves belong to the end of the Mesolithic or to the Neolithic age of the first farmers.

Where large numbers of bones have been found together in passage graves, as at Isbister in Orkney, it has been possible to arrive at an average age for the population. This comes out at less than 20 years from birth, though child mortality would have been high, so many people surviving childhood might expect to reach forty, though few reached fifty. The older bones show much evidence of arthritis but little of dental caries.

The largest and most impressive late Mesolithic or early Neolithic building in the British Isles is located in Ireland. This is the magnificent megalithic passage tomb at Newgrange, County Meath, thought to date from the period 3500-3000 BC. This is a much more sophisticated version of the passage graves found elsewhere in Ireland, and it is a massive structure, estimated to have taken 300 people 20 years to build. It is a kidney-shaped mound covering an area of about an acre, atop walls of dazzling white quartz, reconstructed after 1962 using stone found at the site. It is surrounded by 97 large kerbstones, some of them decorated with megalithic art including the three sculpted whorls which form the best-known symbol of prehistoric Ireland. The passage and chamber are illuminated by the sun at the winter solstice. No one knows who built this mound, but it was certainly not the Celts, who did not arrive till at least 2000 years later.

Another famous passage tomb is Maes Howe in the Orkneys. This is an earth mound, 35 feet high, lined with stone inside. It is linked culturally with Newgrange, with which it shares some architectural features. Once again the sun illuminates the passage and chamber at the midwinter solstice. The estimated date for Maes Howe is also 3500-3000 BC.

Probably also part of this culture are some of the most famous Neolithic ruins in Britain, the homesteads of Skara Brae, also in Orkney. There are few trees in Orkney so the locals were obliged to build in stone. These ruins date from about 3100 BC. There are eight houses, each one consisting of a single room about 20 by 13 feet. On either side of the front door are stone boxes which would have been filled with bracken and heather for use as beds. Each house has stone shelves, a stone hearth and even a stone dresser. The people were farmers, keeping cattle, sheep and pigs, growing barley and wheat, and supplementing their diet with shellfish. About 2450 BC some disaster struck and the inhabitants disappeared, leaving their possessions behind. The excavators even found a pot still standing on a dresser. (See plate, p. 99, Archaeology of the British Isles, Andrew Hayes.) Situated between Maes Howe and Skara Brea is a large and impressive stone circle, the Ring of Brodgar, almost certainly part of the same cultural complex.

Less well-known than Skara Brae but still of significant importance are the timber trackways which have been preserved in the Somerset Levels (marshes), laid down between 4000BC and 2000 BC. These linked up villages and allowed the exploitation of the marshes for fishing, fowling and summertime grazing. The creation of these tracks required large amounts of preparation and planning. A huge volume of timber went into them, and they were carefully maintained after construction. Dating from the same time in England and Wales are long barrows, trapezoidal mounds of earth contain communal burial chambers.

From around 3500 BC a new type of monument is found, the henge. This is a circular bank and a ditch, broken by one or two gaps. From the distribution of post-holes within the henges, it seems that they contained wood-framed buildings, tall at the centre. It has been estimated that the average henge would have required the work of 300 people over one year so clearly these were not small undertakings.

After 500 years or so, henges were no longer built, being replaced by stone circles. One of the largest of these is found at Avebury in Wiltshire, where the sheer size of the megaliths is awe-inspiring today, to say nothing of 5,000 years ago when it is thought to have been built. Only 17 miles to the south is the most famous stone circle of all, Stonehenge, the greatest prehistoric monument in northern Europe. Its construction spanned the Neolithic and early Bronze ages, from about 3000 BC to 1100 BC. Its current spectacular form dates from about 2000 BC. Two types of stone were used to build Stonehenge. The first type was "bluestone", a rock whose source is found in the Presceli mountains of west Wales, 240 miles away. Getting these huge stones into the middle of Salisbury Plain would have been an enormous logistical exercise. However some researchers insist on spoiling a good tale by saying that the stones are erratics, transported by glaciers and dumped when the ice melted. The trilithons (two upright stones topped by a third stone) which are visible today are made from another type of stone, a sandstone cut from the Marlborough Downs 20 miles from the monument.

Every year on midsummer day, modern-day "druids" turn up at Stonehenge, seemingly unaware that it was not a druidic monument. Druidism is a religion which is associated with the Celts, who did not arrive in England until 1000 years or more after the main part of Stonehenge was constructed.

There is strong evidence from the time of Stonehenge that the country was divided between east and west. A map of the distribution of stone circles shows that these are almost all found west of a line drawn north-south between Berwick-on-Tweed and the Isle of Wight, with heavy concentrations in Ireland and eastern Scotland. Clearly at this time, the country was under two cultures. The one in the east, which may have originated in Scandinavia, knew nothing of stone circles.

By custom the Bronze Age is deemed to begin around 2000 BC, but in fact there seems to be little change in the culture of the people until about 500 years later. This is the time when long barrows, which contained communal graves, gave way to round barrows, which held individual burials. Often the round barrows also contained rich grave goods including metallic objects such as swords. The nineteenth-century archaeologists whose passion it was to dig up these barrows could not help noticing that the round barrows also contained bodies with round heads, whilst the long barrows had people with long heads. Hence the expression "Long skulls in long barrows, round skulls in round barrows". Also, the remains of the roundheads were often accompanied by a new type of pot, known as a beaker. The Beaker People had arrived. This culture is known from many sites over Western and Central Europe. It is evident that the social organization of this people featured powerful chieftains. These people used bronze to create new and fearsome weapons quite beyond the technology of the stone axe. These included the first swords – it is not possible to make a stone sword.

It is thought that the Beaker people were originally of Mediterranean stock, but that they moved northwards and came to England from the Rhineland and Brittany. In one of the best-known burials, the "Amesbury Archer", where the grave not only contained a beaker but objects made of bronze and even gold, isotope analysis showed that the man had come from the Alps. The Beakers settled in numbers over the whole of eastern England, from the Yorkshire Wolds to the Thames. They retained the use of flint for common purposes, bronze being reserved for weapons and ceremonial ornaments. Bronze is an alloy of tin and copper. More of it would have become available over time as ores were extracted and smelted, the tin from Cornwall and the copper from the south-west of Ireland. Old and broken bronze items were not thrown away, but remelted into new artifacts. Scrap metal was a valuable commodity and was hoarded as such.

There is some debate in archaeological circles as to whether the Beaker culture spread by diffusion or by migration and conquest. As the skeletons are different shapes, there would seem to be little room for argument. The Stone Age people went with the Stone Age, or many of them did. Of course it is rare for a population to be replaced altogether, as a prehistoric invader was always on the lookout for slaves and fertile women.

There is an Irish tradition that the Beaker people arrived in that country from Greece by way of Scandinavia. This seems unlikely, but it is supported by the distribution of some types of Bronze Age cauldrons. Two hundred years later came the sons of Mil came to Ireland. The story goes that they had migrated up the Danube and down the Rhine, sailing from there to Spain and finally turning back to Ireland. They brought with them the riding of horses, royal forts and tombs. Whilst in Ireland they learnt to smelt gold to make ornaments and brooches. It is worth remarking that at the time of the Roman invasion, the population of Britain was divided into two types of Celts and then the Hibernians, who lived in Ireland and parts of north-west Scotland. This name is of course very similar to Iberia, the Roman name for Spain. Tradition amongst the Silurian tribe of South Wales, found there by the Romans, indicates that the people migrated there from Spain, though at what time is unclear. There is a similar tradition in Scotland that the people came from Scythia, on the shores of the Black Sea, via the Straits of Gibraltar and Spain. This story is even found in Scotland's statement of independence, the Declaration of Arbroath of 1320.

Also of note is that archaeologists recognize a distinctive Atlantic culture in the west of the country, in Cornwall, Wales, Ireland, Western Scotland and also in Brittany and the western part of the Iberian peninsula, lasting from around 1300 BC to 600 BC. Communications by sea would in this period have been much easier than by land so this is quite feasible.

The late Bronze Age passes into the Iron Age at around 500 BC. All archaeologist agree that by the time of the Iron Age, most of the population of the British Isles was Celtic-speaking, so before considering those people, about whom a great deal is known – indeed, they are still with us – it is worth asking, who were the British people up to that point?

The longest-established people in Europe are thought to be the Basques of southern France and northern Spain. Not only is the Basque language quite unlike any other in Europe, but also Basque genes are distinctive. It is possible – indeed likely – that this population was much more widespread than it is today, before the coming of the Indo-Europeans, and Basque-type people may well have been the aboriginal inhabitants of the British Isles. In terms of languages, both Celtic and the Teutonic languages (of which English is one) are Indo-European. It is thought that the previous languages of Britain were from the non-Indo-European Uralo-Altaic group, which today includes Finnish and Hungarian. This group is also known as the Scythian. In any event, it is apparent that a certain portion of the population came originally from the Mediterranean area, and this is reflected today in the physiognomy and in particular the dark hair colouring of many of the people of Scotland, Ireland, Wales and Cornwall.

Talk of large-scale movements of population and of racial types is not fashionable today amongst archaeologists, but there is no doubt that mass migrations did take place, not only in prehistoric times but right through the time of the Roman Empire (when they were well-documented) and well into the medieval period. The fact is that the dislocations of plague and warfare could easily lead to famine and the depopulation of whole regions, giving an opportunity for tribal movement such as scarcely existed in later times. We shall see examples of this when we examine the movements of the Celts and Anglo-Saxons.

Chapter 2 – The Iron Age and the Celts

Celtic is a description of a language rather than a race - the only way to identify a Celt would have been to speak to him. The Celts are also known as the Gauls, and the Galatians (as in St Paul's epistle to the Galatians). As far as the British Celts are concerned, there were (and are) two versions of the language, Q-Celtic and P-Celtic. "Q" is rather misleading as it is the letter that philologists use to distinguish a "K" sound. Thus:

Q-Celtic	P-Celtic	English
Cluv	Pluv	Feather
Mac	Map	Son
Clanna	Plant	Children

Q-Celtic is the language of Ireland, spreading from there to Scotland as Gaelic. Forms of P-Celtic are Welsh, Cornish and Breton. The Q-Celtic speakers are sometimes known as the Goidels, the P-Celtic as the Brythons, or Britons. From this point on in this book, "British" means these people, the Celtic speakers originally of England. The Isle of Man was a P-Celtic area until it was invaded by the Irish in about 400 AD and switched to Q-Celtic.

There is a question mark over the Picts, in this period the people of Scotland. There are no written records of them until a late date, so were they Celts, or not? Certainly by the time written records do emerge, in the ninth century AD, they had become Celtic speakers. Little is known about the Picts, but as Scotland was divided into many kingdoms in medieval times, and different groups were described by the Romans, the "Picts" were hardly one people. It is safe to assume that Scotland was occupied by many different tribes, as England was when the Romans arrived. The main base of at least one of these tribes was the rich agricultural area round the Moray Firth, in eastern Scotland, with its centre at Burghead. Some of these tribes would certainly be Pre-Celtic, but at some point, they learnt the Celtic language. Others would have arrived already speaking the language.

However one people have been identified living in northern Britain known to the Romans as the Atecotti, which translates as the very old people, the aborigines. A small number of inscriptions of their language have been found, written in the Irish Ogham characters. The speakers of this language had made an attempt to express it in Irish characters. The inscriptions appear to be absolute gibberish, undecipherable to any linguist – what could "besmeqqnanammovoez" or "ahehhttan" mean? In early medieval times Scotland was in fact a multilingual place with half a dozen different languages, and one old man turned up at Columba's monastery in Iona speaking a language that no one could recognize.

As the Goidels occupy the western extremities of the British Isles, it is tempting to think that their distribution was once much more widespread, and that they were pushed into the corners by the British, in much the same way as the British were (eventually) pushed into the corners by the Anglo-Saxons. However, archaeologists are wary of jumping to conclusions today, though pre-war historians had no such reservations.

The Celts are identified with two major cultures in central Europe, the first being the Halstatt culture from Austria. Halstatt was the site of salt mining over many generations, between 750 BC and 450 BC. There are many different types of artifact associated with it, so that it is customarily divided into several sub-cultures. The second major Celtic culture is the La Tene from Lake Neuchatel in Switzerland, with dates from 450 BC to 350 BC. From central Europe the Celts fanned out as far as Galatia in Anatolia (modern Turkey), Spain (Galicia), and Italy, where in 390 BC or thereabouts they sacked Rome after the battle of Allia. In fact the Celts made a great impression on the Romans and the Greeks, and some wonderful statuary resulted, most famously the "Dying Celt", thought to be a Roman copy of a Greek statue (see plate p. 360, *Prehistoric Europe*, ed. Barry Cunliffe).

However the main place where the Celts went and stayed was France – Gaul, to the Romans, the land of Celts and druids. From France (and Belgium) they crossed into England, and of course Wales (the Pays de Galles). It is clear that the Celts arrived in these islands in many waves, over a long period, starting perhaps around 550 BC, or earlier. The first invasion colonized the south-east and parts of the north-west of England in the period 550-350 BC and is known as "Iron Age A". The invaders came from the Halstatt tradition. Over the next

200 years was a second phase of invasions, this time of La Tene people – "Iron Age B". The interaction between these two groups may have given rise to that most famous of all British Iron Age features, the hill fort.

Although it is not certain that large numbers of Celts actually replaced the aboriginal population of England, in some cases it is clear that they did. One example is found in East Yorkshire, where burials containing wheeled vehicles mirror La Tene culture. The tribe occupying this area in Roman times was known as the Parisi. The Romans recognized a tribe of the same name in Gaul. There were further movements of Celts into England in the second and first centuries BC (Iron Age C), for whom our witness is none other than Julius Caesar. At the time of his invasions of 55 and 54 BC he states that two of the tribes of south-east England, the Atrebates and the Catevellauni, were recent arrivals, branches of Germanic Belgic tribes on the other side of the Channel who has come as raiders and settled. Some researchers have tried to date this tribal movement later than 54 BC, but it would take a brave archaeologist to contradict Julius Caesar, a contemporary witness with no particular axe to grind. Also, recently some archaeologists have questioned whether the people described by Julius Caesar as the Gauls, living between the Garonne and Somme rivers across central France, really were the successors of the Halstatt and La Tene peoples of central Europe, known to the earlier Greeks. Whether or not they were, there seems little doubt that Celtic speakers did indeed fan out all the way from Ireland to central Turkey, as later writers from Britain expressed immense surprise at finding blond-haired, blue-eyed people in Turkey (the Galatians) who spoke a language similar to their own.

Irish tradition recalls the arrival of the people of Labraid in around 600 BC, early in the Atlantic Iron Age. It is thought that this immigration may have brought the Celtic language to Ireland.

Despite their later reputation as wild Highlanders and Irishmen, the Celts were a relatively sophisticated people, far in advance of the Mesolithic cave-dwellers who had arrived in Britain only a few thousand years earlier. The Halstatt and La Tene cultures were contemporary with the flowering of Ancient Greece in Athens and have produced some wonderful artifacts, in Europe at least. An important collection of these came from a chieftain's grave at Hochdorf near Stuttgart, and included a funerary wagon and a wheeled bronze couch upon which the body was laid.

As a fighting force, the Celts had considerable success. This is the description of a Celtic army given by the Greek historian Polybius, describing the scene at the battle of Telemon in Tuscany in 225 BC. The Roman soldiers were most alarmed by:

"...the fine order of the Celtic host, and the dreadful din, for there were innumerable horn-blowers and trumpeters, and as the whole army were shouting their war-cries out there was such a tumult of sound that is seemed all the country round had got a voice and caught up the cry. Very terrifying too were the gestures of the naked warriors in front, all in the prime of life and finely built men, and all the leading companies richly adorned with gold torcs and armlets."

(Quoted on p. 87, *Iron Age Britain*, Barry Cunliffe)

There are many other contemporary descriptions of Celtic warriors:

"Almost all of the Gauls are of tall stature, fair and ruddy, terrible for the fierceness of their eyes, fond of quarrelling and of overbearing insolence." (Ammianus)

"On whatever pretext you stir them up, you will have them ready to face danger, even if they have nothing on their side but their own strength and courage." (Strabo)

"To the frankness and high-spiritedness of their temperament must be added the traits of childish boastfulness and love of decoration. They wear ornaments of gold, torques on their necks and bracelets of their arms and wrists, while people of high rank wear dyed garments besprinkled with gold. It is this variety which makes them unbearable in victory and so completely downcast in defeat." (Strabo)

(Quoted on p. 362-3 of *Prehistoric Europe*, ed. Barry Cunliffe)

The author Robert Graves literally adds more colour than an archaeologist would dare to do, using contemporary Latin sources (including Julius Caesar). This is how he describes the races of Britain (in *Claudius the God*, pp 211-213, first published in 1934), at the time of the Roman invasion of 43 AD:

21

"The aboriginal inhabitants, a small, dark-haired people, were dispossessed about the time Rome was founded [in 753 BC], by an invasion of Celts from the south-east. Some still maintain themselves independently in small settlements in inaccessible mountains or marshes; the rest became serfs and mixed their blood with that of their conquerors…These Celts, whose language is akin to primitive Latin, were called Goidels – a tall, sandy-haired, big-limbed, boastful, excitable but noble race, gifted in all the arts, including fine metalwork, music and poetry; they still survive, in northern Britain…..Four or five hundred years later another Celtic nation appeared in northern Europe, those tribes we call the Galates….These Galates are also a gifted people; though inferior to the earlier Celts in arts, they are more united in spirit and finer fighting men. They are of middle stature with brown or black hair, round chins and straight noses. At about the time of the Allia disaster [390 BC] some tribes of this nation invaded Britain by way of Kent…and compelled the Goidels to spread out fanwise before them, so that these are now only found, except as serfs, in the North of Britain and in the neighbouring island of Ireland. The Galates who went to Britain became known as Brythons, or painted men, because they used caste-marks of blue dye on their faces and bodies, and have given their name to the whole island. However, 200 years later still came a third race of Celts, moving up the Rhine from Central Europe. These were the people whom we call the Belgians, the same that are now settled along the Channel Coast and are known as the best fighting men in France. They are a mixed race, akin to the Galates but with German blood in them; they have light hair, big chins, and aquiline noses. They invaded Britain by way of Kent and established themselves in the whole southern part of the island with the exception of the south-west corner, which was still occupied by the Brythons and their Goidel serfs."

Note that Graves clearly identifies Iron Ages A, B and C.

When they settled down on the land in Britain, the Iron Age farmers built farmhouses, almost always with storage pits dug into the ground, and granaries capable of storing grain on stilts above the ground. The ard was still in use, but recent experiments with ards fitted with iron shoes on the share show that they could be very effective in turning even heavy clay soil. Improved crops were introduced, spelt wheat replacing the earlier emmer wheat and hulled barley replacing naked barley. These crops yielded twice as much protein as their predecessors and could have supported a much bigger population than was at one time thought possible.

Sheep were kept for their wool and many artifacts were in use to support weaving, including the spindlewhorls and loomweights commonly found on archaeological digs. Metalworking was also widespread. Iron has some great advantages over bronze. Firstly it only requires one ore, iron oxide, and this is much more common in nature than tin or copper. Secondly it is more hard-wearing than bronze, and yields a sharper edge. (However, it does rust!) Whereas bronze artifacts could be created in moulds from melted bronze, iron tools had to be forged and hammered into shape from the mixture of iron and slag that came out of the smelting process. Another new artifact appeared late in this period, in the first century BC – the coin. This of course is a great boon to the archaeologist, who likes nothing better, because coins allow much closer dating of a site than anything else. If a hoard of coins is found bearing the head of say the emperor Trajan but none with the heads of later emperors, then the chances are that the site dates from Trajan's reign.

The most characteristic feature of the Iron Age Britain was of course the hill fort. In fact these massive constructions are mostly located south-west of a line drawn between Chester and Brighton, with heavy concentrations in what became Wessex and in the Welsh borders. By the time the Romans arrived the country was divided up into tribal areas typically the size of two or three counties, so it seems likely that any single tribal area in the south and south-west would have included a number of hill forts.

Some of the hill forts are truly impressive constructions. From what remains of them today (quite a lot), they were by far the largest constructions undertaken up to this time. The best-known of all, Maiden Castle near Dorchester (see plate p. 92, Archaeology of the British Isles, Andrew Hayes), covers 47 acres, the central and relatively flat area being entirely surrounded by three successive sets of massive earth ramparts which at one time would have carried their own fortifications on top. This was the tribal capital of the Durotriges. Hill forts must have been effective at that time because so many were built at such a high cost in labour. Certainly the typical armed chariot rider of the period would have been useless against one. However, they were not effective against Roman tactics. The future emperor Vespasian stormed Maiden Castle through its eastern gate, having softened it up first with catapulted iron bolts. Here archaeologists discovered mass graves, possibly the casualties of this action.

In the north east of England and the southern part of Scotland, few hill forts were built. However the homesteads were still heavily defended with circuits of banks and ditches – these must have been turbulent times. In the north and west of Scotland including the Shetlands and Orkney, there were other types of defensive structures, duns and brochs, built of stone. The brochs, resembling home-made cooling towers up to 50 feet high, are impressive, complicated constructions. They would have required specialist knowledge to build and are quite unlike anything else constructed in Britain. All of them date from the period 100 BC to 100 AD. They are nothing to do with the Romans, being located mainly in the northern mainland and on Orkney and Shetland.

Chapter 3 – The Romans

In 55 BC Julius Caesar had completed the conquest of Gaul and he decided to cross the Channel to England, where the local tribes had been abetting his foes in Gaul and indeed which in some cases recognized the overlordship of Gaulish tribal leaders. His first expedition was a fairly small-scale affair attempted late in the campaigning season. He soon hurried back to France, empty-handed, but returned the following year with five legions (about 25000 men) and 2000 cavalry. This was a serious expedition involving 600 transports and 28 warships, an armada in its day. Caesar fought his way to Wheathampstead (near St Albans), the capital of the Catuvellauni, which he stormed. His army came under heavy pressure and, fearing trouble in Gaul, Caesar once again withdrew back over the Channel. He had been well advised about the situation in Gaul because a major revolt did develop that winter under the leadership of Vercingetorix. This saw Caesar involved in some of the heaviest fighting of his whole career. When that revolt was put down, Caesar returned to Rome and overturned the Republic and the constitution by making himself the effective emperor. This move cost him his life. However an imperial structure was soon set up in Rome, under Augustus. Distractions elsewhere meant that the Romans did not return to Britain until 43 AD.

The inspiration for the invasion of 43 AD was the Emperor Claudius, who had attained his position on the murder of his nephew Caligula two years earlier. He became emperor by default, because he was the only male adult member on the imperial family left, many of the others having been murdered by his grandmother, Lyvia. This story has been told to with great panache by Robert Graves in his books *I Claudius* and *Claudius the God*, and indeed part of it was televised. With a club foot and a pronounced stammer, Claudius was thought to be too feeble physically to be worth murdering. In order to bolster his position, he wanted a military triumph, and the conquest of Britain was his selected objective.

The Britain to which the Romans returned after nearly 90 years had in many respects moved on. The south-east had already begun to resemble a Roman province. Latin traders had established themselves in the main towns, bringing wine, glass, amber and rich ornaments from the continent in exchange for corn, minerals and slaves. Gold and silver coins were being struck in the Roman manner. In the meanwhile, the Belgic Catevellauni under their king Cymbeline (subject of a play by Shakespeare) had continued to expand and give problems to their neighbours. Cymbeline died and was succeeded by his son Bericus. However, Bericus did not command the respect of his people, and was soon ousted by his brothers, Caractacus and Togodumnus, so he sought assistance from the Romans.

Forewarned by the failure of Julius Caesar, this time the Romans were taking no chances. They collected an army of invasion of about 40,000 men, much reinforced in later campaigns. Under Aulus Plautius a successful landing was made, and the Thames was crossed. Closing in for the kill before Colchester, Aulus Plautius sent for Claudius himself, who lead his troops to victory – in fact not only troops, but also a weird assembly of elephants and camels, whose very smell terrified the British cavalry. The Romans won this sort of pitched battle easily, because despite their wild flamboyance, the British chariots represented military tactics by now hundreds of years out of date.

Conquest of the rest of Britain at first ran smoothly, with a defensive line set up along the Fosse Way, the military road that was built between Exeter (Isca) and Lincoln (Lindum), within a few years. After that, things were not so easy. The British leader Caractacus organized a stiff and effective resistance, particularly in the lands across the Severn. He was eventually betrayed and captured in 51 AD. Claudius spared his life and proudly paraded him in Rome, praising the clean campaign he had fought, for Caractacus had not tortured or executed prisoners or poisoned wells. However, the fight did not end with the capture of Caractacus – indeed, it intensified, and lasted for several generations. In 61 there was a major revolt of the Iceni of East Anglia, led by their red-haired queen, Boadicea (Boudicca). Her husband, Prasutagus, had cooperated with the Romans and had the status of a client king. When he died, she offered to share the kingdom with the emperor Nero. However the local Romans had it declared a slave province, as if it had resisted rather than cooperated with the Romans. Boadicea was publicly flogged and her two daughters were raped; this sparked an immediate response. The revolt was truly terrifying for the Romans.

Their main cities at St Albans (Verulamium) and Colchester (Camulodunum) were burnt to the ground. According to Tacitus:

"Something like 70,000 Roman citizens and other friends of Rome died in the places I have mentioned. The Britons took no prisoners, sold no captives as slaves and went in for none of the usual trading of war. They wasted no time in getting down to the bloody business of hanging, burning and crucifying. It was as if they feared that retribution might catch up with them while their vengeance was only half-complete."

(Quoted in *Roman Britain*, Peter Salway)

Retribution did catch up with them. One legion was all but wiped out, but the Romans recovered and suppressed the revolt. Boadicea took her own life rather than fall into the hands of the Romans, and has been remembered as a British heroine ever since.

Gradually Roman rule was established. The most effective early governor was Agricola, who arrived in 78 and was recalled in 86. He had a great deal of difficulty with the Welsh tribes, in particular the Ordovices of north Wales. He solved this problem by massacring the whole tribe. His campaigns took him north of Perth, in Scotland, where he won a victory at Mons Graupius. Agricola gets good notices from the historian Tacitus, but then, Tacitus was his son-in-law. We would find it hard to condone the butchery of the Ordovices, although this type of behaviour was just one of the options considered valid for a Roman general. Julius Caesar had done the same thing at Avaricum in Gaul. The recall of Agricola meant that much of the territory he had conquered was surrendered back to the Picts.

In 122 AD the Emperor Hadrian visited his still-active British front, which by now must have cost Rome a vast fortune to maintain, and decided to cut his losses by building his famous wall, thereby giving up the dream of conquering the whole island after nearly 80 years. The wall stretched 73 miles from Wallsend (appropriately named) outside Newcastle in the east to Bowness on the Solway Firth in the west. This is the largest and most permanent monument left by the Romans in Britain; much of it still survives, partially rebuilt. A full infrastructure was put in to support it, including a military road parallel to it and major forts for garrisons behind it. In time it was manned by soldiers from all over the empire and it is known that the Persian sun god Mithras was worshipped on the wall.

Within 20 years another Roman wall was built, the Antonine Wall, stretching almost 37 miles between the Forth and the Clyde, the narrowest traverse of Scotland. This was a turf wall built on stone foundations, but otherwise it was similar to Hadrian's Wall with a defensive ditch in front of it and a network of milecastles, auxiliary forts and a military road. However the Antonine Wall was only operational for a generation before the defensive line was withdrawn once more to Hadrian's Wall.

Although there was no wall, Wales was scarcely more conquered than Scotland, and major garrisons were maintained at Chester and Caerlon (on the Usk) to keep the Welsh in check. A map of Roman villas shows a very striking distribution. Virtually all of them were south of the Tees-Exe line. There were none or very few indeed in Cornwall, Devon, Cumbria, Lancashire or the West Midlands. While the south-east of the country became thoroughly Romanised with all the paraphernalia of Roman life – the cities, vineyards, villas, mosaics, basilicas – the rest of the country was either unoccupied, or a military zone. The Roman way of life only ever extended to half of what is now England, and a small part of South Wales. (See map, p. 105, *Archaeology of the British Isles*, Andrew Hayes.)

Another enduring aspect of Roman life was the road network, set up at first for military purposes. These were the best roads that Britain had right up to the era of the turnpike roads in the eighteenth century. They ran straight and true wherever possible. The best-known roads are Ermine Street, running from London (Londinium) to York via Lincoln, where it is joined by the Fosse Way (see above); and Watling Street, running from the Kent coast at Richborough via London and St Albans to Wroxeter (Virconium).

Also many new towns were built; up to this time the amount of urban development had been strictly limited. Many of these towns were strategically located and resumed life at some point after the Romans had left. Others, however, were never reoccupied, including Silchester (Calleva Atrebatum) in Hampshire (chief town of the Atrebates) and Wroxeter (near Shrewsbury, a centre for the Cornovii), which is convenient for archaeologists. However, only five towns possessed full civic liberties – Colchester, Gloucester (Glevum), Lincoln, York and St Albans (not London!). The development of towns helped to create commercial agriculture, for the townspeople had to be fed, and a relatively sophisticated market economy sprung up for the first time. Such an economy contains many dependencies and proved too delicate to survive a major upheaval such as took place when the Romans eventually left.

At one time it was thought that the Roman-age farmers confined themselves to the light soils of the chalk and limestone found in southern and eastern England. However there is now evidence that the heavy clays soils so common in the London basin and the Midlands were also exploited during this period.

The booming market economy and the arrival of new and improved strains of cereals, fruit and vegetables plus the availability of a true plough caused something of a population explosion. Villas sprang up, normally at the centre of a country estate, with central heating, baths and mosaic floors. The south-east was transformed, though the taxes must have been punitive as there was a standing army of 50,000 men to pay for. Gold and silver coinage was widespread, facilitating trade. Certain artifacts crop up regularly on digs, particularly a glossy red samian pottery, which was mass-produced in factories in Gaul. The presence of these types of artifact makes Roman remains a dream for archaeologists, so much easier than trying to date Saxon brooches! After the Romans had gone, the British who remained produced nothing that left much in the way of remains, so archaeologically there is little trace of them.

The Roman administration of Britain evolved over time, as did the composition of the army. At first the Romans controlled only southern England directly. There were also three client kingdoms ruled by cooperating natives, in Norfolk, Sussex and the north (this last under Cartimandua, Queen of the Brigantes of the north, the woman who betrayed Caractacus). By the seventies these client kingdoms had disappeared. By the third century the single province of Britain was replaced by two provinces, lower (northern) and upper (southern) Britain. In fact the second and third centuries are something of a dark age and we know little of the detail of what went on in Britannia. However, it is clear that from the Roman point of view, the occupation was hardly a success. It was very expensive to maintain, holding down three legions (as opposed to one in Spain). All the main towns were walled in the second century, indicating that the incursions of the Welsh, Scots, Irish, Saxons and Danes which are familiar from later centuries also took place in Roman times.

During the fourth century, the Christian church became established in Britain. This religion had been given a tremendous boost when it was accepted by the Roman Emperor himself, Constantine (306-337) (his mother was a Christian). Christian cemeteries are a disappointment to archaeologists because they do not contain grave goods. There is a large late Roman one at Poundbury in Dorset, full of east-west inhumations with no grave goods, indicating that Christianity may have become quite well-established in Britain by this period

After about 350 the Roman Empire of the West (based on Rome) had entered its long terminal decline and its British province declined with it. The two military officers in charge were the Duke of Britain, based in York, who commanded the Wall and most of the army with it, and the Count of the Saxon Shore. In order to control piracy and raiding and to discourage disruptive folk movements, the Romans established a string of forts, from Brancaster in Norfolk, round past the Thames estuary as far west as Portchester opposite the Isle of Wight. The Count of the Saxon Shore was the man in charge of these coastal defences and of the fleet. There were more fortifications on the west coast, at Cardiff, Carnarvon and Lancaster. There were watchtowers on the Yorkshire coast and the Bristol Channel, and seven regiments were crammed into Cumberland and Westmorland. The Channel was swarming with Saxon pirates and the Irish Sea with Irish and Picts.

The "Coming of the Anglo-Saxons" (*Adventum Anglorum*) is portrayed by the Venerable Bede as a single event dating from about 450 AD, but we now know that is was not quite so straightforward. Significant numbers of Saxons had already settled round the east coast in the fourth century, a hundred and more years earlier. There was also a strong Germanic component in the army itself, replacing the rag-bag of soldiers from all round the empire which had arrived in the early days. In addition to this there were Germanic soldier-colonies posted outside a number of important towns, hired mercenaries paid to protect the Roman communities, but outside those communities. The legionary strength of the late Roman army is estimated to have fallen drastically to only about 12,000 men, leading to the recruitment of these mercenaries. In the meantime the old legionary centres of York, Caerleon and Chester were largely abandoned as troops moved out to more vulnerable areas.

The towns began to decay and the threats from the Irish, Picts and Saxons became ever more real. In 367 the Picts, the Irish and the Saxons formed an unprecedented alliance for a massive combined raid. The Duke of Britain was captured and the Count of the Saxon Shore was killed, and sacking and raiding stretched from the Midlands to London. However, order was restored. Archaeologists note that the supply of coinage dried up in the last quarter of the fourth century, more evidence of decline. Furnaces and corn dryers were built on top of mosaic floors.

Late in the British Roman period, a Spaniard living in Britain called Magnus Maximus declared himself Roman Emperor. He raised an army in Britain and set off for Gaul in 383, where he did succeed in dethroning Gratian, the current emperor. Maximus held out for five years before he himself was deposed and killed. The main significance of these events is that tradition maintains that the army Maximus had taken with him never returned to Britain. They left their wives, children and property behind and were settled in Brittany, where they formed the nucleus of what was to become a British province.

After this time the disintegrating western Roman Empire came under great pressure from barbarians, and troops were repeatedly withdrawn from Britain by pretenders to the imperial crown. All this culminated in the capture of Rome by Alaric the Visigoth in 410. It was once thought that in this same year, Honorius, the Emperor, wrote to the British civic authorities indicating that they must now make their own arrangements for defence. However it now seems clear that his letter refers not to Britain but to a district in Italy. The Britons themselves were already making their own security arrangements. The Roman Empire was seen as oppressive, cruel and militaristic. It was based on slavery, it taxed its citizens to the maximum and it deliberately prevented social mobility by forcing sons to follow the trade of their fathers. In an age when Christianity was spreading quickly, it was simply out of date in moral terms. In any event, by 410 the last Roman soldier had left Britain and the empire was gone forever. The Dark Ages had begun.

Chapter 4 – The Coming of the Anglo-Saxons

The Dark Ages, the beginning of the medieval period lasting from 410 to 597 or in common parlance throughout the fifth and sixth centuries, have earned their name because so few contemporary accounts of these times in the British Isles survive. It is a Dark Age rather than a completely black one, however, because events can be pieced together from later documents and from archaeology. The period 450-500 is particularly well hidden from our view, and that is when the main body of the Angles and Saxons arrived in England. As well as the Dark Ages, this period is sometimes known as the Age of King Arthur, a shadowy figure portrayed only in much later documents, much embellished by the 12th-century romances of Geoffrey of Monmouth and many later writers. If he existed at all, he was a British general, fighting rough battles and skirmishes against the Picts, Irish and English. Certainly there would be no question of ladies in conical hats, Round Tables, knights in armour attending tournaments on mighty destrier horses, courtly love, Sir Lancelot or Guinevere. All of that is medieval fiction. However, the archaeologists do not want to kill off Arthur. They find it much easier to obtain money for digs and research if his name can be invoked.

There is only one contemporary source available to the historian, *De Excidio et Conquestu Britanniae*, "The Ruin and Conquest of Britain", written in about 540 by the British monk Gildas. He was born in the Strathclyde area, educated at a monastery in Wales, and spent the later part of his life in Brittany. His account infuriates historians because he could have told us so much, yet he tells us little of value. His greatest concern is to castigate the petty Welsh Kings, particularly one Maelgwyn of Gwynedd, for their wickedness in the face of what he sees (correctly) as a serious threat from the "Saxon dogs". The Welsh kings were far too busy fighting one another to care much about the Saxons, a serious mistake. Nevertheless, Gildas does give some valuable information about events within living memory. However, there is one very significant person he does NOT mention – King Arthur. If Arthur had been such a great leader, then it seems unlikely that Gildas would have omitted his name, but then, Gildas was not very good at names and dates.

The second major historical source is a miscellany of documents called the *Historia Britonnum*, compiled from earlier sources by the Welshman Nennius some time around 830, who said "I have made a heap of all that I have found". Some of these documents are fanciful tales, but others such as the Kentish Chronicle give realistic descriptions of events in the fifth century. It is from Nennius that we hear the first account of King Arthur.

The third and most famous book is *Historia Ecclesiastica Gentis Anglorum*, "History of the English Church", written in 731 by the Venerable Bede of Jarrow monastery. Bede is only a secondary historian for the period up to 600, where he relics heavily on Gildas. However, Bede is a much better historian than Gildas! Nevertheless, his is indeed a book of ecclesiastical rather than political history, full of stories of supposed miracles, and seems quaint and naïve by later standards. He believes Hadrian's Wall to have been constructed AFTER the Romans had left (300 years too late) and also he is virtually silent on the vital sixth century. Significantly, Bede sees the English as one distinct people, though of course they were far from one nation. He makes no mention of Arthur either.

In addition to these texts there is the Anglo-Saxon Chronicle, a set of annals (brief entries by year) again compiled years after the event at the time of Alfred the Great, not before about 890 in the form we have now. These do tell us something about the early days of three Saxon kingdoms, Wessex, Sussex and Kent, but they tell us next to nothing about Mercia or Northumberland. The most complete record is for Wessex, but this is of doubtful value as the compilers may have been seeking to glorify the dynasty of their own king. The history of Wessex can be traced almost battle by battle but there is little archaeological support for some of the material.

With reference to the term "Anglo-Saxon", it is to be noted that the Angles and the Saxons came from different parts of Germany, but the term "Saxon" (Sassenach) is frequently used indiscriminately to include not only these people but the other Germanic tribes who were to migrate to Britain alongside them, Jutes and Frisians. Of those who did come, the largest group was almost certainly the Angles, which is the reason why the country came to be called England – Angle-land. The Angles came from what is now Schleswig-Holstein in north Germany, where the district of Angeln is said to have been left swept and empty. The

Jutes came from the Jutland peninsula, in Denmark. The Saxons came from the coastal area between the Weser and the Elbe in north Germany, and the Frisians came from the islands in the Rhine delta. All these people spoke very similar languages, and once they arrived in Britain, they saw themselves as one people, as opposed to the "Welsh" – in their language, "foreigners".

*   *   *   *

When Britain was abandoned to her own resources, it seems that one important resource stayed behind with the British – the soldiers of the northern Wall. These formed a permanent garrison where the soldier's job was handed down from father to son. It would have been very difficult to persuade these men to embark on some risky foreign venture in support of one of the imperial pretenders of the late Roman period, because this would have meant leaving their wives and children to the mercy of the marauding Picts. In any event the defence of the Wall held. Welsh genealogies indicate that the leader of the soldiers was one Coel Hen – Old King Cole.

It is known that there were serious raids by the Picts, the Irish and also the Saxons in the early years following independence, but these were beaten off, and surprisingly, Britain underwent a period of great prosperity for a generation. After 15 years or so stable rule was established in Britain under Vortigern. This is a title (rather than a name), meaning "Overking", but in practice the term applies to one man.

In 428 (all these dates are approximate), Vortigern introduced the "vile unspeakable Saxons" (according to Gildas) in order to protect the Thames estuary from Pictish or any other seaborne raiders. Under their leader Hengist and his brother Horsa, "three keels" of Saxons were settled on the (then) island of Thanet. Hengist was a Danish freebooter of some repute, and the Saxons were the best seamen of the time. Gildas blames Vortigern for letting in the Saxons, but the practice of hiring foreign mercenaries was nothing new; the Romans had done it often enough. There could have been no more than a few hundred of them, and strategically it made sense to plug this gap in the eastern defences of the country when the coast to the north was already covered by local units.

At the same time as Hengist was settling into Thanet, it seems likely that Anglian immigrants were arriving in some strength in Norfolk. In addition to these, Germanic troops were being used to garrison many towns in the east, as they had done in Roman times. To counter the threat of the Picts and the Irish, Hengist is said to have offered more men to Vortigern, and there is some evidence that these did arrive, for example at Dumfries (fortress of the Frisians).

Meanwhile the Irish were becoming well-established in the west. In about 410 they set up their colony at Dalriada (Argyll) on land taken from the Hibernians. This was to become their long-term base in Scotland. In this period the Irish were known as the "Scots", and Scotland was eventually to take its name from them, though it could be argued that it should have been called Pictland. The Irish also took over the Isle of Man and had important settlements on the north coast of Wales, in west Wales and in the south-west of England. To suppress these settlements, Vortigern sent one Cunedda (Kenneth) with his men from the area of the eastern Wall to north Wales. There was a further internal migration of Cornovii (Cornish), from the areas around Wroxeter (near Shrewsbury) to Roman Dumnonia (Devon and Cornwall), again to suppress Irish settlers (though this is disputed – there may have been two tribes both called the Cornovii).

In 429 a French bishop, Germanus of Auxerre, visited Britain. His aim was to head off the Pelagian heresy, named after the influential British Christian, Pelagius, who was born in about 353. The Roman church saw his teachings as a reversion to Druidism. The Roman religion itself was changed by Augustine of Hippo's doctrine of predestination, promulgated just at the time when the Romans were leaving Britain and therefore disregarded in Britain. Germanus found the British holding their own quite comfortably though he is said to have got involved in suppressing a joint Pictish-Saxon raid, no one knows quite where. He returned in 446 to find that the situation had deteriorated drastically.

Civil war rather than foreign invasion caused Vortigern to falter, when he was attacked in the rear by a western aristocrat, Ambrosius. One cause of this conflict was probably the cost of the Saxon mercenaries under Hengist. This colony had grown much larger and was difficult either to feed or to remove. There was at least one battle in the civil war, fought in Hampshire in 437. The outcome is not known, but Vortigern survived. He was now more than ever dependent on Hengist, whose beautiful daughter he married. Hengist obtained the territory of eastern Kent (east of the Medway) as his part of this deal, including the city of Canterbury, which was the only city to pass to the Saxons by treaty.

By 442 Hengist decided to attack his employer Vortigern and the first Saxon revolt broke out. Hengist's motives are not known, but it is possible that it was a case of either revolt or starve to death. In any event, the revolt was a coordinated affair, with the Anglo-Saxon raiders moving out in force from both Kent and East Anglia. The mass of the British were not military people and many fled before the Saxons, abandoning towns which they had occupied for centuries. Colchester and Caistor-by-Norwich were destroyed. In many places Roman life ended suddenly, and forever, during the course of this revolt. One thing to go was mass-produced pottery; the supply of this was suddenly cut off, and did not reappear. The economy was shattered. Gildas does not spare our sensibilities:

"The barbarians...were not slow to put their threats into action. The fire of righteous vengeance, kindled by the sins of the past, blazed from sea to sea, its fuel prepared by the arms of the impious in the east. Once lit, it did not die down. When it had wasted town and country in that area, it burnt up almost the whole surface of the island, until its red and savage tongue licked the western ocean...

All the greater towns fell to the enemy's battering rams; all their inhabitants, bishops, priests and people, were mown down together, while swords flashed and flames crackled. Horrible it was to see the foundation stones of towers and high walls thrown down bottom upward in the squares, mixing with holy altars and fragments of human bodies, as they were covered in a purple crust of clotted blood, as in some fantastic wine-press. There was no burial save in the ruins of the houses, or in the bellies of the beasts and birds."

(P. 75-6, *The Age of Arthur*, John Morris)

Though graphic enough, this is not the sort of detail that we would like to read, and is clearly a gross exaggeration.

In 446 the British sought help from the Roman army commander in Gaul, one Aetius, complaining that:

"The barbarians drive us to the sea and the sea drives us back to the barbarians; death comes by one means or another; we are either slain or drowned."

(From p. 17, *Celt and Saxon*, Peter Berresford Ellis)

Aetius had problems enough of his own with Germanic barbarians, specifically the Franks, and was shortly to have to deal with Attila the Hun, so no help was forthcoming. However, the British rallied and counter-attacked. A number of battles were fought – eventually the war dragged on over 10 years. By the end of it, the revolt had been contained, and the Saxons were confined to Kent and East Anglia, the British holding London to keep the two groups apart. However, the British kingdom was permanently weakened, and a huge wave of British refugees had fled to Brittany (where they were able to form an army of 12,000 men.) Here they joined the descendants of the army of Maximus whose ancestors had settled there towards the end of the previous century. Other smaller groups of refugees also went to Ireland and to northern Spain. One later commentator noted that the existing population of Brittany took pity on the British refugees, who were fellow-Christians, but the British were not grateful, and soon took charge of the country (Ellis p. 103).

After this time we hear no more of Vortigern or Hengist, both said to have died around 460. From 450 until 500, after which Gildas is able to describe events which took place in his own lifetime, a great fog descends, but it is certain that the changes were great. From the contained Saxon revolt of Hengist in 450, we find at the time of Gildas that a series of fully-fledged Anglo-Saxon kingdoms have formed in the east and south, and another series of British kingdoms lined up in the west, with a shadowy no-mans land between them, probably scarcely populated. This was the land of the mysterious British kingdom of Elmet, in Yorkshire and the north Midlands, about which nothing is known. However, it is certain that heavy immigration from northern Germany and Denmark took place during these years, and the archaeologists note the westward march of the pagan Anglo-Saxon cemeteries from which the dead speak eloquently of the migration.

One factor which influenced the migration of the Frisian section of the immigrants was that the sea level was rising (or the sea bed was sinking, a known occurrence in major deltas). It is likely that this caused the Frisians to leave their homes in the islands of the Rhine delta, and make for England. Many of them had built their villages on man-made mounds in the water, which were gradually being engulfed. There is evidence from the archaeology that many mounds were suddenly abandoned about 450. Identical pottery to that found on the mounds then appears in England. This is not the only environmental factor, outside human control, that affected the outcome of Saxon versus Celt, as we shall see.

There has been much debate amongst academics about the extent to which the Anglo-Saxons integrated into existing British communities. However this is a very modern fashion. Until recent years no historian had any doubt that in the east and south-east of England, there was no integration and that the Anglo-Saxons cleared the land of all British people before they occupied it. In the west of the country, taken much later, this was not thought to happen. However it is difficult to see why the integration theory has gained any currency. Place-names in the Anglo-Saxon areas are all from their language, apart from a few rivers. Also the Anglo-Saxon language in use at these times contains only a tiny handful of loan-words from Celtic. It is known that the two communities loathed each other and would not sit at the same table when they met abroad. The evidence from archaeology (especially from the many Saxon cemeteries) is overwhelmingly that there was a complete change in the material culture of the people of southern and eastern England.

Yet archaeologists such as Francis Pryor claim that there was only a small influx of Anglo-Saxon people. However it is to be noted that no German archaeologist agrees with the recent shift in British academic opinion – they still think that the English came from Germany. And after all, it would seem foolish to contradict the only contemporary source, Gildas, as Prior and others now do, especially in view of the fact that, when the dark mist finally cleared at the beginning of the seventh century, all the British kingdoms were lined up in the mountainous west, and the plain of England was indeed occupied by the Anglo-Saxons, just as Gildas had said.

Geneticists such as Stephen Oppenheimer and Brian Sykes have joined the fray, claiming that nearly all the female and most of the male lines in the British Isles pre-date the Saxon conquest. In direct contradiction, another group working from London University in 2011 identified a genetic sequence found on the Y-chromosome of nearly all males of north German and Danish origin which is also found in half British males. The problem here is that the genetic clock ticks too slowly, so that the geneticists are obliged to use statistical manipulation based on very slender data. For example, Julius Caesar noted that the Gauls of northern France were a tall, fair people. Their neighbours were the Belgic tribes who were crossing into England before the Roman Conquest, and their neighbours in turn were the Frisians and Saxons. Is it then possible to separate genetically two sets of immigrants who came from the same geographical region – the mouths of the Scheldt and Rhine - and only four hundred years apart? Of course not, yet Sykes includes the Belgics under "Celts" when in fact it seems likely that they closely resembled the Saxons in appearance. Also, it is thought that the Anglo-Saxons established themselves in England, especially in East Anglia, well before the end of Roman rule. It certainly does seem probable that there was a strong survival rate amongst the female "Celtic" line. Not even Genghis Khan went about slaughtering fertile young woman – on the contrary, he inseminated as many of them as he could, personally (he is thought to have 16 million descendants today).

Also, there are some historians who like to display this struggle as Celt versus Saxon, but the truth is more complicated. The Welsh fought the Welsh, the Saxons fought the Saxons, and the Welsh at times allied with the one group of Saxons to fight another group of Saxons.

During this period Gildas says the leader of the British fight-back was one Ambrosius Aurelianus, who seems to have stabilized the situation in the 460s, with the Anglo-Saxons still confined in the east. The British adopted a new national name for themselves, *Combrogi* or fellow-countryman, in modern form Cymry or Cumbri, still the national name of the Welsh and also still with us in the name of the county of Cumberland. Some Iron-Age forts were refortified and reoccupied, even in western areas far removed from English settlement, so the English may not have been the only problem to the Cymry.

From the evidence of excavated bodies which seem to belong to executed prisoners or warriors dying from fatal wounds, and also of swords and spears found in quantity at river crossings, the main front at this time lay on a line from Wiltshire to Cambridge, along the Roman Icknield Way. Large quantities of old weapons have been found at Wallingford, where the Icknield Way crosses the Thames. The Anglo-Saxons must somehow have moved past London and into the middle Thames area during this period. There is also evidence that Angles had spread into Leicestershire and Northamptonshire, and had become well-established in Lincolnshire and Nottinghamshire. The River Trent formed a major boundary. There are no fifth- or even sixth-century Anglo-Saxon cemeteries on the western side of the river, but there are many on the eastern. During this period the king of the Angles crossed to England, presumably because the majority of his people now lived there. In Germany, Anglo-Saxon burials virtually cease by the end of the fifth century.

Most of the fighting seems to have taken place in the south Midlands. In East Yorkshire, the long-established English colony continued in existence but did not expand. Kent remained isolated and if the trade of London continued in British hands then there must have been some accommodation with the men of Kent. In fact there is no evidence that the Jutes from Kent tried to spread beyond the Medway before 568, and then they were fighting against other Saxons, not the British. However, there is a gap in the history of London itself. It is not known how far it survived as a major centre – after all, what was it to do? The business of trade and administration must have been vastly diminished. A Saxon brooch has been excavated on top of the roof tiles of a collapsed bathhouse in Lower Thames Street, in the heart of the busiest part of the city in the last phase of Roman London. Clearly no one had bothered to clear up the tiles. (This story is taken from The English Settlements, J.N.L. Myres.)

In the meantime, according to the Anglo-Saxon Chronicle, the first Saxon settlers arrived in Sussex under their leader Aelle during the 460s. He landed at Selsey Bill in east Sussex. His landing was opposed, and he did not get far, but held on. His was a tiny kingdom and there is no evidence of a Saxon presence in west Sussex for another hundred years. Chichester is named after one of his descendents, Cissa. A further Saxon kingdom was founded around 480 in the south Hampshire area, the future Wessex. It founder was one Cerdic. The problem here is that Cerdic is a British name, not an Anglo-Saxon one. He has been co-opted as an honorary Englishman by the chroniclers. Another of the leaders was called Maegla, again a British name. One theory is that a group of Jutes (possibly from Kent) formed an alliance with local British chiefs to create an independent kingdom in this area. However the Anglo-Saxon Chronicle is at its shakiest here, because the archaeological evidence is that Wessex was founded from Abingdon in the middle Thames Valley in a settlement very early in the Saxon period.

At this point the misty figure of Arthur appears in the *Historia Britonnum*. Nennius lists twelve of his battles, presumably victories. The sites of these battles can only be guessed at, and at least some of them have names indicating sites in Wales and the north-west. These battles are not likely to have been fought against the English. However, one or more battles were probably located in Lindsey in Lincolnshire, certainly against the English. The culminating battle was fought at Mount Badon. The site of this is much disputed, but since the areas subsequently cleared of Anglo-Saxon population are in the south-east Midlands, that is the most likely region. The one English king known to have been present was Aesc of Kent. The date of the battle is also disputed. Gildas (writing in about 540) says it took place in the year of his birth, 44 years previously, giving a date of around 495, but the Welsh Annals give a date of 516. To the historian who loves a controversy (and what historian does not), Badon is an example of why this era is so fascinating. If the location of its most famous battle is unknown and it cannot be securely dated to within 20 years, the opportunity for argument with fellow historians could scarcely be improved.

Wherever and whenever it took place, it was a major check to the English. After the battle the British had little more trouble with the English for seventy years, so it is likely that a treaty was agreed, and that both sides retired to lick their wounds. That these wounds must have been deep and serious is indicated by the long peace that followed. From the evidence of cemeteries, English settlement was withdrawn from a large area of the south Midlands and Essex. Substantial English settlement only remained in Norfolk, Kent, Sussex and east of the Trent, with smaller scattered settlements elsewhere. There is no sign in the archaeology of this period, for example, of anything that could be called a kingdom of Mercia, Essex or Northumbria.

Where they did exist, Saxon settlements took the form of scattered hamlets and isolated farmsteads rather than nucleated villages; and there is no sign of defensive works. The houses were regularly abandoned and rebuilt elsewhere, presumably to let the land lie fallow. This process is known to archaeologists as the "Saxon Shuffle".

After Badon there were so few opportunities for the English that a considerable number of them emigrated back to Saxony. The majority of the later Saxons are thought to derive their ancestry from this migration. There is also place-name and archaeological evidence of a considerable emigration to France, where over a hundred villages in the country between Boulogne and Lille have English names, now slightly disguised with French spelling. There appears to have been a settlement of East Anglians in this area in the years before 550. The Frankish king Clovis had annexed vast territories in the former Gaul at this time, too large an area to be controlled by just the Franks, and English colonists took lands that the Franks could not use themselves. There are another hundred or so villages behind the coast of Normandy, this time bearing names indicating a south Saxon origin.

For 35 years after Badon, Gildas states that the British territories knew a period of good government. However by that time the country had broken up into a series of petty kingdoms, run unjustly under jumped-up military rulers, warring against each other. It was this situation which caused Gildas to reach for his pen. One problem was the disastrous form of inheritance practised in British territories, where a king would divide his kingdom amongst his male heirs upon his death. These heirs would then fight amongst themselves to regain the whole of the original kingdom. Fratricidal wars were to scar Wales for generations. Nevertheless, there was one dominant Welsh king at this time, Maelgwyn of Gwynedd, whom Gildas clearly regarded as being beyond any hope of redemption. There were other, minor kings in Powys and Merioneth in the north, Brecon, Glamorgan and elsewhere. The Welsh kings were also concerned to take control of Demetia (Dyved), the name given to coastal territories in Pembroke and Carmarthen which were occupied by the Irish. They did regain control, though the Irish population stayed.

Within the remaining British territory there were major kingdoms in the north-east (based at York), the north-west (Reged), and Strathclyde. In the south-west were Dumnonia (Devon, parts of Somerset and Wiltshire) and Cornwall, and in Yorkshire and the north Midlands, Elmet. Gloucester, Cirencester, Wroxeter, Chester and St Albans were also centres of local British kingdoms. London and Colchester show no sign of English settlement before the end of the sixth century and may also have been regional capitals. Not all of these are shadowy and unknown because the comings and goings of kings, wars and battles are recorded in documents of variable reliability. The boundaries of these kingdoms changed constantly as a result of local wars.

One monument which survives from this period is Wansdyke, stretching east-west for 60 miles through the country south of Bath, with a notable gap in the middle. It is known to date from this era because it is partly built on top of a Roman road, and the Anglo-Saxons who came later knew nothing of its origins. It is likely that it was constructed at the northern boundary of Dumnonia.

The disaster which was feared by Gildas was not long in coming, but it did not take the form that he envisaged. Already cursed by him as a force which had weakened the British, plague struck in the 540s and 550s with a virulence which parallels that of the Black Death in 1348. It began in Egypt in about 542. By 544 it had reached Ireland and Britain, but the full force of it was not felt until about 550. However, the disease was selective in its victims, and there is no record that it affected the English, who led simple lives in isolated settlements. There was no contact between the English and the British, and the English did not trade with the continental areas affected - no writer extends it to the Lower Rhine, for example. It was said that plague favoured wars and did not harm rough races. In fact infectious diseases like the plague require a certain density of population to spread themselves; otherwise they fizzle out. One reason why plagues come in waves is that they strike back when the population has built up again. It is possible that the reason that the Anglo-Saxons appeared not to suffer was that there were simply not enough of them.

However there is no doubt that the mainland British were badly affected. One of the plague's victims was Maelgwyn, King of Gwynedd, whom Gildas loathed so heartily, and who was taken in 549. There is archaeological evidence for depopulation around this time. Tintagel in north Cornwall and Cadbury Congresbury on the River Yeo two miles from the Bristol Channel in Somerset were both ports. Thousands of pottery shards originating from the eastern Mediterranean have been dug up in both places, all dating from the first half of the sixth century, none later. The old Roman town of Wroxeter was replanned and rebuilt in the second half of the sixth century on a site reduced from 192 acres to 25 acres (see Catastrophe, David Keys, p. 156).

The plague was notably less severe in its effects in Brittany than in Britain itself, and a third wave of immigration took place from Britain, presumably of families fleeing before the pestilence. After this time the whole of the peninsula of Brittany became British, and the speech and identity of the former population was obliterated. It remained a nominally independent country until the sixteenth century and is Celtic-speaking to this day (there were an estimated 800,000 speakers in 1976).

Chapter 5 – Saxon Expansion

The British did not have to wait long for the English to wake up to their weakness. A small English population had lived in east Hampshire since the fifth century, its grave ornaments indicating that it derived from Sussex, along the coast. This population had expanded northwards to Salisbury and the Berkshire Downs by 550, presumably into territory still controlled by the British. In 552 the second Saxon revolt began when Cynric put the British to flight at Salisbury. This is another Wessex leader who appears not to be English as his name is Irish. However, his people were English.

If the Anglo-Saxon Chronicle is to be believed, then the 570s was one of the most pivotal decades in the whole history of England. The next ruler of note from Wessex is one of the most important of the early Saxons, Ceawlin, for it is he that transformed the western English from a minor people into the masters of the south. However, his first target was not British territory, but English. It must have become clear that London was wide open to conquest. Ceawlin formed an alliance with Cuthwulf of the Angles of Cambridgeshire and attacked the army of Kent which had moved across Medway heading for the same target in 568. Ceawlin won this battle and so took London with its British population. Cuthwulf's Angles then overturned a British kingdom at Bedford in 571 before setting off up the Thames where they liberated a long-established English colony at Abingdon.

The allied Anglian and Wessex army under Ceawlin then headed west where they achieved a famous victory over the British at Dyrham, near Bath, in 577. In this battle they killed the British kings of the lower Severn, and occupied the important towns of Bath, Gloucester and Cirencester. Cirencester, which had been ringed by English villages for a generation or more, became an English town. However there is no sign of any English settlement beyond the Cotswolds in either Gloucester or Bath for another 50 years and nothing is heard of either city for another 100 years. Ceawlin and his Anglian allies marched on, across the Severn, where they wasted the country before being finally checked by the Welsh coming out of Monmouth and Glamorgan in 584. Ceawlin returned home "in anger" (according to the Anglo-Saxon Chronicle). However, his kingdom of Wessex now controlled a large part of southern England. He and his allies had permanently destroyed the southern British kingdoms, and they had done it within 16 years. From his time onwards, the Welsh were separated from the British of Dumnonia in the south-west.

Ceawlin's power did not last long. He was overthrown as leader of the alliance in 591, dying in 593. The men of Wessex and Mercia, the new midland kingdom, took to fighting amongst themselves; possibly the British got involved, but in any event their strength was reduced and the southern overlordship passed to Aethelbert of Kent. It was shortly after this time that the first papal ambassador arrived in Kent. The Pope at this time was Gregory, the man who famously saw slave children on sale in Rome. Told that they were Angles from England, he remarked that they looked more like angels to him. He himself had once been asked to go to England to convert the Saxons, and now he selected his own man, Augustine. Whether this was the right choice is questionable. Aethelbert had been identified by Gregory as a good conversion prospect because he was married to a Christian princess. Augustine duly landed in Aethelbert's Kent in 597, along with forty missionaries. Aethelbert himself accepted Christianity and began to spread literacy amongst his people. The appeal of Christianity – at first a strange choice, a mixture of Jewish and Greek traditions, and very foreign – was that it was fashionable. Although it was already an old religion, it was associated with civilization, in that a Christian could not be regarded as a barbarian. The attitude of many was that they had prayed to the old gods often enough, and that had never worked, so why not try this?

However, there were already many Christians in the British Isles. The best-known Christian missionary in Ireland was of course Patrick. He was a British Celt, born at Dumbarton, a fortress on the Clyde estuary and the later capital of Strathclyde. Captured in an Irish raid at the age of 16, he was taken to Antrim in northern Ireland, but eventually escaped to Gaul, where he went to Auxerre while Germanus was bishop. Germanus was to make two visits to the British in England, as we have already seen. Patrick then went back to northern Ireland to begin his mission, landing at Strangford Loch around 456 (the date is disputed – 432 is another commonly accepted year). He succeeded in spreading the gospel, though it was not until much later, in the 530s, that the mass conversion of the Irish people took place. The importance of Patrick is that he dared to take the cross to Ireland, home of 150 petty and dangerous kings, and beyond the limits of the old Roman Empire, where the Roman church had never taken root.

The organization of Irish Christianity differed from the Roman model in that it was based on rural monasteries rather than urban bishoprics, because there were no towns in Ireland at this time. The monasteries bore a close resemblance to the secular raths, cashels and crannogs, different types of walled round defensive structures built all over Ireland in the early Christian period 500-1000. Some of these sites have been excavated and even restored for tourists. They are not sophisticated structures like later monasteries with their cloisters and chapter houses, but contain a scattering of beehive huts, several small churches and other domestic buildings. A prominent feature is the tall free-standing round tower, which served as a belfry and more importantly as a watch tower. The towers however date from a later period, the tenth century, when Vikings were everywhere.

The next important figure in the Irish church is St Columba. Born the son of a chieftain in Donegal in 521, he got into a scrap with the Irish High King and found himself banished to the Irish kingdom in Argyll in Scotland, Dalriada. Here in 563 when he was 42 years old, he established a monastery and missionary training centre on the island of Iona. This became the setting-off point for the Irish missionaries who fanned out over Strathclyde, Pictland and eventually northern England in the vast work of converting the pagans to Christianity, a job which took 100 years and more. Columba became a man of great influence in both western Scotland and Ireland. He was to die in 597, by coincidence the date of the arrival of Augustine, bringer another version of Christianity to England.

The Irish version of Christianity differed significantly from the Roman. These differences may seem obscure and minor to us, but they were taken very seriously at the time. It is clear that the Roman Christians thought the Irish had gone native and become heretical, but in fact the most important difference concerned the calculation of the date of Easter, which was changed by the Roman church after 455. The Irish adhered to the older tradition. Whilst it is now clear that the Irish were not cut off from Europe and that their holy men did travel to Rome in this period, it is equally clear that Irish Christianity ran beyond the writ of Rome. When Augustine was sent to Britain, one of his top priorities was to stamp out the Irish heresy, but he did not succeed. Though the Roman rules were upheld in Northumbria at the Synod of

Whitby in 664, Irish practices continued long afterwards elsewhere, until 768 in Wales for example, and in Ireland for 500 or more years!

Augustine's attempts to persuade the British Christians to toe the Roman line appear laughable. He had clearly spent too long amongst the Saxons and absorbed their view of the Welsh as foreign savages. A meeting was called near Chepstow. When the seven leading bishops from the British church were ushered in to meet Augustine, he remained seated (a great insult) and immediately launched into a tirade of abusive criticism of their calculation of the date of Easter and other native rites. He also demanded that they accept the authority of Canterbury (i.e. a Saxon establishment), and that they spread the Gospel to the Saxon infidel, their lifelong enemy. Astounded and bemused, the British diplomatically withdrew. They knew there were many older and more venerable religious centres in the Celtic world than the upstart Canterbury, and that their congregations would expect to be consulted about any changes.

A second meeting followed, but this was worse than the first. Augustine again refused to rise to meet his guests, and once again lectured the appalled British clerics on their heretical practices. He finally threatened them with vengeance at the hands of the Saxons if they did not give way. This was too much for the British, who withdrew permanently.

Augustine died after only a few years, but his mission continued. However after the death of Aethelbert in about 616, Christianity in Kent collapsed, confirming the British suspicion that the Saxon commitment to it was skin-deep. However though some missionaries were sent packing, the religion did not disappear entirely, as we shall see.

In the north of England, one Ida established the kingdom of Bernicia in 560, based on a fort at Bamburgh (on the coast north of Newcastle). The British kings of York evidently marched against Ida's successors, in 580, but were beaten and deposed. This left York open to occupation by the much larger English population of Deira, an East Riding community long established nearby. This was the end of the British kings of York, a line which had stretched right back to Old King Cole. The sudden end of this kingdom startled the northern British into a semblance of unity, for up to now they had been fighting amongst themselves in the traditional way. Their leader was Urien, king of Reged in the north-west, and a man much celebrated in the poems of Welsh bards which survive to this day. He marched from his castle at Carlisle to occupy the Yorkist outpost at Catterick, which was (and is) strategically located to control Scots Corner where the road north splits

47

off for Carlisle and Scotland. In or around 590, Urien and his allies pressed on and took Bamburgh, the capital of Bernicia, besieging the Bernicians on the island of Lindisfarne (opposite Bamburgh). However, the Bernicians were saved from annihilation by the British allies, who fell out amongst themselves at this point. Urien was murdered by a rival, the British armies disintegrated and the Bernicians recovered.

However, the Celtic peoples were not finished yet. The next assault on Bernicia came from the "Gododdin", from the Lothians in Scotland. They marched down to Catterick, where a second battle was fought in 598. By this time the king of the Bernicians was Aethelfrith, a strong and rising monarch, by all accounts hungry for glory, and he annihilated the Gododdin.

Meanwhile, in Scotland, a king called Aiden had succeeded to the throne of the Irish kingdom of Dalriada. A contemporary of the famous monk Columba, he was a powerful monarch who extended the political influence of Dalriada over a wide area while Columba was doing the same thing in the spiritual sense. In 603, however, he led a force to help the British against the Aethelfrith of Bernicia. He was so heavily defeated at a place called Degastan ("Degsa's stone") that he was deposed. After this event, according to Bede, no king of the Scots ever dared to meet the English in the field. The Lothians as far as Edinburgh were open for English settlement and a glance at the map today shows the names of hundreds of English villages in this region. The following year, 604, Athelfrith took over the kingdom of Deira, based at York, to create the combined kingdom of Northumbria – England north of the Humber. As the English kingdoms coalesced in this way, this period is sometimes called the Heptarchy or seven kingdoms: three major ones - Northumbria, Mercia and Wessex; and then East Anglia (formerly Norfolk and Suffolk), Essex, Sussex and Kent.

The Northumbrians were now a serious force within Britain. They had faced three attempts to dislodge them, from Urien, the Gododdin and Aiden. None had succeeded, though Urien had come close. Aethelfrith was the undisputed master of the north-east, though the son of the deposed Deiran king of York, Edwin, had escaped his clutches and found refuge (according to some traditions) amongst the Welsh of Gwynned. No wars are reported for 10 years, but in 614 Aethelfrith went after Edwin and fought a combined British force from Gwynned, Shropshire and Powys at Chester. His first target was over a thousand unarmed monks from who had accompanied the British army from their monastery at Bangor-on-Dee. According to Bede, the pagan Aethelfrith justified this attack:

"If these men invoke their god against us, they fight against us, even if they have no arms."

Evidently a hard man, Aethelfrith duly captured Chester, thereby separating Wales from the Pennines and Reged, just as the capture of Gloucester 25 years earlier had separated it from Dumnonia.

However, Aethelfrith had still not managed to catch Edwin, pretender to the throne of Northumberland and always a danger while he lived, because he could encourage Aethelfrith's rivals to overthrow him. To assist him in his enterprise, Edwin had made a dynastic marriage to a daughter of the English king of Mercia. Edwin came eventually to the court of King Redwald of East Anglia, by this time the dominant southern English king. It is thought that the magnificent remains dug up at Sutton Hoo and now in the British Museum, including the famous helmet, ship, chain mail, silver bowls and ornaments in gold, enamel and garnet, may commemorate Redwald. In any event, this time Aethelfrith had gone too far, and was defeated and killed when he attacked Redwald in 616. Edwin was immediately accepted as king by the Northumbrians. In 625 he married Aethelburgh, the daughter of Aethelbert of Kent, his first wife presumably having died. The significance of this marriage was that Aethelburgh had remained a Christian, and brought with her her chaplain Paulinus, who established a church at York.

The Northumbrian armies were still strong, and Edwin next extended his power by removing the last of the Pennine kings, Cerdic of Elmet, in 626, becoming the dominant English king in the process. It is only possible to speculate what happened to the British populations of places like Elmet. As it was partially a Pennine kingdom, it is likely to have been lightly populated, but the area seems to have been overrun by Anglo-Saxon settlement. Odd traces remain, such as the village of Walsden (village of the Welsh), tucked away in a remote Pennine valley.

Edwin also overran north Wales and Anglesey, and took the Isle of Man from the Irish, in doing so becoming more powerful than any previous English king. An under-king king of Wessex, clearly alarmed, sent an assassin to murder him, but the attempt failed. In retaliation, Edwin attacked Wessex in 628, and according to Bede, killed five kings in a battle there. Around this time, and possibly in appreciation for Edwin's escape from the assassin's knife, mass conversions to Christianity began in Northumbria. Edwin was revered in Northumbria as a strong and just king, but the other English kings clearly did not like him, and the wily Cadwallon, the new ruler of Gwynedd, was able to play on their fears. He formed an alliance with Penda, the king of Mercia, which had grown from small beginnings to be a major midland Anglian kingdom based at Tamworth. The new allies marched against Edwin, and fought and beat him at the battle of Hatfield Chase in 633. Edwin was killed; Penda and Cadwallon marched into Northumbria unopposed, and set about devastating the territory so that it could make no further trouble. Bede describes Cadwallon as a man who, though a Christian, "had the temperament and character of a barbarian". He says this period "even today...remains an ill-omened year and hateful to all good people."

However, the Northumbrians bounced back once more. They selected a new king, Oswald, a son of the mighty Aethelfrith, who had been exiled in Iona, perhaps an unlikely place, but at any rate a long way from the clutches of Edwin. Oswald immediately took on Cadwallon, whom he slew personally in a Northumbrian victory near Hexham. Cadwallon is celebrated in Welsh poetry as a most brilliant lord and king who destroyed York, "a man like Maelgwyn". To the Northumbrians he confirmed their worst fears that the Welsh were savages.

Having been brought up amongst Irish Christians, Oswald encouraged missionaries to Northumberland, and an important religious centre was established under the Irish monk Aidan at Lindisfarne. An abbey was built at Whitby under the leadership of Hilda. When Oswald defeated King Cynglis of Wessex in battle, one of his conditions for peace was that Cynglis accept Christianity. From that time onwards missionaries from Ireland arrived to spread the word all over the territories controlled by Oswald. According to Bede:

"In all matters Oswald listened humbly and loyally to bishop Aidan's advice, and showed great concern to build up and extend the Church of Christ within his kingdom. The bishop was not fully conversant with the English language, and on many occasions it was delightful to watch while he preached the gospel, and the king himself, having acquired a perfect knowledge of Irish during his long exile, acted as interpreter of heaven's word for his ealdormen and thanes."

(Quoted in *Celt and Saxon*, Peter Berresford Ellis)

However, Oswald was by no means a man of peace himself, and in fact continued where Edwin had left off, harrying the Welsh and the Scottish borderers as well as the men of Wessex. His power only lasted for eight years, when he was killed at Oswestry (named after him – Oswald's Tree, from which his body was suspended) in 642. His enemy was the old alliance of the Mercian Penda and the Welsh. In these times, not many kings died in their beds. (A surprising number of them withdrew from kingship and retired to monasteries, no doubt aware of the fate of their predecessors.) Oswald's kingdom of Northumbria remained an important political entity, however, his successors pushing into Lancashire (formerly part of Reged) and holding their own until Viking times. The remnant of Northumbria, reconstituted as Bernicia and stretching from the Tees to the Firth of Forth, was still going strong in the tenth century.

The south-west of England remained in British hands for a century or more after the rest of the south had passed to the English. Cenwahl of Wessex defeated the Welsh in Somerset and chased them beyond the River Parrett in 658. Around this time the King of Cornwall (thought to be a separate kingdom at this time) was one Mark, also known as Cunomorus, and a stone standing at Castle Dore near Fowey in Cornwall commemorates his son, reading (in translation from the Latin) "Here lies Drustanus, son of Cunomorus." These characters are traceable to the legend of Tristram (Drustanus) and Isolde (also called Iseult and Isoud), a love triangle involving sea journeys to Ireland and Brittany, and a love potion of course. The story was taken up by many writers, including Malory, and by Wagner in his opera *Tristan*.

Before this period Wessex had been in long decline, beset by civil wars. However the throne was suddenly seized by Caedwalla, a descendant of Ceawlin (and equally Welsh-sounding) in 685. A Saxon thug of the worst type, he began a murderous drive through Sussex and the Isle of Wight, also setting up his brother as king of Kent. Before he was 30, and much to the relief of all concerned, he threw down his arms and abdicated, going to Rome on a pilgrimage of contrition. He was succeeded by Ine as King of Wessex, who in a long reign (688-726) re-established Wessex at parity with the other two great kingdoms, Northumbria and Mercia. In 695, Ine promulgated a set of laws for his recently conquered Dumnonian territory setting out the fines payable for the killing of Britons – up to 600 shillings for a Briton who owned 500 acres. This indicates that in this area at least, the Saxons took over an existing British population.

Ine invaded southern Dumnonia in 710, defeating Geraint, probably the last King of Dumnonia, and advancing to Exeter. English place names indicate heavy colonization inland from the city from this time. Exeter itself was partitioned between the British and the English for long afterwards. Cornwall remained independent.

The kings of Mercia from the time of Penda (victor over Oswald in 642) onwards asserted their ascendancy over all the English kings apart from the Northumbrians, a position they held for the next 150 years. Penda was killed (by Oswald's brother) in 655, but this barely interrupted the long ascendancy of the Mercian kings. During this relatively peaceable period, the English kingdoms settled down and learned to live within their new borders. This period of history was quite unlike the period after 1066 AD, because continental wars were unknown. The only "foreign" wars were small-scale affairs against the Welsh and the Scots.

There most famous later Mercian king was Offa (757-796), who built the massive Offa's dyke between the Dee and the Bristol Channel to keep out the Welsh. This represented 120 miles of earthworks, 25 feet high on average from the bottom of the ditch to the top of the dyke. It represents the largest engineering construction in England before the railways were built. Offa was an important king, with palaces in London, who conducted negotiations with Charlemagne, king of the Franks, and with the Pope. Offa devastated south Wales (twice), annexed the minor kingdoms of Essex and East Anglia, and forced Wessex and Kent to accept his authority. He was loathed in these places, which switched their allegiance to Wessex when Mercia weakened after his death in 796.

*   *   *   *

It is instructive to inquire as to why the Anglo-Saxons eventually won their fight to take over England. After all, they had no superior technology or tactics, in the way that say the Romans had with their catapulted iron bolts and disciplined legions. They were no more sophisticated than the British – indeed less so. The British remained literate and continued to live in towns. The Celtic cultural area centred round the Irish Sea, far from declining, flourished during the early medieval period, producing some memorable artifacts, especially in decorated books and metalwork and in the marvelous carved stones produced by the Picts. Ireland and Irish settlements in Scotland, and monasteries in both Wales and Brittany remained beacons of learning while most of western Europe was succumbing to illiterate barbarians. This is in fact one of the problems – the barbarians, both the Anglo-Saxons and their equivalents in Europe, were first and foremost warriors, full of rude vigour and caring nothing for books. Their arrival caused the complete and permanent dislocation of a delicate economic and political system. After the first shock, in which the barbarians gained important beachheads (and in the case of France, the whole country), the old Romans reorganized and fought back. However, they were then decimated by the plague, opening another window of opportunity for the barbarians. Nevertheless, as Gildas points out, the British were their own worst enemies, and continued to fight one another when they should have been aware of the English menace. The various English kingdoms rarely fought one another until they had each reached a significant size and strength, mainly for the simple reason that they were geographically isolated from each other. However much less effort was wasted on internal dynastic disputes. Only a relatively small number of important battles were fought between English kingdoms.

Once the English kingdoms were organized and of a significant size, they were very powerful and rapidly overran the adjacent British kingdoms. Suddenly in the seventh century the English armies seemed able to move very quickly. Possibly they were moving through a country which was depopulated by internal wars, plague, migration to Brittany and rural famine. Rural economies were very fragile and in years of crop failure or blight, the loss of a husband to war or a cow to raiders could spell starvation and death. Certainly there is precious little British archaeology in the areas conquered in the second Saxon revolt. It could be that the English were simply pressing on an open door. Also there have been suggestions that the British populations welcomed the stability and rule of law brought by their new English masters, and when the opportunity came to rise against them, they did not take it.

The biggest question and most controversial question of all from the Anglo-Saxon era is this: to what extent did the Anglo-Saxons replace the native population? What proportion of today's population has a British rather than an Anglo-Saxon ancestry? Because the fact is, though the different populations of the British Isles have had plenty of time to mix together, they do not in fact seem to have mixed very well, hence the number of really quite different physical types that we find today. This matter is discussed in detail in Chapter 4. At least in the west of England there is good evidence for the survival of the Celtic population, for example from place-names. One thing to bear in mind is the huge expansion of the population since these distant times. The number of Anglo-Saxon immigrants is not thought large, certainly not hundreds of thousands. The Saxon cemeteries are surprisingly small. Many which seem to have been in use over generations contain only a couple of hundred graves, unlike those in say the Rhineland, which can contain thousands. Again, it is likely the early battles that were fought were relatively small-scale affairs, with low numbers killed. It is possible that the reason the Anglo-Saxons waited so long after the battle of Badon (around 495) to begin the main phase of the second Saxon revolt (from around 570) was caused by the need to build up their population after the earlier wars.

Chapter 6 – The Vikings

In 793, raiders from the sea attacked and burned the monastery at Lindisfarne, the holy shrine of St Cuthbert. The same thing happened the following year at Iona, and the year after that at an outpost of Iona in Ireland. The peaceful coastlines of the last 200 years were under a new and terrible threat – the Vikings had arrived. Before long, the king of York would not be called Old King Cole, Edwin or Oswald, but Eric Bloodaxe.

The Norsemen were a new version of the Angles and Saxons of the fifth century, equally vigorous and hungry seamen. They arrived as the Anglo-Saxons did as militant barbarian pagans into a relatively peaceful, literate and religious country, but we know much more about them because they came later, in better recorded times. Certainly some colourful characters appeared at these times, such as Ivar the Boneless, who did quite well for himself as King of Dublin for a man apparently without a skeleton. (Modern physiologists have identified his condition as Osteogenesis imperfecta. In practice this meant that he had cartilage in his legs instead of bones, and so had to be carried about on a shield.) Then there were his brothers, called Ironside and Snake-eye. Ivar's father was said to have been thrown into a snakepit by Aelle of York, whose ribs and lungs were pulled out backwards in retaliation. These were the days of Olaf the White, Sigurd the Powerful, of the obscure Aud the Deep-minded, daughter of Ketil Flatnose and mother of Thorstein the Red, of the Welsh Mervyn Frych "The Freckled", Harold the Fair, Edric Streona "The Grasper", and Ethelred "The Unready".

The best approach to this confusing period, which ran all the way from the first raids in the late eighth century until the time of the Conquest (itself another phase of it) in 1066, is probably to stand back from the detail and pick out the significant motifs of the time. There were two types of Norsemen, the Norwegians, who concentrated their efforts on modern Scotland, Ireland, the Isle of Man and north-west England, and the Danes, whose main strength was to be in Northumbria, East Anglia and the eastern Midlands and Essex – very much the old

Anglian territories. The Norsemen did well against the minor kingdoms and the decadent Northumbria, but they found the going much tougher against the combined weight of Wessex and Mercia under Egbert and his successors, notably of course Alfred. They never succeeded in conquering the whole of England, though they did obtain the monarchy under Sweyn Forkbeard and his son Canute. However no coast was safe from them.

The Norsemen were equally a problem for France, where they established the Duchy of Normandy under Rollo in 911. Between 830 and 900 they sacked London, Paris, Hamburg, Antwerp, Bordeaux, Seville and the Rhone Valley. Also in this period they founded Russia with capitals in Novgorod and Kiev, and they besieged Constantinople. They were to populate Iceland, Greenland and Vinland (in North America), and eventually they took Sicily and Cyprus. Just how many of them were there? Not that many. Why did they come? It is thought that their lands had become overpopulated, and that they suffered from overbearing kings; another theory is that the climate of Scandinavia had become colder and wetter, though it could hardly have been as bad as Greenland. However it seems likely that there was a feedback effect. The first raids against virtually defenceless positions in England and elsewhere (England had no navy) were so successful in terms of booty and slaves, and the losses so few, that the Norsemen decided to make a living out of it. They certainly had no technology that was unavailable to the English or the French. On their side was the fear factor, for they well deserved their reputation for savagery, brutality and mercilessness. The raider who arrived dressed in a wolfcoat and planted his axe in the face of the first man to welcome him was no harmless trader, though the traders came too, eventually.

The invasion of the Norsemen falls into three phases: raiding, settlement and conquest. The first raids came at the end of the eighth century when they fell on carefully picked targets – the coastal monasteries, known to be full of treasure, unarmed monks, and novices who could be taken as slaves. They first made a major impact as settlers in the northern lands. They took over the Orkneys entirely, so that no trace of the original population remained – there are no pre-Norse place names on the map today. They also moved into Shetland, the Hebrides including Argyll, the Scottish Highlands, the Isle of Man and northern and eastern Ireland. By 840 they were firmly established in Dublin, Waterford, Wexford and Limerick. Power was disputed with the High Kings of Ireland for many years afterwards, culminating in the victory of High King Brian at Clontarf in 1014, but in practice the

Norse had come to stay, and intermarried with the local population. Their Dublin Kings, Olaf the White and Ivar the Boneless amongst them, recognized the authority of the King of Norway, and also caused a good deal of trouble in the north of England. A futher group set out for the Faeroes and Iceland, taking their Irish girls with them. Genetic studies have shown that the male genes of Iceland are Norse, but the female genes are Irish.

The Viking attacks had a political impact all over Britain. The first Wessex king to feel the heat of the Viking flame was Egbert (802-839), who by 827 had conquered the Mercians, disunited after the death of Offa in 797. Egbert became the most important English king up to this time, accepted as overlord by the Northumbrians so that his writ ran from Exeter to the Forth of Firth and back to Kent. So in the immortal words of *1066 and all that*, England was ruled by an egg. Egbert beat off a combined force of Norsemen and Cornishmen at Hengist's Down, on the Cornish side of the Tamar, in 836, but a complete change in the political geography of England was not far away.

Just as Wessex expanded, so did Dalriada, the Irish kingdom based in Argyll in Scotland. Three Dalriadan kings ruled over both Dalriada and Pictland, with their base at Fortriu in Perthshire, but their dynasty was overthrown under the weight of Viking attacks. Permanent union dates from 843 when Kenneth MacAlpin, based in Dalriada, took the joint crown in connivance with the Norsemen. From this time the kingdom was known as Alba. The same process was also taking place in Wales, where the northern and central kingdoms coalesced under Rhodri, the king of Gwynedd, from 856.

In 855 the Norsemen overwintered in England for the first time, on the Isle of Sheppey – they were here to stay. Distracted by other temptations in Europe, the full force of the Norsemen was not however felt until 865, when they came from all winds to set about the conquest of England. Full-scale war broke out in the period 865-878, with the English led by Alfred after 871. The fearsome brothers Halfdan and Ivar the Boneless came out of Ireland to take York and most of Northumbria with it, destroying its glorious religion in the process. In 870 Ivar took East Anglia, slaying King Edmund, a righteous and worthy king who would not make terms or renounce his religion to the heathens. He became one of the foremost saints of England and miracles were said to take place at his tomb at Bury St Edmunds for centuries to come.

Meanwhile, Mercia was annihilated. 868 saw the first imposition of the Danegeld, a tax raised at first to fight the Danes, later to buy them off. It proved such a good money-raiser than it continued until the thirteenth century, long after the Danish threat had subsided. Because of it, thousands of English silver coins have been found in Scandinavia and some even in Russia, mainly from the tenth century.

A Dane called Guthrum attacked Wessex, famously pinning Alfred down in the marshes of Athelney in Somerset for three months around Easter in 878 (where he burnt the cakes). However, Alfred raised his militia and came out fighting, defeating Guthrum later that year at the battle of Edington. Guthrum surrendered at Chippenham and agreed to become a Christian. (As Christianity was never a strong suite amongst the Danes, this must have been a blow to his prestige.) The Treaty of Wedmore was agreed. The upshot of this and a later treaty was that the boundary between the Danelaw and what had now effectively become England was set along a wavy line between London and Chester. (The term "England" only dates from this period, to distinguish it from the Norse territories.) There were separate Norse kingdoms in the north, East Anglia and Mercia, so the old geography persisted for the moment. However, this messy boundary, right across the most settled part of the country and recognising no physical barriers, was never going to last, and indeed it did not last long.

*   *   *   *

In England from this period right up until the ascendancy of the Whig aristocracy on the establishment of the Hanoverian dynasty in 1714, when his real power was removed, too much depended on the monarch, be he king, queen or lord protector. In a way it is surprising that such an unsatisfactory system should have been allowed to continue for so long. If the monarch was a strong, mature and long-lived adult, things generally went well. If the monarch was weak, foolish, a minor or short-lived, then there were serious problems. Very rarely was a monarch selected on any other basis than his parentage; the possession of attributes useful to a king did not enter consideration. In Saxon times the heir to the throne was selected by the king, but this choice had then to be approved by the witan, the council of nobles. However if the direct heir – normally the eldest son – was an adult with four limbs and a beating heart, it was very difficult for them to choose another, at the risk of setting off a civil war. So it was that under Alfred (871-899), the only English king ever to earn the epithet "Great", or his grandson Athelstan (925-940), the Danish menace was contained. Under a weak monarch, notably at this time Ethelred the Unready (meaning "lacking advice") (979-1016), all their good work was undone.

Norse settlement is thought to have been extensive, and is identified by place names suffixed by "thwaite", "by", "thorpe" and "toft". There are over 1500 of these, occurring all over the Danelaw, especially on the east coast, but often also far inland. The main strength of the Danes was in the east midlands, in their "five boroughs" – Leicester, Lincoln, Nottingham, Stamford and Derby – and also in the south midlands where they held a number of towns including Bedford and Hertford. The extent to which the existing population was replaced is unknown, but there would certainly have been floods of refugees milling about the country during the long wars. Quite often it appears that Norse villages were created alongside existing villages, but on secondary land rather than on the best land, indicating a degree of co-existence with the native population. Archaeologically speaking the Vikings have left comparatively few remains though there is some evidence of their raiding. Our best idea of what a Viking village looks like come from excavations in Shetland and in their other territories – the Faeroes, Iceland and Norway itself. The geneticist Brian Sykes notes that the signals for male lines coming from Europe after the Roman Conquest are much stronger in the Danelaw area than they are to the south of it. This indicates that the sheer numbers involved in the Danish immigration must have been substantial – probably numerically greater than the Saxon equivalent.

Certainly the Danes soon adopted Christianity and presumably intermarried, and evidence from digs in York shows that they got away from warring and down to trading and craftwork. They also had a profound effect on the English language. Danish and Old English words had similar roots, but different endings. Both were inflected languages, as German still is, with case endings to indicate possession, place and so on. To form one language these word endings were replaced with prepositions. Over 1800 Norse words entered the language (indicating a high degree of mixing), including "they", "them", "their", "get", "both", "give", "take", and remarkably, "are". Many of these words include the "sk" sound – "skirt", "sky", "skin", "whisk." Scandinavian surnames also originated from these times, including those ending in "-son" (Henderson, Davidson) which are very common in the northern England and Scotland.

Norse settlement was proportionately the greatest in Scotland, and its impact on the ethnic mix of the population today is clear to anyone who walks down the street in Glasgow where Nordic features such as the turned-up nose are commonplace. The Norsemen settled thickly all over the Highlands and Islands and the west coast. It was partly from these areas that the lowland industrial towns were populated at the time of the Industrial Revolution.

*   *   *   *

After the treaties ending the war, Alfred understood the political situation perfectly and made no attempt to reconquer the lost territories, instead preferring to consolidate within what was left of England. Considering how bloodthirsty they are supposed to have been (at least in the early days), the Anglo-Saxons built few defences, and there is no such thing as a Saxon hill-fort. The lack of defences was felt very keenly when the Viking raids began, and one of Alfred's initiatives was to create thirty fortified towns or "burhs", right across his kingdom, including Southampton, Oxford, Bath and Totnes. In the long run, these did prove very necessary because the Danes rampaged all over the country. The burhs were laid out internally with a rectangular street-plan and turf walls forty feet high, crowned with a wooden palisade. Taken together the burhs represent the most impressive set of public works since the Roman times. Urbanization was a slow process in Saxon times – there were no towns at all at first – but this process was given a great boost by the need to defend the population against the Vikings.

Alfred, a man of unceasing energy, recodified the laws of what had become "de facto" a united, if shrunken, England by selecting from and combining the laws of Wessex, Mercia and Kent. He also began to codify history for it is under Alfred that the compilation of the Anglo-Saxon Chronicle began. He remodelled the army, created a navy, set up schools and was altogether a Good Egg. There was even a diplomatic rapprochement with the Welsh. Alfred took a Welsh adviser, a wise man by the name of Asser. The Welsh had begun to think that the English might not be so bad after all, when they had had a good dose of the Vikings.

Four more years of war followed in 892 when 800 shiploads of Vikings arrived in the Thames estuary and went berserk (a Viking expression) over the English plain, raising the English Danes. They were finally dispatched to pillage the Franks. By the time he died at the age of 51, Alfred had reigned for 28 years, 16 of those years spent at war.

Alfred's successors did much better than might have been expected and did push back the frontiers until all the important parts of England were under their control. The name of Edgar the Elder (899-925) became a terror to the Norsemen as he and his sister Ethelfleda relentlessly rolled back the frontier. Stafford, Derby, Leicester, Hertford and Bedford were liberated and made the centres of new counties. Athelstan (925-940) his successor did similarly well. One great concerted effort was made to stop him when Athelstan faced a combined army of Scots, Irish, and Norse at Brunaburh in 937 (thought possibly to be Bromborough in the Wirral), but Athelstan was victorious.

Another success for Athelstan was the final subjugation of Cornwall. Although it had been *de facto* part of England for a hundred years, it was nominally independent. In 927, Athelstan attacked the British in Exeter, compelling them to withdraw over the Tamar into Cornwall. William of Malmesbury claims that Athelstan "Cleansed the city of its defilement by wiping out that filthy race." (Quoted from *Celt and Saxon*, Peter Berresford Ellis) Cornish independence disappeared from this time, though it has been claimed that it was not regarded as part of England proper for centuries, but rather as a colonial possession of the English crown. Eventually it was organized into a Duchy to be inherited by each heir apparent to the throne of England.

In Scotland, Strathclyde and Cumberland (the rump of Reged) remained independent kingdoms until the time of Constantine II (900-943) when their rulers accepted his overlordship. Control over this area then changed hands between Alban and English rulers but by the early eleventh century it was firmly in the Alban sphere of influence. The Isle of Man, the whole of the Hebrides (known as the Southern Islands or "Sodor", as in the Bishop of Sodor and Man) and the Orkneys were by this time in Norse hands.

The contemporary of Athelstan in Wales was Hywel Dda ("The Good") (910-950), one of the very few Welsh princes who succeeded in unifying the country and who is famous in Celtic circles for codifying the Welsh laws. These laws were distinctly early medieval in flavour. For example, a man who stole food was pardoned if he had passed by ten houses and none had given him anything to eat. In 927 Hywel acknowledged Athelstan as his overlord, and fixed the boundary of South Wales on the Wye. He was called The Good because of his pilgrimage to Rome in 928/9. However, the obligations of medieval fealty could often be irksome in the extreme, and in 934 Hywel was obliged to accompany Athelstan is his campaigns against the Scottish king, Constantine. Upon his death, Wales broke up into petty principalities once more.

Within England, outside the heartland of greater Wessex, the English kings only had a tenuous hold. The Danes had settled in numbers and were ready to switch allegiance to one of their own at the slightest sign of weakness. They were strong in the five boroughs, in York (the capital of the north for hundreds of years), and they had infiltrated Cumbria and Lancashire to such an extent that these regions were theirs to command. The very year that Athelstan died, Olaf of Dublin was back in control in York. However, English dominance was reasserted, to be consolidated under a second Edgar (959-975), "The Peaceable". In a sense, this was only a lull before the storm, because the Scandinavians were distracted elsewhere.

Chapter 7 – Late Saxon and Danish Rule

Danish piracy was renewed between 980 and 991, in the reign of Ethelred the Unready, who had succeeded to the throne as a child of ten after his mother had organized the murder of his stepbrother. Between 991 and 1016, war was almost continuous. English weakness under Ethelred was there for all to see, and the Danes descended with impunity on every navigable town from Southampton to Chester. The war was immortalised by one Byrhtnoth, the earl of Essex, defending his coast at Maldon in 991. This episode demonstrates that at least one aspect of the English national character, a sense of fair play, had developed by this time. Byrhtnoth caught the Danes at their weakest, when they were disembarking. The Danes protested that this was hardly a fair fight, so Byrhtnoth allowed them to get out of their ships and form up properly. He was then thrashed.

Ethelred resorted to desperate measures, paying out a vast fortune in protection money from the Danegeld in a vain attempt to buy the raiders off. He tried to build a navy to defend his shores, but the ships always seemed to be in the wrong place when the enemy struck. In fact it was to be hundreds of years before the Navy, correctly referred to by W. S. Gilbert as the bulwark of England's greatness, was an effectively organized form of national defence.

Ethelred struck back militarily by devastating Cumbria and the Isle of Man. However, his worst move was to order the murder of the Danes in his own service on 13 November, 1002 in the St Brice's Day Massacre. One of the victims was the sister of Sweyn Forkbeard, King of the Danes, who naturally sought revenge. He invaded the following year, sacking town after town. Ethelred eventually fled the country in 1013, leaving Sweyn in charge. However Sweyn died in 1014, and Ethelred returned; two more years of civil war followed before Canute, son of Sweyn, was acknowledged as king by the London witan. In the last stages of the conflict, Ethelred having died, his son Edmund was betrayed by the murderous Edric Streona, "The Grasper", who changed sides at the last battle. Once in power, Canute executed Streona,

Alderman of Mercia, who could only be trusted to make more trouble. Dane or no, England could now settle down under its best monarch since Alfred.

An event early in the reign of Canute was the permanent secession of the northern part of Berenicia to Scotland. In 1018 the Scots under King Malcolm beat the Northumbrians in a battle at Carham on the Tweed. This confirmed the border on the Tweed, detaching what is now the Scottish part of old Northumbria. Nevertheless, this corner of south-east Scotland had been part of English-speaking Northumbria since the time of Aethelfrith in 603. English, or a form of it, has been spoken in Scotland for almost as long as it has in England.

Canute reigned until 1035. He was soon to inherit Denmark, and during the course of his reign he added Norway to his territories, though this empire broke up on his death. In England, he quickly replaced some of the leading English earls with his own men, but in general he let the well-established administrative machine continue. There were no major changes in the way the country was run; it simply had a Danish ruler. Born a heathen, Canute converted to Christianity and felt safe enough at home to make a long pilgrimage to Rome. However, this may have been simply a political move, because Canute could behave very cynically. In one move of breathtaking cunning, he dumped his wife (claiming, as he was not a Christian at the time, that they had never been properly married) and two sons and married Emma, Ethelred's wife. This was done partly to please the English, but mainly to suppress the claim of her two sons, Edward and Alfred, who were left behind in Normandy. Canute also murdered his brother-in-law, Ulf. He surrounded himself with his Danish housecarls at all times, in fact living amongst them as a fellow-soldier, in the manner of Frederick the Great.

Canute's reign saw the rise of the Godwin, Earl of Wessex, a former Sussex pirate and another of those evil barons that stalked this era of history, like Edric Streona. However, Canute trusted him enough to leave him in charge while he went to Rome. Godwin was the man who kidnapped Alfred, one of the two children that Queen Emma had left behind in Normandy. Alfred was later blinded and left to die in a monastery. This act was to be one of William's excuses for his later invasion. After Canute died, Godwin was the real ruler of England, and the father of its last pre-Norman king, Harold II.

Canute died before he had reached 40, and after a brief extension of Danish rule by short-lived monarchs, the last of whom died of drink by the Thames, the English went back to their old line. They selected Edward ("The Confessor") (1042-1066) as their king. He was the other son of Ethelred and Emma previously left behind in Normandy. Edward was a saintly man, already 37 years old and unmarried. His own mother was not in favour of him accepting the kingship, recommending instead the King of Norway, but Edward's title was good and he was English. However, he was scarcely strong enough to stand up to his barons, notably Earl Godwin, who quickly foisted his daughter Edith on him. There were no children from this marriage, possibly because there was no sex either.

As he had been brought up in Normandy and spoke French, Edward soon filled his court with French-speaking Normans, including his nephew Ralph "The Timid." Things came to a head when, increasingly confident over Godwin, he appointed the Frenchman Robert of Jumieges Archbishop of Canterbury in 1051. There was some justification for this because the Norman clergy was better-educated than the English, but of course the English did not like it. Godwin of Wessex was the head of the English party, and for a time, he was exiled. During this period, William, Duke of Normandy visited Edward. He saw that Normans held great offices, he heard French spoken all around him, and jumped to the obvious conclusion – all this could be mine. However, the Godwin family returned with a fleet, sailing up the Thames unopposed by the English fleet. This forced Edward into a humiliating climbdown; his Frenchmen were expelled. Godwin himself died in 1053, but left his sons behind him in powerful positions, Harold as Earl of Wessex and Tostig as Earl of Northumbria. The family earned a bad reputation for taking land, but in 1063 the brothers won themselves a military reputation by suppressing an insurrection led by Gruffydd of Gwynedd, the most powerful king in Wales. Harold succeeded where many had failed before him. He devastated Gwynedd to the extent that the locals gave up and sent him the neatly severed head of their ruler Gruffydd.

Another man with a bad reputation was ruling in Scotland in this period, Macbeth. Shakespeare dramatised this episode in Scottish history with his notoriously bloodcurdling play, but its basis was only a fairly ordinary dynastic struggle. On the death of King Malcolm II, the last of the MacAlpin dynasty, Macbeth and his queen expected to inherit. However the throne passed instead through Malcolm's daughter to his grandson Duncan, in 1034. Macbeth exercised some independence of power in the Moray area. Having tried and failed to gain military victories against the Northumbrians and the Earl of Orkney, Duncan decided to take an army north to suppress Macbeth.

However he was defeated and slain in battle 1040 – he was not murdered by Macbeth.

Far from being the short-lived, jumpy and guilt-tormented usurper portrayed by the bard, Macbeth then began a seventeen-year reign, not unsuccessful by the standards of the time. Then Duncan's son, another Malcolm, came after him with assistance from Siward, Earl of Northumbria. Macbeth was defeated and killed when Birnam Wood came to Dunsinane, Macbeth's castle. Macbeth was unusual in that he had ruled from the Moray area, north of the Mounth, the physical divide of the Grampian mountains which separates lowland Scotland from the Moray Firth. The lowland nobles did not like this power shift and failed to support Macbeth. As Malcom III (Canmore), his conqueror began a long reign (1057-1093) in which he had to deal with the diplomatic niceties involved with handling the Normans from England. Malcolm's long tenure and the fact that he produced many sons put an end to the dynastic infighting which had plagued the Scottish monarchy up to this time.

When Edward the Confessor died in 1066 it seemed clear to the Witan that William was likely to attempt an invasion. The candidate with the best claim, Edgar Atheling, grandson of Edmund Ironside, was only fourteen years old, so the Witan by-passed the royal family, and simply passed the kingship onto Harold. The nobles felt that he might be able to defend the country from imminent threat. However, Harold had previously gone to France, probably to try to strike some kind of deal. William was in no mood for making deals and obliged Harold to make a feudal oath of homage, under duress, which Harold then ignored. These oaths were taken very seriously in medieval times, and William used this as one of his excuses for launching his attack.

Edward the Confessor had promised the throne to William, a great-nephew of his mother Emma (and so his second cousin), so William had a strong claim. William was the bastard son of Robert, "The Devil", Duke of Normandy and a tanner's daughter from Falaise called Arlette. He had a difficult childhood and had to fight to gain and hold on to power. He was a tall man and a tireless horseman with a fearsome voice. Though able and energetic he could also be cruel and fierce. In 1053 he married Matilda of Flanders. Unusually for these times, this seems to have been a love match, and William had no known mistresses or illegitimate children. He had long subdued rebellions in Normandy and was in a particularly strong position because his main rivals in northern France had been temporarily weakened. His duchy was expanding, and was tightly run on clear and simple principles which everyone understood. It was a highly centralized state in which the leading principle was that William was sovereign and that all important decisions were his. He owned all the land in the first instance. His nobles, bishops and monasteries then took their fiefs from him, and in turn sublet to knightly tenants. There was a clear feudal system of rights and responsibilities, in contrast to the ramshackle state of affairs in England. Note, however, that in some ways, England was better organized that Normandy, notably in its administration.

William was indeed a threat, but he was not the only one. Led by their king Harold Hardrada, the Norwegians, sensing an opportunity, were also on their way back. Harold Hardrada fell in with Tostig, Harold's brother, who had been ousted from Northumbria by the disgusted locals, and the two joined forces for an attack on York. However Harold defeated them at Stamford Bridge, where both men were killed. The date was 25 September. Harold then had to make the best of his way back to the south coast, where three days later, William landed at Pevensey.

He had gathered a fleet and an army in the mouth of the Seine by the first week of August, but he did not set sail until the end of September. This was because his intelligence was good. He knew that Harold Hardrada was also on his way to England. It is thought that William waited until after the Battle of Stamford Bridge, when he knew that he would only have to fight one army, and that that army would be seriously weakened. In the event, William, delayed in any case by unfavorable winds, set sail only when he received news of the battle.

Harold rushed to meet the Normans on the downs behind Hastings, where as we all know, he was defeated and killed in battle on 14 October 1066. His army, composed of fully-armed elite troops, the housecarls, and a poorly-armed peasant militia or fyrd, in contrast to the Normans, was short of archers. Another critical difference was that Harold had no cavalry, only infantry, whereas William had at his disposal a whole division of heavy cavalry, with the horses specially bred for size and trained for warfare. Nevertheless the English army stood its ground all day and only collapsed when a hail of arrows killed Harold himself. His body was identified by his mistress, Edith Swan-Neck, and buried on the beach. According to some critics, Harold made two big mistakes. Firstly he should have waited longer and gathered a larger army before confronting William, so soon after Stamford Bridge. Secondly he should have kept further from the firing line so that his cause could have been saved for another day if he had lost the battle but kept his life. However, the king was expected to physically lead the battle in these times. William himself had three horses killed under him on the day.

It is sometimes claimed (by Norwegians) that if William had landed first, the world would now be learning to speak Norwegian instead of English, because Harold was strong enough to win one battle, but not two. However, that seems unlikely. The Scandinavians had been disputing power in England for over 200 years, since 865, and had never succeeded in holding on to it. William himself would have to face their attacks, but he and his dynasty did hold on, without too much difficulty. The Normans were a far more powerful and sophisticated people than the Scandinavians, or for that matter the English. England was about to find itself jerked fast-forward in a cultural leap into a new era.

Though his involvement at Hastings has cast Harold in a patriotic glow, it is also unlikely that he would have survived for long. He and his family only had strong support in Wessex, and little in Mercia or Northumbria. He represented only a faction and would soon have been overwhelmed by the forces ranged against him, for more Scandinavians – the Danish descendants of Canute – were waiting in the wings, and indeed soon arrived. Furthermore, the disregarded Edgar Atheling would have made a bid for his rights at some point. (William was to see off challenges from both these quarters.)

With the Normans, there is a sense of clear organization. The surprising thing is not so much that William beat Harold, who had not been able to raise much of an army, but that he then held off the enemies – the Scandinavians, the Scots, the Irish and the Welsh – who had troubled England for centuries. William's army was thought to include about 12,000 men. It was not so much a Norman army as a Frankish one, as William had been obliged to trawl all northern France for his soldiers. They came from far and wide in the hope of spoils. This is a far smaller army than the 50,000 brought by the Romans, and this says something for the disorganized military condition of England at this time. A much higher priority for Edward the Confessor had been to build a church, Westminster Abbey. In the event he was buried in it, though it was rebuilt 200 years later in the time of Henry III.

So why was William able to achieve his conquest with a much smaller army than Aulus Plautius and the emperor Claudius? The nature of the enemy had changed. Settled agrarian populations with towns full of civilian and religious functionaries and traders are much easier to conquer than wild tribesman who have been constantly at war with one another for generations (which is what the Romans found).

The same phenomenon can be observed in other countries, notably China and India, which were repeatedly overrun by well-organized horse-based armies from outside their borders. Civilisation is a boon to the conqueror. In contrast, Ireland, land of the warring petty chieftains, the clans and the bogs, proved much more difficult to conquer than England. The Normans never achieved this, and long after them the English Tudors still had the same problems. It was not mastered from England until Oliver Cromwell went there, 600 years after William arrived in England. Again, the Romans had found the settled plains of southern England far easier going than Scotland.

Chapter 8 – The Norman Conquest

William I 1066-1087 (21 years)
Born 1027; married 1053, Matilda of Flanders

The witan bowed to reality with William's army breathing down its neck, and accepted William as king without a fight. If they had known what they were letting themselves in for, they might have thought twice about it, because this was to be no simple switch to a foreign ruler in the manner of Canute. There followed 150 years (to 1215, the year of Magna Carta) in which the English were to be treated as a colonial race, and 300 years in which the English language was regarded as a barbaric gabble. However, the witan recognized that England must have a strong king capable of uniting the country, and William was nothing if not that. William himself, as he did have a dynastic claim, assumed that the English would rally to him with no problem, but soon found out that it was not going to be so easy.

Following the conquest, the Danes occupied both sides of the Humber and penetrated the fenland, but William bought them off. They threatened again under a new King Canute in 1085, this danger stimulating the production of the Domesday Book itself to assess revenue for the coming war. The threat fizzled out with the assassination of Canute, and the Danes never seriously endangered England again – another great benefit of Norman rule. For long periods of time for almost 300 years the Danish menace had stalked the land, but Norman military organization meant that there were no longer easy pickings to be had. All the great lords were now Normans and they were not going to throw in their lot with any Scandinavian adventurer.

William had only defeated Harold and his small army, and soon revolts broke out in Kent, Hereford and the Welsh borders, the Bristol Channel and Northumbria. William found himself in Harold's shoes, having to dash round the country suppressing insurrection. However, the rebellions were uncoordinated, and soon put down. In 1069 there was another serious rising in the north, where 500 knights were murdered at Durham. This time William showed no leniency, as he had with other rebellions, and wasted the country between York and Durham in a winter campaign known as the Harrying of the North.. Much the same happened between Chester and Shrewsbury. Peasants were slaughtered and crops and grain were burnt so that the survivors must starve. This was genocide on the scale of Agricola's massacre of the Ordovices or the first Saxon revolt - William at his most ruthless. At the time of the Domesday Book nearly 20 years later, much of the area was still described as waste.

One figure from legend is known from this time, Hereward the Wake, said to have been an outlawed lord who returned to his estates to find his family destroyed and his property in the hands of Normans. He then led a guerilla campaign from the Fenlands in association with someone who was certainly real enough, Earl Morcar of Northumberland, one of the most important people in Anglo-Saxon England. Their rebellion based on the Isle of Ely was not suppressed until 1071.

Because of widespread confiscations of property following the rebellions, William had vast territories with which to reward his followers. An estimated 4,000 to 5,000 English aristocrats had been deprived of their property. However William did not revive the great earldoms of Wessex, Mercia or Northumbria, fearing that these would put too much power into the hands of the earls. Where one individual received many manors (in the case of one Robert of Mortmain, William's half-brother, 793!) they were spread across the country. In three cases, however, powerful "counties palatinate" were created, where the earl owned the whole county - Cheshire, to guard against the Welsh; Durham, ditto for Scotland; and Kent, to keep an eye on the French. Durham and Kent were allocated to bishops who could not marry and produce legal heirs, only Cheshire going to a layman, as it was thought he would have his hands pretty full anyway. The barons of the Welsh borders were given permission to extend their territories in Wales, and the Normans advanced to Conway in north Wales, Montgomery in east Wales, and Cardiff in the south.

William did not stop with the conquest of England; he invaded Scotland too, trapping King Malcolm III in a pincer movement launched from the Clyde and the Tay in 1072. Malcolm had made the mistake of supporting the claim of the English pretender to the throne, Edgar Atheling. Like many before him, Malcolm was then obliged to acknowledge William as his lord. (As his second wife, Malcolm married Edgar Atheling's sister Margaret. Queensferry on the Forth is named after Margaret – the place where she took the ferry to the abbey at Dunfermline. Born in Hungary and reputed to be the holiest of women, she was later canonized as St Margaret. Her daughter Edith, later called Matilda, became the wife of Henry I of England.)

However, before too long William began to have problems with his own Norman barons, and there were brief rebellions in 1074 and 1078. The real cause of these revolts was that William had limited the powers of the barons, as he did not wish to see them become overmighty, as they had on the continent.

William was to spend much of reign at war with the French in France. In 1073 he led an English army there, against the province of Maine. In 1087 he attacked Mantes, a town on the Seine. By this time an obese man, he fell from his horse, punctured some internal organ (probably his spleen) and died six agonising weeks later.

William left three sons, Robert, William and Henry. He decided to follow the principle that the eldest son should inherit his father's ancestral possessions and the second son the acquired property, so Robert ("Short-Hose") became Duke of Normandy and William (known as William Rufus) became King of England. There was no compulsion on William I to act in this way; probably he would have liked to bequeath all his territory to William Rufus, his favorite, but felt he could not exclude Robert (who had led a rebellion against William in Normandy). Henry had to content himself for the moment with £5,000, though he too was destined to be King of England, in a longer reign than his father or brother. But in the meantime, of course, William I had divided his kingdoms and in so doing had set up the standard conditions for a medieval civil war.

*   *   *   *

The Norman administrators arriving with William I found a mass of archaic rights and privileges. As a result, the country underwent changes more profound that at any other time in its history. Society was completely reshaped on the Norman feudal model, and with it the organs of the state and the church. Relations with Europe changed completely as for the first time, France became the enemy of choice, a relationship that lasted until 1815. Where there had been free villages (as in East Anglia), there was put in place a system where everyone had a lord and knew his place. New castles were built all over the country, very quickly, earth mounds and wood at first, then stone; one of them was the first Tower of London. By way of contrast, glorious new cathedrals of an unprecedented scale were built. Some of the most impressive cathedrals in the country date from the early years of Norman rule – Canterbury (rebuilt from 1070 following a fire), Ely, Peterborough, Lincoln, Durham. The military was reformed. The Exchequer was set up to control government revenue and expenditure. An inventory of the whole country was taken to assess it for revenue, an exercise which created the Domesday Book. No previous monarch would have dreamed of such an enterprise. The barely interrupted chaos of the previous 200 years was replaced by stability. The Normans brought with them the highest culture available in Europe, and without a doubt, hard though it was to bear, England gained far more from defeat at Hastings than it would have done from victory.

The dispossession of the English aristocracy and their replacement by Normans meant that by the time of the Domesday survey in 1086, which compiled data for the country in that year and as it had been in 1066, barely one percent of the tenants-in-chief were English. In fact it is now thought that one of the main purposes of the Domesday survey was to establish title to land. Since the conquest there had been many encroachments by the barons on the lands of both the Anglo-Saxons and the church, and the barons wanted proper title to their gains. The Domesday commissioners sought out the rights and wrongs of each case and fines were levied in some cases.

The replacement of the English aristocracy had been virtually total. However the English held their own as subtenants, and intermarriage over the decades created an Anglo-Norman middle class. By 1177 a chronicler called Scaccario (See The English Language, David Crystal, p.191) was able to say:

"Now that the English and the Normans have been dwelling together, marrying and giving in marriage, the two nations have become so mixed that it is scarcely possible today, speaking of free men, to tell who is English, who is Norman race."

An interesting question from these times is this: had there been no Norman Conquest, would Anglo-Saxon England or Anglo-Danish England have survived? The answer is probably no. By the middle of the thirteen century even the Scottish court was speaking Norman French. The French would have filtered and fought their way into England as they did in Scotland and Ireland. They were bringing with them something new, something modern – the realization that society was getting richer and could afford more specialization, less people on the land. They brought with them a culture that was notably different – great cathedrals, abbeys, cloistered monasteries, castles, walled towns, manors, nucleated villages, the whole feudal system with its carefully measured obligations, and eventually tournaments, courtly love, troubadours, falconers, conical ladies' hats and all the rest of it. This was an irresistible force, partly because it was so much more glamorous than Danish cattle raiders.

William also introduced concepts of Norman law which baffled the Anglo-Saxons. For example, he decreed that:

"If a Frenchman shall charge an Englishman with perjury or murder or theft ...which cannot be denied, the Englishman may defend himself, as he shall prefer, either by the ordeal of hot iron or by wager of battle. But if the Englishman be infirm, let him find another who will take his place. If one of them shall be vanquished, he shall pay a fine of 40 shillings to the king. If an Englishman shall charge a Frenchman and be unwilling to prove his accusation either by ordeal or by wager of battle, I will, nevertheless, that the Frenchman shall acquit himself by a valid oath."

Fighting a battle with your accuser, or providing a champion to fight one for you, seemed to have little to do with sorting out the rights and wrongs and punishing the guilty. Worse, if an Englishman accused a Frenchman of a crime, he then had to back up his accusation by waging a battle with him. Where was the justice of Alfred in this? (The law lasted for a hundred and fifty years before it was replaced with trial by jury.) Punishments were also prescribed including blinding and castration, but the death penalty was banned. Slavery, still in existence (especially in the west country) was abolished as offensive to Norman Christian principles.

As a result of the unification of Normandy and England under one head, another territory came to be ruled from England – the Channel Islands. They were part of the Duchy of Normandy, and never reverted to France, even though they are much nearer to France than England.

*   *   *   *

The most characteristic architectural feature of the Norman landscape was the castle, of which there were two basic types, the motte and bailey and the ringwork. In Saxon times there had been very few castles, but by 1215 there were approximately 900 of them in England alone. These served a function quite unlike any previous defensive installation in England. Whereas Roman forts and walls were built to defend the country from raiders and invaders, and the Saxon burhs to serve as refuges for whole communities, the Norman castles were build in the first instance to protect the Normans from their own subjects. They found later uses as homes for private baronial armies which would then attack similarly fortified armies. The distribution of these castles (see map p. 145, Archaeology of Great Britain, Andrew Hayes) tells us a great deal. The castles are spread fairly evenly over England, but the thickest concentrations are in the Welsh Borders and in West Wales. Piecemeal colonization of Wales was undertaken in Norman times, but it certainly was not a safe occupation. Also there are notable concentrations of Norman castles in southern Scotland, and in the area north of the Tay. These did not represent an occupation; the Normans conquered England militarily, but they also infiltrated Scotland and Ireland, by skirmish and by marriage. The leading families of medieval Scotland and Ireland were Normans.

Other features of the Norman world were the village and the open field system. Saxon settlement had been of scattered farms; over a long period from the Conquest, these were replaced by nuclear villages surrounded by large, subdivided open fields (that is, without hedges or walls). In the basic model there would be three large fields, one producing grain, the other peas or beans, and the third left fallow. In addition there would be common grazing land. Not everyone in the village had a share in the communal pie. At one time it was estimated that landless cottars made up a quarter of the population. Each village would then have its church and of course its manor. It is thought that many of the villages referred to in the Domesday Book were not what we think of as villages, but communities of scattered farms.

Another communal resource was the forest, carefully managed to produce the thin coppiced poles for which so many uses were found, and which served as rough grazing for swine. An innovation of this period was the royal forest. Huge areas of the country were declared royal forest, where no man could take so much as an acorn or a basket of firewood without the risk of punishment by mutilation. The royal forests were a hated institution for many years to come. "Forest" in this sense does not mean a contiguous wooded area, but an area where forest law applied. These forests contained arable land and open grazing as well as trees.

It is also evident from the Domesday Book that England had a very considerable economy. Seven or eight million acres were under the plough in 1086, almost as many as in the 1950s, and all the best cultivable land was already cleared for farming.

*   *   *   *

There has been some speculation concerning the wife of William III, Matilda of Flanders. According to the *Guinness Book of Records* she was England's shortest queen at only four feet two inches tall, yet she produced eleven children for William. Speculation on this matter appears to be long-standing as Matilda's incomplete skeleton was exhumed twice in France, in 1819 and 1959. The conclusion was that Matilda was probably five feet tall after all. Her death at the age of 51 in 1083 led to fears that without her restraining influence, the country would suffer from William's ferocity.

Chapter 9 – The Early Norman Kings

William II 1087-1100 (13 years)
Born 1060

William did not care for his son Robert, much spoiled by his mother, who had grown up to be an irresponsible wastrel, fond only of hawk and hound, the company of harlots and buffoons, and never given any responsibility in the lifetime of his father. On failing to inherit the English crown, Robert encouraged revolt amongst the barons of England. They duly obliged, but William Rufus called on the English to help him, saying that any who did not was a "nithing". The English thought this would be disgraceful, and they did help him. The prime concern of all the early Norman kings was to restrain the power of their barons; and of course the prime concern of the barons was the very opposite, to obtain that power. Into this equation the Norman kings from the Conqueror onwards called on the English people to support them, which they generally did. In his quarrel with his brother Robert, William also invaded Normandy, in 1090, but was persuaded to negotiate by his barons, who had property on both sides of the Channel and who did not want to see it wasted by warfare.

William was an evil-minded but vigorous King. He then invaded Cumbria, the last piece of the English jigsaw to fall into place. It does not appear in the Domesday Book because it was not part of England when that was compiled in 1086. It was eventually annexed by William in 1092; at the time it contained the remnants of the old British population and a large admixture of Norsemen. Large-scale English settlement followed, particularly in Carlisle and the Eden Valley behind it, but Celtic place-names remain a feature of the hillier areas (such as "Helvellyn"). The Scots at this time were partially distracted by their Norse neighbours. The line between what was Scottish and Norwegian territory was settled in 1098 by a treaty between Magnus Barelegs of Norway and Edgar of Scotland, allocating all the Scottish mainland to

Scotland but leaving the western isles and the Isle of Man with a Norwegian king.

William was also concerned with the Welsh threat. He built a string of castles in the borders, and also decreed that any land taken from the Welsh could remain the property of the taker. This policy motivated the unruly border barons and was so successful that most of lowland South Wales was soon in the hands of Norman adventurers.

William Rufus was an unscrupulous man and he employed an extortionate minister, Ranulf Flambard, one of the Normans who had been in England in the reign of Edward the Confessor. Flambard ensured that feudal dues were paid, but he did not stop there. One abuse was the taking of responsibility for minors who had inherited estates, and raking off the revenues in the meantime. Another was maintaining vacancies in bishoprics and abbeys following the death of an incumbent, and again taking the revenue. Bishops and abbots could not have legal heirs, so these vacancies could remain open for years. This caused trouble between the king and the clergy, especially when William refused to appoint an Archbishop of Canterbury for four years. When he thought himself dying, he did appoint one, Anselm. However, William recovered, to find that he now had to deal with this able and pious man who did not approve of his lifestyle at all. The result was that other feature of medieval life, the stand-off between the King and the Archbishop of Canterbury. Anselm left England to take his case to the Pope and William seized his property. Some say that this is one reason why William has had a bad press. He was successful in his conquests and also did well as a builder – one of his projects was Westminster Hall, still with us today. However the medieval "press", such as it was, was written by clerics. William, unlike his father, was not a devout Christian, if he was a Christian at all, and he abused the Church - and the Church wrote the history. Moreover, William was openly criticised by churchmen in his own time, one of them, Orderic Vitalis, saying of him "He had no lawful wife. But he gave himself insatiably to obscene fornications and frequent adulteries. Soiled by his sins, he set a guilty example of shameful debauchery to his subjects". "Obscene fornications" and "shameful debauchery" can be taken as medieval codewords for homosexuality.

In 1096 all Europe was stirred by a completely new phenomenon, the First Crusade. Preparations were under way for the first-ever multinational task force to descend upon Palestine. In 1076 Jerusalem had fallen into the hands of the Muslim Seljuk Turks, who hated Christians and traders, so that Europe began to be filled with the cries of persecuted pilgrims and ruined Italian merchants. There were fears that the Christian Emperor of Constantinople could be next in line. The Normans were already well-established in the Eastern Mediterranean and could provide logistical support, as could the trading fleets of Genoa, Pisa and Venice. So, the Pope Urban II called for a Crusade, and Peter the Hermit crossed Europe preaching holy war. The appeal was amazingly successful, and large armies were gathered to march overland to Palestine. This is not the place to discuss what happened to them, but the effect on Europe itself was profound, because from every land the wild young men, especially the dangerous aristocrats and knights, the disaffected and unemployed, were drained off for this new enterprise. Many crowned heads took up the cross; one of them was Robert, Duke of Normandy, who thought himself the most tremendous gallant. This brought an abrupt end to all trouble between himself and William Rufus.

While Robert was away, William Rufus was killed while hunting in the New Forest. The arrow was said to have been fired by one Walter Tirel, who at once fled on horseback, left the country and never returned. Tirel was married to a daughter of the De Clare family; two of the hunting party were De Clares. Many rumours naturally circulated about this incident. Certainly the immediate benefactor was William's brother Henry. He was also at the hunt in the New Forest, and was conveniently close to the Treasury at Winchester which all new monarchs must secure. After his accession, the De Clare family prospered. Whether it was just a hunting accident or something more sinister we will never know. However, England certainly needed a new king. William had never married. Henry's brother Robert of Normandy, still away on Crusade, had the better claim, but he was nowhere near Winchester.

Henry I 1100-1135 (35 years)
Born 1068; married 1100, Matilda of Scotland, and 1121, Adela of Louvain

So it was that the third of the sons of William the Conqueror came to the throne as Henry I. Anxious to win support against a likely challenge from his brother, his first act was to issue the Coronation Charter repudiating the many revenue-raising abuses of his predecessor; he also threw their chief perpetrator, the extortionist Ranulf Flambard, in the Tower of London. (However Flambard used some of his ill-gotten fortune to have a rope conveyed to him in a jar of wine, and escaped to Normandy.) Next Henry made a strategic marriage to Matilda, the daughter of Malcolm III of Scotland. The purpose of this was not so much to please the Scots as the English, because Matilda's mother came from the royal line of Wessex, so that any issue would combine the Norman and Wessex lines. This may indeed have suited the English, but the Normans laughed at Henry and his Anglo-Scottish queen as "Goodman Godric and his wife Godgifu", after some English tale of the time. In fact Henry was much more of an Englishman than either William I or William II. He was born in England (1068) and went out of his way to learn how to speak and write English, which is more than can be said of either his predecessors or his successors. When the rebellion of one of his unruly barons, Robert of Belleme (Earl of Shrewsbury) was put down and the baron driven out to exile, the English were delighted.

However, at this time Robert Short-Hose returned from the Crusades and claimed the crown of England, as was his right under an agreement he had reached with William Rufus. The English, however, were happy enough with Henry, so Robert had to make do with Normandy. The exiled Robert of Belleme stirred up what trouble he could in Normandy, and Henry determined to put a stop to it. In fact it was his ambition to reunite the realms of his father, so he took an army to Normandy and vanquished the Normans at Tenchebrai in 1106. The English, who formed the majority in Henry's army, saw this as revenge for Hastings, forty years before. Robert was imprisoned and Henry took control in Normandy. This may have seemed a good idea at the time, but with hindsight, it was anything but. The possession of territories within France was to drag the English into countless wars for hundreds of years, until the loss of the last of them, Calais, in the reign of Bloody Mary in 1558. By then the French had become the traditional enemy and there were many more foreign wars against them, through to the defeat of Napoleon in 1815. (In contrast, there were no serious wars against Germans until the eighteenth century, though of course the Spanish were the bogeymen in Tudor times.) These continental wars ultimately did little for England but drain her treasury. European duchies may have suited the transnational Normans and Plantagenets (and later, Hanoverians), but they were bad news for the English, and once more it is surprising that the country did not learn this lesson sooner than it did, and oblige its sovereigns to divest themselves of them as a condition of monarchy. The case of Henry I is typical because although his reign was peaceful in England, Normandy was a constant problem, bordered as it was by hostile neighbours. It is said that in the 35 years of his reign, there were only ten in which he did not go there.

Another popular act early in Henry's reign was the recall of the Archbishop of Canterbury, Anselm. However, while abroad Anselm had noted that the pope was trying to stop the appointment of bishops by kings, and he refused to consecrate Henry's appointments. A compromise was reached whereby the cathedral clergy selected their bishop, who would then do homage to the king for his lands, but it took years to sort out the argument. There were to be many similar arguments about the rights of the clergy in this period of history.

In this relatively quiet reign, Henry replaced the Anglo-Saxon witan with the Great Council. However, this met only on great occasions. Day-to-day business was transacted by the Curia Regis (King's Court), whose members included the heads of administration - the Justiciar (chief officer), Chancellor (chief legal officer), and Treasurer. This court could advise the king on matters of state, when it was called the Ordinary Council; on matters of revenue, when it became the Court of Exchequer; or it could act as a law court, which was the Curia Regis proper. Henry's reforms were popular and earned him the title "The Lion of Justice". There weren't many kings like Henry.

The king had two children by his Scottish wife and 21 more illegitimate ones, whom he installed in earldoms up and down the country. (This was a record number of royal bastards – only Charles II with 14 comes close.) In 1120, he sent his only legitimate son, William, to Normandy to obtain the allegiance of the Norman barons. William was only 18 and his father doted on him. It all came to grief when the ship carrying him home, known as the White Ship, hit rocks and broke up. William was drowned, causing great grief to his father, and in the long run, to the whole country. Henry's only other legitimate child was a woman, Matilda, who had been married to the German emperor, but who had returned to England childless upon his death in 1125. To Henry she was a great political asset because she and any children she might have were now direct heirs to the throne. He arranged that she should be married to Geoffrey of Anjou, whose territory occupied a strategic position between northern and southern France astride the River Loire. This raised the possibility that one day Anjou and Normandy might be united. However this marriage displeased the Normans, because the Angevins (the people of Anjou) were their neighbours and long-standing enemies. It did not much please Matilda either, because Geoffrey was only sixteen (ten years her junior) and was known to have a violent temper. Nevertheless, three sons were born of it, and it proved to have enormous dynastic consequences. Henry himself remarried but had no more legitimate children. In desperation, he bound his nobles to recognize Matilda as his heir. He must have known that it was a long shot, but he also knew that his grandson Henry, son of Matilda (born 1134) had very good prospects.

It is a pity that we hear so little of Henry I today, because he was one of England's best kings. Under him the economy flourished, the towns grew, the monasteries became schools for the sons of the nobility, and cathedrals were built. There were no major foreign wars apart from the invasion of Normandy in 1106 and wars between Normandy itself and its neighbours. The Scandinavian threat did not reappear and there was no trouble from Scotland, Wales or Ireland. Because he treated the English much more tactfully than either of his Norman predecessors, Henry was also the first truly popular Norman king of England.

In short, all the benefits of Norman rule began to flow. An equal pity, then, that Henry had failed to produce a legitimate male heir. He died in 1135, famously from eating a surfeit of lampreys. After that, all hell broke loose.

Stephen 1135-1154 (19 years)
Born 1094; married 1124, Matilda of Boulogne

The barons in England decided to repudiate their oath to Henry. For
one thing, no woman had ever ruled England; for another, Matilda was
married to Geoffrey, the hated Angevin. Moreover she might continue
in the ways of all the Norman monarchs so far, and suppress the power
of the barons. They also claimed that Henry had changed his mind
about Matilda before he died. She had only spent two years in England
since her childhood, and was absent now. Their choice for the king,
subsequently endorsed by the Londoners, fell upon Stephen, Earl of
Leicester. As a grandson of William the Conqueror by his daughter
Adela, he had a very good claim, and was undoubtedly the leading adult
male candidate; but that did not stop Matilda. She herself tried to
secure Normandy first, but met with the same response as in England,
for the same reason, the Normans also accepting Stephen.

Stephen was a brave, energetic and generous man; this last was his
great fault, because early Norman kings had generally administered
their kingdoms wisely but firmly, and certainly not generously. Stephen
allowed the barons to build castles on their own lands, which they did,
with alacrity, so that the king was then obliged to besiege castles which
should never have been built in the first place.

Matilda meantime rallied support, first from Robert, Earl of
Gloucester (the most able of Henry's bastard children), and then from
Milo of Hereford, also in the west. Another of her supporters was her
uncle, King David of Scotland, who invaded the north in 1138. After
dragging off Englishwomen in ropes, he was beaten at the Battle of the
Standard near Northumberland by the north countrymen. However, he
retained control of Cumberland and Northumberland. In the war he
made Carlisle a Scottish royal base, and he also controlled the
Cumbrian mines whose silver was used to mint the very first Scottish
coins.

Matilda's star was rising, and rose further when Stephen alienated
some of his most influential bishops and earls. She came to England to
join her half-brother Robert Earl of Gloucester, and her arrival sparked
the outbreak of a full-scale civil war. The barons had a wonderful
opportunity, settling private scores with their personal armies and
supporting themselves on the pillage of their neighbours. Trade and
agriculture were ruined and the country was ravaged by ruthless foreign
mercenaries. The Welsh rose in revolt. They almost wiped out the
Norman colony that had been established in Pembroke and all security

was lost in South Wales. However, the first full-blooded phase of fighting subsided after two years and settled down to a desultory pace until near the end of Stephen's reign. In France, Stephen had a disastrous time. Normandy was invaded by Geoffrey of Anjou, and the Normans accepted him as their Duke. Geoffrey was careful to keep the local barons on his side, ruling through Normans and local institutions.

The war swayed first one way, then the other for fifteen years. Matilda was her own worst enemy, alienating neutrals with her arrogance and insolence. (For example she insisted on the title of Empress, though her marriage to the German emperor was no more.) At one point she was so closely besieged by Stephen in Oxford that she only escaped by dressing herself in white and fleeing over the ice at midnight. After this she retired to Normandy.

The final outcome was swayed by the death of Matilda's husband, the generally loathed Geoffrey of Anjou. This meant that her son Henry became the Count of Anjou, and he was a very promising young man indeed, for several reasons. Firstly he was not Geoffrey; secondly he was a direct descendant of the line of William I. Within a year, he had married one of the most famous women of the age, Eleanor of Aquitaine, and this made him a most forbidding prospect. From his mother he had title to the disputed throne of England. From his father he held Anjou, to which had been added Normandy and Maine; and from his wife, most of the south-west of France. These were enormous territories, potentially an empire stretching from the Pyrenees to the Cheviots.

It was only by a fluke that Henry secured the hand of Eleanor of Aquitaine, who was the most eligible woman in Europe as she held the Duchy of Aquitaine and County of Poitou in her own right. The political geography of France at the accession of Henry II was very different from that of England. Subject to the varying incursions of the Danes, England had been ruled by one king since the time of Alfred, and his successors from the beginning of the tenth century could claim to rule most of it. The power of the English kings was real, over their whole territories; the Normans in particular ensuring that there were no independent barons. However it was not like that in France, which more resembled England at the time of the Heptarchy and British kingdoms around 600 AD. The country was divided into up to 25 different territories of varying states of independence. In practice these provinces were dominated by six or seven rulers. Inheriting this right from Charlemagne, the King of France was the overlord in these territories, but his own directly controlled state was relatively small, roughly the size of Normandy.

Though the term is used today to indicate the south-west of France, the Duchy of Aquitaine itself was an inland province of central France which bordered the Duchy of Burgundy along the River Rhone. However the southern territories Eleanor brought to her marriage with Henry were much more extensive than this – about a third of France, a much larger territory than the Kingdom of France. Nevertheless, much of this area was in fact controlled by virtually independent barons. The south-western coastal province of Gascony was considered particularly unruly. The power of the ruler of "Aquitaine" really included only the areas round the major cities, Poitiers and Bordeaux. Moreover these southern provinces were not so well developed economically as northern France, though Bordeaux (then as now) was a very important centre for the wine trade. So the territory, though certainly large, did not confer as much weight as centralized England or Normandy.

Eleanor had previously been married to Louis VII, the crusader King of France. That marriage had been dissolved on the grounds of consanguinity, too close kinship, although the real reason was that it had failed to produce a male heir. After twelve years it had only produced two daughters. Eleanor complained that this was no fault of hers, and that being married to Louis was like being married to a monk. Indeed, Louis was far from being a warrior king. He had been very badly chastened when attacking the town of Vitry in Champagne. A thousand or more refugees had crowded into the cathedral to try to escape the violence of his troops. The cathedral then caught fire and all of them perished while Louis looked on, hearing the screams of women and children as they burned. He was never the same again. Louis paid a very high price indeed for his divorce – Aquitaine and Poitou.

It was widely put about at the time that Henry's father Geoffrey had personally validated Eleanor's sexuality before passing her on to Henry. In any event, it was a typical dynastic marriage, in that Henry was only 19 and the lively and forthright Eleanor was 30. The marriage ceremony itself was a quiet affair; the couple had not sought the permission of their overlord, Louis VII, for if they had, they would certainly have been refused. To general amazement, the couple promptly fell in love and produced a large family.

This marriage was probably the most important single act since the Conquest for the future of England. It gave the "English" king French provinces beyond Normandy which were to stay in English hands for hundreds of years, in fact long beyond the loss of Normandy itself. This was bound to lead to endless wars with the French, and was in fact the root cause of the Hundred Years War starting in the fourteenth century.

But first, Henry had to become king of England. He invaded in 1153 and fighting broke out anew. However Stephen, now 60 years old, lost his son Eustace, and with it the appetite for a fight. He agreed to make Henry his successor, and died the following year, 1154, after 19 years of anarchy.

Chapter 10 – Henry II

Henry II 1154-1189 (35 years)
Born 1133; married 1152, Eleanor of Aquitaine

So Henry II became the first Angevin or Plantagenet king of England. The term Plantagenet derives from the yellow broom *Planta Genesta* which appears in the coat of arms of the Count of Anjou. It is often said that here was a king who had everything going for him. Still only a young man, he was the most important monarch in Europe. He controlled not only England and South Wales but also all of the western half of France, apart from Brittany, whose overlord he was (to the extent that he was later able to nominate his son Geoffrey to marry its heiress and become its duke). He was a man of great ability and constant energy, firm as a monarch needed to be, and determined to enforce the law. But it all went so terribly wrong. He was a passionate man, and sometimes his temper got the better of him. So did his sexual appetite, for no woman was too high or too low for him, from a princess to his own ward.

Henry selected Thomas Becket as his Chancellor on the recommendation of Theobald, Archbishop of Canterbury. Becket, thirteen years senior to the king, was the son of a prosperous merchant. He was destined to become the first famous Londoner. He had been picked out and fast-tracked by Theobald, obtaining his higher education in Paris and Bologna. Henry needed a right-hand man; he had been brought up in Anjou and understood little of England and its peculiarities; his English was minimal.

Henry and Becket immediately set about clearing up the mess left behind by Stephen. They began by revoking land grants made by Stephen and Matilda to win support, and by leveling castles, issuing sound coinage and driving out mercenary bands. Henry kicked King Malcolm IV of Scotland out of Cumberland and Northumberland, which he had occupied during the war, and forced his own brother Geoffrey out of Anjou, where he had tried to usurp.

Henry had a scrap in the south of France with the Count of Tolouse which had unforeseen effects. Each knight had a feudal obligation to serve in the king's army for forty days, not counting the travelling there and back to the campaign. Now if the campaign was in the Welsh or Scottish borders, that was of no great consequence, but if it was in Toulouse, that was another matter. Therefore it was arranged that the knight could commute his service for a payment, called scutage. This gave the king flexibility to pay local knights, and also it made his own knights less warlike. It also represents an early move away from the feudal concept of service to a monetary transaction.

When Archbishop Theobald of Canterbury died in 1161, Henry thought to put his own man, Thomas Becket, in his place, though this was not a universally popular choice amongst the senior churchmen. Some of them regarded Becket as not only the king's man but as an outrageous showman. Henry needed support from the Archbishop, because he had decided to abolish a medieval middle-class scam, and as every politician knows who attempts such a thing, trouble was inevitable. William I had allowed the clergy to be tried in their own ecclesiastic courts, and these courts were limited in the punishments they could use – fines, imprisonment in a monastery or ejection from clerical orders. However there were no less than seven orders of clergy which meant that practically all the professional men, the clerks, lawyers, civil servants and so on, apart from the soldiers, were included, and therefore not subject to lay justice. The minor orders could marry and were not subject to the same disciplines as real priests. It is estimated that one in twenty adult males was a clerk.

The Archbishop of Canterbury was a man who must serve two masters, the King and the Pope, and who therefore had some independence from the king. A wronged Archbishop of Canterbury could appeal over the King's head to the Pope, as had Anselm in the reign of William II. Becket promptly refused to cooperate. He took the view that if a clergyman was found guilty of a crime, he could be unfrocked. Then if he committed another crime, he would be tried in lay courts and duly punished. In other words it took one murder to hang a layman but two to hang a clergyman. Henry's position on this issue does seem fair. However, there must have been a lot of pressure on Becket from professional men in clerical orders not to back down.

This was part of a larger power struggle between the King and the Church. During the time of Stephen, the Church like the barons had extended its powers. Henry now proposed to turn back the clock to the time of Henry I, when the agreement between the king and Anselm had effectively left the king in charge. The issue of the ecclesiastic courts was just one of many. For example, Henry was equally unhappy that clergymen could appeal to Rome without his prior approval. To establish a new relationship, he drew up the Constitutions of Clarendon in 1164, which redefined matters in his favour. Becket, to the disgust of his fellow bishops, at first acceded to these new rules. However, he changed his mind. Henry then accused him of a number of crimes and arranged for his trial at Northampton. Here the barons found Becket guilty, but he escaped their clutches and managed to reach Flanders. He found his way to the abbey of Pontigny, south of Paris, where he hoped to enlist the support of the Pope. However, the Pope had been ejected from Rome by Emperor Frederick Barbarossa, who had installed his own pope (or antipope). So the old Pope Alexander III was living in France, and he needed all the support he could get – particularly from Henry – so he could only sympathize.

After five years, Becket and Henry patched up their quarrel and Becket returned, only to reopen the offensive at once. In his absence Archbishop Roger of York, his bitter rival, had crowned Henry's eldest son (a practice meant to secure the succession, copied from France and Germany, but unprecedented in England). Seeing this as an invasion of his prerogative, Becket excommunicated Roger and his other rival, the Bishop of London. This infuriated Henry, who issued the famous words: "Are none of the cowards eating my bread who will rid me of this turbulent priest?" Now it was unthinkable for a medieval French knight to be considered a coward; Henry could not have ordered the murder of Becket more surely if he had written out a death warrant. Four knights immediately detached themselves from the party and set off for Canterbury from Normandy. Their names were Reginald FitzUrse, Hugh de Moreville, William de Tracey and Richard le Breton. There was an angry altercation at the cathedral, where Becket refused to run and hide, though he surely knew what was coming – these were not choirboys after all. So he was murdered in the cathedral in the year 1170.

Whatever the rights and wrongs of the disputes between the king and Becket, everyone knew that it was wrong to order the murder of the Archbishop of Canterbury. Henry had truly shocked the people. Not in all the years since St Augustine set foot on the shores of Kent in 597 had any king done such a thing. Henry's famously short temper had got him into trouble. He found it impossible to implement the Constitutions of Clarendon to regain his grip on the clergy. Meanwhile word got about that miracles were worked at Becket's tomb. Becket the

Londoner was accepted as a national martyr and for years – centuries – afterwards a pilgrimage to his shrine was the event of a lifetime for an Englishman. With hindsight, we can see now that Henry should have left Becket festering in France until he withered away. The Norman barons, knights and senior bishops knew that Becket had been an impossible man to deal with, but nevertheless there was a political backlash. Henry's prestige dropped internationally. He had lost face and popularity, and it was not to be too long before he was faced with an international conspiracy against him.

*   *   *   *

Wales at this time was divided into three kingdoms, Gwynedd in the north, Powys in the centre and Deheubarth in the south, though much of south and west Wales was in the hands of the Normans. It was English policy to keep the Welsh kingdoms apart, rather than letting them unite, and Henry sent a large army into Wales in 1165 to restrain the ambitions of Prince Rhys. The army ran into difficulties as armies did in Wales in those days, when a large army would flounder and a small one would get cut to pieces. Rhys suggested that instead of bothering him, the knights should try Ireland, where they could go in support of the exiled Dermot, King of Leinster (a "bestial savage" in one account – Keith Feiling, History of England). So it was that the barons of Pembroke under Richard "Strongbow" De Clare began the first Norman incursions of Ireland. In this they had some success, reinstating Dermot and taking Dublin and a good part of the east coast in 1169, thereby creating and independent Norman colony. Henry wanted his share of the spoils and so followed them there in 1171 in order to obtain an acknowledgement of his supremacy, which he duly did. In his pocket was a bull from the only English Pope, Nicolas Breakspear (Hadrian IV), authorizing him to conquer Ireland in order to bring the practices of the Irish church into line with those of Rome. This had been sorted out in England at the Synod of Whitby in 664, but 500 years later Ireland had still not fallen in line.

The Normans began to establish themselves in the "Pale", the Dublin region, where the age-old kinship-based clans and petty kings still ruled. Irish law and custom horrified them. For example Irish (and Welsh) law permitted divorce and remarriage, something that the Normans regarded as no more than a licence for wife-swapping. Over the next 50 years, this ancient form of law and government amongst the bogs and cattle-raiders was replaced in the pale with feudalism and all the paraphernalia of Norman life – castles, walled towns, monasteries and manors – and Norman French speech. The landscape of southern and eastern Ireland was permanently changed, filling up with villages, mills, bridges and barns. There was also a tide of English immigration as peasants, soldiers and artisans followed their lords into Ireland. In 1177 Henry's youngest son John, later King John but at this stage known as John Lackland because he had no land or estates of his own, was appointed Lord of Ireland. John actually visited Ireland in 1185, where he upset the local petty kings by pulling their long beards (which indicated to him that they were not yet civilized).

So it was that Henry became the first English ruler (of many) to try to assert his authority over Ireland . One could hardly blame Henry for attempting this, because no one had tried it before. It was the start of a long and sorry saga with repercussions still felt to this day. The fact is that just as England is protected from foreign invasion by the Channel, so to some extent is Ireland insulated from England by the seas between the two countries. It was never going to be easy for the English to subdue Ireland as they could not march directly into it, and it was never fully subdued (and then only temporarily) until the time of Cromwell.

Scotland's ruler at this time was King David I (1124-53), a contemporary and friend of Henry I. He had spent his childhood in England and his sister was the queen of Henry I. Under him, Anglo-Norman influence in Scotland grew rapidly and monasteries were established. Norman barons were also busy establishing themselves as the aristocracy. Sheriffs and other royal officials replaced Celtic clan chiefs, and a council granted taxes. Royal charters established feudalism to replace clan tenures, and conferred trading rights to the main towns (Edinburgh, Stirling, Berwick, Roxburgh). Although the monarchy remained Scottish, the switch from Goidelic Celtic speech to Norman French took place at the Scottish court in the twelfth century. Meanwhile the English language was making steady progress amongst the ordinary people of Scotland. It had been spoken in the Lothians for centuries but by the thirteenth century it had spread north of the Forth, with Gaelic speech in long retreat, never to return.

The west of the country was not part of Scotland, but was rules by the King of Man, who also controlled the Hebrides and varying parts of the mainland. The most famous of these kings was Somerled who led a dreadful invasion in 1164 on Clyde and Renfrew, the territory of the Stewarts. Somerled was killed in this attack. In fact the wild Norse/Gaelic kingdom was kicking against the pricks of progress; the Scots-Normans possessed a far more advanced culture. Scotland was undergoing the same sort of changes as Ireland, but as in Ireland, the new ways did not extend across the whole country.

*   *   *   *

Henry had married Eleanor in 1154 and at first all went stunningly well. She produced eight children by him who grew to maturity, four boys and four girls. This was a great achievement for the times, but it gave Henry II the opposite problem to his grandfather Henry I, whose only son and heir had died young. By 1163, however, Henry and Eleanor were partially estranged. They saw less of each other while Henry dallied with mistresses, notably Rosamund Clifford, whom he set up in a love nest at Woodstock. Eleanor withdrew to her native Aquitaine, where she set up a court at Poitou, complete with troubadours and minstrels. This was the disadvantage of neglecting a wife who had an independent power base. The male children grew up under Eleanor's wing, and abetted by her, began to seek independent power within their father's empire. Henry eventually died when he was only 56, but he would have died a happier man if he had died sooner, for he was to see all his sons betray him. First to break ranks was his eldest son Henry, crowned King of England and Duke of Normandy in 1170 but in practice given no real power by his father, who loved him well enough but found him idle, vain and too much given to gaming. The Young King, as he was known, began to conspire with the King of France, his father-in-law.

Things came to a head in 1173. By this time Henry had England firmly under control, suppressing the power of the baronage with the help of able ministers and soldiers paid for by scutage money. The barons were thoroughly disaffected and sought an uprising. Amongst their allies were the Scots, for the Scottish kings were sometimes rash enough to make trouble even when a strong king sat on the English throne. Henry had kicked Malcolm out of northern England, but his successor William (later called the Lion) (1165-1214) attempted reconquest, in support of the English barons.

However this was only part of a much larger alliance against Henry. He had quarreled with his three eldest sons, Henry, Geoffrey and Richard, and with the support of their mother they made an unholy alliance with Louis VII of France (Eleanor's former husband). Also involved were Henry's Norman barons, his Normandy neighbour to the east, the Count of Flanders, and the Bretons, who chafed at his overlordship. The plan was to invade Normandy and England simultaneously. This was a dangerous time for Henry, but he was ready for the challenge. He beat the French and the Bretons in Normandy, while his ministers Richard de Lucy and William Mandeville routed the barons in England. However, it was not over yet, because the Earl of Norfolk was up in arms and William of Scotland was besieging Alnwick. So great was the danger that Henry felt it expedient to walk to the martyr Becket's tomb in a hair shirt and prostrate himself there, begging forgiveness and allowing himself to be publicly flogged. It worked – that very day William was captured at Alnwick, and the Earl of Norfolk was soon suppressed. The next year, 1174, William was made to pay homage to Henry in the Treaty of Falaise, after he had been paraded as a captive there with his feet tied beneath his horse. One condition of this treaty was that the English would occupy the castles of Lothian. The obligations were later withdrawn by Richard I (the Lionheart) in exchange for a cash sum – Richard needed the money.

Until its closing stages, the remainder of Henry's reign was relatively quiet. However in 1187 news reached Europe that Jerusalem, centre of a Crusader kingdom in Palestine since the end of the previous century, had fallen to the Turk Saladin. Jerusalem had been able to hold its own, given a constant resupply of Crusaders from Europe, against the various petty Muslim states surrounding it. However when Saladin united these states in a kingdom stretching from the Euphrates to the Nile, he took Jerusalem. Crusader towns and forts remained on the coast for a hundred years more, and these served as bases for the new influx of Crusaders.

The news of the fall of Jerusalem stirred Europe profoundly, and had wide-ranging consequences. In what is known as the Crusade of the Kings, the Emperor Frederick Barbarossa raised an army and set off overland (he was accidentally killed on the way). Other heads of state prepared their journeys. Henry himself planned to go, and raised a "Saladin tithe" of a tenth of the value of all the property of his subjects, a massive amount. However, Henry never went to Palestine. His son Henry the Young King, forgiven for his part in the revolt of 1173, had died of dysentery in 1183. His second son Geoffrey, Duke of Brittany, was also dead, having fallen under the hooves of a horse in a tournament, a recreation discouraged by his father. (Tournaments were outlawed by Henry in England but in France they were regarded as serious war games and excellent training for fighting men.) However, that still left Richard and John to make trouble for him.

Henry's third son Richard was made of sterner stuff than his elder brother Henry. Born in 1157, he was brought up in the south of France and spoke the local language, the langue d'oc. His mother's favorite, he was given early responsibilities in her duchy, but like the Young King he chafed at the leash for a larger kingdom. Henry's original plan had been to divide his empire between his sons on his death. Henry the Young King was to have England, Normandy and Anjou; Geoffrey, Brittany; and Richard, Aquitaine. This left the youngest son John with nothing, hence his nickname "Lackland". However, now that Henry the Young King and Geoffrey were dead, Richard wanted his father to acknowledge him as his heir (apart from in Brittany where Geoffrey had left a young son, Arthur). This Henry refused to do, leading to speculation that he was planning a bright future for John Lackland.

In 1189 Richard formed an alliance with the new King of France, Philip Augustus, a much bolder man than his predecessor Louis VII. One motivator might have been that his proposed bride, the French princess Alais, had just given birth do an illegitimate child. According to rumour, the father was none other than Henry. By this time the king was 56 years old and had made many enemies. The war went disastrously for him; watching Philip and Richard set fire Le Mans, his home town, Henry sued for terms. Even as these were agreed he prayed to be spared enough time to gain his revenge. No doubt he would indeed have gained his revenge, but he was not spared the time. Two days later he learned to his horror that his youngest son John, the only one who had never betrayed him, was on the list of noblemen who had agreed to support Philip and Richard. He died, some say of a broken heart. The only son present at his deathbed was an illegitimate one, another Geoffrey. Henry is reported to have remarked as he died that "The others are the real bastards". So now England had to prepare itself for the rule of one of those bastards, Richard the Lionheart.

Toward the end of Henry's reign, from 1180, a new English coin appeared, the Short Cross penny. It had a cross on one side of it to facilitate cutting it in two or four to create halfpennies or farthings (fourths). The discovery of new silver ores in Europe, particularly at Freiberg near Meissen in Germany, had resulted in a large increase in the money supply. This was a boost to the economy and Henry can be credited with improving the coinage (and the lot of the medieval archaeologist).

Also, the second half of the twelfth century was a time of great prosperity in the country. The wool trade with Flanders prospered and with it the ports on the east coast, notably Barton-on-Humber, Boston and Yarmouth. Great Cistercian abbeys were constructed – the most famous, Fountains and Rievaulx in north Yorkshire, but there were many others – which were also important business centres, again particularly in wool production. Everywhere the hunting forests were pushed back – despite the inevitable fines – and in eastern England, a large area of fine arable land became available through the drainage of the Fens, a labour which lasted centuries. The sale and purchase of land – very important as security for loans – was facilitated, and the English peasant prospered.

Had it not been for the Becket debacle, Henry would be regarded as one of the greatest of all the English kings. The country was peaceful, and the administration had become so well-established that the country was strong enough to remain stable through the buffeting it received in the next two reigns. Justice was established as real justice through the king's courts in a system where judges were sent round the country to try cases under "Common" law – the same law everywhere. Unfortunately for Henry, his reign is chiefly remembered today for one thing – the Murder in the Cathedral.

Chapter 11 – The Middle Angevin Kings

Richard I 1189-1199 (10 years)
Born 1157; married 1191, Berengaria of Navarre

For a man known to be a butcher of innocents and a rapist, Richard's reputation as a chivalrous and glamorous monarch and international medieval superstar has survived amazingly well, perhaps because of the comparison with his creepy brother John who succeeded him. However, Richard was a financial calamity for England. His sole aim from the outset was to win glory by recapturing Jerusalem from Saladin. In his whole reign he spent barely ten months in England, to him a foreign country, a place to raise money for his crusade. In the end, that crusade was to cost literally a king's ransom, purely due to Richard's own pettiness while in Palestine. Nevertheless, Richard caught the English public's imagination and there were few who would speak against him during his reign. The country had plenty of saints but was short on military heroes.

Richard's coronation was marred by a pogrom against the Jews of London, and further atrocities in York and Norwich, the first such incidents in England. The Jews were regarded as chattels of the king; they were allowed to settle at his pleasure, and were used by him as a means of raising revenue. As money-lenders they were not popular with the borrowers. Richard tried to stop the massacres, but was only really concerned to collect his money and be on his way. He sold the offices of state in England to the highest bidder and gave up his rights in Scotland for 10,000 pounds, restoring relations with the Scots to the same doubtful uncertainty that had prevailed previously.

Richard anticipated that his little brother John might make trouble in England while he was away, so he assigned to him the revenues of six counties on condition that he kept out of England for three years. Queen Eleanor, delighted that Henry was dead, once more began to play an important role in state affairs, and persuaded Richard not to enforce this condition. The result was that John did come to England and immediately did begin to make trouble, as Richard had anticipated. Government had been left in the hands of William Longchamp, Bishop of Ely and Chancellor, who swiftly used his patronage to put his own relations into the administration. When John arrived, the disaffected flocked to him, and Longchamp was soon sent packing.

Meanwhile, Richard had set off on his crusade in the company of Philip Augustus, King of France. Richard's relations with Philip were to blow hot and cold over the years; sharing a bed on the crusade, waging war once back home. Philip was a much more bellicose character than his father Louis and was to be a great deal more successful. Unlike Richard he was short and stocky, red in the face and with unkempt hair. His primitive notions of personal hygiene may have made sharing a bed and act of chivalry on Richard's part, but after all, this was a feature of French life until very recently. The fact that the pair did sleep together is not a reflection on the sexuality of either, just a sign of comradeship. Richard only managed to create one known bastard, a poor score for a medieval king, but this was not apparently through lack of trying.

On his way to the Holy Land Richard achieved the capture of Cyprus, which was to prove an invaluable base for future crusader operations in the eastern Mediterranean. In 1191 Richard and Philip reached the Holy Land, where they succeeded in taking the coastal city of Acre, which had been under siege for two years. During the capture of the city, a fateful incident occurred. Crusaders under Leopold, Archduke of Austria, planted his flag on one of the towers of the city. To show who was in charge, Richard had it publicly torn down and flung in the latrines. England was to pay very dearly for this action, as Richard had left Leopold humiliated and thirsting for revenge. However, that was not the end of it. The siege left a large number of prisoners in the hands of the Crusaders – figures vary from 2,700 to 3,000. Richard demanded a ransom of 200,000 dinars and the return of the True Cross from Saladin to free these people. Saladin did not receive the demand straight away, and then asked for time to collect what was after all a large sum of money. Richard could not wait, and had the prisoners beheaded, one by one, in full view of Saladin's army outside Acre. This cold-blooded murder was too much for many of the disgusted crusaders, to say nothing of the horrified local population, and did the crusade more harm than good. In justification, Richard could point to the rules of war, which were that if an army approached a fortified place which then surrendered, the lives of the population would be spared. If they did not, they could be massacred at the discretion of the besieging commander. Julius Caesar had committed such a massacre in Gaul, as was Napoleon later to do in Syria.

By now Philip Augustus had gone home, leaving Richard the undisputed leader of the crusade. He failed in his efforts to take Jerusalem, but otherwise his Crusade was a success. He had captured Cyprus and pushed back the frontiers of the Frankish Kingdom of Outremer, what was left of the Kingdom of Jerusalem. His generalship and knightly prowess had won him many admirers, not least Saladin himself. He set off back home, but on his way he was shipwrecked, fetching up on the Adriatic coast near Trieste. Deciding to make his way overland from here with a small group of knights, he tried to slip through Austria in disguise, but was recognized and arrested outside Vienna, then conducted to the presence of his sworn enemy, Archduke Leopold. His life was not in real danger – he was too valuable a catch for that. He was asked to explain his behavior to the Imperial Diet, where he acquitted himself so well that the Emperor (not the Archduke) gave him the kiss of peace. Eventually he arrived back in England, after much negotiation, but the price was high – 150,000 marks – more than the annual income of the crown – but less than Hubert Walter was to raise in a single year to finance Richard's subsequent wars in France.

One reason for Richard's return from the Holy Land was that he had heard (correctly) that his brother John was conspiring with Philip of France to take over his dominions. Richard was received as a returning hero in Normandy, where he sought out his terrified little brother. However he forgave him, saying he was only a child (he was 27) and had been badly advised. Richard could never take his little brother seriously. Richard finally arrived back in England in 1194 and set about raising more money to build castles in France, by the usual methods of fresh taxes and extortion. He stayed for just two months and then went back to France to wage war on Philip, his fellow-crusader, and his rebellious barons. To enrage Philip he built an immense castle, the Chateau Gaillard, right on his borders, on the Seine.

The justiciar at this time was Hubert Walter, also Archbishop of Canterbury. The exactions of his taxation were so severe that the Londoners rose in revolt in 1195. This rebellion was put down, but it showed the limits of revenue raising. Three years later Hugh, Bishop of

Lincoln, was successful in refusing to pay taxes for the French wars, something which had never happened before.

Whilst on crusade, Richard had married Berengaria, daughter of the King of Navarre (which adjoins Aquitaine). However the marriage did not turn out well; the couple saw little of each other and had no children. As is their way, recent historians have questioned Richard's sexuality, but contemporaries never did, and they certainly would have done if they could. In fact as Richard grew older he became careless with women:

"He carried off the wives, daughters and kinswomen of his freemen by force, and made them his concubines, and when he had sated his lust on them, he handed them over to his knights for whoring."

(Quoted in *Eleanor of Aquitaine*, p. 200, Alison Weir)

In 1199 Richard besieged the castle of a petty knight in France, the possessor of some treasure he thought to steal. Here he was rash enough to reconnoitre without body armour within range of the walls. A single archer caught him with an arrow in the angle of his shoulder and neck. Gradually this wound became gangrenous. Before he died, the castle was captured and Richard asked the offending archer what he thought he was doing, what had Richard done to him? The archer replied:

"You slew my father and my two brothers with your own hand, and you had intended now to kill me. Therefore take any revenge on me that you may think fit, for I will readily endure the greatest torments that you can devise, so long as you have met with your end, having inflicted evils so many and so great upon the world."

(p.319, *Eleanor of Aquitaine*, Alison Weir)

Richard liked this response so well that he ordered the archer's life to be spared, but it was not - he was flogged to death for his pains.

Richard was selfish, cruel and vain, but also brave and generous. However his very absence was useful to England, giving time for the legal and administrative reforms of Henry II to bed down.

Richard's reign will always be associated in the public mind with Robin Hood. He was said to be an outlawed aristocrat who supported himself by banditry and highway robbery from his base deep in Sherwood Forest during the "regency" of John. His grave is still maintained in the grounds of the former Kirklees Priory, outside Brighouse in West Yorkshire; it is marked on Ordnance Survey maps, so someone must believe it.

John 1199-1216 (17 years)
Born 1167 married 1189 Hadwissa of Gloucester (divorced); 1200
Isabella of Angouleme

It was always useful to a medieval (or Tudor) monarch to be a tall, imposing man, in the manner of Richard I, Edward I or Henry VIII. John did not start with this advantage, being the only short Plantagenet king, as it were the runt of the litter, the last of four brothers – who would ever have expected him to become king? It is only because Richard died young from his wounds that John came to the throne. Richard wanted his nephew Arthur of Brittany, son of his brother Geoffrey, as his heir, but as he was still only twelve, John was reluctantly accepted in both England and Normandy. By this time his reputation was well-known. He had double-crossed both his brother Richard and Philip of France in the 1190s, he had a string of illegitimate children and when king he was accused of violating the wives and daughters of his barons. Even contemporaries described him as a bad man, cruel and lecherous, so it is hard to take any different view today. Revisionist historians have tried to rescue the reputations of some unlikely people, including the Vikings and Richard III, but no one has done it with this evil king.

Within two years John made trouble for himself by repudiating his wife Hadwissa of Gloucester in favour of a girl of fourteen, Isabella of Angouleme. John's marriage to Hadwissa was a very cynical arrangement and it is thought possible that there was no sex in it. John had no lands and Hadwissa was an heiress, so John was happy to marry her, but the marriage was prohibited by the Archbishop of Canterbury because the couple were too closely related. John appealed to the papal legate against this decision; the papal legate recognized the marriage pending an appeal to Rome. Since John did not pursue this appeal, his marriage remained legal but conveniently voidable.

John's divorce upset the relatives of Hadwissa, who were some of the strongest English barons, and also the equally powerful French baronial family into which Isabella of Angouleme had previously been betrothed. This party appealed to Philip, who made it a pretext for war. Philip sent the young Arthur of Brittany south to his armies there, but he was captured by John's men in Poitou. Meanwhile, Philip was sweeping up in Normandy, which had lost much of its old vitality and operated under subsidy from England.

John then committed a crime which lost him widespread support. In 1203, Arthur disappeared, never to be seen again. He had been murdered by John, and everyone knew it. Then while John idled in bed with his young wife, Philip began knocking out his castles. By 1205 Normandy, Maine, Anjou and Poitou had fallen and John was left with no provinces in northern and central France. Aquitaine and Gascony held on but Philip of France had quadrupled the size of his territories. (It may seem strange that the provinces of south-west France were retained by the English crown when those on the very doorstep of England were lost, but this is to disregard the realities of travel in the early thirteenth century. It was easier to reach Bordeaux from the English ports than it was overland from Paris, and in fact these provinces were not finally surrendered to the French crown until 1453.)

John is widely blamed for these catastrophic losses, and indeed they would never have occurred under Richard. His antics when faced with the threat of military confrontation earned him a new nickname – Softsword. However, the Kingdom of France was expanding. Up until this time it was only one amongst a number of provinces in France, but it would eventually swell to fill all of France as we know it now; within a generation it had also swallowed the County of Toulouse in the south. The Norman territories were right on its borders and controlled access to the sea via the Seine. They would have been lost before long, even under a good English king. In any case their loss was a loss to the Angevin monarchy rather than to England. Many historians take the view that it was actually a Good Thing.

The fact that Philip Augustus did take an aggressive line towards Angevin territories in France (unlike his predecessor Louis VII) changed the political geography of France, more or less permanently. Philip's expansionism was undoubtedly a response to the power of the Anglo-French Plantagenet kings. Until the accession of Henry II, there had been no pressing need for the kings of France to conquer their neighbours, and while Henry II and Richard I were on the Anglo-French throne, little opportunity. But with the accession of the weak John, the French seized their chance. In this way it can be seen that a united England, with French provinces attached, created a united France hundreds of years before unity came to neighbouring Germany and Italy.

(Under the alternative scenario, the Angevin kings would eventually have conquered the whole of France. When it came the turn of the

102

French to have a run of weak kings, the Plantagenets were indeed able to expand their territories once more, a situation which created the Hundred Years War. However once Normandy had been lost, the monarchy was basically an English monarchy. It was never going to be easy to try to run France from England, especially as the English territories remained in south-west France rather than across the Channel. So despite moments of desperate weakness, the French kings held on.)

A dispute then arose in England concerning the appointment of a new Archbishop of Canterbury following the death of Hubert Walter. There were two rival candidates, and both parties sought to involve the Pope, Innocent III, a formidable political operator. He persuaded the electors to accept a compromise candidate, Stephen Langton, an Englishman then resident at the papal court. John refused to accept this choice and the Pope placed the entire country under an interdict in 1208, which meant in practice that there were no church services, church marriages or church burials for the five years in which the interdict remained in force. This was a much more religious age than today, but no one seemed to mind very much and the skies did not fall in. Certainly it did not seem to bother John, who flexed his muscles in Scotland and began helping himself to church property.

During this period, John found time to busy himself in Ireland, which was subjected to the full glare of an English king who was no longer so distracted in France. The settlement of Henry II had long ago lapsed, and the Norman barons had become independent petty kings, intermarrying with the Irish. In 1210 John went to Ireland with an armada of 700 ships. Here he dispossessed some of his Norman enemies, the Lacys and the Briouzes, transferring their estates to himself. This expedition impressed his harshest critics, as no English king had ever extended his power so much in Ireland. John set up mechanisms to enforce English law and the shire system, and introduced English currency.

John also intervened heavily in Wales, extending English territory and building castles. However his actions backfired, causing the previously feuding clans to unite under Llewellyn ap Iorwerth. This prince reasserted Welsh power when the barons revolted against John, making himself the single ruler of Wales until his death in 1240.

Back in England, John's exactions became worse. Henry II had only taken scutage five times in 35 years. John levied the tax every year until 1206 and then again from 1209 onwards. He depended increasingly on foreign mercenaries, some of whom he set up as county sheriffs. His depredations ruined old baronial families, including the de Clares of Gloucester.

Things came to a head when, finding John obdurate, the Pope deposed him – in name at least – and called upon Philip of France to make this a reality. Philip, suspecting that he would find friends enough in England, collected a fleet in preparation for the first invasion of England since 1066. It was clear to John that he needed to divide his enemies, so in an astonishing volte-face he reversed his position with respect to the Pope. In 1213 he agreed to make England a fief of the papacy, to pay the Pope a thousand marks a year in acknowledgement of that relationship, and to accept Stephen Langton as Archbishop of Canterbury. This move was regarded by most as a humiliating climb-down but in its immediate impact it was surprisingly successful. Innocent III withdrew his interdict and his order to depose John, requesting Philip to restrain himself. The English fleet put to sea and defeated the French at Damme (Philip would have ignored the Pope but for this). This was the first in a long line of naval victories against the French.

Elated, John proposed to follow this up by invading France, but received no support from his barons. However an alliance was formed with the Emperor and the Count of Flanders, and war against Philip and his allies resumed in Flanders and Poitou. The allies fell to a complete defeat at Bouvines in Flanders in 1214, one military disaster too far for the English aristocracy.

Bouvines was an example of something extremely rare – a late medieval full-pitched battle. The art of war as practised in these times was to avoid this direct form of confrontation if at all possible. The risks of failure were too great. Henry II never risked a battle and even Richard I only fought in one. Far more common as instruments of war were sieges, skirmishes amongst patrols, and scorched earth policies to deprive the enemy of resources.

All John had to do was to keep on good terms with the few dozen baronial families that controlled the English shires, but by this time, he had abused and alienated so many that he had few friends left. So it was that the news of Bouvines caused civil war to break out in England as the barons, abetted by Stephen Langton, determined to uphold their rights. They could tolerate the incursions of the Angevin kings when they were winners, but when the king was a loser like John, that was another matter. The normal course of aggrieved barons would have been to rally round some prince, probably the next-in-line to the throne. However there was no available figure, so instead they conceived the idea of a charter or bill of rights, harking back to the Coronation Charter issued by Henry I in 1100.

Hostilities broke out, though this was a civil war without a battle. It was soon clear that the rebel barons had the upper hand, as for the first time since the Norman Conquest, the mass of the people ignored the appeal of the king to assist him against the barons. London opened its gates to them and there were risings all over the country. Really this is the worst condemnation of John because the people knew that only the king stood between themselves and anarchy, the reason that they had supported even William the Conqueror.

The result was the Magna Carta, sealed by John at Runnymede in 1215. This was not a new constitution, but a long list of what the king was or was not entitled to do. Its aim was to stop the many abuses and extortions to which Richard, John and their ministers had been quick to resort when they ran out of money. One of its provisions was *Habeas Corpus* – that no man could be arrested and held without a charge being brought against him. This has remained a cornerstone of English law ever since, though it is still withdrawn from time to time, even today. Another provision was that no one should be imprisoned without a legal trial. Again, the charter attempted to limit the scope of the reliefs that the king could demand when a son wished to succeed to his father's estates – a form of inheritance tax which had long been levied but which John abused. Many of the provisions of this type were little more that tax exemptions for the barons and knights, including restrictions on scutages and service abroad. The barons also proposed that 25 of them should sit as a body to monitor the king's compliance to the charter.

The importance of the Magna Carta is that it created the principle that the king was only a part of the machinery of government, and that the rule of law was paramount rather than the whim of the monarch. Although it proved to be an immediate failure, it had a long-term impact. Recourse was made to it whenever future governments stepped out of line. It was repeatedly amended and reissued and the authors of the American constitution had a copy of it in their hands when writing their own document. It also shows up the flaws in the medieval system of government by an autocratic monarch. It is surprising that this obviously faulty system lasted so long – indeed, it was to persist for hundreds of years more. Things had actually gone backwards from early Saxon times, when any sensible king would consult closely with his council before taking an important decision. There were other methods available to select a king. For example, if all the king's children had been eligible for consideration (a system later used in

Turkey), Henry I could have selected an able male heir instead of trying to sell his daughter Matilda to a doubtful aristocracy. If a wider pool other than the next-of-kin had been allowed, then Arthur of Brittany, although a minor of 12 years old, could have been made king instead of John, who was universally regarded as a bad apple even on his accession. It would of course have been necessary to implement the other aspect of the Turkish system – the silken cord to strangle all his brothers once a new Sultan had been selected. This might seem barbaric, but it is much cheaper in terms of human life than the civil wars set off in the reigns of Stephen, John and later John's own son Henry III.

In any event, John had no intention of complying with the charter, which to him was a piece of paper issued to gain time. While he laid siege to Rochester Castle, famously undermining one of it towers, the barons took a desperate step and invited the eldest son of the Philip of France, Louis, to be their king. His wife, Blanche of Castile, was a granddaughter of Henry II and any issue would continue the Plantagenet line. John hired foreign mercenaries and set about attacking his enemies, including the young king Alexander II of Scotland (1214-1249), who had supported the barons. The atrocities of the mercenaries turned regions of England and Scotland into wasteland. Louis arrived in England and made a good impression. Alexander did something no other Scottish king has ever done – he marched an army all the way to Dover to meet up with Louis. Meanwhile John and his mercenaries were still in the field, but not for much longer. Crossing the Wash, a large part of his baggage train was lost, including the royal jewels and cash. Treasure hunters have sought the haul ever since, to no avail. John contracted dysentery, and died when he reached Newark in October, 1216.

The death of John changed everything. He had a son of nine years old, Henry, said to be a pretty little knight. The barons could look forward to a minority when they would be in charge; England would not be a satellite of France. Support for Louis quickly dissipated and the young king was crowned at Gloucester as Henry III.

The universities at Oxford and Cambridge date from the reign of John. There were already a large number of clerics and "academics" in Oxford, but there was no formal university. In 1209 one of the clerics murdered a local woman and then ran away. In the first clash between town and gown, the three students with whom he had shared a house were hanged, even though they were guilty of no crime. At this the clerics of Oxford left the town en masse, many making for Cambridge.

Clearly the economy of Oxford suffered badly because in 1214 the local authorities agreed to do penance and the university was established with its own rules and regulations. Colleges began to be built later in the century, the earliest being University.

There were also important changes in the legal system at this time. At the Fourth Lateran Council of 1215, Pope Innocent III forbade the clergy from taking part in ordeals. Seemingly unfair and barbaric practices such as trial by ordeal and battle were not used as a routine; every attempt was first made to establish the facts of a case from witnesses and evidence. However, in many cases, there were no witnesses – it was simply one man's word against another. There was no fingerprint, forensic or DNA evidence. Trial by battle or ordeal was a last resort when the accused party would not settle the case by paying a fine. From 1215, trial by jury was established in England, where the verdict was given by twelve people who could be expected to be familiar with the facts of the case. Most of Europe opted for another method and tried harder to get the accused to confess - by torture.

Chapter 12 – First Parliament

Henry III 1216-1272 (56 years)
Born 1207 Married 1236, Eleanor of Provence

William Marshall, the eighty-year old Earl of Pembroke, was established as Regent during the minority of the king, supported by Peter des Roches and Guala, the papal legate. These three represented the English barons, the French barons and the Pope, and they formed a council to conduct affairs of state. They had immediate work to do, because Louis of France was not going to give up his claim without a fight. He was defeated at Lincoln in 1217, and a fleet bringing reinforcements from France was also defeated off Sandwich by Hugh de Burgh. Louis went home.

The council also had its work cut out to remove the foreigners brought into the country by John. By now in powerful positions, they proved difficult to dislodge, particularly a fierce little man called Falke de Breaute, the mercenary leader who had become sheriff of six counties. He occupied a number of strong castles and held himself above the law. Not until 1222 was he evicted from his castle at Bedford and sent packing.

Meanwhile, the Pope intended to make his overlordship a reality and attempted to raise taxes for himself in England. The laity refused to pay, but the clergy was obliged to give up a tenth of their income and to pay their first year's income on taking up a posting.

In 1227 King Henry, by now 20 years old, declared himself of age to rule. He kept Hubert de Burgh as his justiciar (a position he had held since 1219). Rivalry grew up when Peter des Roches returned from a crusade in 1231. Peter persuaded the king that Hubert was lining his own pockets, and Hubert was thrown out in 1232. He was the last in a long line of justiciars who, for good or ill, but generally for good, had been the king's chief ministers since the reign of William Rufus. From this time onwards, the chief minister was the Chancellor, but Henry himself took direct control of the government. The fall of Hubert also marked a division in the reign of Henry, because 16 years of stability were followed by 26 years of misrule.

Henry's financial position was much weaker than that of his predecessors. The early Angevins owned vast estates in their own right, which gave them an independent source of wealth. Also they were able to raise taxes and scutages more or less at will because they did not abuse this right. However, all that had now changed. Richard and John between them had sold off much of the crown estate, and their repeated exactions had made the people wary of paying taxes without public agreement. Also, the provisions of the Magna Carta, protecting the rights of the barons, meant that sources of revenue previously available to the monarchy were now effectively illegal.

In the meantime, although Henry did not wage extensive foreign wars, he had a very expensive building program which produced, amongst other marvels, Westminster Abbey. On the other hand, there were tolls, customs and rents to be had from the burgeoning economy. Between 1180 and 1230, fifty-seven new towns were founded in England, and existing towns and cities had also expanded greatly.

In the meantime there were hungry mouths to feed. A large party of Poitevins (from the province of Poitou) was established around Peter des Roche, obtaining offices and benefices from his influence. The English party complained bitterly, but it took the threat of another civil war to persuade Henry to order the Poitevins home. However, they were soon replaced by another set of foreigners. In 1236, Henry married Eleanor of Provence, and more Frenchmen from Provence and Savoy poured into the country seeking and obtaining power and influence. One of Eleanor's uncles was even created Archbishop of Canterbury, the first foreigner to hold the position in over a hundred years. A second body of Poitevins also arrived, connections of the king's mother. The possession of territory in Poitou also led to more expensive French wars in 1242, which resulted in the loss of the province, and meant that more Poitevins arrived in England.

The exactions of the Pope continued, despite the resistance of the English clergy. At the council of Lyons in 1245, the English complained that sixty thousand marks a year was being paid to the pope and foreign clergy. John's quick political fix to make England a fief of the papacy was proving very expensive in the long term. The pope was at this time trying to expand his physical territories in Italy where he acted as a civil ruler, his idea being to raise revenue abroad to pay for this. In 1254 Henry accepted the crown of Sicily on behalf of his younger son Edmund, who was nine years old. Sicily was in fact ruled by German princes, and a war would be needed to get them out. Henry could not finance such a war, but the pope undertook it on his behalf, so that by 1257 Henry owed the pope 135,000 marks. It was this ruinous behavior of the papacy which precipitated a revolution in England. There were many other papal abuses, such as the appointment of hundreds of absentee Italian priests to benefices in England.

Henry's government was hopelessly weak, and the barons and bishops began to demand control over the appointment of ministers in what was by now called Parliament, the successor to the great council. The barons found a new leader in Simon de Montfort, who ironically was also a foreigner. His father, a man of the same name, was a French baron who had taken a leading role in the ruthless suppression of the Albigensian heresy in the south of France. Simon was a second son who could expect no inheritance, so he came to England to pursue a claim to Earldom of Leicester through his mother. This claim was accepted by Henry, who also allowed de Montfort to marry his sister, Eleanor (he consented when he found that she was pregnant). De Montfort was not grateful – he was heard to say that Henry was an imbecile who should be locked up at Windsor. From 1248 to 1253 de Montfort was sent as governor of the king's French provinces in Gascony, where misrule had reigned for a century or more. Gascony was a significant overseas possession for the king with its vineyards and wine trade centred on Bordeaux. Here de Montfort gained such a reputation for severity that he was recalled to England to answer for his behavior, then sent back. The next governor of Gascony was the heir to the throne, Prince Edward, who was a great success, though only 18 years old (born 1239). De Montfort returned to England in 1257 where Henry gave him the magnificent castle at Kenilworth, only to find that he soon emerged as the leader of the opposition.

By now the country was in ferment. Under the leadership of De Montfort and Richard de Clare, the Earl of Gloucester, a Parliament was called at Oxford in 1258. Under the Provisions of Oxford issued by this body, effective control of the government was to pass from Henry to a council which would sort out all the grievances of church and state, and which would then pass on authority to another council to act in future. In the country there was to be a remarkable innovation, elected sheriffs. In this revolutionary atmosphere there were many shades of opinion and many new rules. The feeling was taking hold that there should be consultation on all aspects of government. Absolute monarchy was abolished by the Provisions of Oxford.

The new council was quick to eject the hated Poitevins and other foreigners and to stop the drain of money to Sicily. Its government lasted from 1258 to 1263. Henry tried to repudiate the Provisions, but could not. Eventually appeal was made to Louis IX of France to arbitrate. Louis was an excellent king, but knew nothing of the chaos in England, so he came down on Henry's side, a decision known as the "Mise of Amiens". Open war broke out between the king and his barons. The north and west including Devon and Cornwall, that is the poorer areas, favored the king. The south and in particular London and the Cinque Ports – the richer areas – were overwhelmingly in favour of Simon de Montfort, as was the clergy. (The Queen was pelted by the London mob and forced to take refuge in St Paul's.) The important barons of the Welsh borders, the Mortimers, were for the king; Llewellyn Prince of Wales took the side of De Montfort. First blood went to De Montfort, for at the Battle of Lewes, fought in Sussex in 1264, he vanquished the opposition. Both the king and the heir apparent, Edward, passed into his custody under a treaty called the "Mise of Lewes".

The government was now taken over by De Montfort and the Earl of Gloucester, who summoned the celebrated Parliament of 1265. This was the first body ever set up in England which could claim to be representative of the majority of the country, as two knights were summoned from every shire, and two from each principal city or borough. This represented the high point in the trajectory of Simon de Montfort. By now, his naked ambition was clear to all as he allocated the estates of his enemies to his own family. He was really an adventurer who thought he could make better job of running the country than his brother-in-law Henry. He soon began to lose support. His biggest problem was that while everyone knew that Henry was feeble and incompetent, it was equally obvious that his son and heir, Edward, was the very opposite. Six foot two inches tall, and by now 26 years old, Edward was the very picture of a prince and was the doyen of all the young knights. Clearly capable of running the country, he represented the long-term future. Only a brave man or a fool wanted to get on the wrong side of Edward.

So it was that Edward escaped from the clutches of de Montfort and sought out the Mortimers of the Welsh borders, always royalists, who were already on the march with an army. De Montfort's son was beaten at Kenilworth and then de Montfort himself lost at Evesham, where he was killed (1265).

That might seem the end of the affair, but there were lasting consequences. Firstly, the rebellion saw the end of the pope as the overlord of England. This submission had proved to be a dreadful mistake as the Pope simply used the country as a source of revenue. Secondly, the foreign favorites whom had been sent home were gone for good, as was the troublesome province of Poitou from whence so many of them came. England was henceforth, for the first time since 1066, run by the English and for the English rather than as part of the shaky multi-national Angevin enterprise. Finally the idea of a Parliament representing the whole country was born, a Parliament to which the king's ministers should be responsible. The time of this idea was yet to come, but in its way it was as great a transformation as the French Revolution in 1789, and one which had a long life ahead of it.

Apart from the last two years of the reign after 1270, when he went on a crusade, Prince Edward became the effective ruler of the country, and things settled down quickly. Henry died in 1272. He was certainly unfit to run the country, but he was not an evil or devious man as his father John had been. He only engaged in war in France once in a reign of 56 years, and to him we owe some of our greatest monuments. His hero and role model was Edward the Confessor, whom he emulated by building a magnificent Gothic abbey at Westminster which is still with us today. Henry was personally involved overseeing its construction, as he was at St Albans cathedral and Windsor Castle. Although not undertaken at his initiative, the glorious Salisbury Cathedral was built mostly within Henry's reign. Another legacy from Henry is the powerful outer wall round the Tower of London, for it was in Henry's time that the peripatetic government settled down in one place, Westminster.

It is clear from the events of this reign that the mentality of the ruling classes was still very French. It is unlikely that the Anglo-Danish kings would ever have built England's magnificent cathedrals, but they were very much a part of the French idea of the grand project, as pursued by Henry III. Also this reign produced the first English revolution – an idea for a complete change in the constitution rather than a dynastic struggle as had taken place under Stephen. This of course was led by another Frenchman, Simon de Montfort, in line with the French idea that if you don't like the government, start a revolution.

During this period there had also been important developments in Scotland. The Hebrides were still part of the Kingdom of Norway, though the Scottish kings made various attempts to buy them. In the middle of the thirteenth century the vigorous Norwegian king Haakon IV made strenuous attempts to make his sovereignty a reality, and in doing so clashed with the Scots at the battle of Largs in 1263. However he died shortly afterwards and the Scots were finally able to buy the Hebrides from Norway in 1266. The Scottish king at the time was Alexander III (1249-1286), last of the Canmore line.

Chapter 13 – Hammer of the Scots

Edward I 1272-1307 (35 years)
Born 1239   Married 1254 Eleanor of Castile, 1299 Margaret of France

Edward was in the Holy Land when his father died, and he made his way home via Italy and France, stopping off in Flanders to agree a commercial treaty with the Count of Flanders. The purpose of this was to re-establish and regulate the wool trade between England and Flanders, a matter of the greatest importance to both countries. England was the biggest exporter of wool in western Europe, a trade which remained a keystone of the economy for centuries.

Edward had great military and administrative abilities although he was capable of acting like a thug and a thief when it suited him. He was destined to become one of the most powerful Plantagenet monarchs of England, and as he was not distracted by large continental provinces, it was the rest of Britain that felt the full force of his glare. When his coffin was exhumed from its tomb in Westminster Abbey in 1774, it was found to contain the description *"Hic est malleus Scottorum"* – Here lies the hammer of the Scots; though he was a worse hammer of the Welsh, where it was he (not William) who was remembered as "the Conqueror". Edward was a hard man, chaste, devout and, exceptionally in a medieval monarch, faithful to his wife Eleanor of Castile, a woman of similar characteristics. He had a will of iron and endless endurance, but in the end he took on too much, overtaxed the country and its resources and made himself thoroughly unpopular.

To assist him in the government of the country, Edward recruited Parliament. He did not simply regard this as an impediment to his rule, but took it into his confidence and gained its support. The Provisions of Oxford were here to stay. The composition of Edward's Parliaments varied greatly, according to the business in hand, being drawn from different classes - the knights, the merchants, the burgesses, the barons and the clergy.

A mass of legislation was introduced through Parliament. Legal innovation and reform was a constant necessity as society and the economy evolved, and lawyers found loopholes in old laws and practices which demanded closure. Also, the civil war of the previous reign had left a mass of conflicting claims to property. To obtain a clearer idea of the state of the country, an "Eyre" or survey was conducted in 1274, eventually encoded in the Hundred Rolls, a new form of Domesday Book.

In 1275 Edward's first Parliament granted the king an excise duty on exported wool, at the rate of 7s 6d a sack (which weighed 364 lb). From this dates the start of the regular English customs service. This was a great breakthrough for the monarchy as Edward now had a reliable, regular source of income. He could now borrow against this income to an extent that no previous king had been able to do. Although the duty was at first levied at an acceptable rate, when it rose to 40s a sack in the 1290s it was called the "maltote", the bad tax, and there were howls of protest against it.

One new law was the Statute of Mortmain (1279), which prevented land being given or left to the church without the consent of the king. Church lands were exempt from some feudal services and payments, such as those payable for wardship and consent to marriage. It was widely thought that the church already had too much land, and leaving property to the church could be used as a form of tax evasion. The Statute of Winchester (1278) regulated the military obligations of knights and freeholders. All persons owning land to the value of £20 a year were ordered to be knighted so that these obligations would not be avoided. The first Justices of the Peace were appointed under Edward, mainly to administer this statute. In fact the legal profession as a whole increased in importance, and some statutes and decisions from this period remain in force to this day.

The reign of Edward is most famous for his attempts to annex Wales and Scotland. He did not initiate blatant invasions, but circumstances gave him the opportunities to interfere, and he was not slow to do so. Since the distant days of Hywel Dda in the tenth century, Wales had remained subdivided into petty kingdoms, occasionally coalescing under a strong king, never for long. Its economy recalled the early days of the Anglo-Saxons of the seventh century, pastoral and tribal with little arable tillage outside Anglesey. The English undoubtedly looked upon the Welsh themselves as barbaric savages who would benefit from a dose of civilization. In their relations with Norman England, the Welsh had fallen back before the first onslaught up until the death of

Henry I in 1135. They then retook territory up to 1199, when John succeeded in dividing them amongst themselves. Their prince, Llewellyn (ap Iorworth) (died 1240) almost obliterated English power within Wales itself, though on the borders, the Norman Marcher earls were always powerful, right from the time of William I.

Prince Llewellyn II sided with the barons in the civil war so Edward was never kindly disposed towards him. When Edward was crowned in 1274 Llewellyn failed to attend the coronation to perform his duty as a vassal, to pledge his loyalty to the new king. He refused to answer Edward's summons five times. Also he proposed to marry the daughter of Simon de Montfort. In 1277 Edward detained the young lady in question, declared Llewellyn a rebel, and invaded. He took with him the largest army ever assembled for a Welsh campaign including 800 knights, 15,000 foot soldiers and a train of support staff. Edward fared better than his predecessors, and Llewellyn's principality was cut back to include only Anglesey and the Snowdonia region. Llewellyn was allowed to marry his intended bride. There was peace for three years but Llewellyn must have watched uneasily as a string of new castles was built to surround him. Clearly deciding that it was now or never, he formed an alliance with his brother David, who up to this point had been Edward's ally. David attacked Hawarden Castle near Chester while Llewellyn launched himself on south Wales. However, Llewellyn was killed in single combat with a Shropshire soldier on the Wye. The Englishman was unaware of the identity of his adversary or he would have spared his life for the ransom money. David was captured and gruesomely executed as a traitor. The war dragged on until 1283, the English burning villages and herding away hostages to prevent further resistance.

Llewellyn was the last indigenous Prince of Wales. Edward annexed the country and the title passed to the eldest son of the reigning English monarch, where of course it still remains. Wales was divided into counties and hundreds in the English manner. English law and the English system of the administration of justice were introduced in varying degrees according to region. Edward made a conscious effort to suppress Welsh traditions. He also tried to encourage commerce, and granted charters to towns, but he was under no illusions. The Welsh were a conquered race and were likely to give trouble. To that end, the enormous castles of Wales were built at strategic points, many on the coast where they could be independently supplied from the sea. These castles – Harlech, Conway, Carnarvon and many more – were the largest buildings constructed in Britain up to these times, and were enormously expensive to build. Nothing on this scale had been attempted since Hadrian's Wall and there was no construction program so large anywhere in medieval Europe. Indeed one of the castles, Beaumaris, was never finished because the money simply ran out. The castles were designed to make the annexation of Wales irreversible, and it never was reversed, though there were rebellions. The English lords of the Welsh borders were left in place though Edward tried to reduce their power. These included the Mortimers, Earls of March, who had helped set Edward on his throne, and who in another generation would perform the opposite service for his son. Always something of a law unto themselves, they were to prove more a threat to the monarchy than the Welsh themselves.

So Edward succeeded where so many had failed before him. How did he do it? The real answer is that as an economic power, England had grown enormously in the period of the late middle ages, whereas Wales had not, remaining a rural backwater without towns or commercial infrastructure. The towns that did exist – Cardiff, Neath, Swansea, Cardigan, Pembroke, Carmarthen – were located in areas already controlled by the English. Edward was able to draw on enormous resources – especially borrowed money – and he did not do things by halves. His armies and castle-builders took road makers with them to penetrate the valleys, and the castle builders created fortresses that would not easily be brushed aside when the next weak king sat on the throne, as had happened in previous eras. Also there was an important immigration from various parts of England into the Vale of Clwyd where 10,000 acres were cleared of the native Welsh to make room. The Welsh had to accommodate themselves as best they could in the mountains (the same thing had happened in previous generations at Exeter and Carlisle). But another important factor was the personality of the Edward himself, for he was the most in-your-face Plantagenet of a very in-your-face dynasty, a man to whom power, battles, castles and the iron fist were the very stuff of his existence.

Edward's reign is also notable for the expulsion of the Jews. Usury or the payment of interest was forbidden by the medieval Christian church, so only those outside this religion, that is the Jews, were able to carry out this business. The king used the Jews to borrow money himself, and also taxed them. They were kept apart from the rest of the community in special quarters or Jewries, mainly for their own protection, because they were never popular. Their rates of interest were high, because there were many borrowers, and few lenders. They sold off debtor's land or other securities when loans were not repaid on time.   There had been attacks on them before, at the coronation of Richard and during Simon de Montfort's parliament of 1265.   They were no longer of much use to Edward as he had sucked them dry to finance his Welsh wars.   A community about 3,000 strong, they were ordered to leave in 1290.   Their expulsion in fact increased the power of Parliament, because the king could no longer raise funds from them. They were replaced in time by Italian lenders, who somehow found a way round the ban on usury.

Also in 1290, Edward's wife Eleanor died.   Like his father but most unusually for a medieval monarch, Edward had been a faithful and loyal husband, and her death caused him great grief.   She had born him 15 children, only six of whom survived into adulthood, and only one of them a boy.   The last journey of her body is marked by Eleanor crosses, erected by Edward from Lincoln to Charing Cross, three of which still stand today.

A crisis developed in Scotland at this time.   The thirteenth century had been largely peaceful and prosperous in Scotland − a golden age compared with what was to come.   Under Alexander II and his son Alexander III (1249-1286), the authority of the Scottish kings extended from the Alban heartland to cover most of what is now Scotland, which became a fully independent and unified country for the first time. However, the three children of Alexander III had all died, and only one of them, Margaret, had produced a child of her own.   Margaret had been married to the King of Norway and died giving birth to this child.   One tempestuous night in March, 1286, Alexander set off on a treacherous journey along the north bank of the Forth.   Disregarding warnings to turn back, he was killed falling off his horse.   His death at the age of 44 was a catastrophe for Scotland, which had been peaceful and prosperous during his long reign.   Despite intermittent outbreaks of feuding he had kept the country out of the civil and foreign wars which so dogged England, Ireland and Wales.   The only hope now was to fetch his granddaughter back from Norway.   Known as the Maid of Norway, she was only six years old, so it was likely that there would still be problems.   However she only got as far as Orkney, where in 1290 she too died, plunging Scotland into a dynastic crisis.   This was to plague the country with those civil and foreign wars so feared by Alexander for many years to come.   Nevertheless these Scottish wars of independence helped to form the Scottish nation and are still taught in its schools today.

There were two principal candidates for the Scottish throne, John Balliol, the grandson of Margaret, niece of William the Lion, and

Robert Bruce, son of Margaret's younger sister. Balliol had the better claim by feudal law, but following Roman law, Bruce had the better claim (being one generation shorter), and he was not going to give up without a struggle. Both these men were Norman barons and both of them had fought in Edward's armies in Wales. Balliol was the candidate of his relatives, the Comyns, the most powerful family in Scotland with their strongest castles in the area of the Moray Firth and Galloway. Bruce also was based in Galloway and had extensive estates in north Yorkshire and Durham. Edward was invited by the Scots to arbitrate in this dispute, which he did, on condition that the successful candidate would swear allegiance to him. The affair was known as the Great Cause (1291-2) and earned Robert Bruce the title "The Competitor".

Edward appointed a committee of Scottish barons to advise him, and they selected Balliol to be their king. However, quarrels soon developed between the Balliol and Edward, because some of Balliol's subjects took legal disputes into England when dissatisfied with the results they had obtained in Scotland. They were entitled to do this under feudal law, because Edward was Balliol's superior lord. Balliol went to see Edward to complain, but was subjected to a humiliating, blistering tirade and weakly offered his submission once more. This went down badly in Scotland where a council was set up to oversee a Scottish government independent of Edward. Of course, that would mean war.

Meanwhile a dispute was brewing in France where the French had occupied Bordeaux and the castles of Gascony. Edward was negotiating with the French king, Philip IV (the Fair), for the hand of his sister Blanche. Edward's wife Eleanor had died in 1290 and he had only one surviving son. Negotiations broke down, and in any case Blanche wrote to Edward saying that she did not wish to marry any man, "especially such an old one"! This became public and caused much amusement in the country in the glum year of 1294, when the harvest failed.

War was declared, Scotland allying with France for the first time (this alliance was to become traditional). The war dragged on for four years in France before the French and the English agreed to return to the original frontiers of Gascony. While this was going on, the Welsh under Madog broke out in revolt in 1294 and succeeded in taking Edward's castles, including Carnarvon, the largest of them all. Edward was now in serious need of money, so he summoned a Parliament on the same principles as Simon de Montfort in 1265, calling in representatives from around the country. The Parliament granted him the money he needed, and Edward began to set about the French, the Scots and the Welsh with his customary vigour.

The Welsh revolt was soon put down while Edward set off for Scotland. His first target was Berwick, then the chief town of Scotland. Here 11,000 people were said to have been massacred as a lesson to the rest of the country. Berwick was burned to the ground, to be reinhabited as an English town by the Northumbrians. A battle then took place in 1296 near Dunbar. Edward "Longshanks", now nearly 60 years old with long white hair, was a formidable and experienced warlord. Most of the Scots had never fought a serious battle, and were predictably routed coming out of the Lammermuir Hills. After a campaign of only three weeks, the Scots submitted and the Stone of Scone, on which the Scottish kings were crowned, was hauled off to Westminster. John Balliol went to the Tower of London and Edward showed no inclination to give the Scots another king. After the Scots had come forward in their hundreds to swear fealty, Edward went home, imagining that this was one more problem solved – but it was not to be. The effective ruler left in charge of Scotland was a fat and greedy Exchequer treasurer called Cressingham. The local head of a colonial administration, he was very quick to upset the Scots.

Edward now needed to raise more money in England, but by this time his exactions had gone too far, in the manner of Richard and John. For example he wrung one half of their yearly income from the clergy, then demanded more. Resistance to taxes was growing, and the barons were becoming troublesome. Roger Bigod, Earl of Norfolk, refused to accompany Edward to France. "By God," said Edward, "you shall either go or hang." "By God, sir king, I will neither go nor hang!" replied Bigod, and he did not go, nor did he hang.

Edward left for France to join his Flemish allies. Seizing their opportunity, the barons marched to London, forbade the collection of the latest round of taxes and demanded that the king confirm the Magna Carta, to which they had added a clause forbidding the collection of most taxes without the consent of Parliament. At Ghent in Flanders, Edward did sign this document, known as the "Confirmation of the Charters".

There were now serious problems in Scotland. While the Comyns and their allies amongst the nobility were prepared to accommodate the English, patriots gathered round a knight – a member of the middle classes, not the aristocracy – called William Wallace. He had got into a scrap with the English in the city of Lanark and started a riot. He escaped but left behind his betrothed, Marion, who was then killed by the English sheriff, Haselrig. In true Wild West style, Wallace returned, killed the sheriff and went on the run. Patriots including members of the aristocracy flocked to his banner. He formed an army and in 1297 managed to catch the Earl of Warenne and his army half-way across the Forth at Stirling Bridge. Warenne's army was cut to pieces, but Wallace was not strong enough to take any castles apart from Stirling itself.

Edward came after Wallace in person, defeating his army at Falkirk in 1298. Spurred into action, the Scottish nobility rallied under John Comyn, Balliol's nephew. The nationalists had some success and Edward was obliged to return with his armies for five successive years, grinding down the Scots a castle at a time. By 1304 the Scots had had enough and submitted once more. Wallace remained at large but in 1305 he was captured, taken to London and executed. A Hollywood approximation of his story is told in the film *Braveheart*. Wallace became a martyr of Scottish independence, and is remembered today with an impressive Victorian monument at Stirling. It was he rather than the more successful Robert Bruce who became the martyr, because he was a true Scot (rather than a Norman-Scot) and he was killed by the English.

However, it was still not over in Scotland. Robert Bruce, the son of "The Competitor" of the same name, Earl of Carrick, was an enemy of the dominant Comyn family and for that reason had sided with the English up until this point. Shakespeare could have written a very good play about this character, much more like Macbeth than the real Macbeth. In 1306 he decided, rashly, to revive his father's claim to the throne. Scotland had no king, but Bruce could see that Edward was ailing and might not live much longer. This would create a power vacuum, so he seized his opportunity. His first act was to murder his rival John "Red" Comyn, at the altar of Greyfriars Abbey in Dumfries. He was subsequently crowned by a few very nervous allies at Scone, as he had certainly started a civil war by the murder. His wife told him he would be a "summer king", for one season only. She was very nearly right - with most of the Scots as well as the English against him, he was defeated and forced to take to the hills. His allies at his coronation were not so lucky and a number of them (including his brother Neil) were hung, drawn and quartered in revenge for the murder of Comyn. His sister was kept in a cage at Roxburgh Castle. Bruce then began a guerilla war.

Edward set off to attend to his Scottish affairs in 1307, but he only got as far as Carlisle, where he died at the age of 67. This totally changed the prospects of Robert Bruce. From now on he would no longer have to deal with the military iron fist of Edward I, but with his distinctly unmilitary bisexual son, Edward II.

Why did Edward I fail in Scotland where he had succeeded in Wales? Firstly, Scotland was by this time a very different country from Wales, much larger, more populous and more sophisticated. The Normans were well entrenched, trial by jury was established, and the church flourished with magnificent abbeys at Melrose, Newbattle and Holyrood. Celtic languages were receding in the southern part of the country in the face of French and English. In short, Scotland had been Normanising over a long period, and was far from being a country run by wild Highland clans. Nevertheless in terms of usable agricultural land, towns, infrastructure and population, Scotland was probably little larger than Yorkshire, so this was not the only reason.

Clearly Scotland benefited from distance. It was a long way across relatively lightly populated territory just to reach the Forth and Clyde, but that is still southern Scotland. Armies could march here, passing through English-speaking territory in the Lothians, and still feel at home. But the geography of Scotland allowed for defence in depth, because a large part of the good arable and grazing land lay round the Moray Firth, in the northeast, beyond the "Mounth" or ridge of the Grampian Mountains. Armies from England could enter and conquer the lowlands, and frequently did, as often as not finding no army to fight because the Scottish army had melted away in front of them. However to reach beyond Perth stretched them logistically, to the extent that no English army was able to subdue the area until the second Jacobite revolt of 1745-6.

This lesson seems to have been lost on Edward I and it was not learnt by his successors, who also wasted money and resources on the same futile enterprise. Scotland was just too difficult to conquer and hold, and would remain so for hundreds of years.

Chapter 14 – The Later Angevin Kings

Edward II 1307-1327 (20 years)
Born 1284 Married 1308, Isabella of France

The new king was tall, blond, handsome, engaging and accomplished enough, but even a man of his father's calibre had found running the country and controlling its dangerous satellites difficult. Edward II was to find it impossible. He was lazy, lay in bed late, drank heavily and learned no Latin; he kept bad company, minstrels and grooms; he was to be a thoroughly poor monarch. His father had had to fight for the survival of his dynasty and for his own life, and he had been a prisoner of his own father's enemies. Edward II grew up knowing nothing of this life, and had not developed the appropriate toughness and decision-making abilities, in the manner of the son who takes over the hard-built family business from his parents and loses the lot.

The reason England had so many "bad" kings like Edward II was that the constitution was not sufficiently developed for a country as complicated as England had now become. Too much depended on the king. Other aspects of government – the Parliament, an independent judiciary and body of law, an independent civil service and local government – were not advancing quickly enough to save the country from disaster when the king was incompetent. This problem was not properly sorted out until as late as 1689, after any number of civil wars and lesser internal conflicts. Kings like Edward II and John also call into question the desirability of hereditary monarchy, which is bound to throw up unsuitable monarchs from time to time. However it was widely adopted in Europe. Poland, which reached a peak of prosperity in the fourteenth century, adopted an elective monarchy instead. The result was normally civil war at the death of each king and a decline to such an extent that the country had disappeared off the map by 1795.

Edward's reign was marked by the promotion of his "favorites", who were loathed by the traditionally powerful barons and who caused Edward no end of trouble. The barons looked upon themselves as the traditional advisers to the king and did not take their replacement by upstart nancy-boys kindly. The leader of the opposition to the favorites and to the king was a younger member of the royal family, a tradition which persisted for centuries.

The first of the favorites was one Piers Gaveston, the son of a Gascon knight who had been brought up with the young king. Edward I, who appears to have had no illusions about his son, regarded Gaveston as a bounder and a wastrel, and would not have him at his court. The new king recalled him and gave him the title of Earl of Cornwall. Gaveston had his virtues – he was a brave and able soldier – but he taunted the barons, conferring nicknames upon them such as "the hog" or "the play actor" (Earl of Lancaster), "Joseph the Jew" (Earl of Pembroke) and "the black dog of Arden" (the fierce Earl of Warwick). These were not people to upset. Thomas Earl of Lancaster was the king's cousin; he controlled five counties and was the most powerful subject in the country.

Having withdrawn from the Scottish enterprise, Edward sailed to France to marry the daughter of the French king, Isabella, said to be the most beautiful woman in Europe (as she was the king's daughter, "eligible" might be a more fitting word). Issue of this marriage might then one day have a claim to the throne of France – an eventuality which became a *causus belli* of the Hundred Years War. Edward had originally been betrothed to the Maid of Norway, heiress of the Scottish crown, who died on her way to Scotland in 1290. Had that marriage taken place, there may have been no Hundred Years War, and no Bannockburn!

Gaveston was left as regent, and the barons seized the opportunity to get rid of him. Edward skirted round the problem by sending him to Ireland as Lord-Deputy, but as soon as the pressure was off, he was back, in 1309.

The people knew their king was idle and weak just as they knew that his father was vigorous and strong, and sporadic disorder broke out. Determined to put a stop to this, the barons set up a new council of 21 bishops and barons under the name of the Lords Ordainers to oversee the government of the kingdom. A document called the Ordinances of 1311 was issued, setting out in detail what the king must and must not do.

Possibly able to see the futility of it all, Edward II had abandoned his father's Scottish campaign of 1307 and left the Comyns and their allies to tackle Bruce on their own. As the Comyns were now regarded as the pro-English party, Bruce was able to take Scotland a castle at a time with the patriotic tide behind him. Despite many appeals from the Comyns and others, Edward did not return with an army until 1310-11. This achieved almost nothing, Bruce being too wary to force the issue with a battle. Gaveston went with Edward's army to Scotland and did well enough, but nothing would please the barons, who once again forced his exile, this time to the Netherlands. However, he was soon back. This time the barons had had enough. Separating him from the king, he was taken to the Earl of Warwick (the "black dog") and executed in the presence of the Earl of Lancaster ("the hog") and the Earl of Hereford. The lords were said to have commented that "if you let a fox go, you will have to hunt him again".

Edward was devastated, but could do nothing. With Stirling Castle on the point of falling to Robert Bruce, who already held Edinburgh and Roxburgh, the pressure was now insurmountable to reassert himself in Scotland. So in 1314 Edward invaded Scotland with a splendid army. However, Lancaster refused his support. Edward and his army confronted Bruce near Stirling at Bannockburn. The Scots had the inferior force, and sought to withdraw, but gained heart in the early skirmishes. Robert Bruce was picked out by an English knight, Sir Henry de Bohun, who came at him on his charger while he was disposing his infantry. Robert Bruce, on a poor horse, was unabashed and stood his ground. The knight in his armour and helmet missed his blow, and Bruce stove in his skull with an axe. Overnight the Scots were still nervous of a fight, but were approached in the woods by another Englishman, Sir Alexander de Seton, who told Bruce that the English were disheartened and lacked courage for a fight. Their army in fact included a large number or Welsh and Irish levies of uncertain value and poor morale. In the end, the battle took place, the sword and the claymore clashed together, and the Scots won their most famous victory over the English, so famous that they are still talking about it 700 years later.

The follow-up to Bannockburn was disastrous. The stragglers were picked off as they tried to make their way home. Edward himself escaped to take ship at Dunbar but a number of important barons were killed and others captured and ransomed. Robert Bruce experienced a massive upswing of popular support and over the next few years harried the undefended northern counties of England, driving cattle back to

Scotland. North Yorkshire in particular was ravaged and raided so often that it was exempted from taxes. Berwick was retaken and its English occupiers slaughtered. There are some "historians" for whom the history of Scotland is nothing but a catalogue of grievances against the English, but the murderer and usurper Robert the Bruce showed what the Scots could do when they had the upper hand. But really, Robert the Bruce behaved like a petty king of Ireland. His activity in northern England – looting with no real political motive – contrasted strongly with the civilized courts of Alexander II and III in the previous century, the golden age of medieval Scotland.

Bruce so gained in confidence that he invaded Ireland with the intention of setting up his brother Edward as king. This was partly a diversionary tactic to siphon English resources away from Scotland. However in conditions of starvation in the great famine of 1314-15 (which was equally bad in England), his army acted more like an army of occupation than liberators from the English. The Bruces had a number of successes in their campaign, but their attempt failed. Edward sent Roger Mortimer as his lieutenant to Ireland and provided him with sufficient resources to see off the Bruces. Edward Bruce was killed at Dundalk in 1318 and Robert returned home.

In 1320 the Scots issued the Declaration of Arbroath, an eloquent statement of their intention to remain independent:

"...as long as but a hundred of us remain alive never will we, under any condition, be brought under English rule. It is in truth not for glory nor riches nor honours that we are fighting but for freedom – for that alone which no honest man gives up but with life itself."

The matter was finally settled by a treaty drawn up at Northampton in 1328 when England formally recognized the independence of Scotland. The following year Robert Bruce died of leprosy leaving an heir, David, who was only six years old. With Bruce gone the successors of the Comyns and the Balliols would reassert themselves in the minority.

The result of the disorder, the Scottish defeat and also a famine in 1314-15 was to strengthen the hand of Thomas Earl of Lancaster, who was able to bring members of his own circle into office. One of these was a young nobleman called Hugh Despenser (the younger), the grandson of another Despenser who had served as justiciar under Simon de Montfort. Despenser became the king's chamberlain and before long he had replaced the lamented Piers Gaveston in the king's affections.

He was a much more dangerous man than the insolent butterfly Gaveston had been. Lancaster and his party attacked his former protégé and succeeded in securing the banishment of the Despenser family, but not for long.

It became apparent to the public that the rivalry between different groups of aristocrats was simply self-serving and did the country no good whatever, no matter who had the upper hand. There followed a reaction in favour of the king and against Lancaster. It had been noted that during the pillage of the north by the Scots, the raiders seemed to spare the Lancaster's property, and also that he had failed to accompany Edward to Bannockburn. Now evidence was found that he had indeed been corresponding with the Scots.

Like Simon de Montfort before him, Lancaster was a relative of the king who thought he could run the country better than the king himself, and as this was his real motivation, he lost popular support. In 1322 he withdrew to his northern estates and closer to his Scottish allies, but he was caught at Boroughbridge, then executed at Pontefract. Edward had finally gained his revenge for the death of Gaveston. Roger, Lord Mortimer, another enemy of the king, was thrown into the Tower of London. At York – effective capital of the country during parts of the reigns of both Edward I and Edward II – the hated Ordinances of 1311 were revoked by Parliament (1322).

However, no peace lasted long in this troubled reign. The reinstated Despensers were seizing estates and piling up wealth. The Queen, Isabella of France, fell into conspiracy with Roger Mortimer, who had escaped from the Tower and become her lover. Assembling an army in the Netherlands, she and Mortimer landed in Suffolk in 1325 and set about collecting their friends and the connections of the executed Lancaster about them. The combination was too powerful for Edward. His Despenser friends were caught and executed, and Edward himself was held in custody. Parliament met and decided to replace him with his son. He was then sent to Berkeley Castle, near Bristol, into the hands of his deadliest enemies. Here they attempted to starve him to death. When that took too long, according to legend, they finished him off by shoving a red-hot poker up his anus.

Edward II was the first post-1066 king of England to suffer deposition, though a precedent had been set, and the next-but-one (Richard II) suffered the same fate in 1399, as did Henry VI in 1460. No English king after Harold was to die in battle until Richard III in 1485 – dysentery was a bigger problem; John had died of it and so did Henry V. In fact, rebellion and revolt never lay far beneath the surface, acting as a brake on the actions of the monarch. This was opposition by non-Parliamentary means, in the French style. Even strong kings including William I, Henry II and Edward I had to face baronial rebellions, partly because they were so strong. Weaker kings such as John (in 1215), Henry III (1258-65) and Edward II himself (1310, 1321and 1325-7) suffered full-scale rebellions, though the most frightening and threatening of such disturbances, the Peasants Revolt of 1381, came in a later reign (Richard II).

Edward III 1327-1377 (50 years)
Born 1312 Married 1328, Philippa of Hainault

The new king was only 15 years old and for the first three years of his reign, the country was run by his father's deposer, Mortimer, in association with his mother Queen Isabella. However, in 1330, Mortimer's enemies, led by the Earl of Lancaster, seized Mortimer and had him hanged. Henceforth Edward ruled as well as reigned.

Peace with Scotland after the depredations of Robert the Bruce in the north of England was signed at Northampton in 1328, settling full independence on the rulers of Scotland. However, on the death of Robert the Bruce (1329), a dynastic struggle broke out between the supporters of his son David II, and the Balliol family (whom Robert the Bruce had replaced in the previous generation). Edward intervened on behalf of Edward Balliol, thereby resuming the disastrous policy of his grandfather Edward I. He repeatedly sent armies into Scotland which, despite vicious harryings, refused to concede its independence. At first Edward, anxious to prove that he took after his grandfather, rather than his father, had a great success, taking the town of Berwick after the battle of Halidon Hill (1333). Berwick was at that time the most important town in Scotland. It had changed hands between England and Scotland before, but henceforward it was to remain in English hands permanently.

In their struggle for independence, the Scots called on the assistance of the French. This set off one of the most unedifying sagas in English history, the Hundred Years War with France. This was in essence a pointless and ultimately (for the English) fruitless exercise to turn the clock back, in terms of French territories, to the time of Henry II and Richard I. Most of the fighting took place in northern France (easy to reach from England) or in and around the Gascony region of south-western France, property of the English kings since the inheritance of Eleanor of Aquitaine. France, being four times the size of England, was unified much more slowly. The last pieces did not fall into place until Savoy and Nice were transferred from Italian sovereignty as late as 1860. Gascony was difficult to reach from Paris – easier, in fact, for the English to access by sea – as its principal rivers drain the wrong way, from the Pyrenees to the Atlantic. The old county of Toulouse, to the east, was much more accessible from the north via the Saone and Rhone valleys and so fell under French control much earlier, by 1270.

The Hundred Years War was to run sporadically from 1337 for 116 years until 1453. It was originally started by the French when they attempted to claim Gascony. In retaliation, the English kings claimed the French throne for themselves, and at times came close to snatching it. In fact Edward III WAS the heir to the French throne by descent through the female line, in fact through Isabella, his mother, the daughter of King Philip IV of France and a cousin of the reigning Philip VI. This claim was disputed by the French, of course, who disallowed any claim through the female line under Salic Law – the law which prevailed in the old territories of Charlemagne. The English retorted that the French had in the past allowed the succession to pass through the female line, when it had suited them. The English also disputed whether Salic Law was relevant in Paris as the Franco-German empire of Charlemagne was based at Aachen. A further war aim for the English was to protect Flanders from French ambitions, as Flanders formed the market for that most important of English exports, raw wool.

The war started well enough for the English with the naval victory at Sluys (1340) followed by a famous victory for Edward at Crecy (1346), one of the very few fixed battles of the war. After plundering Normandy, Edward headed for home but only with great difficulty crossed the Somme at its mouth at a ford called Blanchetaque (white shingle). Once over the river he had time to arrange his forces ready to confront the army of Philip, the French king. Edward's forces were not feudal levies, but hired soldiers. They consisted of archers at the front and men-at-arms behind them. Against this small but highly trained army, Philip brought a much larger force of feudal knights, supported by only a few archers. Philip attacked late, after his forces had been marching all day. They were tired and their bowstrings were drenched. Edward's archers quietly stood their ground, pouring arrows into the surging mass of mounted knights in front of them and killing men and horses alike. The stunned Philip had to be led away from the field of battle at the end of the day. The following day a dense mist prevented a French rally and the English were able to follow up their victory, and the slaughter of that day was said to be greater than in the battle itself.

In accordance with tradition, the Scots had entered the war as allies of the French, but in 1346, the same year as Crecy, they were badly beaten by the northern barons Percy and Neville at Neville's Cross near Durham. Here the Scottish king David II, son of Robert the Bruce, was captured and conveyed to London. He was to remain a prisoner for eleven years before being ransomed back to the Scots.

*   *   *   *

However, by 1348 there was an even greater menace than warfare, one which was to ensure that the fourteenth century was to turn out very badly for the English (and indeed for all Europe). The century was certainly punctured by a number of severe bouts of bad harvests and famine, but much worse, in 1348 the first wave of the Black Death struck. The disease was carried by rats, and spread rapidly from the ports to cover the whole of Britain. Anyone catching bubonic or pneumonic plague (both types were reported) could expect to die within days. The original Black Death was followed by renewed visitations in 1361 (striking down especially children born after the first plague, and so without any immunity), 1369 and 1375 and in fact right on into Stuart times. The population fell by a half and did not recover, remaining at about two and a half million from the time of the Poll Tax of 1381 right through until around 1520. In fact the increase in the density of the population (to approximately five million in 1348) was one reason for the severity of the Black Death. Infectious diseases of that type require a dense population to maintain themselves, or else they fizzle out.

The Black Death first struck in Ireland in the same year as in England, 1348, in Dublin and other ports on the east coast. Here and in the towns, its ravages were no less. However the Gaelic countryside, more thinly populated in these times, was notably less affected. So it was the English-dominated colonies which suffered the most. The Scots first attributed the Black Death in England to the avenging hand of God, and even raided Durham in 1349 to take advantage, but they spoke too soon. Their turn for the pestilence duly arrived.

As a side-effect, the Black Death ended English immigration to Ireland. Life in that country was known to be risky to Englishmen. There were now plenty of opportunities at home and some Anglo-Irish took them. Because labour was so scarce, the price of it went up, and the survivors did well. The government of the day tried to curb rapidly rising wages with the Statute of Labourers (1351), a famously doomed attempt to defy the laws of supply and demand. Sometimes whole villages became deserted. The feudal system broke down as villeins – the tied or "unfree" peasants – left the land and their legal lords for better opportunities elsewhere.

*   *   *   *

Legislation passed in this reign also foreshadowed the English Reformation. The Statute of Provisors (1351) made clergymen receiving livings from the Pope in England liable to imprisonment. The Popes had frequently abused their powers by making preferments of English livings on foreigners who were not resident in England, and indeed who had no intention ever of going there, and this law, frequently renewed, made the practice illegal. Also, in 1353 the Statute of Praemunire (meaning to be forewarned) was enacted. This was designed to prevent persons prosecuting suits in foreign courts without the king's leave. It was aimed specifically at the Papacy and indeed it was considered a violation of the statute to receive letters from the Pope without the consent of the king.

*   *   *   *

The two most famous of Edward's sons were the first, also called Edward but better known (after the colour of his body armour) as the Black Prince, and the third, John of Gaunt. Neither of these men were destined to become kings themselves, but children of both of them did. The Black Prince died in 1376, the year before his father, so it was his son who succeeded Edward III as Richard II (1377-1399), at only eleven years old. He was eventually to be deposed by his cousin Henry, Earl of Lancaster and son of John of Gaunt, who became Henry IV (1399-1413).

The Black Prince and John of Gaunt were both heavily involved in looking after their father's continental affairs, in France and also in Spain. In 1355, in territory he was unlikely to conquer and hold, the Black Prince took a scorched earth policy which devastated large areas of the French countryside. This most brutal strategy is very much at odds with the ideas of chivalry which were very fashionable at the time. In 1356 he led the English archers in another famous victory at the Battle of Poitiers (1356). The first phase of the Hundred Years War was ended in 1360 by the Treaty of Bretigny. At this point the Edward had gained the advantage and even ransomed the French king John II after Poitiers.

The Black Prince became involved in Spanish affairs in support of King Pedro (the Cruel) of Castile. Two of his brothers, one of them John of Gaunt, were married to Pedro's daughters. Although he won a victory there at Najera (1367), he came away loaded with debt and stricken with disease – but if an English prince had limited justification for waging war in France, what was he doing in Spain? In any case he had supported the wrongs side, and Pedro was soon ousted by his illegitimate brother, Henry of Trastamare, henceforward an enemy of the English. The taxes levied on the Black Prince's French subjects to pay for these adventures led to the outbreak of a new phase of the Hundred Years War in 1369. An English fleet under the Earl of Pembroke was defeated by Henry of Trastamare's Spaniards off La Rochelle – the reversal of the victory at Sluys in the first phase of the war.

Meanwhile, the French learned their lessons from their defeats at Crecy and Poitiers. Instead of relying on totally undisciplined feudal levies, they hired soldiers who did not have to show off their prowess to their friends or return to their fields. Also, they had learned to avoid pitched battles with the English, instead harassing them without decisive engagements. Under a vigorous king, Charles V, they reversed the earlier English victories. After La Rochelle they made rapid progress, and they harried the English (including those led by John of Gaunt) to the extent that by 1374, of the English possessions in France, only Calais, Bayonne and Bordeaux remained. This phase of the war was to last for twenty years, from 1369 to 1389, though little of note took place in the later years.

An important effect of the war was that it greatly strengthened the hand of Parliament, as the king repeatedly had to ask it to approve taxes to support his campaigns. In 1376 the Good Parliament met. Tired of high taxation to pay for an unsuccessful war, it attempted the impeachment of Edward's ministers. Under the influence of John of Gaunt, the Bad Parliament of 1377 reversed the impeachments.

*   *   *   *

There was one more very significant feature of the reign of Edward III, the rise of the first English Protestants, the Lollards. Disillusionment with the clergy and the state of the Catholic church was widespread (and is very well reflected in Chaucer's *Canterbury Tales*). The leader of the Lollards was a Yorkshireman called John Wycliffe, the master of Balliol College, Oxford. He famously produced the first English translation of the New Testament, and oversaw the translation of the whole Bible. He did what he could to reform the abuses of the clergy. Wycliffe had powerful friends, including in the end John of Gaunt, who was the real ruler of England towards the end of Edward's reign. Otherwise he may not have died, as he did, in his bed.

The long reign of Edward III, which had begun so well, turned sour. The later Whig historians castigated Edward as an irresponsible adventurer, though recent historians have tried to rehabilitate his reputation. It seems that he was very much a family man, devoted to his wife, Queen Philippa of Hainault, and (unusually for a king) never suffering opposition from any of his five adult sons. (I have a personal interest in Queen Philippa – my Oxford college, Queen's, was founded by her chaplain in 1341.) Edward did have a mistress, Alice Perrers, but she did not appear on the scene until the queen was terminally ill. Also, Edward was very popular in his lifetime amongst his own subjects, and was not personally blamed for the failures of the later part of his reign. It says something for him, and for the times, that whilst he reigned for fifty years, the monarchs historically on either side of him – Edward II and Richard II – were both deposed.

*   *   *   *

As the reign of Edward III marks the end of Francophone England, this is a good place to review the impact of the Norman invasion and its aftermath. One important question in this area is this: just how many French-speakers arrived and stayed in England? What impact did they have? Estimates of the numbers vary widely: from "Even including civilians they numbered no more than ten thousand" (Andrew Hayes, Archaeology of the British Isles) to "perhaps 100,000" (Keith Feiling, History of England). There is more agreement on the size of the existing population of England, between one and a half million and two million in 1066. However, an estimate of only 10,000 Frenchmen seems ludicrously low. There were probably that many military men, if not in William's army at Hastings then in the follow-up and consolidation and in the 300 years of Francophone hegemony that followed. We have a better idea of the size of the Roman army that conquered England – 40,000 to 50,000 men - than we do the size of William's, but no one was going to conquer and hold down the country with a few thousand knights.

Then, once a knight or a baron was established in his new property, who was he to talk to all day? Certainly not the English – they had no common language. The clergy knew Latin, but it was not spoken by the mass of the people. The new owner would certainly have brought his friends, family, poor relations and personal servants with him – there were huge numbers of manors to go round, enough to satisfy all the younger sons. He would need the services of estate managers, forest rangers and wine merchants. He would also have wanted a French priest. It is known that the Norman clergy were better-educated than the English. The Domesday Book records 2,000 churches, and there were many larger religious establishments, cathedrals, abbeys, monasteries and seminaries. Again, there must have been a huge demand for teachers of French, interpreters and translators. There were vast opportunities in the patronage of the king and the church and in the military. Also, there was an equally large pool of potential immigrants. These could have come from any part of France, especially after the accession of Henry II in 1154, for his French territories were more extensive than his English.

Right up until the time of Edward IV, whose reign began in 1461, English kings almost invariably married French princesses. These brought with them their own family, friends and hangers-on. The practice was not confined to the monarchy as the aristocrats also married French aristocrats. This was a two-way process, in that English-born princesses and aristocrat girls also married in France. The whole Anglo-French territory acted as a vast marriage pool with a common aristocratic, knightly and religious caste. Up until the arrival of the connections of Eleanor of Provence, wife of Henry III (married in 1236), the French newcomers were not even thought of as foreigners, because so many of their kind were already here, running England as an Anglo-French enterprise. A foreigner like Simon de Montfort slipped effortlessly into the system, so that in his career from 1229 onwards, no one seemed to care that he was in fact French.

Also, in the eleventh and twelfth centuries, it was fashionable to complete one's education in France. The most famous schools were in Paris but there were others in Chartres, Laon, Tours, Poitiers and Orleans. Thousands of Englishmen attended these schools; the universities of Oxford and Cambridge were not established until the thirteenth century. (Another popular centre of learning was Bologna in Italy, especially for the training of lawyers.) A knowledge of French was in any case useful because it gave the English access to a wider world. Over the next few centuries French became established as a *lingua franca* over much of western Europe and the eastern Mediterranean.

Additionally, there was vacant land. The Domesday Book reports the areas in Yorkshire devastated in the harrying of the north as "waste", but it is unlikely that prime agricultural land as is found in the Vale of York would have lain empty for too long. Work carried out by the York Archaeological Trust at the church of St Helen-on-the-Walls on burials from this period revealed a surprising fact. Compared with the Anglo-Scandinavian burials from York, there was a change in the shape of the skulls, from long and narrow to broad and short. This can only mean one thing – there were new people here. The same phenomenon has been observed at other archaeological sites, including Wharram Percy in North Yorkshire. However, the allocation of English resources to Frenchmen was by no means confined to the period of the conquest. Henry III (1216-72) got into trouble with his barons for allowing family connections from Savoy, Provence and Poitou to take up land, castles and offices of state and church.

Over the long period of the Francophone monarchy, probably hundreds of thousands of French speakers came to Britain, temporarily or permanently, the last great external migration of the medieval period. There were to be later ones, of French Huguenots in the seventeenth century, and most notably of Irish in the nineteenth, but none made so great an impact. Ethnically it is likely that most of the incomers were similar to the people already here, because the Normans were of course originally Norsemen, and many of the older inhabitants of Normandy were either Franks or Saxons anyway.

One consequence of the Black Death was the revival of English as the official language of England. Its survival reflects the fact that Norman England remained England with a Norman ruling class. French never became the language of the people, though it was certainly the language of the court and polite society. Like all plagues, the Black Death affected communities which lived close together the most, including those that lived in towns, castles and monasteries. Isolated rural communities were far from immune, but they were much safer. So it was that the Black Death carried off the French ruling class, the French bishops and the French traders, and the French language with them. One place where this is still visible today is in the lists of bishops which appear in many cathedrals. Until about 1350 the names are all Norman French. After that date, they are all English.

The English language re-emerged, marvelously simplified from its original Germanic form, first by the Danish influence, then by Norman. In fact the greatest and most lasting impact the Normans settlers made was on the English language. By the time it emerged from French domination in the fourteenth century, it contained 10,000 loan words from Norman French and had changed its method of forming plurals from the original Germanic form (as in child, children) to the simple addition of –s, the French form. French words came to be used not only for the things one would expect – baron, council, exchequer, government – but for all sorts of everyday things – beef, pork, sausage, dinner, hour, age, city, pain, people, please, dress, use, pen, and so on. In order to communicate with their new masters the mass of the English must have had to learn at least some French, the words for basic things – forest, river, soldier, sir, fine, gaol, table, face (all French). The large number of Anglo-Norman marriages would also have meant that there were two languages spoken in many households.

The most famous English works from this period are *The Canterbury Tales* by Geoffrey Chaucer (1343-1400). They represent Middle English and are riddled with French loan-words such as "visage" and "image". Whereas all but the scholars are baffled by the Old English of Beowolf or the Anglo-Saxon Chronicle, most people can figure out Chaucer with a bit of help.

      *   *   *   *

The economy of England must have taken a severe hit as a result of the Black Death, but prosperity did return in a changing landscape. The high duties on the export of wool, or maltotes, fist levied in the 1290s, reappeared during the early stages of the Hundred Years' War. One unintended consequence was the replacement of the export of raw wool with the export of finished cloth. Wool textile manufacturing sprang up, especially in West Yorkshire, East Anglia and the west of the country, and with it, new or much expanded towns, including Bradford, Halifax and Leeds. Woollen cloth manufacture involves spinning, weaving and then fulling the broadcloths, which were 24 yards long by two and a half yards wide. Fulling meant placing the cloths in troughs filled with water and fuller's earth or alum , to thicken and felt the cloth. This was best done in mills, the first mills built in the wool business, the ruins of which can still be seen by tumbling Pennine streams to this day.

Other industries were growing, notably tin mining in Devon and Cornwall, and coal digging in Newcastle. The coal of Newcastle was known as sea coal because if its method of transport.

On a social note, the reign of Edward III represents the pinnacle of the age of chivalry, of knights on chargers in shining armour, of tremendous jousting tournaments watched by ladies in long gowns and conical hats, of courtly love and of troubadours.

Richard II 1377-1399 (22 years)

Born 1366   Married 1382, Anne of Bohemia, and 1396, Isabella of France

So England moved ahead with yet another regency, as the young king was only 11 years old. The leading man in the country was his uncle, John of Gaunt, but he had made himself thoroughly unpopular in undoing the work of the Good Parliament at the end of the previous reign, so a council was formed to run the country. Amongst its first acts, it levied a series of taxes to support the war with France. The most notorious and by far the heaviest of these was the Poll Tax of 1381, levied at the rate of a shilling a head for all people over the age of 15. The fact that it was not graduated in any way, and so fell equally on the richest and poorest, was greatly resented, and led directly to the Peasants Revolt of the same year. Arising in the prosperous counties of Essex and Kent, this was more than a revolt of the peasants, as it also had support from the middle classes. Its leaders were Wat Tyler and Jack Straw, and its orator was John Ball, who demanded an end to all villeinage or serfdom. One of the victims of the peasants was Simon Sudbury, Lord Chancellor and Archbishop of Canterbury, who was dragged from the Tower of London and killed. Although the revolt was soon suppressed without great violence, it seriously frightened the rulers of the country.

When Richard assumed personal rule in 1389, he found himself struggling to contain the ambitions of many unruly barons. His reign resembles that of Edward II, which followed a similar trajectory. Richard gradually mastered his many enemies, but his rule was seen as arrogant, arbitrary and extravagant, and favoring his friends at the expense of the traditional nobility. Amongst these, Richard made the mistake of alienating his first cousin, Henry, Duke of Lancaster (generally called Bolingbroke after the castle where he was born), whom he banished overseas.

Richard II is the subject of one of Shakespeare's best-known history plays. As he lies on his death-bed, Richard's uncle John of Gaunt is given this famous speech:

> This royal throne of kings, this scepter'd isle
> This earth of majesty, this seat of Mars
> This other Eden, demi-paradise

This fortress built by nature for herself
Against infection and the hand of war
This happy breed of men, this little world
This precious stone set in a silver sea
Which serves in the office of a wall
Or as a moat defensive to a house
Against the evil of less happier lands
This blessed plot, this earth, this realm, this England
This nurse, this teeming womb of royal kings
Fear'd by their breed and famous by their birth

Three years before his death, John of Gaunt did something very unusual for a medieval prince – he married his mistress, Katherine Swynford. His second wife had died two years previously. Katherine was the daughter of a Flemish herald who had acted as a governess to John of Gaunt's children. The late marriage, sanctioned by the Pope, legitimized the four adult children the couple had already had, under the family name of Beaufort. These children and their descendants were to play a prominent part in the politics of the fifteenth century, and were to regain the royal line in 1485 when Henry VII, a direct descendant of Katherine Swynford, ascended the throne.

Matters were brought to a head with the death of John of Gaunt, Bolingbroke's father, in 1399. Richard threatened to disinherit Bolingbroke from his father's estates as he wanted money to fight his wars in Ireland. He duly left for that country, whereupon Bolingbroke promptly returned to England. Support flocked to the new contender, who was thought capable of restoring order. Richard was delayed in sailing back from Ireland by unfavorable winds, and by the time he arrived in Wales, the army which he had caused to be assembled there had dispersed. Richard was legally deposed by Parliament without any battle. After this he was imprisoned, and died the following year, probably from starvation. The first Lancastrian king came to the throne as Henry IV, Richard II being regarded as the last of the Angevin kings.

*   *   *   *

There exists a further famous work of literature from this era, *Sir Gawain and the Green Knight,* an anonymous romance set in the time of King Arthur. Known through a single surviving manuscript, today it is frequently read in translation – one such being the work of J R R

140

Tolkien, author of *Lord of the Rings*, and a man interested in all things medieval and strange.

Chapter 15 – The Kings of Lancaster and York

<u>Henry IV 1399-1413 (14 years)</u>
Born 1366 Married 1380, Mary de Bohun, and 1403, Joan of Navarre

Henry had seized the throne, but his position was not initially a strong one. One problem was that he was not Richard's direct heir. That position belonged to the infant great-grandson of the second son of Edward III, Edmund (later Earl of March), and it was this branch of the family which eventually produced the Yorkist kings. Also, Richard's connections did not take Henry's usurpation of the throne lying down, and there were to be numerous conspiracies and insurrections in this short reign. The two best-known of these are central to Shakespeare's plays, *Henry IV parts I and II* respectively.

In Wales, one Owen Glendower had been in the service of Richard, and he successfully established himself as the first independent ruler of the Welsh heartlands since the time of Edward I. His tactics were to harry the lowlands, then retreat into the Welsh mountains to avoid pitched battle. There were also problems with the Scots, who refused to recognize Henry. After a series of confrontations the Scots were beaten by Percy, the Earl of Northumberland, and his son Henry Hotspur. However, the Percies became dissatisfied at the treatment they received from Henry, and changed sides, allying themselves with the connections of Richard II, the Scots and Owen Glendower. In 1403 battle was joined at Shrewsbury; Henry won the day, Hotspur was killed and Northumberland backed down.

Only two years later there was a further conspiracy, led by Scrope, the Archbishop of York. This too failed, and Scrope was executed. The public execution of an archbishop is rare in English history, and this does show how much the respect for the clergy had fallen since the days of Thomas Becket. Northumberland was forced to flee to the Scots as a result of this conspiracy. He raised another army, but was defeated and killed in 1408. Owen Glendower continued to prosper into the next reign.

However, Henry was then assisted by weakness abroad. The King of Scotland, Robert III, was lame, mad and weak, and the King of France, Charles VI, was mentally unstable. In both cases other ambitious parties tried to assume power and this led to weakness in these countries. The case of Robert III is particularly sad. The Bruce line had died out with the death of David II (1329-70), and was replaced by the Stewarts, later Stuarts, a family which was destined to go a long way in both Scotland and England. The first Stewart king was Robert II (1370-1390), who was then succeeded by Robert III (1390-1406). The latter's reign was dominated by power struggles. His eldest son David was murdered by rivals. The next heir to the throne, his son James (later James I) was captured off Flamborough Head by English pirates when fleeing from defeat at home in 1406, when he was eleven years old. Shortly after this event, Robert III died. When asked for burial instructions by his wife, he said he would prefer to be buried under a midden, describing himself as "the worst of kings and the most wretched of men in the whole kingdom".

At home, however, Henry struggled against his Parliaments. The extravagances of Richard II had impoverished the monarchy, and Parliament was able to exact important concessions on the appointment of ministers.

From 1405 Henry suffered repeated attacks of an unknown but evidently serious illness which involved a disfiguring skin condition. In the later years of the reign his health was so bad that he was barely able to attend to royal business. In the meantime a quarrel brewed with his heir, the Prince of Wales, who certainly considered seizing power while his father was still alive. This proved unnecessary as Henry died of natural causes in 1413.

Henry V 1413-1422 (9 years)
Born 1388 Married 1420, Katherine of France

Lollardism had the favour of the court in the time of Richard II, but it was not tolerated under Henry IV, when the burning of Lollard "heretics" began. Henry V began his reign with the return of the vehemently anti-Lollard Arundel to his duties as Archbishop of Canterbury, and under his influence the persecution of the Lollards intensified. The leader of the Lollards, Sir John Oldcastle, was condemned, but escaped, only to be recaptured and executed in 1417. A Lollard revolt was threatened, but it was nipped in the bud. This is a very unfortunate aspect of Lancastrian rule, given that the Lollards were in fact right, and represented a better form of religion than the thoroughly debased Catholicism. The burning of heretics is a bad sign in any society and it is frequently associated with the forces of reaction and economic decline.

Nevertheless, the reign of Henry is much more famous for the king's renewal of the Hundred Years' War, in its third or "Lancastrian" phase. The war siphoned off unruly subjects, raised immense patriotic fervour and promised glory. In its way, it did give Henry all the glory he could want, especially as his exploits on the field of Agincourt in 1415 were later immortalised by Shakespeare. Henry took advantage of dynastic struggles within France to stake his own claim to the French throne.

Henry's campaign in France began with the seizure of the port of Harfleur in Normandy. His army then set off to march northwards towards Calais, but was decimated by dysentery. After a long diversion round the River Somme, Henry found his much-reduced force confronted by a French army seven times its size. This was the occasion for Shakespeare to give Henry one of his most famous speeches:

> Once more unto the breech, dear friends, once more
> Or close the wall up with our English dead
> ......
> Cry "God for Harry! England and St George!"

Despite its advantage in numbers, the French force lacked archers, and formed three divisions each behind the other. When the English archery poured arrows on the front division, it fell back in confusion on those behind, creating chaos in the French ranks. One unfortunate incident in the battle of Agincourt was a false alarm in the English army of an attack in the rear. This was incorrect, but by the time that was discovered, the French prisoners had been killed. It was considered very poor conduct to kill a captured knight, and it was also very bad business as high ransoms could be obtained. After the great victory, Henry returned triumphantly to England.

Henry returned to France the following year and was making good progress when he received a lucky break. The two factions within France met for purposes of reconciliation, but the leader of one of them, the Duke of Burgundy, was murdered by the other faction, that of the dauphin (the heir to the French throne). This caused the mad King Charles VI and his queen to make a rapid alliance with Henry, known as the Treaty of Troyes (1420). Under this an agreement was made that Henry would marry Charles' daughter Katherine (which he did, in the same year), and that he would succeed to the throne of France on the death of the Charles (who did die in 1422). So Henry was on the verge of achieving the original aim of Edward III at the start of the Hundred Year's War. However, many Frenchmen thought only a king suffering from Charles' mental condition – probably schizophrenia or porphyria – could sign such a disastrous treaty, and it was never going to be easy to enforce it.

Henry returned once more to England, but the situation in France deteriorated. The dauphin beat his army there. Henry returned and took the fortress of Meaux near Paris, and could again have succeeded, but he was taken with dysentery and died at the age of 34. So ended the brief but spectacular career of someone who is sometimes considered one of England's great kings. There has been praise for his courage, valour and sagacity, but he was too severe on the Lollards, and it is difficult to see him today as anything more than another hothead aristocratic adventurer in the manner of Richard I.

Henry VI 1422-1461 (dethroned), (39 years), died 1471
Born 1421 Married 1445, Margaret of Anjou

The son of Henry V by Katherine of France, also called Henry, was only nine months old when he succeeded to the throne. Thus the country once again had to be run by others during the long minority. However, as in the time of Henry III, so it happened that the real problems only started when the king reached adulthood and took control himself.

The leading figure from the early part of the reign was John, Duke of Bedford, uncle of the baby king, and a noble and able man. At this time the English held Paris, and the territories controlled by the French themselves were all south of the Loire, which runs east-west across the centre of France. Bedford was able to consolidate this position. In 1428 he laid siege to Orleans, on the Loire. As part of this campaign Sir John Falstaff beat off a party of French who were attacking a convoy of herrings under his charge.

The French king, Charles VI (called both "The Mad" and "The Well-beloved") died in 1422, the same year as Henry V. This should have caused all the French to rally round the former dauphin, now Charles VII, but this happened only very slowly. In an effort to detach the French from their Scottish allies, the Scottish king James I (1406-1437), in English hands since 1406, was sent home with an English wife in 1423.

However an unexpected figure arose to inspire the French to relieve the siege of Orleans in 1429, Joan of Arc, a patriot girl only 17 years old. Her moment of glory did not last long as she was captured by the English and burnt as a heretic two years later. It is difficult to see what the English meant by the word "heretic"; Joan was subsequently canonized and has been a heroine in France ever since. It was seven years before the French made any further progress in the war.

On the domestic front, in 1430 an act of Parliament was passed which restricted the franchise to persons possessing freeholds to the value of forty shillings a year. This excluded copyholders and villeins from the vote, and the forty-shilling freeholders were the only voters in the counties all the way through until the Reform Act of 1832.

The situation in France held up until the death of Bedford in 1433, but even by this time it was deteriorating, because the two main factions, led by the Charles VII and the Duke of Burgundy, had joined forces against the English. A party in favour of peace gradually formed in England. Henry VI grew up to be a very gentle man, and he favoured this party. The "war" party was led by the noblemen who liked a good fight with the French. In 1445, Henry married Margaret of Anjou, and while he was weak king, she was a strong, not to say a domineering queen, who soon took complete ascendancy over him.

By 1449 the position in France had worsened. The war was fought at a heavy cost in both men and money. By 1453, everything but Calais had been lost and the Hundred Years War was over. In the meantime the government of England itself had degenerated to chaotic conditions. Noblemen took the law into their own hands and their armies of private retainers ran amok. In the midst of all this came Jack Cade's rebellion of Kentishmen in 1450, a new Peasants Revolt. Cade managed to establish himself in London, with his supporters, but this lawless mob soon upset the Londoners, who drove them out themselves. Cade was caught and executed, the fate of all leaders of peasant revolts.

Henry was not strong enough to enforce justice. To this problem was added the loss of France, where many merchants were ruined by the loss of trade with Guienne, where wool had been traded for wine. In the circumstances the Duke of York became an increasingly powerful figure. He was the heir-apparent, as a direct descendant of Edward III by his second son (the Duke of Clarence). To this situation, two new and highly significant developments were added. From 1453 onwards, Henry became subject to bouts of insanity. Almost at the same time Queen Margaret gave birth to a baby son, which deprived York of the succession. By 1455 Henry had recovered, but the seeds had been sown, and so within two years of the end of the Hundred Years War, the Wars of the Roses began. The first battle was a small engagement at St Albans (1455).

These wars never caused serious disruption to the country, unlike the Hundred Years War, which in its late stages had ravaged much of northern and western France, or the earlier depredations of Durham and other northern counties by Robert the Bruce. In a series of relatively small engagements, the war swung first one way, then the other, and it seemed that the Lancastrians, led by the queen, had won it at the battle of Wakefield in 1460, where York was killed. However, his son Edward rallied and reached London before Queen Margaret. Here he was received as king by the citizens (1461) and the disastrous reign of Henry VI was over.

*   *   *   *

In Scotland, James I (1406-37) reasserted his power vigorously on return from his seventeen-year exile in England, and went on to build the magnificent Linlithgow Palace. This still features strongly in Scottish tourist brochures and was to be the birthplace of a number of Scottish monarchs, including Mary, Queen of Scots. However, like all Scottish kings of this period, James I had difficulty with his regional barons, especially Alexander MacDonald, Lord of the Isles, who had territorial ambitions of his own – he intended to take over the mainland province of Ross with its centre at Inverness. James first kidnapped Alexander, then was obliged to release him, then captured him again. This power struggle represented the relatively sophisticated and Europeanized Lowland culture asserting itself over the unsophisticated Gaelic-speaking Highlanders, but "sophisticated" is hardly an appropriate word for the Scottish politics of this era. James was murdered by his nobles in 1437. At this point the MacDonalds succeeded in their attempt to take the Earldom of Ross.

James I was succeeded by James II (1437-1460), notable for the fiery birthmark on his face, but only six years old at his accession. James II was the first Scottish king to make a glittering European marriage, to the niece of the Duke of Burgundy, one of the richest princes in Europe. He had problems with another family of Scottish nobles, the Black Douglases of the south-west. His regents had already murdered the leaders of this family at the bloodcurdling "Black Dinner" in 1440 (having given them an excellent dinner first). James, noted for his fiery temper as well as fiery face, followed suite when he murdered the eighth Earl Douglas at Stirling Castle in 1452. James himself was killed in an accident. At the siege of Roxburgh, a town held by the English in 1460, James was demonstrating a canon, which blew up and killed him. He was succeeded by yet another Scottish minority as his son James III (1460-88) was only nine years old.

Edward IV, 1461-1483 (22 years)
Born 1442 Married 1464, Elizabeth Woodville

So Edward was now the king, but his problems were only beginning. The Lancastrians under Queen Margaret, strong in the north of England, had reached as far as St Albans, which they sacked, to the disgust of the southerners. Until now the Wars of the Roses had been a series of quite small battles, fought between retainers, and had not really involved the people. Now the men of the rich counties of Kent and Essex rallied to Edward, who set off northwards in pursuit of Margaret. The armies met at Towton, between Pontefract and York, in one of the most bloody (but strangely forgotten) battles of English history (1461). In an immense battle, Edward won the day. It is said that thirty-eight thousand bodies were buried on the field. This fight was essentially between the Lancastrian, medieval north, base of the feudal barons, and the Yorkist, modern south, where the rich towns and trades were located. Margaret was eventually obliged to flee to France, and Henry VI was imprisoned in the Tower of London. However, Edward's problems were far from over.

Meanwhile Edward fell in love and married Elizabeth Woodville, daughter of the Lancastrian Earl Rivers. This marriage frustrated the plans of his cousin, the immensely powerful Richard Neville, Earl of Warwick, known as the king-maker because his support had done so much to put Edward on the throne in the first place. By 1469 Edward's position had weakened so much that he fell into Warwick's hands, and was a prisoner until his popularity forced his release. But the wars continued, not so much with the Lancastrians as with rival factions. Matters became so desperate that in 1471 Edward was forced to flee abroad to the sanctuary of the Duke of Burgundy (Charles the Bold), taking his younger brother Richard, Duke of Gloucester with him, whilst his wife took refuge in Westminster. (Edward's sister, Margaret, was the wife of the Duke of Burgundy.) However Edward was soon back. He raised an army and finally put paid to the dreadful Warwick at the battle of Barnet, where Warwick was killed (1471). Edward then turned to face Margaret and her young son Edward, who had landed in Wales. The forces met at Tewkesbury where Edward once again won the day. Margaret's son Edward, direct heir to Henry VI, did not survive the battle – some say he was murdered by Gloucester (later Richard III). From Tewkesbury, Edward marched back to London. The day of his entry saw the death of Henry VI, who was in the Tower. Few attribute this to natural causes; Gloucester is again implicated.

After the tumultuous events of 1471, Edward could settle down to a successful reign. The merchants and industrial classes prospered and the power of the old nobility was curbed. Modern England was dawning and the system whereby the monarch befriended the middle classes and kept the nobility in its place was established, to be continued by the Tudors. Edward also ran a successful spying system, again anticipating the Tudors, notably Elizabeth.

Mistrusting his brother, the Duke of Clarence, who had defected to Warwick in 1469, Edward had him executed in 1478. There is a tradition, faithfully recorded in the Shakespeare play *Richard III*, that he was drowned in a butt of malmsey.

Edward died unexpectedly in 1483 at the age of 40. This was a great pity, because if he had been able to live a few years longer, his children could have succeeded him without any dispute. The greater longevity of the Tudor and Stuart monarchs who were to follow the Yorkists over the next two centuries was to contribute much towards political stability. There must have been advances in medicine and public health as the best doctors were no doubt available in earlier dynasties. As it was, the king's eldest boy, also an Edward, was only 13 years old – not old enough to be able to stand up to a ruthless character like his uncle, Richard, Duke of Gloucester.

There remains to this day doubt about the paternity of Edward IV. It appears that his mother, Cecily Neville, admitted at the time that Richard of York was not his father. Also, Edward was a very tall man, six feet and four inches, and this seemed a difficult match with his official parents. Richard, Duke of Gloucester may have been the direct heir of Richard of York in any case.

Richard III, 1483-1485 (2 years)
Born 1450 Married 1473, Anne Neville

Richard had been a faithful friend to his brother Edward IV, going into exile with him at the age of twenty, and distinguishing himself at the battles of Tewkesbury and Barnet. He acted as the governor of the north of England, based in Yorkshire, and his reputation from this period was high. In any event, Richard simply pushed all rivals aside. The country dreaded another minority and Richard had little difficulty in gaining the title of king. Meanwhile his nephews, the young princes Edward (nominally Edward V) and Richard, disappeared in the Tower of London. It is thought that within two months of the death of their father, they had been killed, on the instructions of Richard. In 1501 a Yorkist knight named John Tyrrell confessed that he had murdered the princes, indeed on the orders of Richard. Historians have never been sure about this confession, but the fact is, they were gone whilst under Richard's protection. As such they would be the third and fourth rivals to the throne he had removed forever. However, this crime was to cost him his throne.

The connections of the murdered princes and other enemies now turned to Henry Tudor, who was directly descended from John of Gaunt and so from Edward III – by now, a very long way back.

Meanwhile Richard settled down to running the country and even held a Parliament, which passed two useful laws. One forbade the collection of benevolences – unofficial taxes which had been levied by Edward IV. The other outlawed the keeping of retainers. However, the enemies of the king were only gathering their strength. Henry Tudor landed an army in Wales and marched into England. The two sides met in a relatively small battle at Bosworth Field in Leicestershire (1485). There was no important difference of principle between the two sides, and little public interest had been excited by the struggle. Richard came close to killing Henry Tudor with his own hand, but it was not to be. He was overwhelmed and killed.

Portrayed as a hunchback in Shakespeare's play *Richard III*, there is no contemporary evidence of this deformity.

        *   *   *   *

The same year saw the end of one of the least attractive of the Stuart kings of Scotland, James III (1460-88) after an unstable reign when the king had to fight off a challenge from his own brother, the Duke of

Albany. The chief event of long-term significance was James' marriage to the daughter of the King of Denmark. Because her dowry payments failed to materialize, Orkney and Shetland were confiscated by the Scots in 1472, and have remained part of Scotland ever since (Denmark had taken over the Kingdom of Norway, previous owners of the islands.) Only at this point was Scotland as we know it today complete. James III was eventually murdered after the Battle of Sauchieburn outside Stirling in 1488. His own son and heir James IV, who was only fifteen years old, fought on the other side.

Chapter 16 – The Early Tudors

Henry VII 1485-1509 (24 years)
Born 1456 Married 1486, Elizabeth of York

The death of Richard III was not quite the end of the line for the Yorkists as Henry Tudor, now Henry VII, married Elizabeth, the daughter and direct heir of Edward IV, who became the mother of the most famous Tudor king, Henry VIII (1509-1547). With the later ending of the Tudor dynasty at the death of Elizabeth in 1603, the Stuart kings came to the throne. They were descended from Margaret, daughter of Henry VII and Elizabeth (and sister of Henry VIII). So it is that the Yorkist bloodline kept going literally for centuries. Nevertheless with Richard III the days of the Yorkist kings themselves were over and the Tudor dynasty began. Although the study of "modern" history, as opposed to the medieval variety, is sometimes begun with the Tudors, the tremendous changes which were looming ahead did not really have much effect until the next reign, that of Henry VIII. The reign of Henry VII was in many ways a more stable version of that of the Yorkist Edward IV, but where Edward had failed to consolidate his dynasty, Henry VII succeeded.

Henry had seized the throne, but his position was not initially secure. Hence his first priority was to destroy all rivals and so secure the throne for himself and his family. In view of the problems which Warwick and others had caused Edward IV, his next priority was to strengthen the monarchy against the nobility, but he also acted firmly against any form of lawlessness. Executions amongst the nobility and thieves were common in this reign, while the middle classes prospered. So it was with all the Tudor monarchs except Mary, so that in spite of their severity, the Tudors were popular in their own lifetimes.

Of the two leading Yorkist contenders to the throne, Edward Plantagenet, son of the Duke of Clarence and nephew of Edward IV, was imprisoned in the Tower of London, where he stayed until his execution in 1499. The other, John de la Pole, Earl of Lincoln, son of Elizabeth (sister of Edward IV) fled to the court of his aunt, Margaret of

Burgundy. From here he organized an insurrection under the name of Edward Plantagenet – in fact an imposter, an Oxford boy called Lambert Simnel. Irish and German mercenaries landed at Ulverston in Lancashire, and marched on London. Henry met and beat them at Stoke, near Nottingham, in 1487. Lincoln was killed, and Henry showed his contempt for Simnel by making him a scullion in his own kitchen.

The next impostor was to prove more troublesome. He was a young man called Perkin Warbeck, again operating under the protection of Edward IV's sister and ally Margaret of Burgundy. Warbeck claimed to be the younger of the princes in the Tower, Richard. Henry could not disprove the story as he could not prove the murder. Warbeck received support from the King of France and later from the Duke of Burgundy. He made some progress in Ireland and Scotland. Meanwhile the Cornish had raised a rebellion against taxes raised by Henry to pay for troops to take on the Scots. Henry put down this rebellion with the assistance of a train of artillery – something new in the armoury of a medieval king. Warbeck landed in Cornwall in an attempt to renew the insurrection, but he was soon captured and imprisoned in the Tower. Here he befriended Edward Plantagenet. Discovering their plot to escape together, Henry had both of them executed in 1499.

The weakness of royal authority in Ireland led Henry to send over as deputy a man called Sir Edward Poynings (1494). He induced the Irish parliament to pass an act forbidding any new legislation unless it had received the consent of the king's council. This is called Poyning's Law, and it remained in force for almost three hundred years, effectively emasculating the Irish parliament.

To deal with troublemakers at home, particularly amongst the nobility, Henry set up a new court which later came to be called the Court of Star Chamber. In this court there was no jury – one reason for setting it up was to deal with cases where the accused was powerful enough to intimidate the jury. Understandably Henry found this court very useful, and equally understandably, its victims were terrified of it.

At Henry's request Parliament renewed Richard's law against the keeping of retainers. In practice this was difficult to enforce, but given the opportunity, Henry did enforce it. One of its victims was the Yorkist Earl of Oxford who was fined £15,000 for not only keeping retainers but daring to show them off in the presence of the king. Henry also executed Sir William Stanley, one of the richest men in the country, for corresponding with Warbeck, and confiscated his estate. In this way Henry ruthlessly enriched himself.

Most famous of Henry's enforcers was the Lord Chancellor and Archbishop of Canterbury, Morton, who operated on the principle of "Morton's Fork" – that if a man spent conspicuously, he could afford to give the king a "benevolence", and if he spent little, then he could give money from his savings. Also Henry enriched himself by obtaining funds to fight the French from Parliament, then securing peace by accepting bribes from the French.

Towards the end of his reign, Henry involved himself in a system of alliances which were designed to restrain the power of France. In order to secure a Spanish alliance, Henry's eldest son and heir, Arthur, was married to Katherine of Aragon, daughter of Ferdinand, King of Spain, in 1501. As Arthur subsequently died, it was only by dispensation from the Pope that Katherine was allowed to marry Arthur's brother, the future Henry VIII. It was the uncertain legality of this marriage which was later to give Henry VIII the excuse to repudiate it and so begin the English Reformation. Henry VII also tried to detach the Scots from the French by marrying his daughter Margaret to James IV of Scotland in 1503, a union known as "The thistle and the rose". Again this had important consequences as the descendants of this marriage included Mary, Queen of Scots and indeed the Stuart dynasty of Scotland and England. James IV (1488-1513) was proving to be the most successful of the Stuart kings of Scotland, and cultivated the image of a Renaissance prince. (He was also the last king of Scotland to speak Gaelic.) However, his reign was to end disastrously ten years later, but not before he had produced a male heir, another James, who was born in 1512.

In the final years his reign Henry VII cut a lonely figure as many of those who had supported him in earlier years had died, including his wife and his eldest son. But no one could doubt the future of the dynasty or the ominous figure of the heir, the future Henry VIII, who like Edward I before him showed every sign that he would be a powerful monarch when his turn came to rule. One parish priest in the Calder Valley prayed earnestly that God might grant him only a short reign, for fear that he would take everything.

*   *   *   *

By the end of the reign of Henry VII some remarkable changes were taking effect, bringing in their train the start of modern history. The first of these changes was the invention of gunpowder, which had slowly been coming into use from the middle of the fourteenth century, and which was to sweep away forever the power of the knights in armour and the famous English archers. The second change was the invention of the printing press, by John Gutenberg of Mainz in 1442. The printing press had movable type and its effect was to make the copying of books vastly cheaper, so that knowledge could be spread much more widely. William Caxton introduced the first printing press into England in 1476. At this time the ancient learning of the Greeks and Romans was disseminating from the east and from Italy in the movement known as the Renaissance, and the printing press assisted greatly in this process.

Also contributing to the Renaissance was the fall of Constantinople to the Ottoman Turks in 1453. This finally brought an end to the Byzantine Empire, formerly the Roman Empire of the east, which had outlasted its western counterpart by a thousand years. The fall of the Constantinople sent scholars scurrying for other centres of learning. There were other important effects. Trade to the east – trade in silks and especially in spices – was impeded by Ottoman extortion. During the fifteen century, the Portuguese under their scholar-prince Henry the Navigator had already begun to explore widely in the Atlantic. They made the important discovery that by swinging westwards almost as far as Brazil, they could use the trade winds to reach southern Africa at the same time avoiding the dreaded Skeleton Coast of south-western Africa. The fall of Constantinople gave a great stimulus to the countries of the Atlantic seaboard to find a maritime route to the East Indies. From this came the discovery of the West Indies by Columbus in 1492 and of the North American mainland by John Cabot (an Italian in an English ship) in 1497. Also in 1497 Vasco da Gama, a Portuguese, finally rounded the Cape of Good Hope and became the first sailor to reach India from Europe by sea. These events brought about momentous changes which led to a power-shift away from the countries of the Mediterranean Sea and towards the countries of the Atlantic seaboard, especially Spain, Portugal, England, Holland and France.

These great developments put an end to the Medieval world forever.

Henry VIII 1509-1547 (38 years)
Born 1491 Married:
1509, Katherine of Aragon, died 1536
1533, Anne Boleyn, executed 1536
1536, Jane Seymour, died 1537
1540, Anne of Cleves, divorced 1540
1540, Katherine Howard, executed 1542
1543, Katherine Parr, survived her husband

Contemporary rulers:

Scotland	France	Spain
James IV d 1513	Louis XII d 1515	Charles V 1516-56
James V d 1542	Francis I d 1547	
Mary deposed 1567		

Henry was only eighteen years old when he succeeded to the throne, but his contemporaries were already well aware that he was likely to be the strongest of kings, and they were not to be disappointed. Their fears were to be justified as Henry lost his youthful idealism and became an overmighty king. But in fact, before modern Britain could be created – a united kingdom, Protestant, seafaring and capitalist – much of the old world had to be swept away, and it was in Henry's reign that this process accelerated rapidly.

At first he followed his father's foreign policy of favoring Spain and making war on France. To this end, he completed his marriage to Katherine of Aragon in the year of his accession. In domestic policy he went further than Henry VII had done, however, in executing the Earl of Suffolk, the nephew of Edward IV and the Yorkist claimant to the throne. Suffolk was the brother of the Earl of Lincoln, John de la Pole (killed at Stoke in 1487) and the son of Elizabeth, sister of Edward IV. Also executed were two of Henry VII's extortionist ministers, Empson and Dudley.

In 1513 Henry invaded France where he won the battle of Guinegaste, known to the French as the "Battle of the Spurs" as their own side made more use of their spurs than their swords. In the same year and in spite of the marriage of James IV to Henry VII's daughter Margaret, the Scots invaded England as allies of the French. However they found themselves outmanoevred by the English under Lord Surrey, who contrived to place his forces behind the Scots at Flodden, just south of the Tweed in the border country. The Scottish retreat back to

Scotland was cut off and their army was destroyed. Amongst those who perished was James IV himself – the last British king to die on the battlefield - and with him the flower of the Scottish aristocracy. James was succeeded by his infant son James V (1513-42), under the care of English Margaret, and for a generation there was little futher trouble from the weakened Scots.

Meanwhile Henry decided not to pursue any idea of creating an empire in France and so made peace with the French in 1514, going so far as to marry his younger sister Mary to King Louis XII. However this king died only three months into the marriage. Mary returned home and married Charles Brandon, the new Duke of Suffolk. Her granddaughter was to be the future Nine Days Queen, Lady Jane Grey. The new French king was Francis I, their first "Renaissance" monarch. (There is a famous portrait of Francis on horseback in the Uffizi Gallery, Florence, by Clouet. It is noteworthy that reliable portraits of monarchs date only from the reigns of Henry VII and Francis I.)

The leading statesman of the first part of Henry's reign was Thomas Wolsey, a middle-class boy originally from Ipswich. Whilst a tutor at Magdalen College, Oxford, he gained the friendship of the Marquess of Dorset, whose three sons he taught, and this connection got him into the royal service, where he rose rapidly to become the Chancellor by 1515. The next year the pope made him a cardinal, and then papal legate. So it was that the chief power in both civil and ecclesiastical affairs was in the hands of this one man, and this situation persisted for fourteen years. Wolsey had three main objectives in mind. The first of these was to continue the policy of Henry VII by increasing the power of the crown, and indeed he showed little scruple in forwarding the views of his king. Secondly he aimed to improve conditions in the church in England. One policy in this area was to abolish some of the smaller monasteries and apply their revenues to the foundation of colleges and schools, where the new learning could be taught. The monastic movement was everywhere in decline, and had been for many years. Thirdly it was Wolsey's ambition to become pope, and so take control over the general reformation of the church which he could see was impending, and indeed which began very soon after he became Chancellor.

In 1519 the Holy Roman Emperor, Maximilian, died, and a new successor had to be elected. The Emperor was effectively the leading monarch within Germany and Austria, but only had direct control over his own hereditary territories, that is, normally the territories controlled by Austria (which for centuries included parts of Italy). Each new emperor was elected by the Archbishops of Mainz, Cologne and Trier and the rulers or Electors of Bohemia, Saxony, Brandenburg and the Palatinate (a Rhineland province, capital Heidelberg). Both Francis I of France and Charles V of Spain put themselves forward as candidates in the election. Charles was elected and thereby came to control the largest empire the world had ever seen, including Spain itself, the Spanish Netherlands (modern Belgium and Holland), Austria, southern Italy (Naples) and the rapidly growing Spanish empire in the Americas. Charles had inherited the territories of three great European dynasties – the Hapsburgs of Austria, the Dukes of Burgundy (who controlled the Netherlands plus Franche-Comte in what is now eastern France) and the Spanish royal family – Ferdinand and Isabella were his maternal grandparents. He had been brought up in the Netherlands and when he went to Spain, took with him many Dutchmen. Once there he was obliged to learn Spanish, and is famous for saying of his polyglot ability "I speak Spanish to God, Italian to women, French to men and German to my horse"!

It was Charles' misfortune to be the principal ruler of Europe when the greatest bombshell in centuries blew up, initiated by Martin Luther in Germany in 1517 – the Reformation of the church, and with it the establishment of Protestant religions all over northern Europe. Dissatisfaction with the papacy had by this time reached epidemic proportions. Meanwhile the Bible was now widely available in vernacular languages, enabling anyone who could read to go back to basics, strip away the centuries of Catholic accretions and concentrate purely on the New Testament and its direct message. They found there no bishops, no church hierarchy, no Pope, no cathedrals and no need for any of these things. None of the well-known corruptions of the church were there – the sale of "indulgences", which purported to shorten the period souls must spend in Purgatory; the idea of Purgatory itself; simony, the practice of paying for church offices; nepotism, the appointment of "nephews" (often illegitimate children) to important church offices – the besetting sin of Renaissance popes; sinecures, jobs for which little or no work was required; absentee priests; and all the rest of it. Because of the wealth of the church and jealousy of the foreigners in charge of it, the new Protestant preachers found no shortage of secular rulers prepared to join and protect them – Martin Luther himself enjoyed the patronage of the Duke of Saxony.

While the Reformation gathered pace, the election of Charles V as Emperor made war between him and Francis I of France inevitable, and both parties courted Henry. Francis entertained the English king at the "Field of Cloth and Gold" in Flanders (1520), and Charles came to

England personally to visit his aunt Katherine, Henry's wife. In the end this relationship and also the importance of the Flemish wool trade, in territory controlled by Charles, prevailed. Henry mounted two small expeditions to France in 1522 and 1523. However, when Charles annihilated Francis' army at Pavia in northern Italy in 1525, he began to look uncomfortably powerful. So Henry and Wolsey changed sides. This was one of the first implementations of the idea of the balance of power within Europe, the concept that states should combine against any overmighty power or alliance. Also noteworthy is the fact that Wolsey and Henry did not use the temporary weakness of France to press any kind of dynastic or territorial claim there, which they certainly would have done a hundred years earlier. In any case, Charles had failed to secure the papacy for Wolsey.

Meanwhile Wolsey was implementing his domestic policies. He gained authority from the pope to suppress some of the smaller monasteries, using the revenue gained to found a school in Ipswich and a large new college in Oxford – Cardinal College, subsequently renamed Christ Church, which went on to become the alma mater of thirteen British prime ministers.

Meanwhile a very serious dynastic situation had arisen at the court of Henry VIII. He and Katherine of Aragon (born 1485) had now been married for many years - since 1509 - and had produced many children, but all of these had died apart from one daughter, Mary. It now began to look as if there would be no male heir – a potentially disastrous situation not only for the Tudor dynasty but for the entire country; the spectre of power struggles and civil wars going back to the time of Matilda was there for all to see. One impact of this looming crisis was the execution of Edward, third Duke of Buckingham, in 1521 – Edward was a descendant of Edward III and a probable claimant in the absence of a male heir. The problem of course eventually led directly to the split of the English from the Roman church, but it would be wrong to accuse Henry of acting cynically as the whole future of the realm was at stake. At first Henry and Wolsey tried to obtain a divorce legally, within the church, and appealed to the Pope, Clement VII. However after the sack of Rome by the troops of the Emperor Charles V in 1525, the pope was little more than a puppet of the emperor, and could not readily give offence by divorcing Charles' aunt from Henry. Having failed to obtain satisfaction from the pope, Henry found that he had no more need of the papal legate, Wolsey, and tried a different tack.

To obtain the support of the English people, in 1529 Henry summoned a Parliament, which sat not as usual for a month or two, but for a full seven years. During this period, and at the bidding of Henry, it carried out one of the greatest revolutions in English history, severing all links with Rome. But Henry could rely on its support in attacking the pope and reforming church abuses. As far back as the time of Henry IV only the authority of the king had prevented Parliament from confiscating church property, and now there was no royal support for the church. Meanwhile Wolsey was replaced by Sir Thomas More, a lawyer already well known for his book *Utopia*, which under the form of a description of an ideal commonwealth satirized the abuses of the times. Within a year Wolsey was accused of treason, under the existing Act of Praemunire, which forbade either appeals to Rome or the receiving of letters from Rome. However he died at Leicester on his way to answer the summons.

By a series of Acts, the parliament replaced the Pope as the head of the English church by the reigning English monarch. Taxes paid by the clergy to the Pope – tithes and firstfruits – were now to be paid to the king's treasury. Any clergy taking the side of Wolsey were themselves threatened with the Act of Preamunire, under which their worldly goods could be forfeited to the king, and themselves imprisoned. The king also became responsible for the appointment of bishops. Finally by the 1535 the Act of Supremacy, Henry took the title of "Supreme Head on earth of the Church in England".

In addition, a series of long-overdue laws was passed to reform the practices of the clergy. The first of these regulated the fees which could be charged for religious services. A second forbade clergymen from holding several livings at once. A third reformed the spiritual courts and strengthened the old mortmain statutes, which forbade lands being given to the church. A fourth finally did away with clerical justice, whereby, since the time of Becket, the clergy were tried by the bishops, and not under the ordinary law of the land.

Meanwhile, having failed in any wider court to have his marriage to Katherine dissolved, Henry had the matter tried before a known symphathiser, Cranmer, whom he had appointed Archbishop of Canterbury. This court allowed the divorce, and Henry immediately married the pregnant Anne Boleyn, to whom he had long been attached. Anne Boleyn was no servant girl – she was a member of the Howard family (the Dukes of Norfolk). In 1533 she bore him a daughter, Elizabeth. Parliament was persuaded to pass an act settling the succession on the children of this marriage, excluding Mary, daughter of Katherine. However, objections were raised, notably by Thomas More, and Fisher, Bishop of Rochester; both were eventually executed on this account. More's story was later told in a famous play by Robert Bolt, *A Man for All Seasons*.

However, Anne Boleyn's ascendancy did not last long. She was accused of adultery, and though the evidence was non-existent, the suspicion was too much for the jealous Henry, and she too was executed. Two days later, Henry was married again, this time to Jane Seymour. In 1537 she bore him a son, Edward. As Katherine had died in 1536 there could be no question whatever about the validity of the marriage, and any problems concerning the succession disappeared for the moment. Jane Seymour herself died giving birth to Edward.

More's place as chief adviser to the king was taken by Thomas Cromwell, who had emerged from Wolsey's entourage. (The later Oliver Cromwell came from the same family – he was descended from Thomas' nephew.) With his assistance, Henry embarked upon his next project – the dissolution of the monasteries.

The monastic system had by this time created a large number of houses of various sizes – over six hundred, occupied by many different orders – the Benedictine, Clugniac, Cistercian, Augustinian, Grey Friar, Black Friar – most of them set up over the centuries to correct the corruption of existing orders. The movement had long been in decline, however, and some of the previous importance of monasteries as centres of learning had been taken over by the universities. However they still provided much in the way of elementary education, health care and poor relief. But in the new capitalist, Protestant England, free from the baggage of the Catholics, this did not justify a sufficient return on their vast wealth. The majority of the population saw them as centres of privilege which belonged to a bygone era. Members of Parliament did not support them because they saw that if their wealth was transferred to the state, there would be less need for taxes.

A commission of enquiry was set up to investigate the state of the monasteries, and as a result an act was passed in 1536 which dissolved the smaller ones. The action was stepped up in the succeeding years, and the abbots of Glastonbury, Colchester and Reading were all executed. In 1539 another act was passed surrendering all remaining monastic property to the king. One result of all this was that some of the country's finest buildings can only be seen as ruins today. It was intended to use some of the revenue for the general benefit of the nation – for example to fund new bishoprics (in fact only six were created), schools and colleges, and to strengthen the coastal defences. In practice much of the money went into the pockets of the king's courtiers, founding the fortunes of a new nobility devoted to the support of the

Reformation. Families including the Russells, Seymours, Dudleys and the Cecils, whose wealth came from this source, began to take the place of the old nobility, in much the same way as a new class of wealthy entrepreneurs, the "oligarchs", suddenly arose following the collapse of the Soviet Union in the 1990s. Above all the dissolution of the monasteries, for better or worse, gave a tremendous boost to capitalism, because the great wealth represented by the former church lands could now be considered general property, readily transferable and available at a price or a rent. Under the church, the taking of a profit from land was not necessarily the first or even the main consideration.

The proceedings of Henry and his Parliaments in religious matters did not pass without disturbance. As early as 1534 a half-witted girl known as the Nun of Kent spoke out against the divorce, was taken up by disaffected priests, and was duly executed. The execution of More and Fisher in 1535 had further repercussions as they were known to be wise and honest men. In 1536 the northern counties, where the monks were much more popular than in the south, rose in revolt against the suppression of the monasteries, under a lawyer, Robert Aske. This movement was called the Pilgrimage of Grace. Aske and other leaders including four abbots were executed, and hundreds of other executions were carried out. One result of this rebellion was the institution of the Council of the North, a committee of the Privy Council, which henceforth sat for four months of the year at York, Hull, Newcastle and Durham. Another result of the rising was the hounding of the last remains of the Yorkists, whereby three of the most prominent remaining members of the family of Edward IV were executed.

The standard of rebellion was also raised, predictably, in Ireland. In 1534 the Fitzgerald family led a revolt which overran the entire country except for Dublin. The English fought back under the Lord Deputy, Grey, and gradually pushed the rebels back. Henry dissolved the Irish monasteries, and tried to enforce the English language and law, with limited success. The problems were far from solved, however, and were to cause endless anguish in the reign of Elizabeth. Also while the English by and large did accept some form of Protestantism, the native Irish emphatically did not, and the Catholic religion became identified with Irish nationalism (as also happened in Poland) – it was a very visible means of separating the Irish from the English.

In the meantime radical movements were afoot to break away from the Catholic liturgy. In particular the teachings of Calvin, based in Geneva, were having a great impact (notably in Scotland), effectively creating a new religion. Henry had wanted to divorce Katherine and to lay his hands on church wealth and privileges, but he had no intention of changing the church liturgy, abolishing the bishoprics or indeed of making any changes in the religion itself. However, the Tudor and Stuart monarchs found that they had a tiger by the tail in the new Protestant religion.

Henry tried to reaffirm the old religious practices by acts of parliament and by the establishment of the Six Articles of doctrine and observance. The most important of these were the belief in transubstantiation, the celibacy of the priesthood and the confession. Note that none of these appear in the New Testament. (Transubstantiation is the belief that communion bread and wine actually change into the flesh and blood of Christ, and was a particularly troublesome doctrine for the new Protestants to accept.)

In 1540, Henry was persuaded by Thomas Cromwell to marry again. Cromwell had selected as a bride one Anne of Cleves, daughter of a minor duke of the Rhineland. Cromwell's idea was to form an alliance with the north German Protestants who were now involved in wars of religion with the Emperor Charles V. A portrait was sent in advance which pleased Henry well enough, but the reality did not match the image (the "Flanders mare", according to Henry). The marriage went ahead but Anne soon found herself divorced, given a pension and some impressive properties (including Hever Castle, former home of Henry's old in-laws, the Boleyns). It was Thomas Cromwell who suffered the consequences; he was attainted – his property confiscated and his head cut off. This was one of Henry's most popular moves as a king; Cromwell had Lutheran sympathies and had harshly repressed the old, Catholic aristocracy, executing many (and opening the way for the new nobility). As he had grown more confident, his later years in power had become a veritable reign of terror in which no one was safe. Also his policy threatened European entanglements with the Emperor, with whom Henry now allied himself once more. The old guard under Thomas Howard, the Duke of Norfolk, now reasserted itself. The Duke produced his beautiful niece, Katherine Howard, as a new bride for the king. After two years Henry discovered that she had taken a lover before the marriage, and she was put to death. Henry finally married Katherine Parr, who survived him.

In 1542, war broke out once again with Scotland, for the first time since Flodden near the start of the reign. James V of Scotland fled the field of battle at Solway Moss, dying shortly afterwards, leaving his throne to his infant daughter Mary (Queen of Scots). Henry's one objective then became to marry this girl to his son Edward, and so unite the crowns of England and Scotland, a prospect which did not appeal to the majority of the Scots themselves. To secure his end Henry sent an army into Scotland – the so-called "rough wooing" – led by Jane Seymour's brother (and his own brother-in-law), the Earl of Hertford (later Duke of Somerset), and Lord Lisle (later Earl of Warwick). The army partially burned down Edinburgh and Leith, but otherwise only infuriated the Scots further. The Scots had allied themselves with the French, and indeed Henry invaded France and took Boulogne. In 1545 King Francis I retaliated by organizing a large fleet (larger than the Spanish Armada 43 years later) and army for the invasion of England. However this only succeeded in landing small bodies of men in Sussex and the Isle of Wight, falling foul of the English fleet in the Battle of the Solent (in which the *Mary Rose*, pride of the English fleet, went down – to be lifted back from the bottom in 1982).

In fact it was no accident that the French invasion failed, because Henry had built up the navy and naval infrastructure to an unprecedented level of strength. In his rule the first of a new type of naval warship was built, firing canon through port-holes in the hull, and so able to deliver devastating broadsides. Before this the canon had fired from the "castles" at the bow and stern. Royal dockyards were established at Deptford and Woolwich, and facilities at Portsmouth were extended. Henry also founded Trinity House, for the organization of pilots, and the Navy Board, precursor of the Admiralty.

Although a third of the monastic lands were still left in royal hands by the end of Henry's reign, money began to run out during the 1540s when the country was at war with France and Scotland, and debasement of the coinage followed – a sure sign of bad government. A small amount of alloy was permitted in order to make silver coins stand wear and tear; but this amount increased from three-quarters of an ounce per twelve ounces of silver to two ounces and by 1546 to eight ounces. The economic consequences were dire, as no one could trust the coinage, so trade ground to a halt. Inflation was set off in the cost of basic provisions, and beggary and robbery became rife following the distress of the poor.

By 1547 it had become apparent that Henry could not survive long, and that regents would have to be appointed to reign in the minority of Edward. Henry had to decide between the old pro-Catholic aristocracy led by the Duke of Norfolk, and the new Protestant nobility under the Earl of Hertford, the uncle of the heir. Henry decided in favour of Hertford, and the Duke of Norfolk and his son the Earl of Surrey were arrested. Surrey was executed and Norfolk was only saved from the same fate by the death of Henry in 1547.

Opinions are divided upon the character and achievements of Henry VIII. That he was ruthless and vindictive is certain, though he was also a conscientious ruler who had the best interests of his country at heart. He ruled absolutely but the major changes wrought by him – some of which dealt with problems outstanding for centuries – were invariably endorsed by Parliament. Henry raised forced loans, and devalued the currency. He swiftly destroyed his ministers, wives, dynastic rivals and even ancient institutions which stood in his way. He was arbitrary, capricious and in private life cold, heartless and unscrupulous. The military achievements of his reign, sometimes overlooked, were not inconsiderable, as the Scots were thrashed twice and naval preparations, in which Henry took great personal interest, saw off the French as well. Above all Henry established the independence of England forever from foreign directions from the Pope, and thereby stopped an important flow of money leaving the country. And he was certainly also a historical character of great force.

It is reasonable to ask the question, what would have happened if Catherine of Aragon had produced a male heir for Henry? There would have been no compelling reason to break with Rome, and it is unlikely that Henry would have done so. However, there seems little doubt that Protestantism would in any case have established itself in England, as it did throughout northern Europe. However the fact that the King was already a Protestant meant that the country was spared the great religious wars which were to disfigure both France and Germany over the next hundred years. A Catholic English dynasty would almost certainly have defended the old faith.

Chapter 17 – Edward VI and Mary I

<u>Edward VI 1547-1553 (6 years)</u>
Born 1537

Contemporary rulers:

Scotland	*France*	*Spain*
Mary deposed 1567	Francis I d 1547	Charles V
	Henry II d 1559	resigned 1556

The son of Jane Seymour, Edward VI was only nine years old when he became king. His father had carefully arranged a ruling council for the regency, which though it excluded the old nobility, included men from the new nobility which represented both old (Catholic) and new (Protestant) opinion. On this council, no one had any priority; but a dead man cannot implement his plans, and this scheme quickly fell apart. The men who held "new" opinions soon gained a majority on the council, and selected Edward Seymour, the Earl of Hertford, uncle of the king, as their leader. The executors then declared that Henry had intended to raise them to higher ranks in the peerage, and also to give them grants out of church lands. Accordingly Hertford became the Duke of Somerset, with the title of Lord Protector, his brother became Lord Seymour, and Dudley (Lord Lisle) the Earl of Warwick. So the new reign certainly did not get off to a good start, and indeed many of the chickens loosed in Henry's reign were to come home to roost.

Henry had tried to make sure that there would be no changes in religion, but the new rulers set about a revolution almost at once. A commission was sent round the country to pull down all images in churches, and to deface pictures. The Catholic Latin mass was abolished and replaced by services in English. These very obvious changes, implemented with great severity, brought home to the common people that there was a new government, and caused great excitement and discontent.

Another change was the confiscation of the property of the guilds, on the grounds that part of it was spent on masses for the dead. Though true, the rest of it was spent on education and training for the guildsmen's children, on supporting sick members, and on feasting and merrymaking. This step was a great blow to the guildsmen, most of whom were artisans, as it took away what was in effect their insurance, and also deprived them of social advantages. This measure was not implemented in London where the mob could have threatened the government.

Equally reckless was Somerset's Scottish policy, where he resumed Henry's "rough wooing", with the aim of securing the marriage of Edward VI and Mary Queen of Scots. He took an army accompanied by a fleet along the east coast, confronting a strong Scottish position near Musselburgh. However, the much larger Scottish army left its position on the river Esk to attack the English, and was beaten in an action known as the Battle of Pinkie (1547). The victory was worse than useless to Somerset's war aims, however. The Scots dispatched their five-year old Queen Mary abroad to the French court for safety (her mother, Mary of Guise, was French). Here she grew up away from the clutches of the English in a carefree atmosphere of luxury which was ill to suit her when she returned to Scotland. Whilst in France she was married to the dauphin, who became King Francis II of France in 1559.

In 1549 Parliament gave its authority to the issue of a new church service book, the First Prayer Book of Edward VI, and an Act of Uniformity was passed to enforce its usage in all church services. Based on the existing Latin Breviary and Missal, the translation was mainly the work of Archbishop Cranmer. It was revised in 1552, 1559, 1603 and 1662, but its general character remained the same. At its introduction it pleased neither the Catholics nor the Calvinists, but the beauty of its language was to endear it to members of the Church of England for centuries to come.

Trouble at home for Somerset came in the form of his own younger brother, Thomas Lord Seymour, a much inferior man. He first married Katherine Parr, widow of Henry VIII, and when she died aspired to the hand of Lady Elizabeth. Caught setting about preparations for armed rebellion, he was executed. Soon more serious trouble arose in Devon and Cornwall where a rebellion arose immediately after the introduction of the new Prayer Book, the rebels demanding the restitution of the Catholic service. The insurrection was put down after a fierce fight at St Mary's Clyst in which over four thousand men were killed. Then another rebellion flared up in East Anglia; this time the causes were agricultural rather than religious. The enclosure of common land for sheep farming had deprived many villagers of their grazing, and everywhere there was indignation at the conduct of the new landowners, who wanted to make money out of their lands and so disregarded ancient privileges formerly extended to the villagers. The peasants of Norfolk rose under Ket, a tanner. The end result was the same as in Devon – three thousand were killed after another fierce fight outside Norwich, with foreign mercenaries led by the Earl of Warwick leading the slaughter.

The credit for the suppression of these rebellions went to the council, which had acted whilst Somerset had dithered. In 1549 Somerset was shunted aside, his rule thought a failure, and replaced by Warwick, and able but unscrupulous man. However, peace was made with France, with which a new war had started, and Boulogne was restored to the French in return for a sum of money. By 1551 Warwick had a new title – the Duke of Northumberland. (This is the name by which he is remembered, but it is his fourth – he was previously Dudley, Lord Lisle and Warwick!) He had his predecessor Somerset tried and executed on a charge of treason. Somerset, though weak, was a man of much finer principle than Northumberland and a sympathetic crowd turned up to see him off.

Meanwhile the state of the country was going from bad to worse. The church lands, the property of the guilds and the bells and plate of the churches had been seized by the state, yet the government had no money, and had debased the currency again. Goods were scarce and expensive and agricultural poverty was widespread. Henry VIII, despite his faults, had always been in sympathy with the people, but the councillors, led by Northumberland, were seen as merely greedy self-seekers who robbed the church and the poor to fill their own pockets.

Meanwhile there was a development which filled Northumberland with alarm – the young king was ailing. No one understood what was wrong with him, but his body was racked by a terrible cough, and his strength declined. Northumberland conceived a desperate plan to set aside the succession of the Catholic Mary, and replace her by the Protestant Lady Jane Grey, whom he married to his youngest son. She was the granddaughter of Mary, sister of Henry VIII, and so a second cousin of Mary. Everyone knew that Mary had the better claim. In fact there seems little logic in Northumberland's move, because if Mary had the better claim, so did Elizabeth, and she was a Protestant; but presumably she would have nothing to do with Northumberland and his schemes.

Then Edward did indeed die, at the age of only 15. Fearing the worst, Mary had already taken flight to the protection of the Howards in Norfolk. Northumberland set off after her, but soon found that the country was rising in favour of Mary, and that his own men would not fight. Northumberland and his supporters had made themselves thoroughly unpopular with the people, the changes in religion were widely disliked, and the harassed country looked back with nostalgia to the rule of Henry VIII. Mary might offer a route back to those days, so with almost universal acceptance, she was proclaimed queen, and Lady Jane Grey, the "Nine Days' Queen", went to the Tower; Northumberland was also imprisoned.

*   *   *   *

The early death of Edward was by no means untypical of this age. The country had simply never recovered to the population levels attained before the Black Death, when there were about five million people. In 1550 there are thought to have been three and a half million. Plague had been the main scourge, but smallpox was also endemic – Elizabeth caught it in 1562, though she recovered. Dysentery, typhus and tuberculosis were rife, as was a condition known as "English sweat" which could carry off its victims in a day. What are nowadays considered minor conditions such as kidney stones and difficult childbirths could easily turn into killers. The worst health was invariably in London, because infectious diseases can transmit themselves so readily in dense populations. London and other cities were evacuated in times of plague through to the 1660s. The capital needed a constant supply of new people from the provinces to maintain its population, though many must have doubted the wisdom of ever going there.

Mary 1553-1558 (5 years)
Born 1516; married, 1554, Philip II of Spain
Contemporary rulers:

Scotland	France	Spain
Mary deposed 1567	Henry II d 1559	Charles V
		resigned 1556
		Philip II, d 1598

Mary was misled from the start by the enthusiasm with which she was welcomed by the majority of the people, who thought that she represented the policies they wanted. In fact their attachment was not so great that their wishes could be disregarded. Meanwhile there was an important minority of determined Protestants who would oppose her every move.

The first step was inevitable – the execution of Northumberland, and his son the Earl of Warwick. (Northumberland's father, Edmund Dudley, minister of Henry VII, had suffered the same fate at the start of the new reign of Henry VIII.) Lady Jane Grey and her husband, after all little but pawns in the hands of Northumberland, were condemned to death, but sent back to the Tower to await her majesty's pleasure. Mary's chief adviser was a foreigner, Renard, who represented the Emperor Charles V. He advised the execution of Lady Jane Grey, but Mary held back. Renard would also have put the Lady Elizabeth to death as well, but even Mary could see how dangerous a step that might be – rebellion would be certain as Elizabeth had committed no crime. Nevertheless this was to be a very dangerous reign for Elizabeth, where she learnt great caution and circumspection – unlike her cousin Mary Queen of Scots, living the high life in Paris.

Renard's main ambition was to secure the match of Mary with Philip, son and heir of his master Charles V. Mary was keen on this match, and rejected the English candidate, Edward Courtenay (great-grandson of Edward IV), much to the disgust of most English parties. Meanwhile Thomas Wyatt, Duke of Suffolk and father of Lady Jane Grey, raised an insurrection, but this was put down without difficulty. After this the execution of Lady Jane Grey was inevitable, and duly took place (it was later famously portrayed by the French Romantic painter Paul Delaroche). (Had Lady Jane survived the reign, her fate may have been no better – both her sisters died young, having been imprisoned, under Elizabeth. These unfortunate sisters were too close to the succession in the brutal world of Tudor politics.) Attempts were made to implicate Elizabeth in the plot, but there was simply no evidence. Nevertheless, she was sent to the Tower, which had proved the final resting place for more than one heir to the throne in the past. Meanwhile Mary had decided upon Philip, though Parliament insisted in the marriage settlement that she was to have sole rule in England, was not to go abroad, and was not to be drawn into any foreign wars on Philip's account.

In religious terms the clock was swiftly wound back to 1529, before the start of the English Reformation, and even the anti-Lollard statutes of Henry IV and V were revived. However, Parliament would not yield up the abbey and church lands which had passed into the hands of the laity. Mary, meanwhile, had married Philip in 1554, and was thought to be pregnant, but it was not to be. She was deceived by the symptoms of an incurable disease. After it became clear that there was no baby, nor was there likely to be one, Mary's hatred of her half-sister and all that she stood for increased to maniacal levels. She saw how the nation watched over Elizabeth, whom she had hated from the cradle, and who appeared fresh and youthful compared to her withered self. Some say the balance of Mary's mind was destroyed by the false pregnancy. At any rate, she was about to earn the epithet by which she was to be known for the rest of history – Bloody Mary.

In 1555 the persecution began, based on the Lollard laws. A succession of bishops and senior churchmen were executed. Philip left England because of the problems of his father, but the pace of the backlash was increased. The next to go were Bishops Ridley (of London) and Latimer (of Worcester). The execution of bishops is never a good sign in any reign, but this was only the start, and many lesser men followed, before it was the turn of Archbishop Cranmer, creator of the English prayer book. At first he agreed to a recantation of his views, but seeing that his enemies would execute him anyway, he thrust the hand that had signed the recantation into the flames. The effect of the burnings on public opinion, however, was to create an admiration for the constancy of the victims, and a belief in a faith for which martyrs were prepared to die. The laity looked on in disgust at this most un-English (some would say Spanish) behaviour on the part of the monarch, and prayed for Elizabeth. The Spanish Inquisition, originally set up to ensure that the converted Moslems and Jews really were Christians, was a byword everywhere for religious cruelty. It was one of the instruments of the Counter-Reformation, the Catholic response to the Reformation. Though the Catholic church still had many adherents in England, many more saw it as a religion of vengeful persecution, and Mary's activities confirmed this view.

Mary's government began to carry out business with no respect for the constitution. Jurors were sent to prison for returning unfavorable verdicts, Members of Parliament for their conduct in the House. Customs duties, unsanctioned by Parliament, were levied and forced loans were raised. Yet still the crown was crippled for money, military stores were rotten and the fleet was unseaworthy. It was becoming a truly wretched reign.

In 1556, the Emperor Charles V, weary after forty years of trying to solve insoluble problems, abdicated his throne and retired to a monastery. His Spanish territories (including the Netherlands) were inherited by Philip II, husband of Mary. (His brother Ferdinand I was already in possession of Charles' Austrian territories, and succeeded him as Emperor, so the mighty Hapsburg empire was split up.) In 1557, in defiance of her marriage settlement, Mary involved the country in a war with France, in support of Spain. This only resulted in the loss of Calais, a fortress which had been in English hands for two hundred years. This was considered an enormous loss at the time, and the government was widely blamed, as its fortifications had been neglected, and its garrison was undermanned and under-armed.

The loss of Calais was the final blow for Mary. Deserted by her husband, disappointed of children, hated by her subjects (who she could see eagerly awaiting the succession of the child of Anne Boleyn) she died. Few monarchs can have lived to see so many hopes blighted in so short a time, and few have been so little lamented.

Chapter 18 – Elizabeth I

Elizabeth I 1558-1603 (45 years)
Born 1533

Contemporary rulers:

Scotland	*France*	*Spain*
Mary deposed 1567	Henry II d 1559	Philip II 1556-98
James VI	Francis II d 1560	
	Charles IX d 1574	
	Henry III d 1589	
	Henry IV d 1610	

Elizabeth ascended the throne at the age of 26. At stake during her reign was the very survival of England as an independent country. It had been seriously weakened since the death of her father. There was every chance that Philip of Spain would try to take over, either by marriage or by invasion – in fact he was to try both – or that Elizabeth would marry the head of another foreign state. The new next-in-line to the succession was her cousin, Mary, Queen of Scots, at this time married to the Dauphin of France. If she had succeeded, then there would have been a union between the crowns of England, France and Scotland, something which would have been too much for Philip of Spain, so despite what was to come later in the reign, Elizabeth started out with the full support of Philip. Indeed, he offered to marry her, but she demurred. It would have meant involving the Pope.

Elizabeth took William Cecil as her main adviser, a sensible, hard-working man who was to serve in this capacity for forty years (a record which has never been equalled). The pair immediately set about resetting the common religion back to the time of Edward VI . The Book of Common Prayer was revised, services in English with an English Bible were ordained, and the forty-two articles of religion as defined by Cranmer were restated, though reduced to thirty-nine. An Act of Uniformity was passed (1559) forbidding any other form of public worship, and attendance at church was made compulsory, with the payment of a fine of one shilling for each offence of non-attendance. The age of religious tolerance was still a long way away – hundreds of years – and any Catholic was considered a potential traitor and source of plots, not without good reason. To supervise the Act of Uniformity, commissions were from time to time granted to bishops and others; in 1583 these arrangements became permanent in the Court of High Commission.

The new rules enabled Elizabeth to clear out Mary's bishops, none of whom would accept them, and appoint her own people, including Matthew Parker, the new Archbishop of Canterbury. Of the common clergy, only two hundred out of nine thousand refused to accept the new order, and so resigned their livings. The vast majority of the public simply got used to the new religious order and a new generation grew up which had known no other. However, there were important minorities of Catholics who refused to attend the services (the recusants), and of Protestants for whom reform had not gone far enough. The chief sects of these were the Presbyterians and the Independents (forerunners of the Congregationalists), together known as the Separatists. Also many who remained within the Church of England agitated for further reform, objecting to the use of the ring in marriage, the cross at baptism, and other practices they regarded as superstitious. This group and the Separatists were called the Puritans. That this was a deadly serious business is shown by the fact that eventually these people were to take over the entire government of the country, under Oliver Cromwell.

In foreign affairs, England was thought too weak to stand alone, and needed either a French or a Spanish alliance. Finding herself technically still at war with the French, Elizabeth made peace, along with the Spanish. One condition was that Calais would be returned to England in eight years – a condition not likely to be kept. In the question of marriage, it seemed best to avoid foreign entanglements, as Spain would remain friendly as long as France supported the claims of Mary, Queen of Scots. Marriage with an Englishman would bring problems at home from the Englishmen Elizabeth did not marry. In any case, in order to restore the condition of the country, a period of stable rule was required. If Elizabeth married and started to produce children, this could by no means be guaranteed, as the rate of death in childbirth was very high for mothers in those times; moreover it rose alarmingly in older mothers – to the extent that it was almost certain in new mothers older than their mid-thirties.

The first change in foreign affairs came from Scotland, where the fiery Protestants were opposed to the regency of Catholic Mary of Guise, who was supported by French troops. Their leading spokesman was John Knox, author of a pamphlet entitled *First Blast of the Trumpet Against the Monstrous Regiment of Women*. Written at the time of Mary but directed against all female rulers, it would hardly endear Knox to Elizabeth. Nevertheless the Scottish Protestants proposed the marriage of Elizabeth to their own Earl of Arran, next-in-line to the Scottish throne. However, Elizabeth did not like the look of the Earl of Arran (who was eventually to be committed as insane) and so the scheme fell through. Even so, led by Knox, the Protestants ousted the Catholics in the Scottish Reformation, established by 1560. This worked on similar lines to the English Reformation in that there was a redistribution of church lands to the laity, but was in other respects very different as Knox and his followers were Calvinists.

Meanwhile in France there were two short-lived reigns, those of Henry II and Francis II, the latter the husband of Mary, but who died in 1560 after only a year on the throne. Upon this, the union of the crowns of France and Scotland was dissolved, and Mary returned to Scotland. Chief power in France fell to the Guise family, to which Mary's mother belonged. This in fact represented a swing to the Catholic faction. In 1562 Elizabeth sent aid to the French Protestants, the Huguenots. The conflict between Catholics and Huguenots in France was to cause many disturbances over the reign of Elizabeth. A similar issue also convulsed the largely Protestant Spanish Netherlands, now in revolt against the arbitrary rule of Spain.

Back in Scotland, developments in the typical Scottish political style, dating back to the days or Robert the Bruce, now unfolded. (It was this sort of thing which caused the later Sir Walter Scott so to abhor the traditional form of Scottish government.) Queen Mary married Henry, Lord Darnley, who was her cousin. In contrast to the cautious Elizabeth, who had barely survived the reign of her sister, Mary was a reckless character, and she soon upset the Scots. At the bottom of it was her Catholic religion, for the Scots had become Protestants of the most persecuting type. However, the cause of her downfall was her husband, Darnley. He became jealous of Mary's secretary and confidant, one David Rizzio. This innocent Italian was dragged from Mary's supper table to his murder – this was Darnley's doing. However, shortly afterwards, Mary gave birth to a son.

The following year Darnley was murdered, and Mary married Lord Bothwell, who had organized this murder – in fact it was widely thought that he had planned it with Mary's connivance. This was demonstrated in the "Casket letters" from Mary to Bothwell, thought by many to be forgeries. The Scottish nobles rose in revolt; Mary made a stand, but was forced to back down at Carberry Hill (1567). She was then imprisoned in Lochleven Castle, and her infant son James VI was crowned king. (Bothwell escaped to the north, where he gathered some ships and began the life of a pirate. However he was soon captured by the King of Denmark, and taken to Scandinavia, where he lived for the rest of his life.) A regency was established in Scotland, but the Scots, whose monarchs regularly met early and violent ends, were used to this. The age at accession of their previous seven monarchs had been: James I, eleven; James II, six: James III, nine; James IV, fifteen; James V, one; Mary, six days; and now James VI, one.

In 1568, Mary escaped and was joined by an army of Catholics. Once again she was beaten, at Langside, and found herself with no alternative but to fly to England to throw herself upon the mercy of Elizabeth. Here she became the most embarrassing of guests, especially as she and her former husband Francis II had styled themselves King and Queen of France, Scotland AND England.

Elizabeth refused to see Mary and kept her confined under careful watch while she decided what to do. However, Mary's presence in the country gave immediate inspiration to the Catholics. Once again, in 1569, the north rose in religious revolt, led by the Dukes of Northumberland and Westmoreland. Mass was sung in Durham Cathedral and the rebels marched on Tutbury in Staffordshire, where Mary was held. Mary was swiftly moved to Coventry and the revolt was savagely put down. The leaders escaped but men were hanged at every market cross and village green from Wetherby to Newcastle. Catholic priests were hunted down.

However, the attempts to enforce the Act of Uniformity were failing to suppress other forms of religion. In 1564 many of the London clergy refused to obey the act, and left the church. There was much sympathy for them, and they had some influential supporters, notably Robert Dudley, Earl of Leicester (the son of the Duke of Northumberland, executed by Mary). Although Elizabeth never did marry, she made it clear that she considered herself available to the right man, and indeed encouraged suitors and favorites, amongst whom Leicester was prominent in the earlier part of her reign. Besides these were the people who were serious civil servants – Cecil (Lord Burleigh), Sir Nicholas Bacon and Sir Francis Walsingham (head of the increasingly omnipresent spy service).

Meanwhile the Catholics began to see that they had nothing to hope from Elizabeth, and indeed Pope Pius V issued a bull excommunicating her, so freeing all English Catholics from allegiance to their monarch. In 1572 there was further religious trouble, this time in France, where the Catholic party murdered thousands of their Protestant opponents on St Bartholomew's Day. But the papal bull and the presence of Mary meant that a series of Catholic plots were planned to replace Elizabeth. This was one reason for the extensive spy network. One of these plots was managed by an Italian called Ridolfi; Thomas Howard, Duke of Norfolk was implicated and so was executed in 1572. (The Howards for many years were England's leading Catholic family. The executed Duke was the grandson of the Duke who narrowly escaped execution himself at the end of the reign of Henry VIII.) Ten years later, another important plot was uncovered, known as the Throgmorton plot after the man who led it. He had been acting with the knowledge of the Spanish ambassador, and was executed after torture in 1584.

Though the government tried hard to fend off a Catholic alliance of France and Spain in Europe, in the New World hostilities between the England and Spain were endemic. The Spaniards attempted to exclude all ships but their own from trade with their American colonies. The response of the English sailors was to trade where they could and plunder where they could not. Sailors such as Sir Francis Drake and Sir John Hawkins were regarded as pirates by the Spaniards, but they were heroes at home. In 1579 Drake sailed through the Straits of Magellan and into the Pacific, where he plundered Valparaiso and other towns on the west coast of South America. He returned via the Cape of Good Hope, loaded with booty, in doing so becoming the first Englishman to circumnavigate the globe (and only the second ever to do it). Other English sailors were engaged in the less profitable enterprise of trying to find the North-West Passage past the north of America, and some of their names are still on the map today – witness the Frobisher and Davis Straits. But they found no way through.

Meanwhile, Sir Humphrey Gilbert and his half-brother Sir Walter Raleigh made a number of attempts at founding a colony in North America. The first attempt came in 1578, but proved a failure. So did the attempt to colonise Newfoundland in 1583, when Gilbert was drowned, the survivors returning home. In 1584 and 1585 Raleigh attempted to found the colony of Virginia, much further south, at the mouth of the Chesapeake River, but the colonists again returned home. Much more famous was his effort of 1587, when 114 colonists settled at Roanoke Island in what is now North Carolina. This venture took place at a very unfortunate time – while the Spanish war and the dramas of the Armada were unfolding back in Europe – so no support ship could be sent. When John White, who had led the colonists but returned to England for help, finally got back to Roanoke in 1590, there were no colonists left. It has always been assumed that they fell victim to the local Indians.

By 1585, Elizabeth had been queen for 17 years and had avoided war. However, conflict with the Spaniards was becoming inevitable, first because of the behaviour of Drake and other seamen, and then because Elizabeth and her ministers elected to support the Protestant revolt and independence movement in the Spanish Netherlands. This long-running war, also called the Dutch Revolt, had begun in 1568 as a Dutch protest against harsh and arbitrary Spanish rule. The rebels, under their leader William of Orange, did not gain their first success until 1572, but by 1585 the northern provinces (modern Holland) were virtually independent as the United Provinces. However, under the rule of the Governor, the Duke of Parma, the Spaniards reconquered much of the south (modern Belgium and French Flanders) and in 1585 retook Antwerp, at that time the largest city in the province. In the north, they found the terrain was much more difficult, as it was riddled with river channels and with dykes which could be flooded by the Dutch in an emergency. Meanwhile the Dutch seamen – the "Sea Beggars" as they styled themselves – successfully blockaded the estuary of the Scheldt, cutting off Antwerp from the sea. Antwerp was the great commercial centre of the Spanish Empire. Much of the Spanish silver mined in the New World passed through it, and it was also the centre of manufacturing

Elizabeth was offered the throne of the United Provinces – the independent Netherlands – but refused it, sensing that it would drag her own country into someone else's wars. However she sent her favorite, Leicester, to aid the Dutch, who made him their chief officer or Stadtholder. However, he failed to distinguish himself, and during the siege of Zutphen one of the most brilliant Englishmen of the day, Sir Philip Sidney, soldier, diplomat and poet (and nephew of Leicester) was killed.

The nation was in a constant state of anxiety lest an assassin should strike down Elizabeth in the name of her cousin Mary. Finally a trap was laid to entangle Mary in a treasonable correspondence involving a Catholic assassination scheme led by a man named Babbington. Mary was found guilty, and though Elizabeth hesitated long over sending one of the crowned heads of Europe to her grave, the execution was carried out at Fotheringay Castle in February, 1587. The nation heaved a collective sigh of relief. The next-in-line to the throne was indeed another Scot, Mary's child James VI of Scotland, but he had been very carefully brought up as a Protestant. Mary herself, however, left her claim not to her son but to the Infanta of Spain, daughter of Philip II, and he at once set about enforcing this claim.

*   *   *   *

In 1580 Philip had succeeded in taking over the throne of Portugal and with it, Brazil and the Portuguese trading empire in the East Indies. With silver flowing in from the mines of Mexico and Peru, he had become immensely powerful, with an annual income ten times anything that could be claimed by Elizabeth. So he set about preparing a great fleet. There was a great setback, however, in 1587, when Francis Drake himself led a fleet right into the harbour at Cadiz and destroyed a large part of the stores and transport waiting there. (By this time, Drake had acquired the reputation of a superman amongst the Spaniards, much as Rommel was to do amongst the English in North Africa in the Second World War.) By the next summer, however, the Armada was ready – or at least as ready as it would ever be; though its leader, the Duke of Medina Sidonia, thought otherwise, Philip insisted that it set sail. The admiral knew from the outset that there would be problems with his slow and ill-equipped fleet, which totalled 150 ships in all. His orders were to sail up the Channel to the Netherlands, where he was to pick up the Duke of Parma and his experienced army, then proceed to England. This strategy meant that he would have to run the gauntlet of the English for the full length of the Channel, then try and cross it once again. Realistically, this was asking a lot. The English seamen would have a wonderful target containing many prizes, right on their own doorstep. Also, Philip was making the same mistake that Napoleon was later to make, and which was then made by both Hitler and the Japanese in the Second World War. Having tired of beating against an increasingly well dug-in foe, in his case the Dutch, he turned on a new enemy before he had defeated the original one, and thus had to face both at once

On the English side, vigorous preparations had been made for the reception of the Spaniards. These had started as far back as 1577 with the appointment of John Hawkins as Treasurer of the Navy. Under his direction, a fleet of new warships had been constructed – relatively lightweight and low in draft, yet heavily gunned, these ships were to be described by the Spaniards as being as easy to manoevre as a horse.

A considerable army was ready to defend London, and the militia of every county was ready to march as beacons lit from hill to hill brought news of the landing. The main reliance however was placed on the fleet, led by Lord Howard of Effingham, a relation of the queen through Anne Boleyn. With him were Drake, Frobisher, Hawkins and all the great English seamen of the day.

The Armada was sighted from the coast of Cornwall on 19 July, 1588. The first battle action took place off Plymouth on 31 July. The Spanish fleet, with its huge heavy galleons, its sheer mass and its good order, inspired awe amongst the English. The Spanish ships had been built to physically grapple with the enemy and they were full of soldiers ready to form boarding parties. However, their gunnery was relatively poor – there were no good cannon makers in Spain itself so the latest, long-range cannon were not available. The English ships were fully equipped with these, so had the better range, and their tactics were to blast away at the Spaniards from a short distance, but on no account to get close enough to allow the Spaniards to board. These tactics infuriated the Spaniards, who called the English cowards and Lutheran hens, but there was nothing they could do about the two-fingered salutes from the English mariners.

The first engagement was inconclusive. After that, the English strategy was to let the main body of the Armada through, then attack any laggards at the back of it. The wind blew up the Channel, so the light English warships could catch the Spanish hulks when they chose, and if they drew off, the Spaniards could not pursue them against the wind. In this way the fight raged all along the Channel, the English re-supplying themselves with powder from captured ships. The Spaniards finally found refuge off Calais, where they waited for the Duke of Parma to assemble his army in nearby Dunkirk; but the army was not ready, and Dunkirk was blockaded by thirty Dutch flyboats of the Sea Beggars. The English, short of provisions and powder, could not let the Armada rest at Calais, and sent fire ships loaded with brimstone, tar and gunpowder at the Spanish fleet to force it out. All was not lost for the Armada if it could make a friendly port in the Netherlands, but the English barred the way. At Gravelines, a small port in the Spanish Netherlands, a naval action was brought by the ferocious English mariners in which five Spanish ships were lost and many more badly damaged. Meanwhile, back at Tilbury, Elizabeth rallied her forces with her most famous speech:

"I know I have the body of a weak and feeble woman; but I have the heart and stomach of a king—and of a king of England too!"

As the wind blew from the south, the only way forward for the Spanish fleet now was northwards. As Norway and Denmark were unfriendly, this meant a journey round the north of Scotland, then southwards into the Atlantic past Ireland, then all the way back through the Bay of Biscay to Spain. To seamen accustomed to Atlantic crossings, this should not have been so fearsome a journey, but most of the ships had been damaged by the constant English bombardment, the seamen were debilitated by a lack of food and fresh water, and great storms blew up in September. So the English fleet did little more, but there was no need for it. Smashed by the storms against rocky coasts, many ships of the Spanish fleet were lost on their way home. In the end, 67 battered ships survived.

If this was to prove the most glorious event of the reign, it was also the last great threat from Spain, which never figured so prominently in the history of England again, and which indeed was destined to sink into reactionary Catholic obscurity and poverty during the next century. Even in the glory days of Philip II, Spain defaulted on its debts four times. In England, the victory gave a tremendous boost to national pride and self-confidence, lasting for many years. The repulse of Spanish naval power also gave heart to the Protestant cause across Europe.

Meanwhile, English sailors and seamen continued to attack Spanish ships where they could find them. Philip did assemble another Armada in Cadiz, in 1596, but this time Howard, Raleigh and Essex sailed into the harbour and destroyed or captured all the ships under the guns of the forts.

The Armada had been a turning point in other ways. No more had the queen to trim between France and Spain. The year after the Armada, Henry IV became King of France. Henry was a Protestant who had agreed to convert to Catholicism to inherit his throne, doing so with the expression "Paris is worth a Mass". In practice, his accession meant a switch back to the Protestant party in France, as he was much more accommodating to Protestants than his predecessors had been, and indeed was proud to accept England as an ally. In 1598 he issued the Edict of Nantes granting freedom of worship to Protestants in France.

Again, within a few months, Leicester died, and Walsingham soon followed. Cecil was growing old, but new figures were appearing on the scene. The most striking of these was Robert Devereux, Earl of Essex, the attractive stepson of the Earl of Leicester. Essex wanted to continue the Spanish war, believing that there was still much to be gained from conquest and colonization; Cecil did not agree. Essex also sought to moderate the queen's stern policies towards the Catholics and Puritans. However, this new influence aroused the jealousy of other courtiers, including Cecil's son Robert and Sir Walter Raleigh. These were powerful men to alienate – Robert Cecil was taking over from his father as chief adviser to the queen (and was to continue in this capacity in the next reign). Yet Essex was an idol of the people and a favorite of the queen.

Meanwhile, trouble was brewing in another quarter, for both the queen and Essex. Elizabeth found Ireland a running sore, and some of the worst failures of her reign were associated with it. Her government was keen to dispossess troublesome native Irish chiefs and replace them with settlers and landowners from England. Sometimes a whole clan was dispossessed in this way. So it was that there were repeated rebellions in which the English were massacred, and their property burnt. Matters came to a head in 1595 when an Irish rebellion led by O'Neal, Earl of Tyrone, defeated all attempts to suppress it. O'Neal was much better aware of local conditions than the generals sent to oppose him and won many victories, at huge expense to Elizabeth's exchequer. Essex talked so much about what he would have done had he been there that he was sent to Ireland to take on O'Neal, and did no better than his predecessors. Fearing that his enemies at home were plotting against him, he suddenly returned home without leave and threw himself on the queen's mercy. He was kept for a time in honourable confinement while his case was investigated.

On his release, Essex did begin treasonable activity. He opened correspondence with James of Scotland and began to form friendships with Puritan separatists, and also collected around him bodies of discontented Catholics and disbanded soldiers. His coup was forestalled; he was arrested before he was ready, tried and executed. His death was said to prey heavily on Elizabeth's mind.

Before the close of the reign, a new deputy in Ireland, Mountjoy, finally put down the Irish rebellion or "Nine Years War". O'Neal and his Spanish allies were defeated at the defining battle at Kinsale in December, 1601 – a battle they had expected to win. After making peace with the English, O'Neal tried once again to rally the Spaniards to his cause. He and another Irish aristocrat, O'Donnell, and their families fled Ireland in the "Flight of the Earls" in 1607. However they failed to raise support overseas and O'Neal died in exile in Rome in 1616.

After the Armada, Parliament became more assertive and less ready to tolerate high-handed conduct on the part of the government. One particular grievance was the sale of monopolies – the right to be the sole seller of sometimes essential commodities (such as salt). This was an easy way for the government to raise money, but the exclusion of competition raised prices and affected the public directly. In 1601 Parliament insisted on the abolition of monopolies. Also in 1601, a new poor law was established. The maintenance of the poor and the setting to work of the able-bodied amongst them in the workhouse was entrusted to regular guardians in each parish, who were allowed to levy a rate for the support of the poor. Although Elizabeth had restored the coinage after the debasements of Henry VIII and Edward VI, enclosures had still continued, and poverty was widespread.

Elizabeth did not care much to think about her successor, as the only real claimant was James VI of Scotland, son of Mary Queen of Scots. It seems that she was satisfied that he was a Protestant who was unlikely much to upset her religious settlement or system of government, so let it be understood that he would be the next king when she died, as she did in 1603, the last of the Tudors. Her reign had brought stability and an improvement in the economy, though like all the Tudor monarchs she was severe enough when there was any trouble. However, as with so many reigns, hers is remembered chiefly for one thing – the glorious defeat of the Spanish Armada, signalling as it did something of the utmost importance for the future – the ascendancy of the English seamanship and of the navy, bulwark of England's strength for centuries to come. In 1607, only four years after the death of Elizabeth, the first successful English colony would be founded in North America, depending as it did on the English navy.

*   *   *   *

The Elizabethan era was also notable for the first flowering of the English theatre, indeed with royal encouragement, as the leading groups of actors performed regularly before the monarch. Shakespeare was born in 1564 and was writing plays throughout the late Elizabethan and Jacobean times. Many of these plays of course are still performed regularly, from noble, high-flown tragedies such as *Hamlet* to low life comedies such as *The Merry Wives of Windsor* (of a type thought by critics to be unworthy of Shakespeare, but still in the repertoire after hundreds of years). However, Shakespeare was not alone. Christopher Marlowe wrote a play which equals anything in Shakespeare, *The Tragical History of Dr Faustus*. Marlowe was linked to Walsingham's spy service. When he was killed in murky circumstances in a brawl (1593), the other three men involved were all connected to the London underworld and to the secret service. Ben Johnson is another contemporary playwright whose works have survived, and another noteworthy name from this era is John Webster, whose *Duchess of Malfi* was first performed in 1614.

Chapter 19 – The Early Stuarts

James I 1603-1625 (22 years)
Born 1566; married 1589, Anne of Denmark

Contemporary rulers:
France   *Spain*
Henry IV d 1610   Philip III d 1621
Louis XIII d 1643   Philip IV d 1665

James I of England and VI of Scotland, son of Mary Queen of Scots, claimed the throne by right of descent from Margaret, daughter of Henry VII. At his accession he was 37 years old. He had been King of Scotland since he was a baby. The Tudors never troubled much about the theory of government, as long as they had the power to do what they wanted, and they generally took care to make sure that their subjects agreed with them. James, on the contrary, thought much of the theory of government, but had little idea of winning respect, while his slovenly and gluttonous habits contrasted badly with the dignity of the Tudors. For all that, James was a learned man, and knew more about foreign affairs, history and religious controversy than most of his contemporaries, but his judgment was not so sound, to the extent that he was called "The wisest fool in Christendom" by the witty Henry IV of France.

James was the first monarch to espouse the idea of the "Divine Right of Kings", and had even written a book about the principle, called *Basilikon Doron*. This was nothing less than a political and religious doctrine of royal absolutism. It asserted that a king is subject to no earthly authority, deriving his right to rule directly from God. So he is not subject to the will of his people, the aristocracy or the church. Any attempt to restrict the powers of the king may constitute treason. The later "Sun" King of France, Louis XIV, was also keen on this idea. However, to anyone familiar with the English constitution, it was a blatant attempt to turn the clock back hundreds of years, to before the evolution of Parliament, and to ignore the Magna Carta. Anyone seriously trying to use it as a principle of government was bound to run straight into trouble in England, as did both James and his son Charles I. Parliament had begun to revive under Elizabeth, and it was not likely to want to give any ground to a pedantic man like James. He, on the other hand, would not want to concede any sovereign rights either, so that disputes between king and Parliament were likely from the outset. On his way down from Scotland, James hanged a pickpocket at Newark without any form of trial, something which violated a host of statutes from the Magna Carta downwards, and this was seen as a fitting prelude to a new era. It was also noticed from the early part of the reign that the many Scots who appeared at court in London were rarely pursued for any crimes of which they were accused, hence the expression "to get off Scot free" – another violation of statute.

James took Robert Cecil, son of William Cecil, as his chief minister – in fact Cecil continued in much the same position as he had held in the last years of Elizabeth's reign. A dwarfish and hump-backed man, he had many enemies, including other courtiers covetous of his position, notably Lord Cobham and Sir Walter Raleigh. The latter in particular was probably too glamorous for the liking of James, and was deprived of his post as captain of the royal guard. Raleigh and Cobham concocted a plan for getting rid of Cecil, and possibly of replacing James on the throne by Lady Arabella Stuart, niece of Lord Darnley. At the same time some Roman Catholics and Puritans, led by a priest, Watson, and Lord Grey de Wilton, a Puritan, who had been friends of Essex, talked of seizing the king and forcing him to grant toleration. These two conspiracies were called the Main and the Bye plots (1603). Cecil heard of them and had the leaders arrested, then tried as if the two plots had been one. Cobham and Raleigh were convicted, condemned to death and thrown into the Tower. Cecil continued as the chief minister for nine years.

Both Catholics and Puritans still hoped to get something from James, who had made vague promises on his way to claim the throne. Judging the temperament of Parliament and no doubt on the advice of Cecil, he soon backed away from this. However in 1604 a conference was held at Hampton Court between the bishops and the Puritans, who could agree on nothing. James sided with the bishops: "No bishop, no king!" However, one thing did come out of this – an order for a new translation of the Bible. Know as the Authorized Version, majestic in its tone, it has lasted for centuries, and - given the standard of other translations - it will probably last for centuries to come.

The more reckless Catholics who had already shared in the Essex conspiracy and in the Bye Plot now embarked upon something much more serious – the Gunpowder Plot. The conspirators, led by Robert Catesby, hired some cellars beneath the House of Lords, planning to blow up the building when James was present to open the Parliament. Unfortunately for the conspirators, the opening was delayed, and more people had to be let into the plot to raise money. This led to its discovery. The meeting of Parliament was fixed for 5 November 1605, and at the last moment the cellars were searched. Guy Fawkes, a Yorkshireman who had fought in the Spanish service, was found ready to fire the gunpowder. The other conspirators were hunted down. The plot gave the Catholics a terrible reputation in the country so that for years afterwards any evil was attributed to them, and Parliament, instead of relaxing the rules against them, made them more severe.

Relations between James and his Parliaments were bad from the outset. In his first summons in 1604, James warned the electors not to pick outlaws or men of extreme religious views. However, an outlaw called Goodwin was elected for Buckinghamshire. The Chancellor ordered a new election, but the Commons remonstrated against a violation of their rights, and the king had to give way. This victory gave Parliament the right to settle the merits of all disputed elections, and was of great importance. In the case of another member called Shirley, who had been imprisoned for debt, it was established that no member could be arrested except on a charge of treason, felony or breach of the peace.

By 1608 the extravagance of his court led James to run short of money, and because of this he began – in the view of Parliament – to violate the law. Tonnage was a tax levied on each tun of wine or liquor coming into or going out of the country, and poundage was a similar tax on dry goods. These taxes were granted to James for life. However, James chose to increase the rates of these taxes – measures known as the Impositions. As this infringed the right of Parliament to control taxation, Parliament protested, but the Impositions stayed. However, Parliament had an independent power base of its own. London had grown rapidly as a centre of for the organization of trade. Many merchants companies were established there, notably the East India Company, founded in 1600 to further trade with India and the lands of the east; but there were many such companies. The merchants were great supporters of Parliament against the king, something which was to become increasingly significant.

In terms of domestic policy, in 1607 Parliament also thwarted James' plan for a united kingdom of England and Scotland, instead of just a union of the crowns. It did abolish some hostile border laws; but full union had to wait another hundred years. In foreign policy, James favoured an alliance with Spain, with whom an undeclared war was still being fought, but this was not a popular idea as the English were doing well by plundering Spanish property abroad. Cecil preferred Elizabeth's French alliance, and managed to keep James on his side. This policy was advanced by the marriage of James' daughter Elizabeth to the anti-Spanish Elector of the Palatinate, Frederick. However, after this marriage, Cecil died, shortly to be followed to the grave by James' eldest son Henry, a prince of great promise and known to favour the policy of Cecil. After this James drifted rapidly towards a Spanish alliance.

There were further developments in Ireland. In 1608, confiscated lands within Ulster were handed over to energetic settlers from Scotland. This province, formerly the wildest province of a wild enough country, became the most prosperous, but the wrongs of the dispossessed were never forgotten, and revenge would come one day.

There were also very important developments in North America. In 1607 the Virginia Company finally succeeded in establishing a permanent colony at Jamestown, Virginia, on the south-eastern coast of what is now the United States. The leader of the colonists was John Smith, who managed to obtain food from the local Indians when his people were starving. However at one point he was captured by these Indians, and, according to him, only saved from execution by the intervention of the chief's daughter, Pocahontas. (Pocahontas subsequently married another of the settlers, John Rolfe, and returned with him to England, though she died soon after her arrival, aged only 22.) Also settled by the English at this time were the West Indian islands of Bermuda – still in British hands to this day. Just as significant was the arrival of English colonists in what was to become New England, on the north-east coast of America. In 1608 a body of Nottingham Independents left England to practise their religion in peace at Leyden in the United Provinces (Holland). However, they found after some time that there were things they did not like there – for one thing, their children were growing up into little Dutchmen. So they headed back to England and embarked from Southampton in the *Mayflower* for a life in the temperate part of America, beginning at New Plymouth, Massachusetts where they landed in 1620. Here there was no gold, and no climate suitable for growing sugar or tobacco, but conditions were close enough to allow them to plant European crops and to prosper. The example of the first colonists soon attracted others and flourishing colonies grew up, always strongly agricultural and Puritan in character at first.

After the death of Cecil, whose advice had generally been sound enough, James began upon a downhill trajectory. For advice he turned to inexperienced favorites, bound to raise the hackles of those better placed, as in the days of Edward II. The first of these was a worthless young man called Robert Carr, created Earl of Somerset, who was disgraced after his wife was found guilty of the poisoning and murder of Carr's former friend Sir Thomas Overbury (in which Carr was also concerned). The next favorite was George Villiers (later the Duke of Buckingham), with whom James was said to be infatuated. Under the influence of these favorites, court expenses rose threefold, and by 1614 James found himself obliged to summon a Parliament to provide more money. Despite attempts to procure friendly members, the new Parliament proved to be so hostile to James that it was dissolved before it had passed a single measure, and became known as the Addled Parliament.

For seven years James ruled without a Parliament, and used the opportunity to remodel the government after his own ideas. In legal matters his chief adviser was Sir Francis Bacon, who rose to be Chancellor in 1618. Bacon was simply too weak to take a strong line against James, and willing to see his advice disregarded so long as he kept his place. His chief rival was Edward Coke, who was dismissed from his post as Chief Justice in 1616, as a warning to judges that they only held their positions so long as they pleased the king.

The greatest hero in the country – at least in the eyes of the people – was Sir Walter Raleigh, who was still languishing in the Tower, writing a history of the world. An agreement was reached that he would be released to go and find the fabled city of gold, El Dorado, in South America, thought by Raleigh to be located up the Orinoco River. A condition of this expedition was that it did not enter into hostilities with James' friends, the Spaniards. However, as it represented a thrust into the heart of their American territories, it is difficult to see how this was to be avoided. Certainly the expedition failed to locate El Dorado, and of course there was a clash with the Spaniards, in which Raleigh's son was killed. The expedition returned home, the captains having failed to fall in with Raleigh's request that they attack the Spanish treasure fleet. The blame for the failure of the expedition and the hostilities with the Spanish was attributed entirely to Raleigh, and the Spanish Ambassador demanded his head. So Raleigh, now 66 years old, was executed on his old sentence, which had never been commuted (1618). As he saw the blade which was to be used for his execution, Raleigh famously mused "This is a sharp Medicine, but it is a Physician for all diseases and miseries".

In 1618 began the first great pan-European war, the Thirty Years War (1618-48), a gigantic convulsion of central Europe. The major conflict was between the Protestants of the north and the Catholics of the south, but embedded in it was also the rivalry between the Hapsburgs of Austria (who supported the Catholics) and the Bourbons of France (who were Catholics, but who supported the Protestants). Another major impact was made by the Swedes, under their King Gustavus Adolphus, setting upon the northern plains to establish an empire there, and there were many strange leaders appearing from the Transylvanian mists and from other points of the compass. The Spaniards were involved from their presence in the Spanish Netherlands, the Italians because of French and Austrian territories and ambitions there, and also the Poles, Bohemians, Germans and Dutch. The combination of warfare, starvation and disease resulted in a decline of about a third in the population of Germany and there were also major declines in the Low Countries and Italy. The best thing that can be said about it from the British point of view is that the British nations kept out of it – only to get involved in a Civil War which overlapped the end of the Thirty Years War. However, one person who was involved in the war was the Elector of the Palatinate, who had married James' daughter, and in the early stages of the war it did seem as if England would get involved. In 1620 the Spaniards ejected Frederick from his Rhineland Palatinate and there was a widespread clamour to support him in England, by attacking Spain.

The disgraceful sacrifice of Raleigh, the extravagance of the court and the influence of favorites had brought James' government into utter contempt. However because of the situation in the Palatinate, James thought he might persuade his subjects to forgive the past by going to support Frederick, so he called a Parliament. By the time it met, however, James had changed his mind, and tried to rely on negotiations to thwart Spanish policy without a war. Finding that James had no real intention of fighting, the Parliament of 1621 turned its attention to abuses at home, and set about the impeachment of some of James' ministers. This process – trial before the House of Lords of offenders accused by the Commons – had lapsed since 1450. It was now revived, and Sir Giles Mompesson, accused of holding monopolies, and Sir

Francis Bacon, accused of taking bribes, were both impeached and found guilty. Infuriated, James imprisoned four members – Coke, Phelps, Pym and Mallory. John Pym was to go on to be one of the main leaders of the opposition to Charles I, into the Civil War.

Negotiations were re-opened with Spain with a view to securing an alliance by the marriage of James' heir Charles with the Spanish Infanta. Charles and Buckingham (formerly Villiers) went off to Spain in disguise in a ludicrous attempt, worthy of a Shakespeare comedy, to win the hand of the Infanta. They came back predictably empty-handed, denouncing the perfidy of the Spaniards, and for the only time in his life Charles found himself popular. Parliament met and eagerly voted supplies for a war with Spain. Charles now pursued the opposite alliance and a treaty was made for him to marry the sister of the king of France (Louis XIII) and daughter of Henry IV, Henrietta Maria. At this point James died.

History has few kind words for James, thought a fool and slovenly and unkingly in his personal habits. However, the years of his reign were not without significance. James did establish a new dynasty in the face of serious conspiracies in the early years, and he did produce a male heir. He kept his joint crowns out of European war for the best part of a generation and there were no wars between England and Scotland (the same cannot be said of the next reign). Also during his reign, the first solid steps were taken to establish the British Empire in both North America and India, and there was produced a translation of the Bible which is still found in millions of households and churches.

Charles I 1625-1649 (24 years)
Born 1600; married 1625, Henrietta Maria of France

Contemporary rulers:

France	Sweden	Spain
Louis XIII d 1643	Gustavus Adolphus	Philip IV d 1665
Louis XIV d 1715	1611-32	

Charles had not grown up expecting to be king. He was very slow to walk and talk as a child, and was delicate in health. He adored his elder brother, Henry, but Henry died at the age of only 18, in 1612, just before Charles' twelfth birthday. If Henry had lived, there may well have been no Civil War. When Charles did grow up, he was still a small man, only five feet and three inches, harking back to the problems with that other small king, John. In his manner he was much more dignified than his father James, but unlike James he had no special knowledge of state or religious affairs. He was inflexible in character, and also, like John, devious - his subjects soon found that his word could not be trusted. Also, though never a professed Catholic himself, he showed leanings towards Catholicism, and he was married to a Catholic. Never a competent man or king, however, he really frightened his subjects when he hired men to carry out his wishes who were only too competent – Wentworth and Laud.

The first thing Charles did was to implement the French treaty and marry the wife that came with it, Henrietta Maria, and open hostilities with the Spanish. To this end he lent Cardinal Richelieu of France eight ships. To the consternation of the English, Richelieu then used these ships to attack the Huguenots in La Rochelle. Parliament, assembled to vote taxes, soon took a dim view of the new policy towards the Catholics. Not only had Henrietta Maria been given complete freedom of worship, but convicted priests were being pardoned. As soon as Parliament began to criticise his minister, Buckingham, Charles did what his father did, and dissolved it. In 1626 Charles, running out of money, tried once more and called a second Parliament, but it proved just as troublesome as the first, again attacking Buckingham, and so had to be dismissed as well.

Meanwhile war continued against Spain, but somehow Charles quarelled with France as well. To help the Huguenots, a great expedition was organized to occupy the Isle de Rhe, off La Rochelle, led by Buckingham in person. Forced loans were raised to pay for it, but it was a failure, and gave the nation further proof of the incompetence of the government.

Still Charles had to apply for funds, so in 1628 his third Parliament met. Tired of Stuart abuses, under Thomas Wentworth and John Pym, it drew up the Petition of Rights, specifically aimed at the recent behaviour of the government. This set out that (1) no freeman must be required give any gift, loan or tax without the consent of Parliament; (2) no freeman must be imprisoned contrary to the law of the land; (3) soldiers and marines must not be billeted in private houses (Charles had been sending them to live with his critics); and (4) commissions to punish soldiers and sailors by martial law must be withdrawn. Charles reluctantly agreed to the Petition and in return was granted funds.

Charles favoured what we would now call the High Church, and disliked the Puritans. He now moved a man of similar principles, Laud, from the bishopric of Bath and Wells to London. Although he did not become Archbishop of Canterbury until 1633, he immediately became Charles' principal adviser on religious matters. Laud was a pious and earnest man, but he was narrow-minded and his dislike of the Puritans was very well know to them, and equally reciprocated. At about the same time, Thomas Wentworth (later the Earl of Strafford), one of the chief promoters of the Petition of Rights, changed sides. He disliked the rule of Buckingham but he disliked still more the tendency he saw in Parliament to take upon itself the king's business of governing the country. Parliament was only a legislative body, not an executive one, and in those times the members of the government itself were not also members of Parliament. It so happened that Buckingham was then murdered by a private enemy called Felton, and Wentworth from this time took a leading place in the king's councils.

In 1629 Charles called his third Parliament, the course of which ran on similar lines to the previous ones. It objected to the collection of tonnage and poundage. At the start of his reign Parliament had granted these taxes to Charles for one year only, instead of for life, as under James. Charles had continued to collect them regardless of the lack of any further approval by Parliament, but in some ways he was within his rights, because the attempt to approve expenditure annually by Parliament represented an increase in its constitutional power to which he had never agreed. The 1629 Parliament was a stormy affair in which the Speaker had at one point to be held in his chair (to prevent adjournments) until resolutions had been passed. Such resolutions stated that those who made innovations in religion or exacted taxes not granted by Parliament were enemies of the kingdom. This was incendiary, almost revolutionary talk. Several members were sent to the Tower, including Sir John Eliot, who never made his peace with the king and died there, his health undermined.

Eleven years of arbitrary government followed, with no Parliaments. During this period, Wentworth and Laud were the chief advisers of the king. Wentworth could see clearly enough that money problems were at the heart of Charles' difficulties. The wars with France and Spain were terminated. (One of the people involved in the diplomatic missions concerning this peace was the Flemish painter Peter Paul Rubens, the finest artist of his generation, who was knighted by Charles.) Tax receipts were increased by greater strictness in collection. Still Charles was short of money, so he revived a lapsed statute that all holders of land to the value of £40 a year must be knighted. Those who complied paid a fee for the privilege, and those who did not, a fine. Again, from time immemorial landowners whose property adjoined the royal forests had encroached upon them. In 1633 Charles sent out a commission to reclaim the land or fine the current holders. In this way large tracts of land were reclaimed for the crown and considerable sums secured for the treasury. However the irritation to the nobility, who had been the main offenders, was great. For example the Earl of Essex found himself stripped of the greater part of his property; Essex was to go on to be the head of the Roundhead army in the Civil War. Long forgotten statutes were revived to raise money. For example some were fined for pulling down houses on their property, others for building houses in London. Also the king attacked the corporation of London, and confiscated property in Ulster given to it by James I on the grounds of mismanagement. No doubt there had been mismanagement, but it was unwise for Charles to alienate the richest city in the country. There were further abuses in the establishment of monopolies for basic commodities including starch, beer, bricks and soap.

In 1633 Wentworth became Lord-Deputy for Ireland. Here, amongst other things, he reformed the government, created an efficient army, established linen manufacture, and secured large tracts of land for the crown. However, he tyrannically pursued the English against the Irish interest, storing up trouble for the inevitable reaction.

In England Charles made heavy use of two courts, both of which operated without juries. One was the Court of Star Chamber, set up under Henry VII and now used as a general-purpose vehicle to suppress malcontents. The other was the Court of High Commission, used to enforce the Act of Uniformity (of religious worship), but which in fact represented a frontal attack on the (very numerous) Puritans. These courts had genuine, useful functions as well – Star Chamber tried cases between private individuals quickly and well, and High Commission fought hard against immorality; but the usage of the courts became increasingly political.

In 1634, at the advice of William Noy, his attorney-general, Charles levied ship money, a tax on seaports to furnish ships, in this case to protect English shipping from Algerian pirates, or alternatively to strengthen the fleet in case of war with the Dutch. The tax dated back to Tudor times and was raised without much complaint. However, the following year, ship money was levied on inland towns as well. This was quite unconstitutional, especially because there was no pretence of any immediate danger. The money was paid, with complaints. However, when a further demand was made the following year, it became clear that Charles intended to make ship money a perpetual tax, which could be levied without the consent of Parliament. This would have undermined the constitution completely. A Buckingham gentleman called John Hampden refused to pay, and was taken to court. He lost his case, but made his point. Hampden's trial was a turning point in the downward spiral to civil war. Hampden himself, a cousin of Oliver Cromwell, went on to be one of the main opponents of Charles in both Parliament and the Civil War.

In North America, the new colony of Massachusetts Bay was founded in 1629 for the distinct purpose of providing a refuge for those who disliked Stuart rule in England. In the single year of 1635, 3000 new settlers joined it. Laud tried to interfere in the colony, but his action only tended to make the new colonies more bigoted and Puritanical than they were before.

Laud also attempted to enforce an Episcopal system in Scotland. Greatly against the wishes of the people, James I had already reintroduced bishops, but they had little power and the Scots clung firmly to their dislike of a regular liturgy. In 1637, Laud determined to introduce the Prayer Book. The first attempt to use it ended in a riot in which the reader barely escaped with his life. Within a year almost the whole Scottish nation had bound itself in a new Convenant to preserve Presbyterianism. From this point onwards, Scottish Presbyterians were usually called Covenanters. In 1638 Episcopacy was abolished in Scotland by the General Assembly, and as Charles was not expected to agree, preparations were made for war. This was the first sign of armed resistance to Charles' government and was watched with great interest from England. Charles' call to arms was met without enthusiasm, but he collected a force and marched towards Scotland. Many of the Scots, however, had seen service abroad in the Netherlands and Germany, and a formidable army of them gathered together. The two armies met at Berwick. Charles sensed his weakness, and backed down, negotiating the Pacification of Berwick – in fact, a temporary truce.

Charles now needed money to build up his forces, so after a gap of eleven years, he called his fourth Parliament, known as the Short Parliament, which met in April, 1640. Charles hoped that hostility to the Scots would lead it to support him, but it did not. The members, led by Pym (previously imprisoned by James I in 1621 for opposition to the government), applied themselves to English grievances, and refused to recognise the legality of ship money. So once again the king hastily dissolved Parliament before it had sat a month.

Noting the weakness of the king, the Scottish army marched into England. Charles' soldiers had no fight in them, and were beaten at Newburn on the Tyne, allowing the Scots to advance en masse into Yorkshire. Charles found himself obliged to summon Parliament yet again, and made another truce with the Scots.

The "Long Parliament" met in November, 1640. Amongst its members were John Pym and John Hampden, who had already suffered for the cause of freedom, plus Oliver Cromwell, Edward Hyde and Lord Falkland, all of whom were later to attain celebrity (and of whom only Hyde, later Lord Clarendon, lasted into the Restoration). Most of the members were country gentlemen, so unlikely revolutionaries, but they had taken up the role of the nobility in the Middle Ages to resist arbitrary power. Others were lawyers who were certainly not men to support violent changes in the constitution. Yet Charles must have known what to expect from these people. Their first priority was the impeachment of Wentworth (now Lord Strafford) and Laud. The ecclesiastical policy of Laud was reversed, with orders sent out to deface and demolish images in churches. A Triennial Act was passed by which it was ordered that no more than three years should pass between Parliaments. It was felt that Charles and his ministers would not have dared to act as they had if they had been certain of scrutiny by Parliament.

Strafford was tried in the early part of 1641. Impeachment could not be made to stick, because he could not really be accused of treason when carrying out the wishes of the king, so a bill of attainder was passed instead. By this time Strafford had run out of friends in high places. Charles abandoned him and signed the Act, and Strafford was executed in May, 1641. Charles had lost the ablest of his ministers and his greatest opponent of the revolutionaries.

Meanwhile Charles consented to a bill which stated that Parliament could only be dissolved with its own consent. The idea of this was to induce lenders to support the government with greater confidence in the credit of Parliament. However, this act was to form the legal basis of the Parliamentary side in the war which followed. During the spring and summer of 1641, Parliament passed a series of measures aimed directly at the rule of the previous eleven years. The Courts of Star Chamber and High Commission were abolished. Statutes were passed against the collection of ship money, distraint of knighthood, and illegal customs duties, and the extent of the royal forests was set back as it had been before the late commission.

All these measures passed with practical unanimity, but there was no such agreement on church matters. The advanced Puritans went so far as to introduce a bill called the Root and Branch bill aimed at abolishing episcopacy altogether. This failed, but a bill to exclude the bishops from the House of Lords only failed in the Lords itself. Moderate men who were happy with the church as it stood began to question the behaviour of the extremists. Similarly in state affairs a party arose which thought that reform had gone far enough, and that the king should now be given a fair chance.

Suddenly in the autumn of 1641, a new crisis arose in Ireland. The Irish, who had long smarted under the loss of their land and the degradation of their religion, took advantage of the removal of Strafford and of the turmoil across in England and Scotland, and rose in rebellion. A terrible massacre of new landowners and of Protestants followed. It was apparent that quick action was needed if English rule was to be maintained. An army must be sent, but Parliament did not dare trust Charles with an army. Led by Pym (by this point known as King Pym), Parliament produced the Grand Remonstrance – in practice little more than a list of complaints against the king, and an appeal to the nation against him. The growing influence of the moderates was shown by the fact that this passed by only eleven votes.

Arriving back in London, Charles was pleased to find that he now had the support of a party in Parliament, led by Falkland and Hyde. However he overplayed his hand, sending soldiers into the House to arrest Pym, Hampden and three others, in January, 1642. They escaped but his reversion to type and his clear intention of using force meant that war was all but inevitable. Meanwhile the Londonners protected the members of Parliament and a triumphant return to Westminster was planned. To avoid seeing his own humiliation, Charles left London, never to return as a free man.

Chapter 20 – The Civil War, Commonwealth and Protectorate

Both sides now prepared for war. Charles withdrew to York, and demanded admission to Hull, where the arms for the Scottish campaign were stored, but was refused. Parliament named the Earl of Essex (son of the Elizabethan favorite) as its commander-in-chief. He was a fair soldier, but was to prove too cautious as a leader. To pay for troops the Commons made an order for tonnage and poundage. Charles had to rely on the generosity of his supporters.

In terms of geography, if a line is drawn from Hull to Gloucester, then to Bristol and then back to Weymouth, the majority to the south and east of it were for Parliament, and to the north and west of it for the king. There were two important exceptions: the University of Oxford supported the king, and the clothing towns of the West Riding supported Parliament. These divisions were in fact similar to those at the time of the Wars of the Roses – in fact the towns and richer districts favoured Parliament, as they had the Yorkists, and the poorer areas followed the king. Within this divide, the Catholics and High Churchmen supported Charles and the Puritans and Separatists, Parliament.

By the autumn of 1642, both sides were ready. Charles gathered his army at Shrewsbury and set off on a march to London, hoping to bring the war to an early close by a decisive success. Essex barred the way, investing towns in the Midlands. At one of them, Worcester, there was a skirmish with Prince Rupert, son of the Princess Elizabeth of the Palatinate, who had come over to help his uncle, and who was 22 years old. Moving towards London, the two armies met at Edgehill outside Banbury. Here Prince Rupert and his cavalry carried all before them on the Royalist right, but Essex and his infantry held the centre. Essex won the day and marched on to London, while Charles fell back on Oxford.

The two sides sat out the winter, gathering more forces, and in 1643 fighting broke out all over the country. There was a disastrous start for the Parliamentarians. The two southern armies met at

Chalgrove Field, near Oxford. The Royalists won the day, and Hampden was killed trying to cut off a troop of Rupert's horse. At Roundaway Down, near Devizes, the Parliamentarian Sir William Waller was utterly defeated. The Royalists under Rupert moved on to take Bristol, but with the loss of many men. The Parliamentarians of Bristol were subjected to such pillage that their resistance elsewhere became much more desperate. In the north, Lord Fairfax and his son, also Parliamentarians, were defeated at Atherton Moor, and forced to take refuge in Hull. Then the tide began to turn in favour of the Parliamentarians. In the east, Cromwell and the Earl of Manchester were fighting the Royalists for control of the fens, and Cromwell finally defeated the Royalists at Gainsborough. At Newbury, the king tried to stop the march of Essex back to London, but the attempt failed, and one of his leading supporters, Lord Falkland, was killed. In the north, the Royalist Marquess of Newcastle was forced to raise the siege of Hull.

In the winter lull, both sides sought new allies. Parliament, under the guidance of Pym, signed the Solemn League and Convenant with the Scots. This committed the Parliamentarians to adopt the Scottish system of church government in England. It did not specifically commit the English side to Presbyterianism, as the Independents would also be accommodated, but certainly it meant the end of episcopacy. After the treaty, an army of 21,000 Scots crossed the border to fight in Parliament's pay. This was Pym's last achievement as he died at the end of the year. Charles, meanwhile, wintered in Oxford with his leading adviser, Edward Hyde. From here he organized a truce with the Irish rebels. This freed up a part of his Irish army to join the war at home, and a contingent landed in Wales.

1644 opened well for Parliament. In January Sir Thomas Fairfax (son of Lord Fairfax) defeated the newly arrived army from Ireland at Nantwich, then turning north and east, evicted an outpost of Newcastle's troops at Selby. Newcastle was then besieged in York by the combined army of Fairfax, the Scots and the army from the eastern counties under Manchester and Cromwell. In the south the king had the upper hand, winning a battle at Cropredy Bridge, near Banbury, and driving Essex as far as Cornwall, where his army surrendered at Lostwithiel. Essex himself escaped by sea to London. If successful in the south, however, the Royalists suffered disaster in the north. Charles sent Prince Rupert and his troops to relieve the siege of York. After much maneuvering, the two sides met at Marston Moor outside the city on 2 July, 1644. Rupert's Cavaliers were routed at the first charge, and though Newcastle's foot made a stout resistance, the Royalists were routed. The battle ruined the king's cause in the north. Rupert escaped back to the south, and Newcastle fled to the Continent. Cromwell and Manchester followed Rupert, were joined by Waller, and confronted the Royalists at the second battle of Newbury. Due to Manchester's hesitation, Cromwell and Waller failed to achieve a decisive success, and the king regained Oxford.

The failure at Newbury brought discontent amongst the Parliamentarians to a head. The more energetic of these were Independent in religion, as distinct from the more moderate Presbyterians. The leaders of the moderates were Essex, Manchester and Waller. The leader of the Independents was Cromwell, who had risen rapidly to prominence. At first, the Parliamentary army was strong in infantry but weak in cavalry. Cromwell had found amongst the sons of yeomen farmers of the east people who could ride just as well as the Cavalier gentry, but also men inspired with the utmost zeal for their religion. From these he formed his Ironsides, and drilled them into the finest body of cavalry the country had ever known. These men carried the day at Marston Moor and would have done so at Newbury but for Manchester's hesitation. So the Independents now came forward and demanded that all the old generals should retire. As they were in fact members of Parliament, a Self-Denying Ordinance was passed, by which all members were deprived of their commands. Thus Essex, Waller and Manchester were removed. Only Cromwell, whose services were too valuable to lose, was spared the Ordinance. This reorganization was critical to the outcome of the war, which could have lasted as long as the Wars of the Roses, but which in fact ended much sooner.

Negotiations with Charles were conducted over the winter, but nothing came of them. In January 1645, his old ally Archbishop Laud was executed by the Parliamentarians. As he was innocent of any crime, this shows that extremism was taking over. By the summer of 1645, the New Model Army was ready to take the field. It consisted of 14,000 foot and 7,000 horse, under the overall command of Sir Thomas Fairfax (the younger Fairfax). This was very much the army of the Independents, and thought itself the army of God (most of its officers were Independents, but by no means all of the men). Whatever else, it was a real professional army. Cromwell had purged his troops of men who would not fight. However, it was, certainly in modern terms, only a small army. Much larger armies than this had taken the field before in England, for example at Towton in 1461. In these times, however, large armies could not be kept together for long – the men had to get back to their fields and occupations. The unmechanised and largely unimproved agriculture and industry of the day could not spare many men for long periods. Also, a large army was very difficult to keep supplied in the field. Again, it seems likely that many men were essentially neutral, and simply kept out of the way when the press gangs came calling. In any event, Charles faced this army at Naseby, near Leicester, on 14 June 1645, and was completely routed.

Charles now pinned his hopes on a Scottish army under the Marquess of Montrose, which had won three victories in Scotland against the Covenanters and their leader the Marquess of Argyll. Three months after Naseby, however, Montrose was defeated at Philiphaugh. Ten days later Charles himself saw his last army defeated at Rowton Heath outside Chester. All next winter Charles roamed the country, before finally giving himself up to the Scottish army at Newark in May, 1646. When Parliament paid the Scots the first £400,000 of their expenses, they handed over Charles. He was treated with respect and kept at Holmby House in Northamptonshire.

Serious disputes now arose between two of the three parties involved in the victory – Parliament, now predominantly Presbyterian, and the army, predominantly Independent (the third party, the Scots, had gone home). Parliament tried to install Presbyterianism as the established religion of England, and to disband the army, paying the soldiers only one-sixth of their arrears of pay. It also passed ordinances to make all remaining officers take the Convenant and to deprive members of Parliament (that is, Cromwell) of their commands. In response, Cromwell sent Cornet Joyce and a body of horse to collect Charles from Holmby House. The army commanders then offered very generous terms to Charles, on the basis of restoring his throne and episcopacy, but with toleration for other sects. However, they found Charles a very slippery customer, in two ways. Suspecting that hostilities might break out again, this time amongst the victors, Charles refused the terms, then escaped from Hampton Court to the Isle of Wight. This behaviour was to cost him his life.

So a second civil war began in 1648. Royalist insurrections broke out in Kent and Wales, while the Duke of Hamilton invaded England from Scotland with an army of Presbyterians. The New Model Army reacted with great energy. Fairfax put down the rebellion in Kent and Essex, Cromwell that in Wales. Marching north, Cromwell cut Hamilton's army in two at Preston, the last full battle of the civil war, then completed its destruction at Wigan and Warrington. The army came back from Warrington and tore up agreements made between

Parliament and Charles. The Presbyterian members were simply expelled from Parliament. From this time it had no claim to represent the nation, but the 53 Independents who were left, known as the Rump, carried on conducting business, the first object of which was to get rid of Charles. He was tried before a court of Independent leaders, whose authority he claimed not to recognise – a familiar plea! Found guilty of high treason, he was beheaded in January, 1649.

Charles could have won the civil war if his army, and especially his cavalry, had acted with more discipline. His officers behaved with insolence and insubordination. Throughout the war, the Royalist cavalry could never be mustered for a second charge. Once the Parliamentary side had reorganized, it quickly saw off the Royalists. Its cavalry at both the decisive battles, Marston Moor and Naseby, did rally. In fact Charles' armies suffered defeat for much the same reason as the French feudal levies at Crecy and Agincourt. However, even if he had lost the war, his enemies were so divided that Charles could have won the peace. Had he taken up the terms offered to him by the army, he would have survived. But he did not, so another Stuart king of desperately poor judgment went to his grave.

So, the revolution produced the most unexpected winners – the Independents, who comprised a small minority of the population. As with the later French Revolution (1789) and Russian Revolution (1917), the people who started it – in all three cases, essentially middle-class moderates – were eventually pushed aside by extremists.

So England became, for the first and only time in its history, a military dictatorship. Whatever the rights and wrongs of the execution of Charles, it did not go down well politically. Charles himself was utterly discredited, but his death rallied the Royalists round the Prince of Wales, against whom no harm was known. Hardly had Charles been executed than an account appeared of his life in prison, *Eikon Basilike* (the Royal Likeness), purportedly written by Charles himself. Portraying the king as an innocent Christian martyr, it was a phenomenal best-seller, and produced such a reaction that the poet Milton was engaged to answer it.

Also, the expulsion of the Presbyterians in 1648 had thrown them into opposition. So it was certain that the new government could not rely on popular support, which meant in practice that it was obliged to rely upon the terror inspired by the New Model Army. However, the revolutionaries and regicides started confidently enough, abolishing the monarchy and the House of Lords, and proclaiming a "Commonwealth". The leaders of the Royalist rising of 1648 were executed, as was Hamilton, leader of the Scottish invasion.

The new government found itself surrounded with difficulties. In England a dangerous mutiny broke out in the army. In Ireland the rebels and the Royalists, now making common cause, hemmed in the Parliamentarians at Dublin. In Scotland the Covenanters were levying troops and corresponding with the Prince of Wales. In response, the ruling council in England acted with great energy. The mutineers were sternly put down, and Cromwell himself was dispatched to Ireland. He set out not only to quell the rebellion, but also to exact his revenge for the Irish alliance with Charles, which had allowed Charles to put another army into the English conflict. At this time, there was a great fear of the Catholic Irish bogeyman in England. At around two million, the population of Ireland was a quarter of that of England – a much higher proportion than today – and the country was seen (quite rightly) as a considerable Royalist threat. The tide had already turned before Cromwell arrived in Ireland, with a government victory at Rathmines, near Dublin. Upon that the Royalists quit the field and invested the town, in order to protract the war by making the English undertake a number of sieges.

Cromwell first ordered the surrender of Drogheda. This was refused, whereupon he stormed the town and put the garrison to the sword (as, under the rules of war from Julius Caesar to Napoleon, he was entitled to do). The same thing happened at Wexford; after this, the other towns did surrender. Meanwhile, determined to solve the Ulster problem for once and for all (faint hope!), Cromwell drove as much of the native Catholic population as he could away to the west, answering all pleas for mercy with the words "Hell, or Connaught!" His name is still reviled in Ireland to this day. Of all the countries involved in the Civil War, the population of Ireland fell by far the largest proportion – it is estimated by one third.

In Scotland, the Scottish Parliament proclaimed Charles (Prince of Wales) their king in 1649. Then there was a mini-civil war between the Royalists under Montrose and the Covenanters under Argyll. Charles waited to see which side won. The side he would probably have preferred, the Royalists, were defeated at Carbisdale. So Charles threw in his lot with the Covenanters and was crowned king at Scone in January, 1651. This was the last coronation ever to take place in Scotland. The ruling council in England thought the Scots likely to invade. While Fairfax dithered, the other council members sent Cromwell with an army to strike the first blow. Despite encountering serious difficulties, Cromwell eventually brought the Scottish army to an action at Dunbar. After his victory here he invested Edinburgh and chased the Scots beyond the Forth to Stirling. This left the road to England open. Seizing his opportunity, Charles raised an army and set off for London. Cromwell, caught by surprise, sent Lambert after him on forced marches. Lambert diverted Charles westward. Coming up behind him, Cromwell caught Charles at Worcester (September, 1651) and crushed his army. Charles himself escaped through Cromwell's lines and after a number of hair-raising adventures, during one of which he only evaded capture by hiding in an oak tree, reached safety in France.

In 1652 there was trouble from another quarter when a maritime war with the Dutch broke out. Entering their "Golden Age", the Dutch had become a powerful commercial and maritime nation and there was frequent rivalry with the English in foreign seas, especially in the East Indies. In this quarter there had been the notorious execution of ten English merchants by the Dutch authorities in the Moluccas in 1623, known as the Massacre of Amboina, which the English had neither forgiven or forgotten. The Dutch also did a good business in shipping goods in and out of England. However, in retaliation for perceived abuses by Dutch shipping, Parliament passed the Navigation Act. This forbade the importation of goods into England except in English ships, or in the ships of the country producing the goods. So broke out what was to be the first of three wars with the Dutch in the second half of the seventeenth century. In the seas between the two countries the English inflicted devastating defeats on the Dutch (Battle of Kentish Knock, 1652). However in more distant waters, the Dutch succeeded in excluding English ships from both the Baltic and the Mediterranean and brought much of England's trade to a standstill. A peace was signed in 1653, but this was little better than a truce as the main grievances of both sides, and in particular the Navigation Act, remained in place.

Back at home, the army became much dissatisfied with Parliament, which it thought should be replaced with a house more in harmony with its views. In 1653, Cromwell went in person and finally dismissed the old house, in the famous words "In the name of God, go!" A new house was formed by members nominated by Independent ministers. This is usually referred to as Barebones' Parliament, named after one of its members for London. Many of the measures put forward by this Parliament were worthy enough, but many also were too violent for Cromwell. The army was again dissatisfied. At the end of 1653 the members resigned their power into Cromwell's hands. Cromwell was made Lord Protector, to rule the country supported by a council of 21 members.

The council tried to stamp out the Church of England. As early as 1645 an Act of Parliament suppressed the Book of Common Prayer. Presbyterianism was established by law, but in practice never gained any real hold in England outside of London, Lancashire, Bristol and Hull. Cromwell dispatched a commission to enquire into the character of ministers of religion. As immorality, frivolity, the use of the Prayer Book and loyalty to the Stuarts were all regarded as scandalous, much iniquity was done to ordinary men. Each person nominated for a church living had to pass a board of triers consisting of Presbyterians, Independents and Baptists, who of course had little time for Royalist sympathisers.

In the later period of the Commonwealth, 1654 to 1659, Ireland was ruled by Henry Cromwell, second son of the Lord Protector. Under him the property of Catholics and Royalists was confiscated, and divided amongst those who had lent money for the war, and retired soldiery. The new settlers, like the Ulsterman, were vigorous improvers, but the confiscations were as unjust as they had been in 1608. Scotland in this period was administered by one of Cromwell's generals, George Monk, who pacified the Highlands. In contrast to Ireland, Cromwell's rule in Scotland was a period of peace and prosperity.

The first Protectorate Parliament met in September of 1654. This was a parliament which, for the first time, contained members for Scotland and Ireland. It proved to be almost as troublesome to Cromwell as Charles' Parliaments had been to the former king, insisting, for example, on debating the desirability of rule by a single person. Cromwell, who had in fact shown himself to be a vigorous and able administrator, both at home and abroad, was understandably vexed, and first excluded a hundred members, then dissolved the Parliament. Meanwhile a Royalist rising took place at Salisbury in 1655, led by a man called Penruddock. Although easily suppressed, it gave Cromwell the excuse for dividing England into eleven military districts, each under the control of a major-general, who paid himself and his men out of the estates of the Royalists, and ruled with despotic power. England really was under a military dictatorship.

In terms of foreign policy, Cromwell reverted to Elizabethan ideas. The Stuart Spanish alliances had never been popular in the country. So Cromwell chose war with Spain, in alliance with France. The best prospects seemed to be amongst the Spanish colonies, and in 1655 Jamaica was taken from Spain. It has remained a British possession or Commonwealth member ever since. Meanwhile Cromwell's troops were much sought after abroad, as for the first time in history, England had the best army in Europe. In alliance with the French, the army took Dunkirk from the Spanish Netherlands (Battle of the Dunes, 1658). (In some ways the reign of Cromwell 1653-8 is a kind of mirror image of the reign of Mary, exactly 100 years earlier; opposite in religion and opposite in the results of warfare, as Mary lost Calais and Cromwell gained Dunkirk.)

As he did not wish to be an arbitrary ruler, Cromwell called a second Parliament in 1656. To avoid the difficulties of the previous Parliament, above ninety Republicans and Presbyterians were excluded from the outset. The new Parliament wanted Cromwell to accept the title of King. One reason for this was that it would protect office-holders from prosecution in any subsequent reign, as under the statutes of Henry VII, no one could be prosecuted for treason for holding office under a reigning king. However, the title was still distasteful to the Army, so Cromwell declined it. Instead he accepted the Humble

Petition and Advice, by which the office of Lord Protector was made hereditary. Also by the acts of this Parliament, all forms of religion were tolerated except Catholicism.

Only shortly afterwards, Cromwell died, in 1658 (he is sometimes said to be the last person in England to die of locally contracted malaria, though he also seems to have suffered kidney failure). He is generally considered a great man, and indeed as late as 2002 was amongst ten contenders for the title of Greatest Briton in a BBC competition (he came tenth). In military terms, he carried all before him, and never lost a battle. His peacetime administration was as successful as could be expected, given that, at any time since the beginning of the Civil War, a freely elected Parliament would have left his own party of Independents a small minority in a mass of Royalists and Presbyterians. Cromwell was also a realist and is well remembered for his instructions to the famous painter Lely to "Remark all these roughnesses, pimples, warts, and everything as you see me, otherwise I will never pay a farthing for it!"

The succession was left to Cromwell's son, Richard. It would have been much better for the Independents if the second son, Henry could have succeeded, as he was a capable soldier and statesman, but Richard was a retiring gentleman incapable of inspiring the respect of the zealots. His accession, however, passed off without incident. When his first Parliament met, all the old dissensions broke out, and Richard found that he must trust to the support of either Parliament or the army. He preferred the army, and Parliament was dissolved. The army then took matters into its own hands, and recalled the remains of the Long Parliament – the Rump. Finding himself neglected, Richard retired to private life. These events naturally encouraged insurrection. There was a rising in Cheshire, promptly put down by Lambert, who then dismissed the Rump for a second time. Meanwhile, Cromwell's man in Scotland, General Monk, keeping his own counsel as to his exact intentions, began a cautious advance into England. Lambert marched north to fight, but Lord Fairfax mustered the Yorkshire militia and threatened to join Monk. Lambert's troops dispersed and Monk marched without opposition into London, declaring for a free Parliament. So a free Parliament was elected, known as the Convention (because it was not summoned by a king). Composed almost entirely of Royalists and Presbyterians, it met in April 1660. With one voice the Convention determined to recall Charles, who was in no way responsible for the ill deeds of his father. Charles was only too happy to respond, and so he landed at Dover in May, 1660. The feeling of the lifting of a dreadful suppression was everywhere experienced, and Charles was welcomed with great enthusiasm by the whole nation.

Yet in one of those "what if" questions of history, it is instructive to question what would have happened if Cromwell had been succeeded by his second surviving son, Henry, who had made a good impression as the lord deputy of (effective ruler) of Ireland. He would have been much more difficult to replace than Richard Cromwell – there could have been a renewal of civil war, or Henry could have gradually softened the severity of his father's rule and gained general acceptance, establishing a new dynasty. In that case, Charles II may never have been restored.

Despite the general atmosphere of Puritan bigotry and severity which pervades this age, it did produce one of England's greatest poets, John Milton (1608-1674). Not widely read today, his poetry is nevertheless accessible in language. Milton served as Latin secretary to the Commonwealth – it was his job to produce correspondence with foreign powers, in those days written in Latin. His most famous work is the epic poem, *Paradise Lost*, but more readable today are shorter works such as *Comus*, in which something surprising can be noted – the devil has the good lines!

Chapter 21 – The Restoration

Charles II 1660-85 (25 years)
Born 1630; married 1662, Katherine of Portugal

Contemporary rulers:

France	*Holland*
Louis XIV	William of Orange, Stadtholder
1643-1715	1672-1702

Charles became king at the age of thirty. He had lived abroad for the previous nine years, in France and Holland. He was a man of great natural sagacity and his chequered career had given him considerable experience. More able than his father and more worldly-wise than his grandfather, he brought back with him the fixed determination never to set out on his travels again. At the same time, he was determined to secure as much power as possible, and his easy-going manner, which blinded observers to his real character, enabled him to gain a large measure of success. And indeed Charles found himself in a very good position, because if he needed England, England needed him even more. No one wanted anything more to do with the most un-English Puritanical government, which had even sold off most of the magnificent art collection of Charles I (which included paintings by Titian, Raphael, Mantegna and Rubens). This sentiment is expressed very clearly by contemporary writers, including Samuel Pepys (27 years old at the time of the Restoration) in his *Diaries*.

After his accession Charles gave his confidence to Edward Hyde of the Long Parliament, now Lord Clarendon, who after steady adherence to the royal family in its adversity, returned as Lord Chancellor. Indeed, the Hyde family was doing well – in 1660 Hyde's daughter Anne married James, Duke of York, Charles' younger brother and heir to the throne (one of very few such heirs to marry an

Englishwoman), so that as Lord Clarendon, Hyde was to become the grandfather of two queens, Mary II and Anne.

The first step of the Convention was to pass an Act of Indemnity and Oblivion for offences committed during the civil war and Commonwealth; this specifically excluded those connected with the trial and execution of Charles I. Ten of these were executed. Two of the leading men of the Commonwealth, General Lambert and Sir Henry Vane, though not regicides, where also imprisoned. Vane, a former member of the council, had refused to sanction the regicide, but still he was executed.

The Convention conducted certain other business, amongst other things sweeping away the remains of feudalism by abolishing the practice of holding land on military tenure (which involved the payment of feudal dues). It also established for the first time a standing army of 5000 men. There comes a point in the development of a country when a permanent army of professional soldiers becomes a necessity, as men could no longer be expected to be called away from their trades at short notice, and as the development of the arts of war became more complex, requiring special training. Continental countries had long had standing armies.

The Convention was dissolved in 1661 and replaced by a newly elected Parliament whose members, such was the enthusiasm for the Restoration, were almost entirely Royalist. The new body reinstated the Church of England as the established church, and went so far as to pass an Act of Uniformity, requiring all holders of benefices to be ordained by a bishop and to use only the Book of Common Prayer. This was very hard on the Presbyterians, the alliance with whom had brought about the Restoration. As a result of the Act, it is estimated that fifteen hundred clergymen left their livings on St Bartholomew's Day, 1662. The selection of this day was particularly vindictive upon the departing clergy as it fell just before they were about to receive their annual tithes, so they lost a year's income as well as a job.

Not content with this, in 1664 Parliament imitated the bad example of Cromwell by passing the Conventicle Act, which forbade all assemblies for worship other than those in a church, the idea being to stop the informal ceremonies which were taking place elsewhere. Parliament also passed the Five Mile Act, which forbade any ministers who would not conform with the Act of Uniformity from earning a living by teaching, and also forbade them from settling within five miles of any corporate town. Again, it was known that the political strength of the Nonconformist sects – Presbyterians, Independents, Baptists and

Quakers – lay in the corporations of small towns. To deprive them of this, the Corporation Act was passed, ordering all holders of municipal office to renounce the Covenant and take the sacraments of the Church of England. The Uniformity, Conventicle, Five Mile and Corporation Acts together came to be called the Clarendon Code. Under the Commonwealth, in fact, similar rules had been applied, but against the Church of England rather than in its favour. This demonstrates very clearly that in the seventeenth century there was still no conception of religious toleration, nor would there be for a very long time. However, unlike in Tudor times, if they felt sufficiently strongly, the Nonconformists did have somewhere else to go – North America. During this reign three new colonies were established under a syndicate headed by William Penn, a Quaker – New Jersey, Delaware and Pennsylvania.

In foreign policy, Clarendon favoured the French alliance against Spain. In furtherance of this Charles married Katherine of Portugal. This country had broken away from Spanish rule (1580-1640) but in fact the alliance with Portugal went right back to the fourteenth century. With Katherine Charles received the island of Bombay in India, and Tangiers in north Africa. The possession of these places gave new opportunities for trade, which Charles, like the rest of the Stuarts, was keen to encourage. The same year Clarendon also sold Dunkirk to the French. This was probably wise (or they may have taken it for nothing for themselves), but it made Clarendon very unpopular. It was said that he had been bribed, and a new house he was building for himself was nicknamed Dunkirk House.

In 1664 the second Dutch war broke out, caused like the first by continuing colonial and commercial rivalry, to which was added the annoyance felt by Charles because the Dutch states would not recognise the claims of his nephew Prince William (of Orange) to the title of Stadtholder designate. Prince William was a minor, born in 1650; his father was the Stadtholder William II, who died of smallpox before his son was born, and his mother was Charles' sister Mary. At first the war went well, and Sir Robert Holmer seized the Dutch colony of New Amsterdam (1664). The last Dutch governor had a famous name – Peter Stuyvesant. The colony was subsequently renamed New York in honour of the Duke of York, the king's brother, who was the head of the Navy. In 1665 the Duke himself won a great victory over the Dutch off Lowestoft (thought to be the worst naval defeat in Dutch history).

In 1665, meanwhile, disaster struck – the Great Plague, the last of the great pestilences which from time to time struck the filthy alleys and narrow streets which formed the cities of Europe. It was during this plague that Isaac Newton (born 1643) withdrew from the city – in his case, Cambridge – and went home to Grantham, where he worked out the principles of gravity and the laws of motion, according to myth by observing an apple fall from a tree. In September, 1666, the plague was followed by a second disaster, the Great Fire of London, which destroyed the greater part of the city, including St Paul's Cathedral. In 1667 there was a naval disaster when the Dutch sailed up the Thames and burnt the ships lying in the Medway. The Dutch admiral on the day was de Ruyter, who was a great scourge of the English in three naval wars. The Dutch caused such panic that Samuel Pepys records in his diary that he packed his wife and father off to the country with a bag of gold, and lay awake all night worrying about his remaining bag of gold. This little vignette illustrates the important difference between England and the United Provinces. The English fleet had fallen into disrepair because Parliament, not trusting Charles to use it wisely, had refused to vote him funds for the fleet. Charles was then obliged to raise what funds he could at ruinous rates of interest. The Dutch, meanwhile, had established a proper banking and commercial system, without which a real navy cannot flourish, and its citizens left their bags of gold at the bank, where they could be used to finance the government's wars.

After this, peace was made by the Treaty of Breda. However by this time Clarendon had become thoroughly unpopular, not only with the people, but with Charles, of whose dissipated lifestyle he disapproved. As impeachment loomed and on the advice of Charles, he fled abroad, never to return (died 1674).

The new government was no more tolerant in Scotland and Ireland than it had been at home. In Scotland, in spite of the wishes of the people (who would have preferred a Calvinist theocracy), the old form of government was restored, episcopacy was reestablished and persecution of the Puritans begun. In Ireland an Act of Settlement was passed, whereby certain of the lands confiscated by Cromwell were restored to Catholics and Royalists. Unhappily, the English did all they could to injure Irish trade to the benefit of their own. The Irish were forbidden to trade with the colonies, or to enjoy the benefits of the Navigation Act. Nor were they allowed to export their main produce to England – cattle, meat and butter.

After the fall of Clarendon, power devolved to the "Cabal" (thought to be formed from the first letters of their names): Clifford, Arlington, Buckingham, Ashley and Lauderdale, operating as a cabinet. Baron Clifford was a Catholic. George Villiers, second Duke of

Buckingham, was the son of the favorite of James I. His father was murdered when he was only four months old and he and his brother had been brought up with the children of Charles I. The Duke of Lauderdale was responsible for Scotland. In foreign policy this group forged an alliance with the United Provinces and Sweden – the Triple Alliance – against France, which under its king Louis XIV (the "Sun King") had now become the most powerful and dangerous country in Europe. Coming so soon after Breda, this represented a complete change of attitude towards the Dutch.

With Clarendon out of the way, Charles began to act like a typical Stuart king. He did not like the Triple Alliance. Under his mother's influence (Henrietta Maria of France), both he and his brother James were very attached to Catholicism. Charles went so far as to make the secret treaty of Dover with Louis in 1670, pledging to declare himself a Catholic and to make war on the United Provinces in return for a bribe of £300,000, most of it to be used for naval spending. This sordid treaty illustrates very clearly the divergence between England and the United Provinces in the hundred years since they had together fought off the Spanish. Amsterdam had become the undisputed financial and commercial capital of the world, while Charles had to go cap-in-hand to the King of France for his money.

The treaty was in direct contradiction of what the Cabal was trying to achieve. Under Louis XIV and his minister Colbert, France had shaken off its troubles and had become a great power. It had built up a navy to rival the English and the Dutch and was seen by the Cabal and indeed the country as a whole as the main threat to England. Charles induced Parliament to make a liberal grant for the Navy, on the understanding that war was to be declared against France. He then prorogued Parliament, which did not meet again for two years. His next move was to announce that loans due for repayment would not be repaid that year, but only interest on the loans would be paid. This appeared tantamount to national bankruptcy and caused great consternation amongst the lenders.

In religious matters the Duke of York was received openly into the Catholic church, then a Declaration of Indulgence was proclaimed in 1672, by which the king suspended the operation of all acts of Parliament against Nonconformists and Catholics. This again caused general consternation. Finally there was great surprise when the English fleet suddenly issued forth from Portsmouth, and without any declaration of war, attacked the Dutch spice fleet which was anchored peacefully off the Isle of Wight. The Dutch beat off the attack, but then war was declared against them simultaneously by the English and the French, in line with the secret treaty of Dover, and the very opposite of the terms of the Triple Alliance. Unlike the previous two Dutch wars, this new conflict had little to do with commercial rivalry at sea. Rather its aim was to support the political purposes of Charles, who had agreed a share of the spoils with the French, including ports in Zeeland and Flanders.

The combined English and French fleets fought an almighty naval battle against the Dutch in Sole Bay off Southwold, but the result was indecisive (1672). The Dutch admiral was once again de Ruyter, while the Duke of York, the future James II, led the English. James won the respect of his men in this battle, being described by one of them as "General, soldier, pilot, master, seaman; to say all, everything that a man can be, and most pleasant when great shots are thundering about his ears." It was the Dutch, however, who gained the tactical advantage, keeping the English and French fleets away from their shores and so allowing them to fight on against the French at home. (This war was to see the emergence of William III, future king of England, as Stadtholder in the United Provinces, where he managed to beat off Louis XIV.)

When Parliament met at the start of 1673, it at once began to undo the recent acts by the government. It passed a Test Act which stipulated that anyone holding an office under the crown must follow Church of England rites and make a declaration against transubstantiation. The act made it impossible for a declared Catholic to hold office. The Cabal broke up: Clifford (a Catholic) resigned, Ashley (Lord Shaftesbury) and Buckingham joined the opposition and Arlington's influence declined. Only Lauderdale remained, in Scotland. Also as a result of the Test Act, the Duke of York stood down from his office of High Admiral.

Sir Thomas Osborne, later Earl of Danby and then Duke of Leeds, now became the chief minister. It was during his time that the forerunner of the party system came into being. Since 1661 there had been no election, but the temper of Parliament had changed greatly as disillusionment with Charles set in. The most discontented members usually belonged to the country, and so were called the country party – the forerunners of the Whigs and then the Liberals, and at this time the opposition party. The policy of the country party was strongly in favour of the Anglican church and against the Catholics and Nonconformists (this attitude towards the Nonconformists was later to change). It favoured peace with the United Provinces and war with France, but did not trust any standing army. On the other side was the court party, forerunner of the Tories and later the Conservatives, which supported the king. Louis XIV of France dreaded that the country party would push Charles into a war against him, so when he thought the opposition likely to get its way, he paid Charles money so that he could prorogue Parliament. If he thought that Charles was becoming too independent, he would help the opposition to attack him

In 1674, peace was made with the United Provinces in the Treaty of Westminster. In territorial terms, there was a reversion to the *status quo ante bellum*. This meant that the Dutch returned New York, which they had retaken in 1673. The useful Atlantic naval staging island of St Helena was confirmed as an English possession, and the territory of Surinam in South America, captured by the Dutch in the previous conflict, became legally their colony. The treaty ended the last of three sharp predominantly naval conflicts with the Dutch in this period – indeed within fifteen years, there was the equivalent of a joint monarchy. However, the immense future significance of New York was yet to be realised. At the time it seemed that little of substance had been gained by the third Dutch war, against a high cost in money, men and ships. Charles had only succeeded in building up a formidable opposition at home.

Danby favoured the anti-French Triple Alliance, and strengthened it by arranging the marriage of Mary, daughter of James Duke of York (and Anne Hyde) to William of Orange, her cousin, who had by now become the leader or Stadtholder of Holland. This was of great importance because Mary was the second-in-line to the throne, and Charles had produced no legitimate children. Particularly as William was a Protestant, the marriage was very popular in the country, but it was very unpopular at the French court. Danby and Charles then made another secret treaty with Louis XIV whereby Charles was to receive £300,000 a year for three years, in return for which he would dissolve Parliament, disband the army (and so not make war), and promise not to assist the Dutch, whom Louis was still fighting. As soon as Louis concluded a peace treaty with the Dutch, he revenged himself on Danby by revealing his part in the secret treaty to the leaders of the country party. The same Parliament had sat since 1661. In 1679 it was dissolved and new elections were held. The country party was much stronger in the new house, and Danby was impeached, and sent to the Tower for the remainder of the reign.

As three administrations – those of Clarendon, the Cabal and Danby had all now been overthrown by the votes of Parliament, many thought that such sharp disagreements between king and Parliament should be avoided, and a plan was adopted to give the whole Privy Council – instead of just a small body within it, as the Cabal had been – a much more central role, so that it might act as a check on both the king and Parliament. However this did not work and before long, a new cabal had emerged.

In 1678 there was much consternation about a fictitious Popish plot, invented by one Titus Oates. Ever since the Gunpowder plot of 1605 the country had been ready enough to believe any rumours of Catholics plots and some attributed the Great Fire of London to them. There was no doubt also that Charles and James were secretly working in favour of the Catholics. Oates came forward with an absurd story that the Papists had hatched a scheme to murder Charles and James, who were their best friends. In the excitement hundreds of Catholics were arrested and many were executed, including some eminent victims such as Viscount Stafford.

One result of the Titus Oates "plot" was the introduction of an Exclusion bill in Parliament to keep James from the succession, in favour of his own daughter Mary and her husband William. It would have saved a lot of trouble if it had been passed, but Charles would not sacrifice his brother's interests. The final Act passed before the dissolution was Habeas Corpus, ever since one of the mainstays of the British constitution, which laid down that no man could be arrested and held without charge, and gave facilities for a prisoner to obtain either a trial or release on bail.

The new, fourth Parliament met in 1680 with the country in uproar. In the new Parliament, the names Whig and Tory were first used. Both names were originally insults, Whig being derived from the term Whigamoor, a Scottish Presbyterian, and a Tory being an Irish brigand. Members of both parties were drawn from all classes of society – unlike Labour and Conservative, they did not denote any class distinction, but different principles. The Tories were pro-monarchy and Anglican. The Whigs were exclusionist and leaned to an alliance with the Nonconformists. In the 1680 Parliament a further attempt was made by the Whigs, who had a majority in the Commons, to introduce an Exclusion bill. It was rejected in the Lords under the influence of the Prince of Orange himself, who would come to the throne sooner or later anyway. He discouraged the bill because some extreme Whigs were now pushing the claims of the Duke of Monmouth, illegitimate son of Charles. Meanwhile in Scotland, the Covenanters rose in revolt, but were defeated in battle at Bothwell Bridge

In 1682 the country was still in a ferment over the exclusion question. Parliament was dissolved twice and it seemed as if another civil war would start. Charles managed without Parliament thanks to another hefty subsidy from Louis XIV, and passions cooled for the moment. Lord Shaftesbury (former Cabal member Ashley), leader of the Whig opposition, was prosecuted. His scheme to exclude James had been very nearly successful and had only failed on account of his foolish substitution of the Duke of Monmouth for William and Mary. Shaftesbury left the country (to die the following year) but Monmouth, by no means deterred, made a pseudo-royal progress round the country to gather support. Tired of constant Whig opposition, Charles himself began to cancel the charters of the town and city corporations from which the Whigs drew their chief support. He then restored the charters and replaced the officials with new men favorable to himself. In effect, this allowed Charles to pack the House of Commons.

Although the Whig leaders had resisted any resort to arms, some of their supporters did not, and a plot emerged led by an old soldier called Rumbold. The plan was to murder Charles and James when they stopped at the Rye House on their way back from the races at Newmarket on 1 April 1683. Then there was a fire in Newmarket which burned down half the town, so Charles and James returned early and the plot misfired, but it was discovered. The government tried the conspirators, but included amongst them two opposition leaders, Lord Russell and Algernon Sidney. The latter, son of the Earl of Leicester, was a lifelong republican who had served in the New Model Army. Russell was the grandson of Robert Carr, favorite of James I. The judge at his trial was Jeffries, destined to become infamous in the next reign. The evidence against them was ridiculously slight but the pressure was put on the juries and judges, and the two were executed. Thereafter they were looked upon as martyrs to the Whig cause.

By 1685 Charles had seen off his opponents and become little less than an absolute monarch, especially after he had successfully remodelled the corporations. He also exerted all the control he wanted over the processes of justice. Just at the height of his power, he suddenly died. On his deathbed he did or said three notable things. On behalf of his most famous mistress, Nell Gwyn, he asked "Let not poor Nelly starve". He received the final sacraments from a Catholic priest, and finally apologised for taking such an unconscionable time dying. He had been a king of great ability, concealing under the appearance of frivolity a talent for intrigue which baffled the statesmen of the day. However his attempts to establish a kingship on the model of his patron

Louis XIV were ultimately doomed to failure in England. He left behind him a large number of illegitimate children, most of whom were raised to the peerage, but no legitimate heir, so the throne passed to his brother James II.

Chapter 22 – The Glorious Revolution

James II 1685-88 (3 years)
Born 1633; married 1662, Anne Hyde and 1673 Mary of Modena

Contemporary rulers:
France   *Holland*
Louis XIV   William of Orange, Stadtholder
1643-1715   1672-1702

James was a very different man to his elder brother, being more narrow-minded but also more conscientious, and he shared with his father an inability to understand what the nation wanted. As the first declared Catholic monarch since the disastrous Mary, 130 years previously, he should have realised that he would have to tread very carefully, but he did not do so. In fact, his personality deteriorated as he aged. From the energetic if imperceptive sailor he once had been, he turned into an obstinate, hard-hearted and bigoted man, indecisive in a crisis. Nevertheless things began quite well; James was welcomed as the new sovereign, just as Mary had been, as people thought he should be given his chance. So James appointed as his ministers his brother-in-law, Rochester, Clarendon's son; Lord Halifax, whose speech in the House of Lords had brought about the defeat of the Exclusion Bill; and Lord Godolphin, a most able financier.

One of his James' first acts was to take his revenge on Titus Oates, who was accused of perjury in the Popish Plot, and then flogged and imprisoned. Roman Catholic dignitaries still in prison because of the plot were released.   However there was to be no quarter for the Nonconformists: Baxter, one of their leading ministers, was convicted after a grossly unfair trial under Judge Jeffries.

Charles' new powers in the boroughs had proved so successful in eliminating recalcitrant Whigs that when a new Parliament was elected, James himself exclaimed that "there were not above forty members but such as he himself wished for". James had continued to collect custom duties before Parliament had met to approve them – sensible, but unconstitutional – but this proved no problem within Parliament, which also voted new taxes on sugar and tobacco.

Meanwhile Charles' illegitimate son Monmouth made a bid for power, in association with his fellow exile, Argyll. Argyll landed in Scotland but was quickly captured and executed. Monmouth landed in Dorset and set off for the manufacturing districts of Somerset, where he was popular with the clothiers. He gathered around him a rag-tag army of peasants, weavers and colliers, but received no support from the nobility and was soon confronted by the standing army of trained troops, led by Faversham and Churchill (later Marlborough). The two sides met at Sedgemoor in the last pitched battle ever fought on English soil. The result was a predictable defeat for Monmouth (1685). The army showed little mercy on the field, and the battle was followed by something just as bad. Judge Jeffries was sent to try the prisoners, and his cruelty gained him eternal infamy as the author of the Bloody Assize. More than three hundred men were executed, including Monmouth, and eight hundred others were transported to the American colonies.

The failure of the insurrection gave James confidence, and he set about his scheme for securing the ascendancy of the Catholics. His first step was to remove Halifax from the Privy Council (Halifax had also been a leading minister under Charles), then he made Jeffries Lord Chancellor. Then drastic news was received from abroad – Louis XIV revoked the Edict of Nantes (1685), which had granted toleration to the French Protestants from the time of Henry IV in 1598. This move greatly alarmed the English Protestants, and it had other, major impacts. The Huguenots were some of the most industrious and energetic people in France. Hundreds of thousands of them left the country, including approximately 40,000 finding their way to England and 10,000 to Ireland. Many more went to Prussia, Holland, North America and elsewhere. They formed an important addition to the relatively small population in the Cape of Good Hope where a Dutch colony had been founded in 1652. Their departure seriously damaged the French economy over the long term.

James now began to go about promoting Catholics in earnest. The main obstacle was the Test Act of 1673, but James believed it was his prerogative to grant dispensations from this to private individuals. He brought a test case in front of his judges (who were never independent of the king in these times) and won the verdict. After this he began to put Catholics into many positions, for example replacing the Protestant

Lord Deputy of Ireland by a Catholic, Tyrconnel. Rochester refused to change his religion and was removed from the Treasury. To secure his hold over the church, James also illegally set up a new court of Ecclesiastical Commission, with Jeffreys at its head. To overawe the capital, James formed an army of 13,000 men on Hounslow Heath.

Armed with his Ecclesiastical Commission, James now suspended the Bishop of London, then tackled the universities, firstly Cambridge where the Vice-Chancellor was deprived of his office for failing to award a degree to a Benedictine monk, which he could not legally do. At Oxford the Fellows of Magdalen were all replaced by Catholics when they refused to appoint a Catholic as their president. In this way, James contrived to alienate the Church of England and the universities. In 1687 there was more of the same when James issued a Declaration of Indulgence to suspend the penal statutes against both Catholics and Nonconformists. He then appointed a Jesuit to the Privy Council and it was clear enough that, though the Catholics did not number more than one in thirty of the population, they would soon have a disproportionate amount of power.

For two years no Parliament had sat. However James had great confidence in the influence of the crown, which had the power to remodel the corporations which selected the members, so he thought he could assemble a Parliament which would confirm his Declaration of Indulgence. So he wrote to the lords-lieutenant of the counties and to magistrates, asking them to put forward and support Catholic and Nonconformist candidates. Ominously, though many had fought for Charles I, many did not reply, and some resigned, only to be immediately replaced by Catholics. James also hoped for support from the Nonconformists, but they judged the temper of the nation better than he did, concluding that no free Parliament would accept the Declaration of Indulgence, and so rebuffed James.

There now happened an event which sealed the fate of James. Up until now the nation had been patient with him because it was assumed that he would soon be succeeded by Mary and William. Then it was announced that James' second wife, Mary of Modena, was pregnant. If the child was a boy it would be the heir to the throne and would of course be another Catholic, so the present system would become perpetual.

James now pushed the Anglican clergy too far. In April 1688 he issued a second Declaration of Indulgence and required that it be read out in all established churches on successive Sundays. To be asked to publish this unlawful decree to their own parishioners was more than the most strenuous supporters of non-resistance could bear. Seven of the bishops asked to be excused, and were sent to the Tower. Then on 10 June, a baby boy was born to the queen. The king was foolish enough not to ask his Protestant daughter, Anne, or any other Protestant lady, to be present, though the palace was crowded with enthusiastic Catholics. So the Protestants put about a rumour that the queen had not been pregnant and that a baby had been smuggled into the palace in a bedpan. This story was widely believed. Three weeks later the seven bishops were tried for libel, but despite the most strenuous efforts on the part of the crown, a verdict of Not Guilty was returned. There were huge celebrations in London.

Still James may have been safe if he had retained the support of his army on Hounslow Heath. However, the camp had become a picnic ground. The soldiers mixed with the common people, shared their sympathies and supported the acquittal of the bishops with enthusiasm. James visited the camp and discovered these sentiments. That very night, a letter was sent to William of Orange, inviting him to bring an army and take over the country. This was signed not only by the leading Whigs including Russell (cousin of the Lord Russell executed in 1683) and Sidney, but also by Danby and the leading Tories, and the Archbishop of Canterbury. Though wary of moves against him by Louis XIV, William set about preparations. He was concerned that Louis might stir up trouble amongst William's own enemies in Holland, but Louis then alienated the Dutch burghers by passing a law against their trade. William also worried that bringing over a Dutch army could arouse the patriotism of the English against him, but James brought over Irish regiments, which disgusted the English soldiery. So William then issued a declaration that he was bringing an army to secure a free and legal Parliament, by whose decisions he would abide.

Now the danger was clear, James began to reverse his rash decisions, but it was too late. William and his large fleet set sail, hoping to land in Yorkshire, far away from James' army, and gather support from the country. However, once at sea the fleet was driven down the Channel by a north-east wind, as far as Devon, where the wind turned and blew it into shore at Torbay on 5 November 1688. William had been lucky as the same north-east wind confined the English fleet which was to intercept him, and whose affiliations were uncertain, in the Thames estuary. So this wind was known as the Protestant wind. James led his army out to meet William at Salisbury, but Churchill and many other officers and men walked over to William's side. Princess Anne deserted her father and joined insurgents in the north. James sent his wife and baby away, then fled himself, throwing his great seal of office into the Thames on his way. This relieved William of much embarrassment. In fact, James was apprehended as a suspected smuggler by fishermen, and brought back to London, but was then allowed to escape once more to safety at the court of Louis XIV in France.

William arrived in London and summoned a Convention – a Parliament in all but name – which met at the beginning of 1689. This offered the crown jointly to William and Mary. It also drew up a Declaration of Rights to affirm the fundamental principles of the constitution. This brought to a close the struggle between king and Parliament which had carried on throughout Stuart times. Amongst other things, it excluded from the throne all who were "Papists", or who were married to Papists. It abolished the Ecclesiastical Commission and the standing army in times of peace. It called for free elections of members of Parliaments, regular Parliaments and free speech within Parliament.

The Glorious Revolution or Whig Succession destroyed the Stuart idea of the divine right of kings, and changed the succession in favour of a king and queen who owed their position to the choice of Parliament. So here effectively began the reign of Parliament. Up until this point, the main force in directing the policy of the nation had been the king, but after the Revolution, it was Parliament. But there was no doubt that the Revolution also meant war with Louis XIV of France.

* * * *

It was during the reign of James II, in fact in 1687, that one of the greatest scientific works of all time was published in England. This was the *Principia Mathematica*, or to give it its full title in English, *The Mathematical Principles of Natural Philosophy*. This difficult book, written in three volumes and in Latin, swept away forever the mumbo-jumbo of astronomical ideas derived from Aristotle and the Greeks. It established the laws of motion and the principles of gravity, and made possible the more-or-less exact prediction of the movements of the heavenly bodies in the solar system. Newton (1643-1727) had evolved the main ideas behind the book in his twenties, but now he set them down to be available to all learned men. He himself said that if he had seen further than others, it was by standing on the shoulders of giants.

By this he particularly meant the Italian Galileo, who in the previous generation had begun the real development of the laws of motion and who invented a telescope by which he identified the first four moons of Jupiter. Other notable contributors had been Copernicus and Kepler.

One reason the book was written in Latin was to stop ignorant busybodies reading it, but of course it did make it immediately available to anyone in Europe who understood Latin. The importance of the work was immediately recognised throughout Europe, and Newton became a celebrity. One of the greatest minds ever to come out of England, his was a flawed nature. He delved deeply and unsuccessfully into alchemy, spent a great deal of time on religion, and was almost certainly a homosexual. Nevertheless his great work stood the test of time, only receiving any serious modification at the time of Einstein. It was the latter who realised that more rules where needed when motion approached the speed of light. Newton also made important contributions in other fields, notably optics. In the next reign, he got a good job from the government.

Chapter 23 – The Later Stuarts

<u>William and Mary 1689-1702 (13 years)</u>
William, born 1650, married 1677. Mary, born 1662, died 1694

Contemporary rulers:
France
Louis XIV
1643-1715

Foreign, lacking the common touch and small in height, William was never likely to be especially popular, unlike his wife Mary, who was engaging in her character and of direct descent. Within England there was still a lingering dislike of the Dutch after three recent wars – the last ending only 15 years previously – and great commercial rivalry throughout the century. Also William always preferred a Dutchman ahead of an Englishman, be it as a councillor or a soldier. However, he was certainly a Protestant, of Calvinistic leanings, and favoured toleration in religion. The most important thing which defined him was his anti-French foreign policy. He rightly regarded the overmighty and ambitious Louis XIV as a threat to the interests of both Holland and England. The critical point in his life had come in 1672, when Louis XIV invaded the Low Countries. Up until that point, the Dutch burghers had contrived to keep William from the post of Stadtholder – effectively, king – of the United Provinces (Holland). However, they now needed a leader, and William, whose father had held the position, was their man. William organized an alliance with Spain (still in charge in the Spanish Netherlands, modern Belgium) and Austria, and so managed to drive the French out of Holland.

William's views inclined him naturally to the Whigs, who agreed with him that it would be preferable to take on Louis abroad than give him peace to organize an invasion of England. At the same time, William did not wish to alienate the Tories, who had joined with the Whigs to invite him to England, so he formed a ministry of the leaders of both parties. Danby came back as President of the Council, Halifax was Privy Seal and Godolphin was put in charge of the Treasury Board. James' servile judges were dismissed and replace by twelve new ones.

The Convention continued business as a real Parliament. It voted an annual revenue of £1,200,000 of which £700,000 was given for the support of the crown, the rest being voted from time to time according to estimates drawn up by the ministers. The first of these sums was called the Civil List. In this way, Parliament secured a much firmer hold on royal expenditure than it had ever had previously.

In order to weed out all persons disaffected with the new arrangements, a new oath of allegiance and supremacy was imposed on all office-holders in both church and state. Many refused to take the oath, including seven bishops and three hundred clergy. These people were known as the non-jurors, and were deprived of their places.

The Declaration of Rights had outlawed the standing army in times of peace, but more sensible counsel now prevailed as it was clearly too dangerous to try to survive without one, so two measures were agreed by Parliament to control such an army. One was the Mutiny Act, to be passed annually, so that if it was not renewed, the legal authority of the government over the soldiers would cease. Secondly it was agreed that money for the army would only be voted annually.

The Nonconformists were rewarded for their refusal to support James by the passing of a Toleration Act, which gave them freedom of worship. However, their political disabilities were left untouched, and nothing at all was done for the Catholics.

In 1690, a new Parliament met, with a Tory majority that could still be partially put down to the remodeling of the corporations which had taken place under Charles. The leader of the government was once again Danby, now created Marquess of Carmarthen. It passed an Act of Grace, indemnifying from prosecution all but a handful of people who had been involved in the shenanigans of the two previous reigns. For the times, this was a very small number, and showed what a quiet revolution it had been.

In Ireland, the revolution in England brought about events which reverberate to this day. Trouble could only be expected because James II had favoured the Catholics. A rebellion against the English duly arose, led by Tyrconnel, James' own Lord Deputy, the aim being complete independence. The Protestants of Ulster came under attack.

The Scottish settlers retired into Londonderry and the Cromwellians into Enniskillen, while James himself arrived to take charge. However after a hard siege of four months, Londonderry was relieved, and the Irish were beaten outside Enniskillen. Then in the summer of 1690 there was a full-scale confrontation between William's troops and an Irish army under James at the River Boyne, north of Dublin. William won the day, called the Battle of the Boyne (1690) and James fled back to France.

As expected war between England and Holland on the one side and France on the other had been declared in 1689. The French got much the best of a naval engagement, the Battle of Beachy Head (1690), but the Anglo-Dutch fleet managed to withdraw in reasonable order into the Thames. The French withdrew after burning Teignmouth. The Dutch came off much the worst. They had failed to follow their battle instructions, but their anger afterwards caused Mary to send the most humiliating apology ever sent to an ally. This is probably the only naval battle in history after which both admirals were disgraced. The loser, Torrington, was court-martialled because he failed to engage the enemy with his own squadron. The French admiral was dismissed because he meekly withdrew most of his fleet to Brest after the battle. He did not succeed in supporting James in Ireland, or interfere with William's movements across the Irish Sea, and handed back control of the Channel to the English and Dutch. (Torrington was not a popular man. Pepys said of him "Of all the worst men living, he is the only man that I do not know to have any one virtue to compound for all his vices". However, he was acquitted at court-martial.)

William returned to England as a war hero while mopping up operations in Ireland were left under Ginkel, a Dutchman, and Churchill, now Lord Marlborough. Ginkel forced his way across the Shannon into Connaught, where he beat the Irish at the Battle of Aughrim (1691). Limerick was besieged and fell. Meanwhile, Marlborough subdued the south. Protestant rule was restored and the Catholics found themselves worse off than they had been before the rebellion.

The greater part of the fighting with France took place in the Netherlands, where Louis secured a number of strong fortresses, the most important of which was Namur. English troops fought in this theatre alongside the Dutch, and this is another example, to be repeated under the Hanoverians, of England being dragged into Continental entanglements because of their sovereign's overseas possessions. However it also serves as an example of the policy of keeping the Low

Countries – the mouths of the Rhine, Maas and Scheldt – neutral, and out of the hands of major powers, this time France, but in the twentieth century Germany.

In Scotland the majority, the Presbyterians, had been subjected to severe persecution in the previous two reigns. A Convention was called which accepted William and Mary virtually without opposition. There was however a Highland rebellion in favour of James. The Highlanders beat an army of regular troops in the Battle of Killiecrankie, but their leader was killed and they dispersed. A proclamation was then issued, ordering all Highland chiefs to swear allegiance to William and Mary by 1 January, 1692. By a series of accidents, one of them, Alastair Maclain, chief of the MacDonald clan, failed to meet this date. His enemies, the rival Campbell clan, took advantage to obtain an order to "extirpate" the MacDonalds. Sufficient enquiry was not made before the order was issued. Soldiers were sent into the glens and lived with the MacDonalds on the most friendly terms until word was received that all the passes were secured. They then turned on their hosts in the middle of the night, and 38 of the MacDonalds were killed, with another 40 dying later of cold and hunger. This was the infamous Massacre of Glencoe (1692), and it embittered the Highlanders against the government and the remaining MacDonalds against the Campbells for a very long time – some would say to this day.

In the spring of 1692, James and the French prepared an invasion of England, collecting a large fleet at Brest and an army on the Normandy coast, for which transports were ready in La Hogue. The danger was pressing and it was known that the English admiral, Russell, was in correspondence with the exiled king. However James then issued a proclamation in which he declared that if he was successful, then a large number of people of all classes would feel his vengeance. This was circulated by Queen Mary in England, where it roused the whole country in indignation. Suitably maddened, the English sailors under Russell attacked the French fleet ferociously off Cape Barfleur on the Cotentin peninsula. The French fleet was utterly destroyed, as were the transports which had been collected for the army. James himself watched the action from a vantage point onshore, and was filled with patriotic pride as the English fleet attacked, exclaiming "Ah, none but my brave English could do so brave an action!" The Battle of La Hogue/Barfleur (1692) was the most important English naval victory from the Armada to Trafalgar and put to an end any French ideas of invasion. The French admiral, Tourville, had known that he was hopelessly outgunned, and was forced into action by military thinkers in

Paris with little understanding of the unpredictability of sea battles, dependent as they were on the vagaries of the wind and the weather. Louis XIV did not blame Tourville for the defeat, however – in fact he pinned a medal on him for the glorious way his ships had borne down so bravely on the enemy against impossible odds. After this defeat, Louis switched from naval construction to raids against enemy merchant ships by small, fast squadrons, at first with a great deal of success.

Things were not going so well in Europe, however. Many thought that William would not be able to stand up to James and Louis XIV, and some of the most important statesmen of the day kept up a correspondence with James in case he should return, including Marlborough and Shrewsbury. William was in fact fully aware of this, and by 1692 felt strong enough to dismiss Marlborough from all his offices.

It was certainly the case that the English contingent in Europe did not have the experience to match Louis' veterans, though they were acquiring it for good use later on. William spent each summer campaigning in the Netherlands, but he conceded defeats in 1692 and 1693. In 1694 an English attempt to storm the port of Brest in France was beaten off – the French had been tipped off by the disgraced Marlborough. The tide finally turned when William took Namur in 1695. This was the last major confrontation of the war, which was ended two years later by the Peace of Ryswick (1697). Under this, France conceded all territorial gains made since the previous Treaty of Nijmegen in 1678, and acknowledged William as King of England. The treaty was the cause of great rejoicing in England, but not in France. Louis had intervened in territorial disputes and with the monarchy in England at enormous expense and had come away with nothing. If James had been reinstalled then he would have been little more than a French puppet. The ambitions of Louis XIV were as costly and as fruitless to France as the Hundred Years War had been to England, because when they saw the balance of power tipping against them, his neighbours formed alliances against him, and he made no progress. (In fact the conflict of 1688-1697 is sometimes known as the War of the Grand Alliance, or the War of the League of Augsburg.) However, the main reason that all wars came to an end after six or seven years in this period is that both sides ran out of money.

1693 saw the institution of another permanent feature of the economic landscape, the National Debt, brainchild of Montague, Chancellor of the Exchequer, the idea being that money would be lent to the nation rather than to the king personally. William's position was so precarious – depending as it did on the outcome of the next battle in the Netherlands – that it would have been very difficult for him to raise money on his own credit for the heavy expenses of the war. So the National Debt was guaranteed by Parliament, not by the king, and it voted specific taxes to pay for it. It would have been poor politics to try to fund the war from heavy taxation. The National Debt was good politics, because people who lent money were eager supporters of the Revolution, fearing that if William were deposed, the debt might be repudiated. All governments since this time have found the National Debt extremely useful, because it can be increased rapidly to meet sudden heavy expenditure – as in wartime – and paid down in more stable times.

In 1694 another great national institution was founded by a Scotsman, William Paterson – the Bank of England, at first a private company. It received deposits and was allowed to issue promises to pay on demand – the first English banknotes. People with capital felt they could safely deposit it with the Bank, which in turn could lend to people it felt it could trust, to the benefit of both parties. But first and foremost, the Bank existed to lend to the government. Economic conditions were so dire at the time of its foundation that its first loans of this type were struck at the rate of eight percent. It also supervised the National Debt. In 1695 the Scots, seizing a good idea, founded the Bank of Scotland, but this was primarily a trading bank.

The National Debt and the Bank of England resulted from the introduction of Dutch-style financial methods following the accession of William and Mary. There was to be no more of the monarch scrabbling around for expensive credit. In practice, their existence made the funding of wars and naval expenditure much easier, and from their foundation dates the real growth of England as a major European power.

Another boost to trade from 1696 was the renewal of the coinage. Coins were not issued with milled edges, but were smooth, and clipping was common. This was bad for trade, partly because merchants wished to weigh the money before accepting it, and therefore found it difficult to trade at a distance. All the bad coinage was called in and paid for with new coins to the full value, the nation taking the cost of the difference. This may have been a costly exercise but it was a great boon to trade. After the renewal, the great mathematician Sir Isaac Newton was made Warden of the Royal Mint (itself an ancient institution), whose job was to ensure the purity of the coinage, and to pursue counterfeiters. He worked in this capacity from 1699 until his death in 1727.

In 1694 there were further developments in the constitution when the Triennial Act was passed. The purpose of this was to limit the length of one Parliament to three years, after which there must be an election to select a new one. The Whigs worried that if the king obtained a House which was favorable to himself, he would not dissolve it for years; indeed Charles II had kept one Parliament sitting for seventeen years without dissolution. In the matter of the freedom of the press, a Licensing Act had been passed at the Restoration, limiting the printing of books and pamphlets to certain specific centres. This was to try and stem the flood of seditious pamphlets. In 1695 this act expired, and was not renewed by Parliament, establishing the freedom of the press (subject to the laws of libel).

As might be expected, in these times there were a number of plots aiming to assassinate the king. After Mary died of smallpox, the danger increased, because his single life might be thought to stand in the way of a restoration. In 1696 a plot to kill William was organized by one Sir George Barclay, who planned to murder him on his return from hunting in a lane near Newbury. There is little doubt that James was well aware of this plot, for a large French army had been assembled ready to cross the Channel had it succeeded. However it was uncovered, and caused great indignation in the country.

To protect people accused of treason, the law was changed to allow them more rights. By the law of Edward VI there had to be at least two witnesses, yet Algernon Sidney had been condemned under Charles II on the evidence of only one, and the testimony afforded by some unpublished papers found on his desk. The new provisions also allowed for witnesses of the accused to be questioned under oath; this had not been possible previously. The new provisions, though they did protect the innocent, actually made it much harder to convict the guilty. In the case of Sir John Fenwick, tried in 1697, a guilty man nearly escaped – his wife contrived to convey one of the two witnesses against him out of the country. As in the case of Strafford, a bill of attainder had to be used instead.

One effect of Mary's death was to bring about the rapprochement of William and Marlborough. The heir to the throne was Anne, second daughter of James II, and Marlborough's wife Sarah was her best friend and had great influence over her. Marlborough (rightly) foresaw the prospect of unfettered power in her accession.

The peace of Ryswick had a great effect on William's position, as it removed all fear of a French invasion. In 1698 there was a general election, which returned a Tory majority unsympathetic to William. The Tories were smarting under the heavy taxation which had fallen on the landed gentry, who had not shared in the trade boom with the mercantile classes. Moreover the Tories did not live in constant fear of the bogeyman Louis XIV, as William did. Accordingly Parliament at once reduced the size of the army to 10,000 men, and in 1699, much to William's disgust, sent home the Dutch guards, his favorite soldiers. There were also gripes about the way William had granted land from dispossessed Irish rebels to his Dutch favorites. Nevertheless, in line with the new system, William dismissed his Whig advisers and appointed a Tory administration in its place, led by Rochester and Godolphin.

The heir to the throne, James II's second surviving daughter Anne, had nineteen children, but the last surviving one of these died in 1700. Therefore it became necessary to make new arrangements for the succession. James II and all Catholics were disregarded, and by the Act of Settlement (1701) the choice of the succession after Anne fell to Sophia, wife of the Elector of Hanover. She was the daughter of Elizabeth, Queen of Bohemia, and granddaughter of James I. Also, the Act of Settlement established the independence of the judiciary. Judges were to be appointed for life, were to receive a fixed salary, and could not be removed except on conviction of some offence. These arrangements cleared away the abuses of the judicial system which had taken place under the earlier Stuarts, and in fact continue in place to this day.

In the new century, all Europe was arming. The problem was the Spanish succession. In 1700 the Spanish king Charles II died with no direct heir. There were two leading candidates for the throne. One of these was a Bourbon, Philip, grandson of Louis XIV. The Spaniards offered him the throne as Philip IV – an offer which delighted Louis XIV, who declared that "the Pyrenees have ceased to exist". To add fuel to the flames, Louis poured troops into the Spanish Netherlands. Also, one of his opening moves after the accession of his Philip IV in Spain was to exclude the English and the Dutch from trade with Spain and her colonies. The "asiento" to supply the Spanish colonies with slaves was awarded to a French company. One of the principal war aims of the English was to reestablish this Spanish trade. Meanwhile James II died, and Louis, in spite of the Treaty of Ryswick, recognised his son as James III. Not having recovered financially from the last

234

war, which had finally concluded only in 1697, no nation wanted to fight another, but Louis, who could afford it least of all, made it inevitable by his actions.

The other candidate for the Spanish throne was a Hapsburg, the Archduke Charles of Austria, and the Austrians were surely not going to take the selection of a rival Bourbon lying down. However, just as the stage was set for a pan-European war, William fell from his horse and broke his collar bone. He should have survived such a minor injury, but he did not, dying shortly afterwards.

William never won the warmth of national sympathy, in a way that say the severe Elizabeth had done. He was after all a foreigner. However, he had led the country successfully through a great crisis, and had for the first time shared power successfully with Parliament, so he is still counted amongst the most successful kings of England.

One intriguing question – a "what if" of history – is, what would have happened if William and Mary had produced heirs? William had been the King of England and the Stadtholder of the Netherlands. This form of joint monarchy could easily have been continued, when in fact it was dissolved with the death of William. Given the common interests of England and the Netherlands in fighting back French ambitions, it is possible that this link could have continued over generations, as did that between England and Scotland, eventually leading to political union between the two countries.

Anne 1702-1714 (12 years)
Born 1665, married 1683, Prince George of Denmark

Contemporary rulers:
France
Louis XIV
1643-1715

Anne was a very different sovereign from her predecessor. William had towered head and shoulders above the his domestic statesmen in political stature. He had been his own foreign minister and commander-in-chief, and his wishes had been the main influence on domestic and foreign policy. Anne, however, took her ideas from others, and had long been under the dominating influence of Sarah Churchill, wife of Marlborough. So the most important person for the first part of the reign was Marlborough – a soldier, not a politician. By inclination a Tory, he set up a mixed ministry with himself as commander-in-chief, Nottingham as Secretary of State and the perennial (Tory) Godolphin as Lord Treasurer. But this reign was destined to be a continuation of the last one, because there had been no regime change in France, and the bogeyman Louis XIV was making his latest foray.

The War of the Spanish Succession opened at once in the campaigning season of 1702. It was indeed wide ranging, having four main theatres: Spain; the Netherlands, overrun in the first instance by the French; the Rhineland, where several small German states joined the Austrians to take on the French; and Italy, where the French hoped to occupy the Spanish-held Duchy of Milan. From the English point of view, this war was to be quite untypical of other wars in the eighteenth century, when it became the custom to subsidise foreign armies in Europe, whilst fighting the good fight at sea. In this war, there were no great sea battles, but an English army under an English general stayed in the field.

Marlborough's first great exploit was to seize Liege, in the Low Countries, in 1702, and a line of forts, removing the French threat to Holland. For this he was made a duke and given a pension of £5000 a year. The next year he made himself the master of the lower course of the Rhine, of which Bonn was the chief fortress.

The next summer, 1704, the Elector of Bavaria joined the French, and combined with a large French army under Talland which was making for Vienna. Marching south and joining the Austrians under Prince Eugene of Savoy, Marlborough then led the combined army to beat a Bavarian force at Donauwerth. The Anglo-Dutch-Austrian army then confronted and crushed the French and Bavarians at Blenheim, on the Danube (1704). Bavaria was knocked out of the war, the road to Vienna was closed to the French, and the French borders themselves would come under pressure. It was indeed a great victory – the greatest by an English army in Europe since Agincourt – but what were they doing fighting on the Danube? Marlborough had taken a great risk in marching the English army further away from home than any since the Black Prince in his Spanish campaign, by now three hundred years earlier. It could be argued that Marlborough should have confined himself to the Low Countries where the English interest was clear for all to see. Still it was a gamble which paid off. A grateful English Parliament granted the Duke an estate near Woodstock, where Blenheim Palace was subsequently constructed and where Winston Churchill was later born.

Of much greater long-term strategic significance was the capture from Spain in the same year of Gibraltar by an English naval force under Sir George Rooke and the wonderfully-named Sir Cloudesley Shovel. This fortified rock guards the narrow entrance to the Mediterranean and proved to be of incalculable value in the centuries ahead, most notably in the Second World War. During this war, the English fleet overwintered for the first time in the Mediterranean – a sure sign of its growing size and importance. A sea battle was fought against the French off Malaga in 1704, but it was indecisive.

Returning to the Low Countries, Marlborough won another famous victory against the French at Ramillies in 1706. Adept at manoeuvre and quick to spot an opportunity on the battlefield, he was becoming one of England's great generals. This victory obliged the French to quit Antwerp and Brussels, forcing them back to the border fortresses of the Spanish Netherlands. In 1708 Marlborough, combining once again with Prince Eugene, beat the French again at Oudenarde, and so was able to occupy the city of Lille. In 1709 Marlborough confronted the French once more at Malplaquet and recorded yet another victory in a scene of great slaughter. He lost 24,000 men to French losses of 10,000, causing the French general, Villars, to comment that he could use a few more defeats like that, and shocking public opinion in Britain and Holland. Nevertheless, Lille, Tournai and Mons were now in Marlborough's hands and the road to France was open.

The English also took the war to mainland Spain with an army of allies, at one point even taking Madrid, which they then lost to an army led by the Duke of Berwick, a natural son of James II (Battle of Almanza, 1708). The English also took Barcelona and the island of Minorca. They also attacked French colonies overseas, taking Newfoundland and Nova Scotia in North America, though an attack on Canada itself failed.

Whilst the English fought the war, the Scots were trying to recover from some murky business of their own in what is now Panama, Central America. An ambitious plan was created by William Paterson, the same man who had founded the Bank of England, to establish a Scottish colony at Darien, with the hope of creating a new trade route to the Far East. The first expedition set off with 1200 people in 1698. They found the place pestilential, humid and hot and very quickly large numbers began to die of malaria and other tropical fevers. King William instructed the English colonies in that part of the world not to supply the Scots, for fear of upsetting the Spaniards. After only eight months the colony was abandoned, with only 300 people returning home. Word of this failure did not get back until a second expedition with 2500 on board had already set off. Few of these survived. The Scots tried to blame the English; one desperate returning ship from the first expedition had been turned away from Jamaica on the orders of the English government, but really the Scots should have ensured the cooperation of the English, if not the Spaniards, before embarking on the adventure at all.

The Scots had invested heavily in the Darien fiasco and were now desperately short of money, so the idea was mooted of a full union with England and Wales. It had long been the desire of the Scots to participate in trade with the English colonies, from which they were excluded by the Navigation Acts. It is this commercial interest which brought Scotland into the Union and which has kept it there ever since. The Scots, on the other hand, worried that their Presbyterian Church might suffer in a union, and that the laws and customs peculiar to them might be altered. As temperatures rose on both sides of the border, each side began to implement measures against the other. However, saner counsel prevailed. A Commission set up to enquire into the matter gave the Scots the assurances they needed concerning their church and their laws. A payment of £398,000 was made from the English to the Scots, which was used to pay off the Scottish national debt and to indemnify the shareholders of the Darien company, and which offset the future liability of the Scots for their share of the existing English national debt. At least it represented ready money for some of the most influential people in Scotland.

The Act of Union was completed in 1707 and at first was most unpopular in Scotland, where it was felt that there had been a sellout of the whole nation in the interests of a small minority of money men. However, Scotland soon began to reap the benefits of participation in the English trading and colonial systems. The Union was to make the fortune of Scotland. The rapid growth of Glasgow and the whole Strathclyde area followed its completion. For the English, there was far less need to worry about the threat from the north, present for centuries, or of any more Scottish alliances with the French. It greatly lessened the force of wars with the French, which henceforth were confined to the Continent.

The Whigs had gained the ascendancy in Marlborough's administration, but the long war tried the patience of the nation and the ministry lost popularity. Nevertheless the Whigs held their own by the support of the commercial and middle classes. However by 1708 the Tories had managed to replace Sarah Churchill in the affections of Queen Anne by one of their own supporters, Mrs Abigail Hill. In 1710 the Whigs made a great mistake by prosecuting a Tory minister of the church, one Dr Sacheverell. This made a martyr of him and 40,000 copies of his sermon attacking the government were sold. Anne seized this turn of the tide to dismiss the Whigs and replace them by Tories, led by Harley and St John. Marlborough alone remained as commander-in-chief of the army, though he too was replaced (by the Duke of Ormond, a Tory) before long. The Tories represented the country party, which detested the money men of London, the high taxes needed to support the war and the whole idea of deficit financing by the Bank of England, which threatened to upset the old order of things completely (as indeed it did). Also by this stage England had developed a highly efficient, nationwide revenue collection service. Taxes were high as a result of the war, but they were fairly distributed across the different classes of society, and were seen to be so. The contrast with France, a much more populous country, could not have been greater. There, a large part of the nobility and clergy had gained exemption from taxation, there were huge regional disparities, and collection was shambolic and unfair. Debts for earlier wars had been partly cleared by the sale of tax-exempt offices, often hereditary, which both deprived the French government of long-term tax revenue and locked it into the permanent payment of annuities and salaries. But to the Tories, the revenue men were yet another sign of the times, and one that they did not like.

The Tories soon lost support, however, by attempting to convict Marlborough for peculation – taking a percentage of the large amount of money which had passed through his hands. Everyone knew that the Duke was fond of money, but nothing irregular could be proved. The Tories did succeed in impeaching Robert Walpole for similar offences. He had supported Marlborough as Secretary for War. Though his guilt was doubtful he was sent to the Tower. These vindictive attacks alienated the public from the Tories.

In 1711, after several failed attempts in previous years, the Occasional Conformity Act was passed, mainly under the influence of the Whigs. Under the Test and Corporation Acts, no one except an Anglican could hold public or military office. This obviously excluded Nonconformists, a good many of whom were otherwise very well qualified for the public service, and many of whom were prepared to take Anglican sacraments once, or occasionally, then simply resume attendance at their own chapels. The new act allowed them to do so and let this be a sufficient qualification for public service. This old-fashioned British compromise was really a large step towards toleration. No one was pretending that the Nonconformists had started to conform, but at the same time it was recognised that they formed part of the backbone of the supporters of the Revolution and the Act of Settlement – an act which was likely to need to rally all the support it could get when Anne, the last Protestant Stuart, died, and a completely alien dynasty was imposed. An attempt at a Restoration was inevitable.

The War of the Spanish Succession was finally ended by the Treaty of Utrecht in 1713. In 1711, the Hapsburg candidate, the Archduke Charles, had become Emperor, so his accession would have been as dangerous as that of the Bourbon Philip of France. So Philip was accepted as the king of Spain, on condition that the crowns of Spain and France should never be united. However, as a result of the war, he lost some important territories. The Spanish Netherlands now became the Austrian Netherlands. Their line of fortresses were partly to be garrisoned by Dutch troops and it was hoped that these would act as a barrier between France and Holland. Austria also gained the Duchy of Milan, Naples and Sardinia from Spain. Sicily passed to Savoy, and England kept both Gibraltar and Minorca. In the New World England was given a monopoly of the slave trade (the asiento) and the right (subsequently much abused) to send one ship a year to trade with the Spanish colonies. England kept Nova Scotia, Newfoundland and the island of St Christopher in the West Indies. Louis acknowledged the Protestant succession in England.

These advantages gained by England were very real, notably as the possessions which passed to England were not transferred elsewhere in the next war. Louis got his man onto the throne of Spain, but at great cost as the Spaniards lost their European possessions, notably to Austria, and even a small but strategically important part of their mainland. On the whole the Spaniards were the biggest losers, but Louis XIV, whose over-ambition had cost his country so dear, had fought yet another war at enormous expense and for limited returns. It would have been better for France if their magnificent king had had a shorter reign, as his foolishness and intolerance had also cost the country its Huguenot population. The Treaty of Utrecht was almost the last act in his reign of sixty-two years, as he was to die in 1715. Also amongst the losers were the Dutch, who had fought alongside Marlborough. They were on the winning side but they had seen their naval supremacy and dominance in trade pass to the English, or since the Union of 1707, the British.

Marlborough's star long having faded, the last few years of Anne's reign were dominated by the two Tories, Bolingbroke (formerly St John) and the Earl of Oxford (formerly Harley). Under Bolingbroke, a Schism Act was passed, by which only Anglicans could run schools – a return to the old intolerance. In the question of the succession, there was no real enthusiasm for either the Pretender James "III" or for Sophia of Hanover. The latter was now an old lady, and her grandson George (later George II) was invited to England to represent his family. Bolingbroke prevaricated.

As Anne lay dying in 1714, the Whig nobility acted decisively against Bolingbroke. Shrewsbury was made Lord Treasurer, a move which destroyed Bolingbroke's power. When Anne died the new team implemented the plans which had been made to enthrone the Hanoverians. As Sophia had died two months before Anne, the new king was her son, and was acclaimed as George I. The dithering Tories had been trounced by the Whigs who for the second time had acted to secure a Protestant succession.

Chapter 24 – The Early Hanoverians

George I 1714-27 (13 years)
Born 1660, married 1682, Sophia of Brunswick

Contemporary rulers:
France
Louis XIV 1643-1715
Louis XV 1715-1774

At the time of his accession, George I was already 54 years old, and very much set in his Germanic ways; indeed he did not speak English. So he was never likely to be a popular king. However, his departure was much regretted by his old Hanoverian subjects. In the matter of politics he continued to take a great interest in their affairs, and liked to have his own way there. In England, however, he trusted his ministers to do what they thought best, and in this way the system of constitutional party government became thoroughly well established. As the second monarch to be imposed on the country by the will of Parliament in less than thirty years, George was very much beholden to his connections there, but his unostentatious rule suited the country well enough. His personal morality was however questioned, as he arrived with two German mistresses, one immensely tall and the other very fat – christened the maypole and the elephant – whilst his wife was locked up for adultery!

This period – the Whig supremacy – was still a long way from modern politics. No prime minister calling himself a Tory was to take office for nearly fifty years. However in both major parties there were factions likely to vote against their own government. In the absence of anything resembling a Whip's Office, the members could do this with impunity. The Whigs were equally as aristocratic as the Tories, and elections to Parliament were widely rigged and could not necessarily be said to represent public opinion.

George made no attempt to form a mixed ministry, but installed the Whigs under Townshend, Stanhope and Walpole. This team immediately began the attack on the previous Tory incumbents, whom they accused of sacrificing English interests at the Treaty of Utrecht and of having intrigued to restore the Pretender. Bolingbroke and Ormond fled to France – where the Pretender resided. They were attainted in their absence, and Oxford was put in the Tower – all still rather medieval. An election then took place in such an atmosphere of disorder that a Riot Act was passed. This empowered the magistrates to employ soldiers to break up any gathering of more than twelve people who refused to disperse, and remains on the statute book to this day.

As expected, the accession of the Hanoverians was followed by a Jacobite rebellion. Though sympathy with the Stuarts was widespread, no insurrection in England had any hope of success without the backing of the regular army (which William III had had). In Scotland it was another matter, given the dissatisfaction with the Act of Union and the antagonism of the Highland clans to any form of constituted authority. The loyalist Argyll and his men stopped the advance of the clans in a battle at Sherriffmuir (1715) on the road from Perth to Stirling. The Pretender James Stuart, the "bedpan baby" who had taken over the claim of his father James II on his death in 1701, came to Scotland, but there was little he could do, so he soon returned to France. In England the small insurrection raised in the north was put down at the battle of Preston.

These miserable failures made it clear that no insurrection could succeed without foreign assistance. However, Louis XIV of France had finally died in 1715, to be succeeded by his great grandson Louis XV, a small boy in delicate health. The regent, his cousin the Duke of Orleans, was much more favorably disposed towards Britain than the previous regime, so no help was forthcoming to the Jacobites from France. There were however hostilities against Spain, unhappy with the loss of her territories in the Treaty of Utrecht. Admiral Byng destroyed the Spanish fleet, which was threatening Sicily, off Cape Passaro in 1718. The Spaniards landed a small force in Scotland which was defeated without difficulty.

At home the Septennial Act was passed in 1717, extending the term of Parliaments to seven years maximum. It replaced the Triennial Act of 1694, which had limited that term to three years, not thought enough to allow for a stable government to pass unpopular but necessary measures. This new, longer term did however allow the party in power plenty of time to consolidate its position and so favoured the incumbent Whigs. Now led by Stanhope, the Whigs proposed another measure to limit the extention of the peerage – the Peerage Bill – but this was rejected in the Commons, under the influence of Walpole, as it could have kept the Whig oligarchy in power indefinitely.

The South Sea Company was founded by act of Parliament in 1711 with exclusive rights to trade along the east coast of South America, from the Orinoco to Cape Horn, and in the Pacific – rights which included the slave trade, a monopoly of which was granted to Britain by the Treaty of Utrecht in 1713. One of the sponsors of the company was the Lord Treasurer himself, Robert Harley (Earl of Oxford), who was looking for a means to fund the government debts incurred in the war. The company prospered, to the extent that it made an offer to the Government to allow holders of the National Debt to transfer their holdings into South Sea Company shares. The government undertook to pay the company 5% on the loans it thus acquired – much less than the average level of interest on the National Debt. The shareholders meanwhile would be paid a dividend expected to be in excess of their old debt interest.

As there were so few investment opportunities available during this period, the scheme was a wild success, and shares in the company rocketed from £100 to £1000. This became known as the South Sea Bubble – the first of many such stock market bubbles right up to the dot.com bubble of 2000. The dividend yield for anyone paying £1000 a share was likely to be minimal – 5% would become .5% on level payments. Many rival schemes were soon mooted, many of them vague or ridiculous – such as a prospectus "for a wheel of perpetual motion" or "an undertaking of great advantage, but nobody to know what it is". The South Sea Company itself prosecuted some of the more absurd swindles in court, and the bubble quickly burst. South Sea shares fell to £135 – still a good premium on the issue price – and stayed at that level, which demonstrated the soundness of the original proposition. However many thousands of wealthy citizens had paid much more for their shares, and a general ruination followed. A few however had sold out in time, and these included Robert Walpole. He had opposed the South Sea bill in Parliament, but as he opposed everything put forward by his fellow Whig Stanhope, he got no credit for that. However it emerged that bribes had been given about the court and to certain members of Parliament by the company. Stanhope – who was not implicated – defended the government, but burst a blood vessel in doing so, collapsed and died. The government collapsed with him, and Walpole became the First Lord of the Treasury and Prime Minister (1721). Walpole was the first politician to whom this title was given. By 1724 Walpole had been joined by the Duke of Newcastle and his brother Henry Pelham, a pair who were to have a long run in government.

In 1724 problems flared up in Ireland. A Parliament sat in Dublin, but it was severely restricted in its powers. When Walpole tried to renew the Irish coinage, fierce agitation broke out in Ireland, as its Parliament had not been consulted. Feelings were fanned by the pamphleteer Dean Swift, writing under the title "Drapier". Walpole withdrew his scheme when he saw that the trouble was serious. However in 1727 a measure was passed, removing the franchise from all Catholic voters in Ireland. This measure meant that the Dublin Parliament could only represent one-sixth of the population.

By 1725 a regular opposition to the Walpole administration had formed in Parliament, under the disillusioned ex-Whig Pulteney and the Tory Bolingbroke. A daily opposition newspaper was printed to attack Walpole at every opportunity. Under the banner *The Craftsman*, it was the first paper of this type. Opposition centred around the Prince of Wales, the heir to the throne. This was to become a regular feature of Hanoverian politics, and while it did not reflect particularly well on the Hanoverians themselves, at least it stopped the Opposition leaders turning to the Pretender. As the attempts to remove Walpole continued, George I died suddenly in Hanover in 1727.

*   *   *   *

A little-remembered but important migration which went on throughout the eighteenth century reached a peak in the 1720s. This was the movement of Ulster Presbyterians to the North American colonies. As they suffered discrimination under the Test Acts, one motive was religious freedom from any such hindrances. More important was the simple opportunity the opening up of the New World offered to this largely poor rural population. The migration was given an impetus in the Irish famine of 1740-1, and then peaked again in the 1760s. It is thought that as many as 400,000 emigrants left Ulster in the course of the eighteenth century, the vast majority bound for North America, where they have formed a significant part of the community ever since.

George II 1727-60 (33 years)
Born 1683, married 1705, Caroline of Anspach

Like his father before him, George II was very much a German, having spent most of his 44 years in that country. Unlike his father, however, he was totally under the influence of his wife, Caroline of Anspach, who exercised as much influence on him as the Duchess of Marlborough had on Anne. In line with his sentiments as Prince of Wales, George's first act was to dismiss Walpole. In his place he appointed Sir Spencer Compton, the Speaker, but Compton proved so incompetent that Walpole was soon back in office – with the backing of Caroline.

In the years 1726-9 there was a small war with Spain – still smarting under the terms of the Treaty of Utrecht – but there were no major actions and a peace was concluded in 1729. The following year Lord Townshend – Walpole's brother-in-law – left the ministry, tired of his relation's overbearing conduct. Instead of going into opposition, Townsend devoted his time to agriculture, introducing the turnip into crop rotations. Turnips can be grown on land exhausted by cereals and indeed with a four-crop rotation (wheat, barley, turnips and clover) a fallow year was no longer needed. So Townshend has gone down in history as Turnip Townshend.

Following the Jacobite Revolt of 1715, steps were taken to improve access within the Highland area by the construction of roads, bridges and barracks. This work was undertaken under the supervision of General Wade in the period 1725-37, when 250 miles of roads were constructed. This military infrastructure was to prove its value in the second Jacobite Revolt of 1745-6.

In 1733 the opposition under Pulteney and Bolingbroke achieved its first real success against Walpole. He proposed a scheme to replace the excise duty levied on tobacco and wine at the ports with a much more widespread, smaller duty levied in the shops. One motive for this was to reduce smuggling. One impact of this scheme would have been an increase in the number of excisemen required to inspect goods liable to the tax. The idea of having the exciseman knocking at the door of any

246

Englishman's home was too much for the opposition and for the mob. It was also put about that the real purpose of the scheme was to create an army of excisemen who would be eligible to vote for the government in elections. Seeing trouble ahead, Walpole withdrew the bill. The measures were then introduced gradually without comment. The fact that fifty years later, it was found that seventy elections depended on the votes of excisemen, showed that the second argument against the scheme was not without foundation!

In 1736 Scotland was inflamed by the Porteous Riots. Captain Porteus had ordered his men to fire on an Edinburgh mob demonstrating in favour of a smuggler who was being hung. Porteous was condemned to death, then reprieved by the government, but the mob broke open the gaol and hanged him anyway. The city of Edinburgh was fined. These events form the background to *The Heart of Midlothian*, a novel by Sir Walter Scott.

The religious life of the country was revived in the reign of George II by the rise of the Methodists under John and Charles Wesley and George Whitfield, beginning in Oxford in 1730. At first the Methodists regarded themselves as a wing within the Church of England, but eventually they became an independent church, noted for their energy and clean living. The new religious movement was assisted by the immense popularity of Handel's "Messiah", first performed in 1742. A source of real religious inspiration, it caught hold all over the country very quickly. Its centrepiece, the "Hallelujah Chorus" was and remains the most forthright declaration of the Christian faith ever set to music. As Methodist churches were gradually constructed in every town and village to house the meetings formerly held in the open air and in barns, the "Messiah" is the only piece of music ever to change the landscape in England!

1739 saw the opening of the War of Jenkins' Ear, so-called after a British sea captain who had his ear cut off by Spanish coast guards in 1731. Conflicts over trade with the Spanish American colonies were endemic. The English had the right to send one ship a year to trade, but abused this right by repeatedly replenishing the ship from tenders, kept out of sight of land. The English colonies in North America and the Caribbean were always trying to set up contraband trade with the Spanish colonies. The Spaniards tried to stop this by searching English vessels and these many disputes eventually dragged Walpole into a war he had wished to avoid. When church bells rang to celebrate the declaration of war, he observed "They are ringing their bells now, but soon they will be ringing their hands." In the manner of James I,

Walpole was averse to continental conflicts. When asked by Queen Caroline why he kept Britain out of the War of the Polish Succession in 1734, he had replied, "Madam, there are fifty thousand dead in Europe this year, and not one English"

At first the war went well, Admiral Vernon capturing Porto Bello, a silver-exporting town on the coast of Panama. At a dinner held to celebrate this victory in London in 1741, "Rule Britannia" was sung in public for the first time. Portobello Road also takes its name from the victory. The success at Porto Bello encouraged Vernon to release a squadron of eight ships under Commodore Anson to attack Spanish possessions on the Pacific side of Spanish America. This famous expedition did capture a Spanish Acapulco galleon and with it much gold and other treasure. Setting off in 1740, Anson eventually returned to England in 1744 via the (Spanish) Philippines and China. Only one-tenth of his original complement of 1854 men survived the journey.

Meanwhile the war in the Caribbean continued. In the biggest action of the war, Vernon failed to take the port of Cartagena (in what is now Colombia) (1741). Disillusionment with the war set in at home. Despite extensive vote-rigging in the many rotten boroughs, Walpole could hold on no longer and was finally defeated in Parliament after the election of 1742.

The new prime minister was Spencer Compton, now ennobled as Lord Wilmington. The Duke of Newcastle and his brother Henry Pelham kept their places, the latter becoming prime minister himself on Wilmington's death in 1743.

After 1742 the Spanish war was subsumed by a larger conflict, the War of the Austrian Succession, when for the first time Britain was drawn into a continental conflict in support of Hanover and its ally, Austria. In 1740 the Austrian Emperor Charles VI had died, leaving his dominions to his daughter Maria Theresa. Questions were raised about a woman's right to become Emperor. Austria was at once attacked by Frederick II of Prussia (later Frederick the Great), who had chafed under Austrian domination of the court at Berlin during the reign of his more cautious father. For the first time, Prussia emerged as the dominant power in northern Europe, supplanting Sweden in that role. It had formed from the old Electorate of Brandenburg (capital Berlin) and the Duchy of Prussia (capital Koenigsberg), a Junker territory once run by the Teutonic Knights, which had passed to the rulers of Brandenburg - the Hohenzollerns. Frederick, flute-playing and almost certainly homosexual, had quarelled seriously with his father, but on succeeding him in 1742 showed unexpected flair in invading Austrian Silesia, a territory which was to remain in Prussian and then German hands until it was transferred to Poland at the end of the Second World War. Until Prussia itself was subsumed into Germany in 1871, it regularly allied with Britain against France, but in this war, it allied with France and so against England.

So France and also Bavaria joined Frederick. George II himself and his second son William, Duke of Cumberland, went in person to defend the Hanoverian interest, in an alliance with Maria Theresa. Their army of Hanoverians and Hessians caught the French at Dettingen in the Main valley and achieved a resounding victory (1743). This has gone down in history as the last major battle at which an English monarch was present. The victory gave great credit to the government, which was increased the following year by Anson's return from his circumnavigation with an enormous treasure of £1,250,000.

1745 saw defeat at the hands of the French at Fontenoy near Tournai in the Austrian Netherlands, a fortress garrisoned by Dutch troops. Lacking in support from the Dutch and the Hessians, the English under the Duke of Cumberland nevertheless fought with great credit. The next French move was an attempt at the invasion of Britain itself in support of the Young Pretender, Prince Charles Edward Stuart (1720-1788) (Bonny Prince Charlie), grandson of James II. A fleet was gathered and loaded with soldiers and equipment at Dunkirk, but this was scattered by a storm as it embarked (1744). Charles was then obliged to set off with only one armed support ship, loaded with arms and ammunition – but this was attacked by an English ship and ran for home. So Charles landed almost alone in Scotland in 1745. The clan chiefs were not impressed, and one of them advised him to return home. "I am come home, sir" replied Charles.

Here he raised the Highland clans and set off for Edinburgh. His tartan army met with government forces beside the Firth of Forth at Preston Pans. The Highlanders won the day, enormously increasing the prestige of the Pretender in Scotland, though most of the canny Lowlanders demurred to join him. Undeterred, Charles set off on the high road to England, where he marched as far as Derby and caused panic in London. Sensing themselves about to be trapped, his officers refused to continue and he was obliged to order the retreat back to Scotland. Here he managed to beat off a pursuing English army at Falkirk. In 1746, withdrawing as far north as Inverness, Charles' army finally succumbed to government troops under the Duke of Cumberland at Culloden Moor. So ended the Second Jacobite Revolt, or '45.

The Pretender spent five months evading capture in the Highlands, protected by loyal supporters (including the famous Flora Macdonald) before escaping back to France. His followers were not so fortunate as they were hunted down and executed by the "Butcher" Cumberland and his men. The clans were disarmed and forbidden to wear the kilt, and the hereditary jurisdiction of their chiefs was abolished. In addition a large and enormously expensive new castle was built near Inverness on the Moray Firth, called Fort George, in the period 1748-69. It survives to this day in its original Georgian form.

The War of the Austrian Succession continued until 1748 when it was concluded by the Treaty of Aix-la-Chapelle. This recognised the right of Maria Theresa to her dominions and for the most part restored the territorial *status quo ante bellum*, though Frederick II kept his gains in Silesia.

In domestic politics, the '45 saw the emergence of two new faces, William Pitt (the Elder) and Henry Fox. Pitt came from a family whose money had been made in India, and despite a lack of connections to the Whig grandees, he made rapid progress in Parliament, where his speaking abilities and freedom from mercenary motives were soon widely noted. Fox was an excellent debater and man of business. The opposition of these two young statesmen – and their obvious ability – was such a problem to Pelham and his ministers that they were brought into the administration in 1746. This was despite the objections of the king, who disliked Pitt intensely because of his attacks on the Hanoverian policy of taking soldiers from Hanover and Hesse onto the English payroll.

In 1751 the heir to the throne, Frederick, was killed by the ball whilst playing cricket. He is remembered in the epitaph:

Here lies poor Fred who was alive and is dead,
Had it been his father I had much rather,
Had it been his sister nobody would have missed her,
Had it been his brother, still better than another,
Had it been the whole generation, so much better for the nation,
But since it is Fred who was alive and is dead,
There is no more to be said!

In 1752 an important change was made to the calendar. Britain adhered to the old Julian calendar, which did not make sufficient allowance for leap years. Mainland Europe had switched to the Gregorian calendar, arranged by Pope Gregory XIII, in 1582. At the time, the English were too bigoted to accept anything from the Pope, and stuck to the old calendar, so that by 1752 the English date was eleven days behind the European date. The switchover was now made, so that September 2 was immediately followed by September 14. The change was much disliked: "Give us back our eleven days!" was the popular cry. This is the reason why the financial year now begins on April 6 (budget day) instead of on the old date, March 25 or Lady Day. Rents, traditionally due on Lady Day, Midsummer Day (24 June), Michaelmass (29 September) and Christmas (25 December) stuck to the old dates.

In 1754 Henry Pelham died. Though not regarded as a brilliant man, he had been a very sensible and safe pair of hands for his monarch George II, who on hearing of his death, exclaimed – prophetically enough – "now I shall have no more peace!" Pelham was succeeded by his brother, the great Parliamentary fixer the Duke of Newcastle, a far inferior statesman. Upon this change, Fox was admitted to the cabinet, but – much to his chagrin – Pitt remained outside it.

In 1756 began the most successful war in British history, the Seven Years War. It started in Europe, where the Austrians, bent on revenge for his success in the previous war, had arranged a formidable alliance against Frederick II of Prussia, including Saxony, France and Russia. The main reason the English joined in – on Frederick's side – was to sort out colonial problems with France in India, North America and the Caribbean.

In North America the French controlled Canada and all the known interior east of the Appalachian Mountains, including the Mississippi Valley all the way to New Orleans. In attempting to enforce this control, and to prevent the English on the coast trading with the natives of the interior, the French were in the process of building a string of forts. The most important of these was Fort Duquesne (at the junction of the Allegheny and Monongahela rivers in what is now Pittsburgh, Pennsylvania), completed in 1754. Undeclared warfare was already endemic in this area.

In India, the French and English East India Companies had long coexisted, working from widely separated bases or factories, the English at Calcutta, Bombay and Madras, the French at Pondicherry and Trichinopoly (an inland town south of Madras). Seeking to exploit the weakness of the decadent Mogul Empire, the French governor of Pondicherry, Dupleix, began to arm and drill Indian soldiers – sepoys – with a view to taking sides in local quarrels, and so extending his power. The English followed suit. Their champion was Robert Clive, who had gone out to India as a clerk, but soon exchanged the pen for the sword. A courageous man and excellent diplomat, he proved to be too much for Dupleix. In 1751 they had clashed at Arcot, in southern India, where Clive emerged victorious. In 1756 the French stirred up Surajah Dowlah, the Nabob (Nawab) of Bengal, to overrun Calcutta. Most of the English traders fled, but 146 traders and soldiers were captured and held overnight in a tiny prison – the Black Hole of Calcutta. Many of them – figures vary from 46 to 123 – died of suffocation. Clive was dispatched from Madras to retake Calcutta, which he duly did in 1757. Later the same year his small force of a thousand English and four thousand sepoys beat the 50,000 native troops of Sùrajah Dowlah at Plassey. English hegemony in India – certainly in Bengal – is traditionally dated to this battle.

In Europe the war started badly for the English. Minorca, taken from the Spanish in 1708, was captured by the French. Admiral Byng, the victor of Passaro in 1718, in charge of an English squadron, had declined to engage a superior French fleet. He was court-martialled and shot for this decision. Voltaire remarked that "In England, they kill one admiral to encourage the others!"

As a result of the loss of Minorca, the Duke of Newcastle resigned, to be replaced by the Duke of Devonshire. Newcastle returned to power in 1757 and – after a dispute with George II – so did Pitt, as Secretary of State but now the real power in the land. He was a man of great self-confidence, saying "I can save the country – and I know that no one else can." He had a clear policy – to subsidise Frederick to keep the French busy in Europe, and to attack the French at sea, to prevent support going out to the French colonists. The disastrous Duke of Cumberland was replaced in the European theatre by one of Frederick's best generals, Ferdinand of Brunswick. The Toulon fleet was beaten at the Battle of Lagos, off Portugal, and the Brest fleet in the Battle of Quiberon Bay, leaving the French troops in India and America without help from home (1757).

In North America the war had also started badly when an English attack on Fort Duquesne was repulsed in 1756, but with the arrival of Pitt everything changed and the fort was taken (and renamed Pittsburg in his honour) in 1758. In Canada, Louisburg and Cape Breton also fell to the English.

More was to follow in 1759, the "Year of Victories". In the West Indies, the rich sugar island of Guadeloupe fell to the English. Ferdinand of Brunswick achieved a great victory over the French at Minden. Advancing down the St Lawrence River following the capture of Cape Breton and Louisville, General Wolfe captured the city of Quebec from the French under Montcalm in a famous battle. There had been questions about Wolfe, described as "mad" to George II, who replied "Mad, is he? Then I wish he would BITE some of my other generals!" He was killed at Quebec, as was Montcalm, who predicted (correctly) that the English would not hold onto their conquests for long. The following year an English army under Sir Eyre Coote (another wonderful name!) vanquished a French army at Wandewash near Madras, and the English domination of the French in both North America and India was complete. In the midst of these victories George II died, aged 77.

Chapter 25 – George III

Born 1738, married 1761, Charlotte Sophia of Mecklenburg-Strelitz

At his accession George III, grandson of George II and son of the lamented Fred, was only 22 years old. Unlike his two Hanoverian predecessors, he was an Englishman down to the toes, and as he said himself, "gloried in the name of Britain"; English was his native tongue. Unfortunately, his character had many defects, and his limited understanding of the British constitution was to cause many problems. He had not been brought up to the notion that the monarch should stay above party – or if he had, chose to ignore it. His chief tutors had been Tories, and their views were opposed to those of the great Whig ministers who had just made England so glorious. Instead of selecting his ministers from the party which was most numerous in parliament, George wanted to name his own ministers and implement his own policy – he wanted not only to reign, but to govern himself.

In many respects, George was right to question the Whig hierarchy which had governed for so long, because Walpole and the Pelhams had ruthlessly exploited the rotten boroughs and the royal patronage to obtain Parliaments favorable to themselves. In doing so they had been able to pursue their own policies without regard to the wishes of the king, as they did by forcing Pitt upon a reluctant George II. So George III hoped to break up the idea of party rule, and govern through men who would be acceptable to the country as a whole. His first step was to plant Lord Bute into Newcastle's ministry. Bute was a Scottish Tory who had managed George's own household. Meanwhile, Pitt wished to extend the war by attacking Spain, but he was unable to persuade his colleagues to follow him, and resigned in disgust. He was followed in 1762 by Newcastle. The long series of Whig ministries was finally over, replaced by Lord Bute, a man of no political experience who happened to be a personal friend of the king. The next few years were notable for ministerial instability, in the manner of post-war Italian politics, with ministers switching in and out of power.

War with Spain duly followed in any case, and was prosecuted successfully with the capture of Havana in Cuba and Manila in the Philippines. However, George and Bute had no heart for it, and the burden of debt it was causing grew alarmingly, so the subsidy to Frederick of Prussia was stopped. All but overwhelmed by the vast alliance against him, Frederick had barely managed to hold on to his territories until he was saved by the "Miracle of the House of Brandenburg" when the Empress of Russia, Elizabeth, died, to be replaced by the Emperor Peter III, who hero-worshipped Frederick.

The Peace of Paris (1763) was duly agreed between England, France and Spain. England secured Canada, and in the West Indies, Tobago, Dominica, St Vincent and Grenada. However much the most valuable island – Martinique, taken in 1762 – was handed back to the French, as were Guadeloupe and Pondicherry, and Havana and Manila to Spain. On the other hand, Minorca was returned to the British. The terms of the treaty exasperated the Whigs, and it was said that the Peace of Paris was "as the Peace of God – it passeth all understanding". Presumably George and Bute thought that by taking too much from the French and the Spaniards, they would invite another war in very short order. Despite the protests, Henry Fox, who had changed sides to join Bute, secured the agreement of Parliament to the Peace, by the usual methods of bribery and corruption. In the meantime, Whig supporters were being turned out of offices high (lord-lieutenancies) and low all over the country. This encountered strong opposition, so that when Bute proposed a tax on cider to help pay for the war, he encountered such a flood of abuse that he resigned his post.

Bute was succeeded by Pitt's brother-in-law, Henry Grenville. By this time George had managed to organize what was effectively his own party in Parliament, the "King's friends", which made government very difficult for the Whigs, split as they were into factions of their own. Grenville himself held on until 1765, but he was hardly a successful prime minister. His first mistake was the prosecution of John Wilkes, a clever but profligate MP who printed his own scurrilous magazine, the *North Briton*. Issue 45 of this magazine stated the king's speech contained a lie in reference to the King of Prussia. George and Grenville went after Wilkes, and had him arrested. They had no right to do this, as an MP could only be arrested for treason, felony or breach of the peace. Because of this, Wilkes freed himself with no difficulty, and successfully sued the king's messengers for illegal imprisonment. George and Grenville then acted vindictively in expelling Wilkes from Parliament, an act which led to riots on Wilkes' behalf.

In 1764 the first salvoes were fired in what was to prove a long-running battle when Grenville imposed customs duties and stamp duty on the American colonies. By the Stamp Act the government raised revenue by requiring the purchase of a stamp to legalise certain transactions, including cashing cheques and leaving money in a will. It was the first attempt to levy an inland revenue as opposed to customs. The reason for these impositions was the need to pay the debts raised in the Seven Years War, and it seemed only fair that the Americans should pay their fair share. However, they did not like the idea. They claimed they should not have to pay taxes without their own representation in parliament, and they refused to use the stamped paper.

Bored by his long speeches, George replaced Grenville by the leader of another Whig faction, the Marquess of Rockingham. The new administration repealed the Stamp Act. One man who spoke against it was Pitt, who said that the American trade was worth £3 million a year to England, and it was not worth risking that for the pittance the stamp duty would raise. Also involved in the repeal was Edmund Burke, a rising politician.

In 1766 Pitt – never far from power in these times – combined with the King to turn out Rockingham and form a new ministry under the Duke of Grafton. Pitt himself took office as Lord Privy Seal and went to the Lords as the Earl of Chatham. This proved a mistake as the great power of his speeches was wasted in the Lords, and because he was no longer the "Great Commoner". However Pitt became ill and withdrew from public life. In the meantime the row over American duties rumbled on – the Chancellor imposed customs duties meant to raise only small sums but also to demonstrate the government's right to tax the American colonies in this way.

More trouble occurred when John Wilkes was reelected to parliament as the member for Middlesex. Because of the interference of George, who refused to allow the result, the election was held four times, and each time Wilkes was returned. At one point there were riots in which twenty people were killed. The pamphleteers were kept busy, notably the *Public Advertiser* in which the "Letter of Junius" attacked the government in violent language.

In 1770 Grafton was sent packing and replaced by Lord North, a Tory of great administrative ability but whose long ministry – twelve years – was to include one of the greatest debacles of the century, the loss of the American colonies. North relieved the colonies of all customs duties except a small charge on imported tea. However the colonists, thoroughly inflamed and angry with George III by now, would not accept even that – they were simply opposed in principle, or they said they were. In the Boston Tea Party of 1773 the ships of the East India company were boarded by colonists, not very well disguised as Indians, who threw the tea overboard. This caused the government to annul the charter of Massachusetts (of which Boston was the capital), placing the colony under the direct rule of the crown. Also the customs house was removed from Boston to Salem, a deliberate attempt to ruin the merchants of Boston. Everyone who understood colonial feeling – and in Britain that in practice meant Chatham (Pitt) and Burke – knew that the colonists would fight rather than submit to these measures, and a war of independence became inevitable.

The colonists quickly organized themselves for action. George Washington, from Virginia, who had distinguished himself during the Seven Years War, emerged as one of the early leaders. The first fighting took place at Lexington in 1775. The colonists, who made excellent irregular soldiers, gained the advantage here, then seized Bunker's Hill, overlooking Boston. They were expelled by the British, but at great loss of life, and the war began in earnest.

The Americans under George Washington beat off a British attempt to capture the New England states, and, encouraged, the colonists declared their independence (1776). The following year, the British struck back in the middle tier of states, and took both New York and Philadelphia. The army there under General Clinton then arranged to move up the Hudson Valley to join hands with another army advancing southwards from Canada under General Burgoyne. However, Clinton was so slow that Burgoyne was caught with only his own forces and overwhelmed at Saratoga Springs (1777). This defeat encouraged Britain's enemies in Europe to exploit the situation, and France, Spain and even Holland declared war. This time there would be no support from the Prussians – abandoned at the end of the previous war – so Britain faced a formidable alliance of old enemies bent on revenge for their losses in previous conflicts. Suddenly not only was North America at risk, but the Caribbean as well.

The failures of the war led to an increase in the opposition to the king and his ministers at home. A parliamentarian called Dunning brought a motion to the House of Commons stating that "The power of the crown has increased, is increasing and ought to be diminished". This was passed by a large majority but the king and North remained unmoved. Meanwhile there was much agitation to loosen the grip of the ruling party by parliamentary reform – mainly of the rotten boroughs. This was not actually achieved until 1832, 50 years later! Also on the domestic front, measures were passed to ease the condition of the Roman Catholics, who still laboured under many restrictions. These, however, ran up against terrific prejudice in the country, and led to the anti-popish Gordon Riots (1780), named after Lord George Gordon, President of the Protestant Association. Property was destroyed in London on a scale not seen since Cade's rebellion in 1450.

1779 saw the death in Hawaii of one of the most famous Englishmen of all time, the Yorkshireman Captain James Cook. His three great voyages – 1768-71, 1772-5 and 1776-9 led to the discovery and mapping of a large area of the Pacific Ocean and its bordering coasts, touching on the Americas, Australia and even Antarctica. On his second and third voyages, he had the advantage of a brand new navigational aid, invented by another great Yorkshireman, the clockmaker John Harrison - the watch chronometer ("H4"). Finding the correct longitude had been the greatest scientific challenge of the century. Inaccurate measurements had cost the lives of thousands of seamen, including Sir Cloudesley Shovel, the man who took Gibraltar but whose ship was wrecked on the Scillies in 1707. Harrison was awarded a prize of over £20,000 for his work by the Board of Longitude – eventually.

In the war, the French and Spanish fleets besieged Gibraltar. In 1780 the fort was resupplied by Admiral Rodney, who defeated the Spanish fleet off Cape St Vincent. The siege continued but Gibraltar held on. In North America the British were obliged to abandon Philadelphia and fall back to New York. From here a force was detached to Charleston in South Carolina to try to secure the southern states, under the leadership of Lord Cornwallis. Marching back northwards along the coast, this army was hemmed in at Yorktown by Washington. An inconclusive naval action was fought in the Battle of Chesapeake Bay (1781) between the British under Admiral Graves and the French under De Grasse. However the important strategic consequence was that the British fleet was then unable to reinforce or evacuate Cornwallis and his army. So Cornwallis was obliged to surrender (1781). This disaster brought the fighting on land to a virtual close. In the maritime war, the Spanish captured Minorca (1782). At home, this event led to the fall of the North government. The Whig Rockingham returned for his second term as prime minister. In accordance with Whig policy, fighting in North America was discontinued at once, but the naval war against France and Spain was prosecuted with vigour. In 1782 Rodney won a famous victory in the Battle of the Saints in the West Indies, securing the English colonies there against the French.

Rockingham died in 1782 after only a few months in office, to be succeeded by Shelburne. The new administration concluded the Peace of Versailles (1783) to terminate the war. The independence of the United States was recognized. England also lost Minorca and Tobago. The severance of the American colonies was a severe blow to English commerce, as the former colonists could now trade with whomever they pleased. However, the position of the new country was at first precarious, as it had been up until this point utterly dependent on the protection of the Royal Navy. Many did not expect United States to survive in its newly independent form, but survive it did, and indeed prospered. Its democratic form of government and lack of either king or aristocracy was noted in Europe – especially in France – with dramatic consequences only six years later. Some, however, had no love for the new republic. About 100,000 of its citizens emigrated – the United Empire Loyalists – the majority to Canada, which, though mainly still French, had remained loyal throughout the conflict.

The Rockingham administration, under Edmund Burke, had also initiated important changes at home. The civil list – the revenue of the king – was severely cut back by the abolition of many sinecures. Persons holding government contracts were forbidden from sitting in the Commons – thus abolishing a frequently used means of bribery. The franchise was removed from revenue officers after it was shown that elections in seventy constituencies depended on their votes. Concessions were also made in Ireland, where the Dublin parliament gained its independence and also where restrictions on trade were removed.

Shelburne was soon ousted from office by a combination of former rivals – Lord North, Charles James Fox (son of Henry Fox, who had died in 1774) and Burke. These – all now regarded as bitter enemies by the king – formed a new administration under the nominal leadership of the Duke of Portland (1783). George determined to be rid of this unwanted ministry at the first opportunity, which was not long in coming.

The rule of the East India Company – which was supposed to be a commercial organization, not a colonial government – had now extended *de facto* to cover much of north-east India, including Bengal, Orissa and Bihar. In the south a threat arose from Hyder Ali of Mysore. He was defeated by Sir Eyre Coote (victor at Wandewash in the Seven Years War) at Porto Novo in 1781. To raise money for the campaign, the Governor-General, Warren Hastings (generally an honest man by the standards of India) had resorted to unprincipled means, including cajoling nabobs distant from the conflict into forced loans. When word of his conduct reached England, an attempt was made by Burke in

Parliament to change the political administration of the Indian possessions. This was to be placed under a board of seven persons nominated by Parliament for four years, and by the king after that. The opposition – including the king – saw that this would provide the government with a gigantic engine of patronage with which to secure its ill-gotten power. George put it about that "Whoever voted for the India Bill was not only not his friend, but would be considered by him as an enemy". This misuse of influence was enough to secure the rejection of the bill, and the king, overjoyed by his success, demanded the seals of office from the government that very night.

The new Prime Minister was William Pitt, son of Chatham (Pitt the Elder) and, at 24, by far the youngest English prime minister of all time. There were many jibes – "England entrusted to a schoolboy's care" – but Pitt stood firm and soon won friends inside and outside parliament. A Tory supported originally by the king's friends and his father's followers, he gained the confidence of the country to the extent that he won a large majority in the election of 1784. The many supporters of the previous coalition now deprived of their seats were called "Fox's Martyrs". Pitt himself was to prove one of England's great prime ministers, and to his delight George found his own popularity increasing – for the first time in his reign – on the back of Pitt's success.

One of Pitt's first actions was to resolve the India issue by an India Act. This established a board of control, but left Indian patronage in the hands of the East India Company. On the same issue, in 1785 Warren Hastings returned from India, only to face impeachment before the Lords for corruption whilst Governor General. The trial dragged on over six years as the Lords rarely sat. In the end, Hastings was acquitted. The trial served as a warning to other officers to be more careful in their behavior than Hasting had been, and the Indian civil service henceforward ran at a much higher standard.

Pitt's reputation is founded upon his success as a financier, but here he had the benefit of a compete re-thinking of traditional economics in the Scot Adam Smith's *Wealth of Nations*, first published in 1776. The book demonstrated that national economies would do best where individuals were allowed to pursue their own self-interest, and that all nations would benefit by a free exchange of their goods. Up until this time it had been the practice of governments to discourage foreign trade for fear that it would reduce the stocks of gold in the country. The new scheme was known as Free Trade. In 1786 Pitt concluded a commercial treaty with France, lowering customs duties and benefitting trade in both countries.

Also, at this time, the Industrial Revolution in Britain was coming into full swing, and production from the new mills and factories was rising rapidly. The inventions of Arkwright, Hargreaves and Crompton in textile manufacture, of Wilkinson the ironmaster, and of Watt in steam engines were being widely installed. James Brindley was busy building the early canal network, and Telford improving the roads. The new wealth generated by this activity was to have a tremendous impact on Pitt's ability to finance the long wars which lay ahead – wars which were to make the expense of the American war seem like a mere trifle.

Pitt pressed ahead with a scheme to reform some of the rotten boroughs, which was eventually rejected. Also at this time came the first stirrings of action against the slave trade, led by William Wilberforce, an MP and son of a Hull merchant. A bill was passed for the better regulation of the slave ships. However all was thrown into confusion when George III became completely mad in 1788. Moves were made to install his son George as regent – an action which would certainly have led to the replacement of Pitt by Fox. However, the Prince of Wales was not a popular man in the country. He had married a Mrs Fitzherbert – a Catholic – illegally, then tried to disown his own marriage because it contravened the Royal Marriage Act (whereby the consent of the king was required for royal marriages). Also the Prince was known to have run up immense debts and to be addicted to gambling. Fortunately for Pitt, George III recovered – this time – and was able to resume his rule.

     *   *   *   *

In Scotland at this time, two important movements are to be noted. The first of these began around 1780 and continued for fifty years of more – the Highland Clearances. The Scottish lairds made little money from the Highland peasantry on their vast estates. Much more was to be made from stocking the land with new breeds of hardy sheep, and cattle. Also – and this is particularly important – there was a reasonable alternative for the Highlanders – emigration to Canada or to the newly forming industrial areas of the Scottish Lowlands.

A brutal policy of eviction was implemented on estate after estate, with the population moved to the coast, where it was expected to gain a meagre living from fishing, or simply moved away completely. The landscape of the Highlands is still full of the deserted villages. In England, this same policy, called the Enclosure Movement, had been going on over a much longer period, and its immediate impact was less. The long-term effect was the same – marginal agricultural land reverted to moorland, grazed by sheep, as can for example be seen on the moors and their flanks in the Pennines today. However in Scotland the late timing, the abruptness of the movement, the lack of legal protection for the old tenants, and the sudden breakup of the clan system made its impact so much greater, and the laments have echoed down the centuries. But this is the reason that there are so many Scandinavian faces on the streets of Glasgow and in the whole Strathclyde area today.

On a brighter note, Scotland became one of the intellectual beacons of Europe during the second half of the eighteenth century, a period known as the Scottish Enlightenment. There were noted achievements in philosophy (David Hume), political economy (Adam Smith), engineering (James Watt), chemistry (Joseph Black), geology (James Hutton) and of course poetry (Robert Burns).

*   *   *   *

In 1788 an event of great long-term importance occurred when the first colonists arrived in Australia. There were almost a thousand of them – mainly convicts – carried in eleven ships under the command of Captain Arthur Phillip. Settling initially at the site of modern Sydney, following a recommendation from Captain Cook, the new settlers were in for a difficult start, as the first settlers in North America had been. After a few "hungry years", however, the colony grew quickly, by 1815 spreading along the coast and out to Norfolk Island and Tasmania. It is thought that over a period of 80 years, over 165,000 convicts were transported to Australia, although their numbers were swamped by free immigrants arriving after 1850 in the Australian gold rush.

*   *   *   *

The Industrial Revolution in Britain not only transformed the economy but also the ethnic map of the country, because large new urban populations were required in previously rural areas. What was once the Anglian kingdom of Mercia became the home of the West Midlands metal industries centred on Birmingham. It is thought that a large proportion of the new workers came from nearby mid-Wales, a fact which is reflected on the streets of the city to this day; some found their way later to the motor industry in Oxford. It is known that people were drawn from poor rural areas of Suffolk far away to the new mills of Lancashire. South Wales drew many immigrants from the west of England, particularly Somerset, and also overseas immigrant populations arrived from Italy, Africa and even China, so that Welsh was never the native language of many of its citizens. Partly as a result of the later famines, many Irish arrived and stayed in Lancashire. West Yorkshire – already densely populated with wool workers before the Industrial Revolution proper – drew in more workers from the Yorkshire Dales.

*   *   *   *

One of the most significant cultural figures who casts a long shadow over the Georgian age is Dr Samuel Johnson (1709-1784). He is most noted for producing the first real dictionary of the English language, which is often quoted today for its idiosyncratic definitions, for example: "Oats – a grain which in England is generally given to horses, but which in Scotland appears to support the people". Johnson was a lively character, originally from Lichfield, but living for most of his life in London: "A man who is tired of London is tired of life". In any anthology of quotations, Samuel Johnson is the first name to seek – along with a later character from this book, the Duke of Wellington!

Chapter 26 – The French Revolutionary and Napoleonic Wars

In 1789 all Europe was stirred by the greatest historical event since the Reformation – the French Revolution, the impact of which was to reverberate right around the world. France and indeed many countries of continental Europe retained feudal customs. These may have had their uses in medieval times, but by the last quarter of the eighteenth century, only the abuses remained. In France, nearly all the wealth and privilege belonged to the nobility and higher clergy, perhaps one in thirty of the population. A rural tenant existed on much the same basis as a villein had in the time of Edward III in England, and had to render services to his lord, such as the arduous roadwork or *corvee*. Again the seigneur might keep a dovecote with a thousand doves, which preyed on the peasant's fields at will, even if the peasant had to sow his crop three times. The seigneur also owned all the hunting rights. In the towns, all trades were dominated by closed guilds, and entry into any of these required a substantial payment. In the army, only nobles could be officers, and in the church, no one but a noble could rise above the level of a poor *cure* or parish priest. So at every turn, the ordinary man with the ability to rise in society was thwarted by inherited privilege.

However, by far the most burdensome load upon the peasantry was taxation, needed especially to pay for the useless wars entered upon quite capriciously and very frequently under Louis XIV and Louis XV. The nobility and clergy paid very little in taxation – they were able to obtain hereditary exemptions by making one-off payments to a government desperate for ready cash. So that burden fell on the rest of the population. Taxation was farmed out to tax-gatherers whose extortions were uneven and unavoidable by the peasant. Also each province of France had its own system of customs houses, which greatly interfered with trade by making the movement of goods between provinces expensive. Again, the wars against the English had resulted in the loss of many colonies and the loss of foreign trade.

Moreover, there was no new economy in France, generating new wealth, as the Industrial Revolution did in England. New business suffocated in the stultifying rules of privilege. There had been no reform of the banking system, such as had taken place with the foundation of the Bank of England and National Debt in England, so that government fundraising remained chaotic and expensive. Generation after generation of leading ministers had tried to remedy this situation, but the result was always the same – more unpaid debt and more taxes for the common man. Under the noses of the most extravagant court in Europe, he was getting poorer and poorer.

In the meantime, this was the age of the European Enlightenment, when French writers such as Diderot and Rousseau were preaching a doctrine of liberty and equality – a doctrine which had just been implemented in real life by the United States! The French aristocrats had ground the noses of the poor into the soil for far too long, and they were about to pay for this behavior with their lives.

Note that there are some parallels between the French Revolution and the English Revolution and Civil War of the seventeenth century – in both cases the power of the king was challenged, that king lost his head, and was followed eventually by a dictator. However the English revolution, if about the respective powers of the people and the king, was also about religion, whereas the French revolution was all about privileges. There is a much stronger parallel with the Russian Revolution of 1917, as a similar system of inherited wealth and privilege was swept away in that country too.

Matters came to a head in 1789 when a National Assembly was convened. While this was sitting, the Revolution got off to its symbolic start with the storming of the Bastille – the French equivalent of the Tower of London – by the Paris mob. Insurrections followed all over the country in which the nobles were ill-treated, their manor houses burnt and their feudal rights ignored. The National Assembly then abolished all privileges, and later titles of nobility, and also caused the lands of the church to be forfeited. Many amongst the nobility fled the country and attempted to persuade Austria and Prussia to invade France and restore their privileges. The king, Louis XVI, and his wife Marie Antoinette (an Austrian) attempted to join the *émigrés*, but were caught and held prisoner. This was likely to mean trouble for Marie Antoinette – when told that the people were rioting because they had no bread to eat, she said "Then let them eat cake"! The execution of aristocrats became an everyday occurrence in Paris.

In the meantime the Legislative Assembly, successor to the National Assembly, had been taken over by the Corporation of Paris and extremists known as the Jacobins. The invasion by Austria and Prussia duly followed in 1792 – it was thought that given the chaotic state of France, this would be a straight march to Paris. However, that is not what happened. The invaders were repelled by the Revolutionary army at Valmy in north-east France. By 1793 the Jacobins had increased their stranglehold on power, and the king and queen were executed – this was the Reign of Terror.

The Revolution was widely welcomed at first in England, but disillusionment set in rapidly. In his *Reflections on the French Revolution* (1790), Edmund Burke accurately foretold that the movement would result in the complete destruction of society as previously constituted in France, and its replacement with a military dictatorship. The English aristocracy took fright, as it was widely expected that the Revolution would spread to England, though the conditions which had caused it hardly existed here. Even the king had become popular. Burke demanded war with France to put down the new evil empire. War he demanded, and war he eventually got, more war than ever he could have wanted!

Meanwhile repressive measures were taken to suppress any idea of revolution in England. The repeal of the Test and Corporation Acts was thrown out, and an Aliens Act was passed to control the movement of foreigners (i.e. Frenchmen). In 1794 Habeas Corpus (outlawing imprisonment without trial) was suspended (for eight years) and a Treasonable Practices Bill and a Seditious Meetings Bill were enacted. So it was said that because the Frenchmen had abused their liberty, the Englishmen were being deprived of theirs.

After the regicide, Britain joined a coalition including Austria, Prussia, Spain and Holland to make war on the Revolutionaries in France (1793). In former times, the French might expect to be overwhelmed by such an alliance, but this time – especially in Italy – the French were seen as liberators against ancient oppressors, and the French soldiers were – in the manner of Cromwell's Ironsides – filled with revolutionary zeal.

Pitt organized subsidies for his continental allies. The navy attacked and destroyed the French Mediterranean fleet at Toulon (1793), but failed to hold the harbour. It was in this action that a young Corsican officer called Napoleon Bonaparte first came to prominence, in rallying the French troops. Meanwhile the Duke of York contrived to lose an action in support of the Dutch. Then a British fleet under the command of Lord Howe beat the Atlantic (Brest) French fleet in the Battle of the Glorious First of June (1794). This was to set a pattern for the rest of the war – the British were successful at sea, but could not stop the

French in the land war. The naval situation became more serious when the French overran Holland (meeting almost no resistance), causing the Dutch fleet to fall into their hands; the Spanish changed sides; and Prussia dropped out of the war (1795). This threat was removed by victories against the combined Spanish and French fleets off Cape St Vincent (Jervis, assisted by Nelson), and against the Dutch off Camperdown (both 1797). These victories gave the Royal Navy command of the oceans, and so enabled the capture of Trinidad from Spain in 1797 and the retention of Ceylon, taken from the Dutch in 1795.

By 1797 the expense of the war, and the domestic inflation it produced, was causing Pitt to seek an end to it, but the French, buoyed up by their success along the Rhine and into Germany, and in Italy, were in no mood to stop. What is more, they were (for once) not short of money. The Revolutionary government had repudiated the old debts and money was raised by selling off the confiscated property of the nobles and clergy. Pitt was obliged to make a great financial innovation to meet his own government's expense – income tax, levied for the first time in 1798, on a graduated scale from two pence to two shillings in the pound.

Seeking new adventures during the lull on the European fronts in this period, the rapidly rising General Napoleon Bonaparte led an amazing expedition to Egypt, with a view either to attacking India overland from there or of taking the lands of the Levant for France. He and his army embarked, gave Nelson and the British Mediterranean squadron the slip, and reached Egypt successfully. Once there the French easily beat the army of the Mamelukes, the soldier caste that ruled the country, in the Battle of the Pyramids (1798). However, by this time Nelson had located the French fleet lying in Aboukir Bay off the mouth of the Nile. His squadron completely annihilated the French ships in the Battle of the Nile (1798). Undeterred for the moment, Napoleon turned up the coast and invaded Syria (1799). His way, however, was blocked by the Turkish fort of Acre – in the same town successfully besieged by Richard the Lionheart in 1191. Very ably assisted by an English naval force under Sir Sidney Smith, the defenders repelled Napoleon. He was obliged to return to Egypt, where he abandoned his army and slipped away back to France. He always said of Sir Sidney Smith, "That man made me miss my destiny."

The impact of the Battle of the Nile was to encourage the enemies of France, notably Britain, Austria and Russia, to form a second coalition to resume the war in Europe. Russia is certainly a long way away from

France, only emerging from the boreal forests with the establishment of St Petersburg on the Baltic in 1703, but its Tsar Paul I agreed to send an army to support the Austrians. Many French aristocrats were by now established in Russia, including "King" Louis XVIII, and the manners of the old French court were held in great esteem in that country.

The armies of this coalition met the French in Switzerland, overrun by the French at this time. The alliance was defeated at the Battle of Zurich (1799). Napoleon, meanwhile, had succeeded in overthrowing the rulers of France – the Directory – and replacing them with himself under the title of First Consul. Very soon his government was as despotic as that of the old monarchy, though it was certainly much more liberal. The old privileges were not restored. In the war, his success continued with the defeat of the Austrians at Marengo (1800). This secured the north of Italy for the French and led the Austrians to withdraw from the war, leaving Britain to continue single-handed.

In 1800 a British army under Abercrombie defeated the French army in Egypt at the Battle of Alexandria. The French army was then repatriated in British ships. In the meantime Britain's attempt to cut off all maritime trade with France had upset the neutral northern states – Russia, Denmark, Sweden and Prussia – which then formed the "armed neutrality" to oppose the rough British tactics. This led to England's first conflict with Denmark since the days of Canute. Fearing that the new alliance was only a stepping-stone to joining the French, Pitt sent Nelson to Copenhagen to sort out the Danish fleet, which was destroyed in the action (1801). This caused the dissolution of the armed neutrality – now not so well armed – and was shortly followed by peace between Britain and France, formalised in the Treaty of Amiens (1802).

Pitt, meanwhile, had himself fallen from grace over the affairs of Ireland. The French Revolution caused great excitement in that country. The French attempted an invasion and there were several rebellions, one led by Wolf Tone. Pitt formed a plan to abolish the Dublin parliament and instead have the Irish electorate directly represented in the Westminster parliament. This was enacted in 1800 as the Act of Union. The similar act which had brought together Scotland and England in 1707 had proved a great success for the Scots, despite its initial unpopularity. This new Act of Union, however, was to prove a disaster for the Irish in the coming century.

Part of the bargain was to be the relief of the restrictions placed on the Catholics. Pitt thought they should be allowed the franchise, as Catholic MPs would always form a minority in the new British parliament. These measures were very distasteful to George III, who claimed that to accept them would cause him to violate his coronation oath. As this issue could not be resolved, Pitt resigned, to be replaced by Henry Addington. Also on the domestic front, the first modern census was conducted in Great Britain in 1801, when the population was counted at 11 million.

In India the French Jacobins began to consort with the southern ruler Tipu Sahib, son of Hyder Ali. The governor general, Lord Mornington (Richard Wellesley) ordered a march on Tipu's capital, Seringapatam. Under the direction of General Harris, this town was taken in 1799, when Tipu was killed. The policy of the English at this time was to form alliances with native princes where possible. The prince would be left to look after his domestic affairs whilst external matters fell under the direction of a British resident. This forward policy aroused the next group in line, the Marattas of the north-western Deccan, fierce cavalrymen. Sir Arthur Wellesley, who had distinguished himself at Seringapatam, and whose brother Richard was the governor general, beat the Marattas at the battle of Assaye (1803). Approaching from another direction, General Lake recorded a further victory at Laswaree. These defeats reduced the Marattas to a state of subjection. Even the decrepit Mogul in Delhi became a pensioner of the East India Company, so the whole of the Ganges Valley and the south of India were now under British control. There were many at home, however, who believed that the likes of the Wellesleys were adventurers bent on extending political power when they should have been overseeing peaceful commerce.

The Peace of Amiens proved to be little more than a truce and war was resumed in 1803. The first war had been an attempt by the old monarchies of Europe to put down the French Republic. This time, France was the aggressor. This brought about a strong feeling within England that Pitt should be brought back as prime minister, according to the ditty:

Pitt is to Addington

As London is to Paddington

So Pitt replaced Addington in 1804. New alliances were formed, Britain with Austria and Russia, and France with Spain. Napoleon hoped to combine the French and Spanish navies to neutralise the English navy and so carry out his first great scheme of the war – the invasion of England. "Let us be masters of the Channel for six hours," he said, "and we are masters of the world." He contrived to send the Toulon fleet under Villeneuve to the West Indies as a bait for Nelson to follow, but with instructions to return immediately, then link up with the

Brest and Spanish fleets ready for the invasion. Meanwhile an immense army was collected at Boulogne, and small craft of all types were assembled there from every harbour along the south Channel coast. Villeneuve duly turned about in the West Indies, but was unable to combine with the blockaded Brest fleet, so he made for Spain. He was intercepted by an English squadron and ran for Cadiz. The English remained in complete command of the Channel and Napoleon was obliged to break up his army of invasion.

After a short visit home, Nelson resumed his pursuit of Villeneuve, finally confronting the combined French and Spanish fleets in the terrific naval battle of Trafalgar in October, 1805. Nelson sent out his message before the battle – "England expects every man to do his duty". Sailing his ships in two lines at right angles through the enemy line, Nelson annihilated the combined fleet. Wearing his bright uniform on the deck of his flagship the *Victory*, Nelson made a conspicuous target for snipers and was killed in the action. Nevertheless this victory made the English fleets the masters of every ocean.

In the land war the Austrians and the Russians were comprehensively beaten at the battles of Ulm and Austerlitz (1805). These defeats caused dismay in Britain. Pitt observed, "Roll up the map of Europe, it will not be wanted these ten years". Worn out by overwork, Pitt died shortly afterwards, in January 1806. His last words were said to have been "I think I could eat one of Bellamy's veal pies!" He was only 46 years old – twenty of those years having been spent as prime minister.

Pitt was succeeded by William Grenville, his cousin (whose father had also briefly been prime minister), and Fox. The new government sought to unite the best men of all parties and was called the ministry of "All the talents". It passed a resolution condemning slavery, on which the 1807 Act for the abolition of slavery was based. Hitherto Wilberforce and his friends, although having the goodwill of Pitt, had always been thwarted in the Lords. However, once in power, Fox found it impossible to negotiate with Napoleon (something he had always recommended up to this point); but in six months he followed Pitt to the grave.

In the war, Napoleon had bribed the Prussians to stay out of an alliance with Austria and Russia by offering them Hanover, still ruled by George III. They now paid the price, as having seen off the allies, Napoleon crushed the Prussians at Jena (1806) and marched into Berlin. Here he issued his Berlin Decrees, forbidding any country under his control from trading with the British – the "Continental system". This was outright economic warfare. However, he had no navy, and so limited means of enforcing the decrees. In retaliation England issued Orders in Council forbidding all trade with French or French-occupied ports. These Orders severely constrained maritime trade with France, but they certainly did not make England popular with neutrals wishing to carry out that trade, including Denmark, Sweden and the United States.

In 1807 Grenville's administration put forward proposals to allow Roman Catholics to hold the higher commissions in the army. This did not go down well with the king, who dismissed Grenville and installed the Duke of Portland in his place. The Duke had been prime minister before, nearly a quarter of a century earlier, when he was a Whig, but by this time he was certainly a Tory. His cabinet included some famous names of the nineteenth century – Perceval (Chancellor), Canning (Foreign Secretary), Castlereagh (War and Colonial Secretary) and Huskisson (Secretary to the Treasury).

Fearing that the French had designs to seize the (rebuilt) Danish fleet, the British sent another expedition out to Copenhagen, capturing the ships before the French got there (1807). The island of Heligoland, a convenient station in the North Sea commanding the mouth of the Elbe, was also taken. The Cape of Good Hope was retaken from the Dutch in 1806, and the island of Mauritius (in the Indian Ocean) from the French in 1810.

Napoleon and his *Grand Armee* were nearly defeated by the Russians at the battle of Eylau in East Prussia (February 1807), but recovered to rout the Russians at the battle of Friedland, also in East Prussia, in the summer of that same year. This led to the Treaty of Tilsit (1807), virtually halving the size of Prussia and drawing the Russians in on the side of the French against the English. This meant that Russia was to be included in the Continental system.

At the other end of Europe an imbroglio began to unfold which was to prove impossible for Napoleon to resolve. Napoleon wished to attack yet another country, England's oldest ally, Portugal. To do this, his army under Junot needed to march through Spain. This they did, leaving French troops in command of all important military posts in northern Spain. Having expelled the King of Portugal to Brazil, Napoleon calmly installed his own brother Joseph as King of Spain.

From the point of view of any observer at the start of 1808, Napoleon's position must now have appeared impregnable – Pitt would certainly not have liked it. The borders of France itself now stretched far to the east, into Germany and the Low Countries, and there were cowed or client states established all along the North Sea coast and the Baltic. The whole of Italy and Spain were also under French domination. Yet Napoleon had already sown the seeds of his own destruction. He was about to become involved in fighting in totally alien environments as a result of the events of 1807. His armies always survived by living off the land, simply stealing provisions by plunder wherever they went. In the lush plains of central Europe and northern Italy, this had worked well enough, but it would not work in Russia or in Spain, at opposite ends – one freezing, the other torrid in summer, brutal in winter – of the continent. The Russians would not comply with the Continental system, which would eventually force Napoleon to invade to enforce it. There his armies would starve and freeze to death as they advanced across the scorched earth. His exposed position in Spain soon meant his first serious confrontation with British troops in Europe, in a land where a small army would get beaten and a large one would starve. Also he had committed an error of military strategy which was to cost the Germans so much in the next century – war on two fronts.

King Joseph did not last long in Spain. A popular insurrection, also involving units of the Spanish army, drove him back to France (1808). Although he was not present personally, this was the first major defeat for Napoleon – one he did not intend to take lying down. Meanwhile Junot and his army were still in Portugal, so the British shipped out an army under Arthur Wellesley, victor of Assaye, to take advantage of the situation. Wellesley promptly did just that, defeating Junot at Vimeiro (1808). After this battle it was agreed in the Convention of Cintra that the French could be repatriated on English ships, and leave Portugal with all its fortresses for the English. This treaty was negotiated by generals superior in rank to Wellesley, and though it secured Portugal without another fight, it was very unpopular back in England, where the French soldiers were expected back as prisoners of war.

Napoleon now took charge personally in Spain, marching rapidly into Madrid with a large force. Declaring the job done, he then retired to France, leaving the mopping up operations to Soult and Ney – but the job was not done – far from it. The small British force, now under General Sir John Moore, had advanced beyond Salamanca, but was now obliged to retreat north-westwards to the coast at Corunna. This army beat off the French whilst waiting for transport home (1808), though Moore was killed in the action. Encouraged by victories against the French at Alexandria, Vimeiro and now Corunna, the British government soon reembarked the troops under Wellesley. Advancing through Portugal, Wellesley approached to within 80 miles of Madrid, where he beat a French army at Talavera (1809), before withdrawing into Portugal in the face of superior numbers. This is a very notable feature of Wellesley campaign – he was never afraid to retreat, and so kept his forces in the field. He said himself that the real test of a general was "to know when to retreat, and to dare to do it". This was one reason why the Peninsular War, as this war in Spain and Portugal became known, was the longest campaign of the Revolutionary wars. For his victory at Talavera, Wellesley was made Viscount (later the Duke of) Wellington.

The year 1809 also witnessed the largest and most unsuccessful expedition by an English army since Bannockburn. Forty thousand soldiers were embarked for the Low Countries under the command of a holiday general, Lord Cobham, in an attempt to capture of the port of Antwerp. Most of the soldiers got no further than the low, sandy and fever-stricken island of Walcheren, off the mouth of the Scheldt, where they died in their thousands from disease. Virtually no medication of any kind was available and the expedition was a complete fiasco.

At home this disaster led to a duel between Castlereagh (Secretary for War) and Canning (Foreign Secretary) to decide who was responsible! Both survived, but the prime minister, Portland, who had long been ailing, resigned, being replaced by Spencer Perceval (1809). A year later George III – thought now to be suffering from porphyria – became permanently insane, and had to be replaced by his son, the enormously fat, overindulged and thoroughly disreputable George, Prince Regent.

Napoleon ended his campaign of 1809 with another great victory over the Austrians at Wagram. This forced the Austrian Emperor to make peace, and to give his daughter – Archduchess Marie Louise, niece of Marie Antoinette – to Napoleon in marriage. (Napoleon had tired of Empress Josephine, who had failed to produce any children, and divorced her to make this new match. The phase "Not tonight, Josephine", attributed to Napoleon, is thought to be apocryphal!)

Freed now to concentrate resources on the Peninsular campaign, a large army under Massena was dispatched to deal with Wellington. Anticipating this, Wellington had constructed massive siege defences known as the lines of Torres Vedras at Lisbon. Withdrawing behind these lines and burning and destroying all provisions as he went, his plan was to draw in the French army and starve it into withdrawal. Unfortunately about 50,000 Portuguese peasants are thought to have starved to death as well. Wellington beat a French force at Busaco

(1810), then withdrew behind his lines. One sight of the fortifications was enough to convince Massena that they were impregnable, so he retreated. After intermittent fighting in 1811, Wellington's army finally took the Spanish frontier fortresses of Ciudad Rodrigo and Bajadoz in 1812. Supplied from the sea, he then invaded Spain along the northern road, but had to fall back once more when confronted with the concentrated French army at Burgos.

Back at home, Castlereagh, a very determined character, had become foreign secretary. He was to prove a decisive figure in the last stages of the war, rallying his continental allies and providing subsidies for their armies on an even larger scale than Pitt. Shortly after his appointment, Perceval achieved the distinction of becoming the only British prime minister in history to be assassinated, by a merchant called Bellingham (1812). His place was taken by Lord Liverpool, who had a long run ahead of him in the job – until 1827.

The British had reacted to the closed ports of the North Sea coast by diverting much of their European trade through the Baltic, kept open throughout this period by a British squadron under Admiral Saumarez (Nelson's deputy at the Battle of the Nile). This trade grew enormously though the course of the war, but 1811 was a bad year for Britain. The continental blockade was reinforced as Napoleon's officers had access to most of the ports of northern Europe. The American trade, flourishing early in the war, was also severely disrupted. Inflation and rioting were taking a grip in England, where the first outbreaks of Luddism took place. Named after the mythical Ned Ludd, the handloom weavers broke into factories and destroyed the machines which were taking their work.

Then in 1812 Napoleon took his fateful decision to invade the Russia of Tsar Alexander I. This was not his intention – he thought he was fighting the "third Polish war" – but following Wellington's example, the Russians simply withdrew before his armies, removing or burning everything they could as they went. The reason that Napoleon wanted to beat the Russians was to enforce his continental system and so defeat Britain by choking off her trade. This had proved impossible for him to impose on the Baltic coasts which he did not control.

So Napoleon recruited a huge *Grand Armee* of 450,000 men from all over Europe and followed the retreating Russians. By the time he reached Smolensk, scarcely half-way to Moscow, he had already lost 10,000 horses. Horses do not succumb to wet weather, but to repeated forced marches and a lack of good fodder. To the good general (such as Wellington) at these times, the health of his horses was critical, so this

274

loss was a very bad omen. Napoleon finally fought the Russians, under General Kutuzov, in front of Moscow at Borodino (1812). Napoleon won the day but failed to destroy the Russian army, which retreated – only to come back later. The Russians withdrew from Moscow and Napoleon took the city. There was enough food and clothing left in Moscow to carry the *Grand Armee* through the winter, but the city was soon burned down by careless, undisciplined troops, looting and destroying. So the French army, facing starvation, was obliged to make its retreat through the winter months, harried all the way by Russian partisans and regular troops. It is thought that only about 25,000 men made it home. Napoleon had been so badly beaten that he was never able to recover. Like Hitler in the next century, it had taken the invasion of Russia to break him. The question then arises – how long would either dictator have lasted if they had not taken this step? It could have proved impossible to dislodge them. As it was, the French wars of this period ran for 23 years!

Meanwhile, war had broken out between the British and the Americans. The Americans had been generally supportive in the earlier stages of the Revolutionary Wars, but by 1812 the irritation caused by the interference to their shipping through the application of the Orders in Council was so great that the Americans declared war. This is another great difference between the Revolutionary Wars and the First and Second World Wars, which were both quickly over once the Americans joined the English, instead of fighting them.

The defeat in Russia meant that Napoleon had to deplete his forces in Spain to continue his campaigns in central Europe in the 1813 season. Wellington was quick to take advantage, chasing the French back through Spain and smashing their army at the battle of Vittoria, south of Bilbao. The French retreated back over the Pyrenees. Napoleon held his own on the eastern front through the summer, but in the autumn the Austrians, sensing blood, joined the allies and *le petit caporal* was finally defeated at Leipzig in the Battle of the Nations.

In 1814 France itself was invaded by the Prussians, Russians and Austrians. Despite a series of checks from the ever-resourceful Napoleon, they were in Paris by March. Wellington by this time had advanced to take Bordeaux and Toulouse. Napoleon was replaced by an interim government in Paris and eventually by the Bourbon Louis XVIII, brother of the executed Louis XVI. By the Peace of Paris (1814), Napoleon was exiled to be the ruler of the small island of Elba, off the coast of Tuscany. France reverted close to her borders of 1792.

Britain retained possession of Mauritius, the Cape of Good Hope, Malta and Ceylon.

The conflict with the Americans, begun in 1812, took on a very different light after the defeat of Napoleon. In practice it had amounted to a series of minor naval engagements in American and Caribbean waters. These at least proved that the Americans did not need the British to teach them anything about sailing warships. The British at one point took Washington itself, and failed in the attempt to take New Orleans. The Americans also failed in their attempts to take Canada – one of their war aims. Their war party had hoped to find easy pickings whilst the British were distracted in Europe; instead they found their trade blockaded and ruined by the Royal Navy, which became overwhelmingly powerful at the end of hostilities in Europe. The American president, James Madison, who had started the war with high hopes, became desperate to finish it. Peace was concluded at Ghent in Belgium towards the end of 1814.

The statesmen of Europe then convened at the Congress of Vienna to decide on the future map of Europe. Britain was represented by Castlereagh. Whilst they deliberated, they received an unpleasant surprise – Napoleon was back in Paris. Louis XVIII had fled into exile.

Napoleon, knowing he would be attacked, took the initiative by invading Belgium, where he found the British under Wellington and the Prussians under Blucher. His opinion of Wellington was that he was a "sepoy general" – but his own senior generals, all of whom had been defeated by the Englishman in Spain and the south of France, knew better. Wellington, who was destined never to lose a battle, was a master of battlefield tactics. In Spain much of this had come down to selecting a site where troops could be concealed from the enemy over the brow of a hill, only to swoop down to join what had appeared to be a much smaller force when battle began. The French generals, who believed that soldiers should stand up and be counted, didn't think much of this – but they lost every time.

After smaller engagements at Ligny, where the French beat the Prussians, and at Quatre Bras, where the British barely held them off, the main confrontation took place at Waterloo on a single day, 18 June 1815. Wellington reviewed his troops – whom he had once described as the "scum of the earth": "I don't know what effect these men will have on the enemy, but, by God, they frighten me!" About one fifth of his force of 67,000 men were his veterans from the Peninsular War.

Finding the British steadfast where they had formed up overnight, Napoleon attacked head-on. The battle carried on all day and could have gone to the French. "Would that night or Blucher come!" exclaimed Wellington. Blucher and his Prussians did come, late in a very long day, and that was the end of Napoleon. In this, probably the most famous battle in British history, the combined army of the British, Dutch and their German allies suffered 16,000 men killed or wounded – almost a quarter of those engaged. The Prussians lost another 7,000, and the French 30,000. As Wellington well knew, "It has been a damned nice thing - the nearest run thing you ever saw in your life!" He was well aware of his own role – "Up guards and at them again!" – and – "By God, I don't think it would have been done if I had not been there."

After the battle, Napoleon was conducted to the British warship *HMS Bellerophon*, and thence to a lonely island in the South Atlantic, Saint Helena, where he died aged only 51 in 1821. Wellington became a celebrity for the rest of his long life. He and Napoleon had both been born in the same year, 1769, but Wellington finally died in 1852, becoming prime minister in the years 1828-30 and briefly in 1834. However, he was not always popular, and attracted much criticism for his opposition to parliamentary reform.

This heroic age of warfare and empire was accompanied by a great blossoming of the arts in England. notably in poetry. One of the people directly affected by the French Revolution was the Romantic poet William Wordsworth (1770-1850), who was in France in 1791 and who fathered a child by a Frenchwoman, Annette Vallon. Wordsworth was enthralled by the Revolution, then subsequently appalled by the Reign of Terror. In any event, as war had broken out, he was only able to return to France to see Annette and his child Caroline during the brief lull provided by the Peace of Amiens in 1802. Here he made what arrangements he could so that he could marry Mary Hutchinson back in England. Another poet was Samuel Taylor Coleridge (1772-1834), author of *The Rime of the Ancient Mariner* and *Kubla Khan*, and one-time friend of Wordsworth. The other famous Romantic poets of this era are John Keats (1795-1821), Percy Bysshe Shelley (1792-1822) and Lord Byron (1788-1824). From an earlier generation is the mystic poet and painter William Blake (1757-1827), author of *Jerusalem*. In painting, too, William Turner (1775-1851) and John Constable (1776-1837) were active in this period. In literature, the most enduring name from the Revolutionary years is that of Jane Austen (1775-1817), whose novels – artfully written comedies of manners – seem a million miles from the bloody battlefields of Europe. Her most famous work, *Pride and Prejudice*, was published in 1813, the year of the defining Battle of the Nations at Leipzig. It has probably the most famous opening line of any novel in the English language: "It is a truth universally acknowledged, that a single man, in possession of a good fortune, must be in want of a wife".

This period is also remarkable for the construction of the canal network in Great Britain, which transformed the transportation of heavy goods. The canals, the motorways of their day, were mainly built to transport coal, other heavy materials such as limestone, and fragile goods such as pottery from Stoke-on-Trent. The 1790s were the years of Canal Mania, when many projects were undertaken and the principal engineers of the day – Thomas Telford (1757-1834), John Rennie and William Jessop amongst them – were kept busy with multiple projects running simultaneously. The main construction phase lasted into the 1820s when the potential of railways began to be realised.

Over a longer period in the eighteenth and nineteenth centuries, the road were also being substantially improved. The establishment of turnpike trusts enabled road maintenance and improvement to be taken from parish administration and passed to trusts, which collected tolls to pay their way. There were also technological improvements, chiefly associated with the name of John McAdam. Up until this time, the roads had been little more than earth tracks. When appointed surveyor to the Bristol Turnpike Trust in 1816, McAdam remade the roads under his care with crushed stone bound with gravel on a firm base of larger stones. His roads also featured a camber, making the surface slightly convex to allow water to drain off rapidly. The roads were also built raised above the level of the surrounding ground. These techniques represented the greatest advance in road construction since Roman times, and greatly reduced journey times.

The French wars stimulated a boom in agriculture, already being established on more scientific principles in the eighteenth century. The improving landlords of the period, such as Coke of Norfolk (1752-1842) spent vast amounts on their estates, and as a result enjoyed great increases in rent. The old open fields with their scattered strips had already undergone consolidation earlier in the century, and in many areas wasteland and common land had also been enclosed. The result was greatly improved agricultural productivity, at the expense of the creation of a large, landless labouring class in the countryside. To offset the dire effects of rural poverty, the Speenhamland System was set up in 1795 to provide outdoor relief to the rural poor.

Chapter 27 – The Late Georgian Period

The peace of 1815 marked a great turning point in British history. No observer from those times would have guessed that the country would never again fight the French, or that in fact France would be an ally in the major wars of the future. No one would have even considered that the military strategy and foreign policy of the country for the next 132 years would come to be overshadowed by the security requirements of one country, which barely registered a blip on the national screen in 1815 – India. It is unlikely that anyone would imagine that the country would fight three wars against the Chinese, the first within a generation. That the country itself would continue its rapid industrialization, a process which continued apace throughout the nineteenth century – many of the industrial towns of the north were largely unbuilt before 1870 – was easier to foretell. That the agricultural life of the country would collapse as a result of developments in international shipping would have been harder to foresee. But most difficult of all would have been the realization that for the next hundred years, the country would not be involved in a single major war in continental Europe; in fact in just one second-ranking conflict, and that – of all places – in Russia.

By 1815, however, the first glimmers of light had penetrated two of the darkest places on earth, both of which were to figure prominently in British history for the first time in the nineteenth century – the interior of Africa, and China. On a journey undertaken between 1795 and 1797, a Scottish explorer called Mungo Park had located and sailed down the River Niger, key to all West Africa. Turning back before he reached the delta, he tried again in 1805, but never returned. In the same era, an embassy was sent to China in 1793 under the leadership of Lord Macartney, carrying with it the wonders of western technology, including one of John Harrison's chronometers. Its mission was to open China to British trade. The Ching Emperor and his courtiers, however, saw no need for China to become involved with the foreign devils, and the mission was politely but firmly rebuffed. With or without their permission, however, the foreign devils meant to open the Chinese trade, and were about to do so, not with chronometers, but with opium.

The postwar years from 1815 were marked by a profound depression in both agriculture and industry. Continental production revived, creating competition for British goods. The prospect of this had already caused the Corn Law to be passed in 1815 to protect home farmers. This established that no corn (wheat) could be imported until the price reached 80 shillings a quarter. However this did mean that in good years, the supply was high and the price well below this – on the average, only 45 shillings, and so not profitable. In a year of bad harvests, the farmers had little to sell and could not recoup their losses because of foreign imports keeping the price down. Furthermore, in the biggest volcanic eruption for 1600 years, Mount Tabora in what is now Indonesia exploded and sent such volume of debris into the atmosphere that the following year, 1816, was described as the "Year without a summer" in much of the northern hemisphere. Harvests were disastrous and hunger and starvation stalked the land.

Meanwhile Luddite rioting, which had first broken out in Nottinghamshire in 1811, had spread throughout the manufacturing districts. The year 1817 saw riots in Spa Fields in London and a planned insurrection in Derbyshire. Habeas Corpus was suspended again. The more sensible amongst the working classes were now creating pressure for parliamentary reform. What had by now become huge cities, including Manchester, Birmingham and Leeds, were simply not represented in parliament, an absurd situation. Large meetings were called to demand a change. These alarmed the government, which issued proclamations against "seditious" meetings. One such was then held in August, 1819 in St Peter's Fields in Manchester. A large crowd had gathered – men, women and children – marching in processions with flags flying: a gala day, with a speech by the famous pro-reform orator Henry Hunt. The magistrates became alarmed and ordered cavalry and yeomanry to charge the unarmed crowd. It is thought that fifteen people were killed outright and literally hundreds were injured. This incident became known as the Peterloo Massacre.

Parliament was hardly deflected by the massacre, passing the "Six Acts" of repressive measures, as if the country was on the verge of a revolution. These banned training in military exercises, seditious publications and unauthorized meetings, amongst other things. The rising leader of the Whigs, Lord John Russell, said in parliament that what the people wanted was representation in parliament. However, what was really needed was an improvement in the economy following the post-war slump. Measures were taken by Robert Peel in 1819 to resume cash payments of banknotes on demand. This put trade on a firmer footing, and an economic recovery began. Peel is notable as the first important member of any government to originate in the northern "millocracy" – his father was a Lancashire cotton magnate.

Amidst the uproar, George III, long detached from any reality, died at the age of 81.

George IV 1820-1830 (10 years)
Born 1762, married 1795, Caroline of Brunswick

A real plot was discovered right at the start of the reign of George IV, known as the Cato Street conspiracy. An ex-army officer called Thistlewood planned to murder Lord Liverpool and his ministers when they were dining at the house of Lord Barrowby. The conspirators – mainly draymen and butchers – were arrested before any action could be taken. Thistlewood and four others were executed.

The royal household very quickly became involved in the first real royal scandal of the Hanoverian period, of the type which has become common enough today. George IV had shaken off Mrs Fitzherbert, as his marriage to her was illegal, and as long ago as 1795 had made a dynastic marriage to Caroline of Brunswick. This new union produced one daughter, Charlotte, but it was an unhappy marriage, and Princess Caroline moved abroad in 1814. Charlotte grew up and married a German prince, but then died herself in childbirth. This meant that the succession would eventually fall to George's niece, Victoria, born in 1819.

Whilst Caroline had been abroad, stories had got back to England about improprieties in her conduct, namely her involvement with her Italian "servant". Accordingly, when it came to the coronation, George tried to exclude her from the ceremony, and from the title of Queen. This upset public opinion, which saw her as an injured woman. However, the evidence brought forward to support her exclusion was so strong that public opinion turned against her. Said to be broken-hearted at missing the ceremony at Westminster Abbey, she died shortly afterwards.

In the meantime it had become clear that there was to be no immediate revolution in the country, and restrictions began to relax. A new, moderate force was making itself felt in the Tory party, symbolized by the appointment of Robert Peel, as Home Secretary. Another sign of the times was the suicide of the reactionary foreign secretary, Lord Castlereagh in 1822 – an event which was greeted with unseemly joy in the country. The new foreign secretary was the much more liberal George Canning. He supported the former South American colonies of Spain, busy at this time in winning their independence – most achieved this by 1825, including (Portuguese) Brazil. This would obviously benefit British trade, which the Spanish had tried to exclude for so long, and it was indeed to do so. Also the new countries were to turn to Britain for capital in future years, falling heavily under British influence. Another man to support the new countries was President Monroe of the United States. His "Monroe Doctrine" – America for the Americans – was intended to stop European countries taking over the old Spanish colonies, but really meant "Latin America for the United States".

Canning also supported the Greeks in their fight to gain independence from the Ottoman Empire. This struggle that lasted right through until 1832; Lord Byron famously involved himself in it, and died of fever in Greece in 1824.

In parallel to Canning at the foreign office was a new broom at the Board of Trade, William Huskisson. He vastly reduced the scope of the Navigation Laws, whose intention was to exclude foreign shipping, and also removed restrictions on the movement of labour, wages and both trade unions and cartels. He also reduced customs duties on imported raw material such as silk and wool. The object of these policies was to assist the manufacturing interest, rapidly growing in both economic and political importance. However the boom of the 1820s, accompanied by bubble companies and overtrading, collapsed in 1825 when a new recession set in, accompanied by more riots and Luddism.

Several political issues ran over decades at this time. One was Catholic emancipation. The Catholics had support within parliament, but legislation to relieve them of their restrictions could never pass the Lords, or the king. In 1823 a vigorous Irishman called Daniel O'Connell formed the Catholic Association to advocate Catholic claims. This became a vast organization and almost superseded the government in Ireland. The Westminster government suppressed the Catholic Association but it soon reappeared under another name, and agitation in favour of the Catholics continued – but it was not a cause which had much support in England.

Another recurring theme was the attempt to stop Russia from taking advantage of the rotten Ottoman Empire to extend its own empire to Constantinople. The British became involved with the Greeks in their struggle for independence from the Turks. An attempt by the Turks to take the Ionian Islands was defeated at the Battle of Navarino (1827), the last naval battle ever fought entirely with sailing ships. The Ionian Islands – a group to the west of Greece – were at this time a British possession. A Russian squadron fought with the British on this occasion. On land the Russians extended their territory down both the west and east coasts of the Black Sea, at the expense of the Turks, but they failed to reach Constantinople. This issue was ultimately to be the cause of the Crimean War, thirty years later.

During the later 1820s, home governments changed at bewildering speed. Lord Liverpool, prime minister since 1812, finally resigned (in ill-health) in 1827, to be followed by George Canning, who died within months. Then it was briefly the turn of Lord Goderich, before the Duke of Wellington himself took on the job in 1828. The first event of the new ministry was the final repeal of the Test and Corporation Acts, by which Nonconformists were admitted to full political rights. This was promoted from outside the government by the Whig Russell. It was widely recognised that the government was not doing itself any good by excluding so many able Nonconformists from their full participation in society.

In 1829 the Home Secretary Robert Peel established the Metropolitan Police, the first professional policemen in the country, initially 1000 constables – known after him as bobbies or peelers. The innovation proved so successful in curtailing crime that it later spread to all urban areas.

Having been put in office on the promise of refusing Catholic emancipation, Wellington and Peel then found that they were obliged to bow to pressure and grant it after all. This immediate cause was O'Connell's election as MP for Clare – a seat he could not take up because of his religion. Widespread disorder was expected to follow in Ireland. So the Irish franchise was extended to include Catholics, but the qualifying rate was increase from forty shillings to ten pounds a year, which automatically excluded most of them again. O'Connell. then extended his campaign into one for the outright dissolution of the union between Ireland and England.

At this juncture (1830), George IV died. He was described as "a bad son, a bad husband, a bad father, a bad subject, a bad monarch and a bad friend". He was succeeded by his brother, William, Duke of Clarence.

William IV 1830-1837 (7 years)
Born 1765, married 1818, Adelaide of Saxe Meiningen

Already 64 years old on his accession, William – known as the "Sailor King" from his earlier years in the Navy – was a much more popular man than his brother had been, and was thought to be in favour of reform. His reign was indeed to witness some great changes.

The first of these was the coming of the railways, which made fast, reliable transport possible for the first time, anywhere on the planet. The first railway with a steam-driven locomotive was the Stockton to Darlington, opened in 1825, but the first real commercial passenger-carrying railway was the Liverpool to Manchester, opened to great ceremony in 1830. An important politician, William Huskisson, managed to get himself knocked down and killed. The engineer was a self-taught northern workman, George Stephenson, and his locomotive the famous *Rocket*. The Duke of Wellington, who also attended, feared to get out in Manchester – where he was deeply unpopular, due to his attitude to parliamentary and other reform – and so stayed in his carriage for the return journey. The speed restrictions on the early trains were lifted and very soon, trains were travelling at 60 mph and faster.

The next great change was parliamentary reform. Wellington and many other aristocrats who controlled the House of Lords thought that, for all its imperfections, the old system worked well enough in practice, and generally secured a House of Commons which reflected opinion in the country. By now, however, the tide of history was against them. The Duke was replaced as prime minister by the Whig Lord Grey, and after a tremendous battle with the Lords, riots and near revolution in the cities, Russell secured the passage of the Great Reform Bill in 1832. 143 rotten boroughs were deprived of their seats, which were then distributed amongst the larger cities and towns across the country, especially in the manufacturing districts but also in the London suburbs. This was the main reform. The franchise was increased by fifty percent, but still excluded most of the population. However it was standardized, so that for example in the towns those paying an annual rental of £10 were entitled to vote. Similar reform bills were enacted for Scotland and Ireland, though the rural Catholics were still largely excluded in Ireland. Scotland had 53 seats, Ireland 105, indicating that at that point in the century, Ireland was much the more populous country.

The new franchise meant that the power of the aristocracy in the towns was gone, though less so in the country. A new parliament was elected and the Tories under Peel and Wellington only obtained 172 seats to the Whigs' 486. Wellington reviewed the newly elected parliament and commented – "I've never seen so many bad hats in all my life!" The new parliament immediately abolished slavery in the Empire. The slave trade had already been abolished in 1807. Compensation to the tune of £20 million was paid to the slave owners of the Caribbean. Ashley-Cooper (later Earl of Shaftesbury) enacted a famous bill outlawing the employment of children under the age of nine in factories (1833 Factory Act). A later Factory Act (1847), introduced by mill owner John Fielden, limited working hours to ten a day.

In 1834 by the Poor Law Amendment Act, outdoor relief was forbidden to the able-bodied poor. From now on they would have to get their dole indoors, in the workhouse. Also, in 1833 an act was passed to reform the Irish (Protestant) church, reducing the number of archbishops and bishops to reflect reality, though as always in Irish affairs, there were disagreements and defections from the government.

Tired of reform and the Whigs, William IV attempted to replace them with the Tories – now calling themselves the Conservatives – in 1834, under the Duke of Wellington and then Peel. However, at the election then called, the Whigs were still in a majority of 107, and so returned to office under Lord Melbourne. Lord John Russell became home secretary, and Lord Palmerston foreign secretary. Both were to be future prime ministers. The most important act of the new administration was the Municipal Corporation Act, passed in 1835. This provided for elections for municipal councils, which had hitherto filled up vacancies by nomination. This was an important advance in local democracy which removed many abuses. The Corporation of London was the only important exemption to the new act.

In 1836 the circulation of newspapers was much increased when the duty upon them was reduced to one penny.

The following year, the old king died, to be succeeded by his eighteen year-old niece, Victoria. Though seen as honest, William was widely regarded as a weak, ignorant and commonplace sort of man. He was the last in a line of unattractive Hanoverians.

Chapter 28 – The Early Victorian Period

Victoria 1837-1901 (64 years)
Born 1819, married 1840, Albert of Saxe-Coburg

The new queen had led a sheltered existence until her accession to the throne, but she made a good first impression and hopes for a prosperous reign were raised. A top priority was to find a suitable husband. Several early suitors were soon sent packing, but one was not – Prince Albert of Saxe-Coburg. It was widely thought that the young queen doted on him – she admitted that "It was with some emotion that I beheld Albert – who is so beautiful". The couple were married in 1840. Interested in the moral and intellectual well-being of the people, he turned out to be a very good choice, and municipal statues of him abound to this day.

The accession of Victoria meant that the long association with Hanover came to an end, as in the area of Salic law – the old territories of Charlemagne – no woman could succeed. Her uncle the Duke of Cumberland took her place. The loss of Hanover was hardly regretted, as the territory had brought neither profit nor honour, but only the constant danger of Britain being dragged into German wars.

Melbourne's ministry soon ran into trouble in Canada. Pitt had divided the colony into Lower and Upper parts, dominated by French and British settlers respectively. There were constant difficulties with this arrangement, and in 1837 Lower Canada was in revolt. The government sent out special commissioners – the first, Lord Durham – with unlimited powers to sort out the difficulties. The ringleaders were deported to Bermuda, and new political arrangements united the two Canadas in a legislative union. This paved the way for a federal union of all the Canadian territories.

The Melbourne government showed many signs of weakness and pleased no one, but carried on in power because it did have a large majority in the Commons. There were many in the country by now who wanted further reforms. The most important of these were Anti-Corn Law agitators. The Corn Laws of 1815 kept the price of wheat artificially high and so favoured the agricultural over the manufacturing interest. At the same time the Radicals wanted futher parliamentary reform. The Whigs saw the Reform Act of 1832 as settling the question, but to the Radicals, this was only the first step. The Whigs believed that Parliament should represent the ownership of property, but the Radicals believed it should represent the people – all of them.

Another important group opposing the government (Whig or Tory) was the Chartists. These people created a "Charter" containing six demands: (1) universal male suffrage regardless of any property qualification; (2) vote by secret ballot, to prevent intimidation; (3) annual parliaments; (4) payment of members, to allow the working classes to send their own representatives; (5) the abolition of the property qualification for MPs; and (6) equal electoral districts, so that every person's vote would be worth the same. It is not difficult to see that for the time, the Charter was a revolutionary document, although all its clauses except for annual parliaments were implemented eventually. It horrified the governing aristocrats, but it proved very popular with the working man. The leader of the Chartists was an MP, Feargus O'Connor. The Chartists held many public meetings up and down the country and the movement generated much excitement both amongst the government and the governed. In an era of great public agitation, the Anti-Corn Law League, under its eloquent leaders Richard Cobden and John Bright, with its narrower platform, was to achieve its goals first.

The trade union movement was also becoming established in this era. The Combination Laws of 1799, outlawing such bodies, were repealed in 1824, then temporarily reimposed in the following year. In one notorious case, a group of farm workers from Dorset – the Tolpuddle Martyrs – were sentenced to transportation to Australia for forming a union, in 1834. After a public campaign the martyrs were released in 1836.

In the face of heavy opposition, Melbourne resigned in 1839 and Peel attempted to form a ministry, only to be foiled by a most unexpected problem. The personal attendants of the monarch – known as the ladies of the bedchamber – were supposed to resign with the old ministry, to be replaced by the connections of the new government. However the young queen was much distressed at this proposal, as her household would be broken up. This became known as the Bedchamber Crisis. Peel backed down, and Melbourne staggered on for two more years. By that time, Victoria was married, and no longer cared about the ladies.

In 1840 the Penny Post was introduced by Rowland Hill, whereby a letter could be sent anywhere in the country for just one penny, which could be pre-paid using the first postage stamp, the Penny Black. This revolutionized the postal service and provided great benefits for both business and the public. It represents the third important step in democratizing the country and allowing public opinion to form quickly – cheap post, following cheap newspapers and cheap, fast travel by train. It was, of course, the development of the rail network which made the Penny Post possible.

There were also colonial developments. In 1836, South Australia was colonised for the first time, taking the name of its capital from the wife of William IV, Adelaide. The next year Natal was colonised by Dutch settlers moving up from the Cape in South Africa; this territory became a colony in 1841. In 1839 Aden was acquired, with its strategic position at the entrance to the Red Sea. In the same year, New Zealand was first permanently colonised. Meanwhile there were futher extensions to the Empire around the borders of British India, as Nepal was added in 1813, Burma in 1824 and Assam in 1826. Elsewhere in Asia, Singapore was added in 1819. Just an island off the coast of Malaya, Thomas Raffles of the East India Company realised the potential of the site, one of the world's geopolitical pinch-points commanding the Straits of Singapore between the island and the Dutch East Indies. He negotiated a treaty with the local sultan to found a port. (Bombay and Hong Kong are similarly situated on islands with continental access.)

The charter of the East India company was renewed in 1833, but its monopoly of trade in India and China was withdrawn. By 1839, however, it was at the centre of a dispute which arose with the Ching (Qing) emperors of China. The main commodity it shipped from China was tea, for which the Chinese demanded payment in silver – they would not buy any tradable goods from the Company. However, the Company found one commodity that could easily be sold in China – opium. It organized the cultivation and shipment of this commodity to China in huge amounts. The importation of the drug was forbidden in China, but bribes were paid to customs officials, and after the drug left port, its distribution was entirely in the hands of Chinamen. In this way the opium trade resembled the slave trade in reverse, because it was Africans who delivered the slaves from the interior to the coast, and accepted payment for them.

The First Opium War began when the Chinese, in the shape of Commissioner Lin at Canton, decided to crack down on the trade. 20,000 chests weighing about 55 kg each were seized and destroyed, the greatest drugs bust of all time. The men of the East India Company were not amused. Lord Palmerston, the Whig Foreign Secretary, sent an expeditionary force to deal with the problem. This force took Canton and Shanghai, and moved to a point on the Yangtze where it took command of the junction between the river and the Grand Canal. The Chinese, appalled at the disastrous results of Lin's actions, sued for peace. Under the terms of the Treaty of Nanking (1842) China was opened to British trade, and Hong Kong was handed over to become a British possession. This was the first of the "unequal treaties" still bemoaned by the Chinese.

British imperial power did however suffer one major setback – in Afghanistan. At the same time as Britain was expanding its empire overseas, Russia was extending an empire of its own across Central Asia, and had reached close to the borders of Afghanistan, sending an envoy to the capital, Kabul, where the ruler was the Emir, Dost Mahomed. This was getting very close to British Indian territory. The interplay between the Russians and the British in this area came to be known as the Great Game, and continued over several decades. The British demanded the withdrawal of the Russian envoy, but Dost Mahomed refused. Setting off from Quetta in the south at the end of 1838, a British force of 21,000 men – mostly sepoys – then penetrated the Bolan Pass, and took Kandahar and Kabul. Dost Mahomed was deposed and a puppet called Shah Sujah was set up in his place. The British then learnt a lesson which several later invaders of Afghanistan have failed to remember – it is much easier to invade the country than it is to hold on to it. Most of the army was sent back, and wives and dependents moved in the opposite direction. By the start of 1842 the troops were under fire from all sides. William Elphinstone, leader of the expedition, was thoroughly outwitted by Akbar Khan, son of Dost Mahomed, and his troops were obliged to retreat down the Khyber Pass in the depths of winter. There were approximately 4,500 fighting men and 12,000 civilian camp followers. Only one man reached the fort of Jallalabad at the Indian end of the pass, a Dr Brydon. This tale is told in stirring, if fictionalised fashion in *Flashman* by George Macdonald Fraser. New armies were sent to try to atone for this disgrace. Kabul was recaptured but in the end, Dost Mahomed was restored.

Barely was the First Afghan War over when the British took another Indian territory, Scinde, which lies at the mouth of the Indus in what is now Pakistan. The general, a Peninsular War veteran called Sir Charles Napier, is said to have sent a one-word message on completing his victory – "Peccavi" – Latin for "I have sinned" – one of the most famous (if apocryphal) puns in history (1843). Very quickly the British moved on to the next territory, the Punjab, an area of northern India (now spilt between India and Pakistan) through which the five major tributaries of the Indus flow, and the homeland of the Sikhs. There were four major battles fought here against the warlike Punjabis, two in 1846 and two more in 1849, before the territory was annexed. The sepoys subsequently recruited from the Punjab were to prove some of the best soldiers in the Indian army.

Peel had finally returned to office with the Conservatives after the general election of 1841, promising to maintain the Corn Laws. His high reputation as a financier had helped him win over some of the towns. In Scotland, a great secession took place from the established Presbyterian church when the Free Church of Scotland was founded. In Ireland, Peel gave financial support to the Catholic college at Maynooth, just outside Dublin, a seminary for priests. Religious tolerance was spreading at last. William Gladstone, who had been a member of the Conservative government up to this time, resigned over the issue (he returned in 1846). Gladstone started his parliamentary career as a High Tory in the Reform parliament of 1832, then became a Peelite Conservative before becoming a Liberal prime minister.

Although elected to retain the Corn Laws, Peel was deflected by a completely unexpected event – a potato famine in Ireland. The crop of 1845 failed, and it was certain that there would be a great famine in 1846. In the circumstances the Irish would need cheap corn. Peel offered to resign over the issue, but the opposition could not or would not form a government, so it was left to Peel to repeal the Corn Laws in 1846. Thus for a second time, Peel had been obliged to renege on a key election commitment – the previous occasion was in granting emancipation to the Irish Catholics in 1829. In any event, the price of corn immediately fell. The agricultural interest did not forgive Peel, however. He was defeated in Parliament, to be replaced by Lord John Russell as prime minister (1846).

Famine duly struck in Ireland with an even greater ferocity than expected. A third of all families had been utterly dependent on the potato. Although any crop grown in monoculture and not hybridized is liable to blight, the potato had been reliably planted in Ireland for generations. The problem was exacerbated because a large section of the population had no source of income, and so no money to pay for alternative foodstuffs. Abject rural poverty was the norm in the south and west of the country. The land was normally owned by Anglo-Irish landowners, most of them absentees, so the rural poor had no assets to sell either. It was simply a hand-to-mouth existence. Many attempts had been made by the British government to improve the situation, with commission after commission making recommendations, but by the time the famine arrived, nothing substantial had been achieved. In addition, Ireland was grossly overpopulated for an almost entirely rural country, and in these circumstances, a famine due to one natural cause or another was inevitable. It was thought that the population stood at about eight million in 1846, up from two million at the time of the Civil War. There had already been a major famine in the years 1741-2, simply due to terrible, cold weather.

The attitude of the government in England was influenced by the writings of Thomas Malthus, who in 1798 published *An Essay on the Principle of Population*. In this he stated that human populations increase exponentially, and could double with every generation, whereas food production can only increase at lower, arithmetic rates. Therefore sooner or later the population would have to be reduced by famine, warfare or disease. Many people in England, and the more prosperous in Ireland, took the Malthusian view that the potato famine was an accident waiting to happen. There was in any case no welfare state as such in either England or Ireland, and there was widespread resentment amongst the hard-working element of the population at the able-bodied poor who for generations had simply cultivated their "lazy beds" – for potatoes require very little work – whilst doing nothing to improve their miserable living conditions. Within Ireland, on the other hand, amazement was expressed that food crops were being exported from the country – but the Government just saw this as the normal operation of the market, where those crops were beyond the reach of people with no money to buy them.

Irish people of influence, such as Daniel O'Connell, pleaded for help and the government did take some action. Before his resignation, Peel imported maize to distribute amongst the Irish, though this unfamiliar grain proved difficult to handle. Under Russell a program of public works – mainly road-building – was set up, administered by Lord Trevelyan. At one point this employed half a million people, most of them too weak to break rocks. The scheme was abandoned in favour of soup kitchens where the food was given away.

The upshot of the Great Famine was that around one million people starved to death and two million more emigrated, most of them to England, Scotland and North America. The social landscape of the country was changed permanently and new social norms (such as late marriage, or no marriage) meant that the population continued to decline right through until 1930. So if the English enclosure movement had been spread over centuries and the Highland Clearances over two or three generations, in Ireland this process happened within a decade, and only half a century after the Act of Union which had joined Ireland to England. The Irish never forgave the English for their callousness during the famine. But England and Scotland were themselves changed by the Irish diaspora. The great industrial cities of the west – Glasgow, Liverpool and Manchester – were expanding and jobs were available, so these cities and their satellites even today have a much higher proportion of Irish names and Irish faces than other parts of the north.

The period 1846-1874 was dominated by a succession of Whig ministries in which the most prominent figure (until his death in 1865) was the pugnacious Lord Palmerston, first as Foreign Secretary, later Prime Minister. 1848 was the Year of Revolutions in Europe where governments were replaced in France, Austria, and state capitals within Germany and Italy. Naturally this caused consternation in Britain, but at least a part of what the revolutionaries sought in Europe had already been conceded in Britain. The British share of all this was to be a relatively minor rebellion in Ireland, and a great Chartist demonstration in London. The Chartist meeting took place on Kennington Common, but the planned procession into Westminster fizzled out. The Duke of Wellington himself had organized military precautions against it. The Chartists had prepared a monster petition, but many of the names on it turned out to be fictitious, including the Duke of Wellington, Prince Albert and Punch. Chartism receded into history in favour of piecemeal reform.

1851 was the year of the Great Exhibition, housed in the Crystal Palace in Hyde Park and organized under the auspices of Prince Albert. It was a tremendous success, drawing visitors from all over the country on cheap railway specials, and indeed from abroad. The prefabricated glass and iron structure was re-erected on Sydenham Hill in south London after the exhibition, but it burnt down in 1936.

In 1852 a new coalition ministry formed with Lord Aberdeen as Prime Minister. It included both Conservative Peelites such as Gladstone and Whigs such as Palmerston. Within a year, this new government found itself involved in a war with Russia. The Russians were keen to exploit the weakness of the Ottoman Empire, known as the "sick man of Europe" throughout the nineteenth century. They demanded of the Sultan that he acknowledge the right of the Tsar Nicholas I to act as protector of the many (Orthodox) Christians within the Ottoman Empire. This would have made Russia all-powerful in the Christian provinces in the Balkans – Serbia, Bulgaria, Macedonia and others – but Russia had territorial ambitions as well, aimed at the warm-sea port of Constantinople. The British always feared this move, so found themselves supporting a decrepit, oppressive Muslim State against a Christian one. Their allies in the adventure were the French, where the new Emperor, Louis Napoleon III, nephew of Napoleon, was keen on the idea of military glory.

It is said of this war that it took six months deciding where to fight it, but the eventual strategy was a good one, concentrating on the Russian Black Sea fleet based in the Crimea, but also bottling up the Baltic and strangling Russian trade. The main target was the arsenal of Sebastopol on the Crimea. Russian logistics were stretched to support the city and the English, French and Turkish allies registered a victory at the battle of Alma on landing in the Crimea (1854). There were further victories at Balaclava and Inkerman in the same year. Balaclava was made infamous by the Charge of the Light Brigade, ordered by Lord Cardigan, where 600 cavalrymen charged straight across the line of Russian fire. A watching French general noted "C'est Magnifique, mais ce ne'est pas la guerre!"

The Charge seemed typical of the early incompetence shown by the allies. Conditions in the Crimea were poor, especially in winter, and the miserable arrangements made by the home government caused unnecessary suffering amongst the soldiers. These failings were highlighted by the first real modern war correspondent, William Russell of the *Times*. More soldiers were dying of infections and improperly treated wounds than in battle. Conditions at the war hospital at Scutari outside Constantinople were notorious. So it was that the famous nursing sister Florence Nightingale was sent to Scutari to institute proper care for the men. It was noted, however, that the death rate did not fall significantly until the later arrival of sanitary and public health engineers from England. Another famous nurse was the Jamaican Mary Seacole, who made her own way to the battlefront and nursed the wounded men.

By the beginning of 1856 it had become clear that the continuation of the war would bankrupt Russia. Her trade had been ruined by the blockade and she was obliged to raise money in Europe at unaffordable rates. Nicholas I had died in 1855, to be replaced by Alexander II. The fighting had reached a stalemate. So peace was concluded in Paris in 1856, where Russia agreed to the neutralization of the Black Sea and Danube delta. The real result of the war was to cripple Russia for years to come, but she would be back, in 1877.

In 1856 another war began in China, the Second Opium War. Chinese customs officials boarded a ship called the *Arrow*, manned by Chinese but formerly registered as British. Palmerston (Prime Minister since 1855) used this as an excuse to begin hostilities, in which he was once again joined by the French. After fighting in the Canton area the attacks spread up the coast and eventually the allies captured Peking itself, looting and destroying the emperor's summer palace nearby. As a result of a new treaty signed in 1860, the foreigners – including the Americans – established the right to travel anywhere in China, to navigate the Yangtze, to send ambassadors to the imperial court, to import opium legally, to work as missionaries within China, and to be paid a large indemnity against their war costs. Only a truly supine government could have yielded so much after so many years of resistance – clearly the Ching dynasty was tottering, and this treaty (Tientsin/Tianjin) was seen by many as the prelude to the partition of China amongst its enemies, the foreign devils.

In the meantime, and much more serious for the British, a mutiny had broken out in India in 1857. There were rumours amongst the sepoys that the British intended to force Christianity upon them. There was consternation at the recent annexation of the province of Oudh, from which many of the Bengal sepoys came. There was a prophecy that British rule would come to an end after 100 years – and the battle of Plassey, marking the start of it, had been in 1757. Most famously, the sepoys had been issued with new cartridges wrapped in greased rags. This grease was said to come from the fat of cows and pigs, the one sacred to the Hindus, the other an abomination to the Muslims. The mutiny broke out at Meerut where the sepoys murdered their officers. It spread rapidly along the valley of the Ganges and the soldiers were soon in control of Delhi itself. The city of Cawnpore fell to the rebels with the slaughter of 200 Europeans. Lucknow, the capital of Oudh, was besieged.

The problem sepoy regiments were Bengali, and the East India Company was able to bring in loyal troops from other areas, especially Sikhs, Punjabi Muslims and Gurkhas. Lucknow was relieved by General Havelock. Delhi was retaken after strenuous efforts. Reinforcements arrived from Britain and the mutiny was put down by 1858. The insurgents had lacked leadership and coordination and made little headway outside the Ganges Valley. Today they are remembered within India as the country's first freedom fighters.

As a result of the mutiny, the proportion of British soldiers in the Indian regiments was increased permanently. The powers of the East India Company were transferred to the crown, bringing down the curtain on its activities going back to the reign of Elizabeth. At one point it had accounted for ten percent of the economy of England.

Henceforward a Viceroy or Governor-General appointed by the government in Westminster would run the administration of India.

1858 was the year of something distinctly domestic – the Great Stink of London. The Thames was literally an open sewer and the population pressure meant that it became so polluted that it was not possible to sit in the House of Commons without being exposed to the appalling stench of the river. It was finally decided that this time, something must be done, and plans were made for the construction of a modern sewerage system for London. There was a further motivation. The capital was subject to severe epidemics of cholera. For years the cause had been unknown, the most popular idea being that the disease was caused by bad air, or "miasma". However after the 1854 epidemic, work by one Dr John Snow showed that this was not the case, and the disease was associated with bad water. In streets drawing their water from one well, cholera had struck; in adjacent streets using another well, it had not. It became an urgent matter of public health to remedy the situation – but it took the Great Stink in the House of Commons to get the job started. A truly massive feat of engineering, the main work was completed in the six years starting from 1859 under the supervision of John Bazelgette, Chief Engineer of the Metropolitan Board of Works.

Another great engineering work of this period was the rebuilding of the Houses of Parliament. The old Palace of Westminster had burnt down in 1834, so the construction of a replacement was begun in 1840. The architect was Sir Charles Barry, and the interior designer, Augustus Pugin. The work was to continue for thirty years, and gave England its most iconic building.

The establishment of limited liability companies was made possible by legislation in 1855-6. Under this system, investors were only liable for the capital invested in a company, and could not be held personally responsible for unpaid debts beyond that amount. This proved a great boon to business set-ups, and following the Companies Act of 1862, a large number of public joint-stock companies were established, or converted from previously private concerns.

Prince Albert sadly died in 1861, aged only 42, leaving a grieving Queen Victoria and ten children. Otherwise the great events of the next few years all happened abroad. The first was the unification of Italy, mostly achieved in 1861. The second was the American Civil War of 1861-5. In this conflict, Britain remained neutral. However a warship, the *Alabama*, was built at Birkenhead for the southern Confederacy. The Northern Union regarded this as an infringement of neutrality. After it had won the war, compensation was demanded. This was settled by arbitration at a value of three million pounds. The third great event was the defeat of Austria by Prussia in 1866, paving the way for the unification of Germany five years later.

Chapter 29 – The Later Victorian Period

The late Victorian era saw many important demographic changes in the country. A great depression affected agriculture in Britain, lasting from 1870 until the start of the Great War in 1914. Poor harvests and animal diseases at home were compounded by a much greater problem, the growing import of foodstuffs from abroad. The great prairies of the American Midwest and Canada had been opened up for farming. The development of the steamship and the establishment of a railway network in the USA and Canada, together with the invention of the refrigerated wagon and ship, allowed North American farmers to export grain and meat to Britain at a price that undercut the home producers. The American farmers made heavy use of machinery, and benefitted from economies of scale because of their huge fields on the open prairies. At the same time, large amounts of cheap corned beef started to arrive from Argentina, and the completion of the Suez Canal in 1869 reduced the price of lamb and wool from Australia and New Zealand. By 1900 half the meat eaten in Britain came from abroad. Domestic cereal output fell and remained in a depressed condition, though dairy farmers were less affected. There was also a shift to higher-cost produce such as fruit and vegetables. Nevertheless much arable land reverted to pasture, and 400,000 agricultural labourers left the land between 1870 and 1900. Many migrated from rural areas of the south into the fast-growing industrial towns of the north.

Another great change taking place in these times was the depopulation of the mining areas of the south-west, particularly Cornwall. Employment in the tin and copper mines reached its zenith in the middle of the nineteenth century, before the opening of new mines overseas made the mines of the south-west unprofitable. However, the miners found that their skills were in great demand in the new mines, for example in northern Michigan, but also in many other places, including South Africa, Australia and Chile, so many emigrated, taking their families with them. It is estimated that half a million people left the mining communities, the greatest numbers leaving in the 1870s.

       *   *   *   *

After numerous attempts, a second Reform Act was passed in 1867. It was introduced by the Conservatives under Lord Derby and Benjamin Disraeli. The vote was extended to all householders in towns, and to all £12 householders in the counties. There was a further redistribution of seats to reflect the changing pattern of population. The new franchise was still far from universal, but it did give the vote to many previously unfranchised groups such as schoolteachers.

Also in 1867, the government of Canada was remodelled by the British North America Act, which set up a new federal government there and gave the country "Dominion" status – in practice fully independent, but remaining cooperative with the home country. Following in the steps of the Durham Report of 1839, this meant that actual fighting between the British and the French Canadian settlers was avoided. In contrast, two wars were to follow between the British and the Dutch settlers in South Africa

In 1868, Gladstone came to power as the leader of the Whigs, now renamed the Liberals, on a reforming ticket. In fact this was to be one of the most important reforming ministries of the century The first priority was Ireland, a country which was to haunt Gladstone. There had been outrages committed by a newly formed group, the Fenians, but Gladstone recognised that some of the Irish grievances were genuine. He disestablished and partly disendowed the Irish Protestant Church, which had little support in most of the country. He also passed a Land Act giving Irish tenants the power to sell their tenancies and any unexhausted improvements to the incoming tenant. It was hoped this would assuage the ill-feeling between landlord and tenant in Ireland.

Another most important measure was Forster's Education Act of 1870, making education available to every child in the country between the ages of five and twelve. This was done by the establishment of "Board" schools, that is, supervised by an elected board of governors rather than by a church, and supported by a local authority rate. Also in education, the University Test Act of 1871 allowed Nonconformists and Catholics to take degrees at Oxford and Cambridge. 1870 saw the introduction of competitive examinations for civil servants, and with it the end of a system of patronage running back hundreds of years. Then in 1871 the sale and purchase of commissions in the army was discontinued. The Ballot Act of 1872 created secret ballots at elections – one of the original demands of the Chartists.

The Franco-Prussian War took place in 1870-1. This represented the French attempt to prevent the unification of Germany, but the Prussians won after only a short campaign. The French government of Louis Napoleon III fell as a result. France had good reason to fear a united Germany, as events of the next century were to show. During the war the Italians took Rome from the Pope, finally ending the temporal power of the papacy. In all the excitement, Britain reaffirmed the neutrality of Belgium, first guaranteed in 1839. This was a clear warning to Germany that any invasion of France through that small country – the easy route into France – would mean war with Britain. That is indeed what took place in 1914 when Germany breached the neutrality of Belgium.

Gladstone was replaced by the Conservative Disraeli in 1874. Apart from a brief spell in 1868, Disraeli had only one term as Prime Minister, which lasted until 1880. Of Jewish origin, he was a practising Christian, and a witty character who delighted Queen Victoria. She complained that Gladstone "addresses me as if I were a public meeting". One of Disraeli's first acts was to buy a share of the Suez Canal. Begun as a French project under De Lesseps in 1859 and completed ten years later, the canal had proved a success. Disraeli bought a large shareholding from the Khedive of Egypt in 1874, giving the British government a share of control. A further development in the field of communications was the establishment of an undersea network of telegraph cables, from 1870 onwards, allowing messages to be transmitted round the world at the press of a key.

In 1877 another war broke out between Russia and Turkey. Russia would have annexed Constantinople in this conflict, but Disraeli sent a Royal Navy squadron to Constantinople, and brought soldiers to Malta, to make it clear that the British would oppose the annexation with force. In the course of the war the Turks committed one of their infamous massacres when 15,000 Bulgarians were killed in an uprising. The Treaty of Berlin (1878) concluded the war, recognising the independence of Serbia, Montenegro and Romania and the partial independence of Bulgaria. Britain assumed control of Cyprus. This war gave rise to the term Jingoism, or excessive patriotism, from a popular song of the time:

We don't want to fight but by Jingo if we do
We've got the ships, we've got the men, we've got the money too
We've fought the Bear before, and while we're Britons true
The Russians shall not have Constantinople.

Thwarted in the Balkans, the Russians decided once more to play the Great Game in Asia, and sent another envoy to Afghanistan. This precipitated the Second Afghan War (1878-80), where the British once again invaded the country and took the capital, Kabul. The British had to invade twice, the second time under Frederick Roberts. The Emir, one Sher Ali Khan, son of Dost Mohammed, had then to concede control of his foreign policy but otherwise maintained his sovereignty.

In 1880 Gladstone and the Liberals returned to power, partly on the back of a series of powerful speeches made in Scotland by Gladstone himself and known collectively as the Midlothian Campaign. The Irish immediately began to make more trouble under a new leader, Charles Parnell. They now demanded Home Rule. Gladstone tried to placate them with the Irish Land Act (1881), creating a new way of setting rents by tribunal. The troubles continued and the government was obliged to pass two Coercion Acts, this being a generic term for the many acts passed specifically to establish law and order in Ireland. In practice this meant the suspension of Habeas Corpus. Parnell and others were imprisoned without trial for a short time. The new Irish Secretary, Lord Frederick Cavendish, was murdered by Irish nationalists immediately upon his arrival in Dublin.

Suddenly events in Africa began to move quickly. The British, moving north into Natal in southern Africa, ran up against the warlike Zulu nation. War ensued in 1879. British forces, underestimating the enemy, suffered a famous defeat at Isandlwana, a British version of Custer's last stand (in fact Lord Chelmsford's last stand). A section of the troops held on at Rorke's Drift. Reinforcements were brought up, and after the battle of Ulundi (1879) the Zulus under their king Cetswayo lost their independence.

Elsewhere in southern Africa, the Dutch Afrikaaner settlers or Boers had moved northwards in the "Great Trek", and had settled in the area known as the Transvaal. One reason for moving was to get away from British rule, and under their leader Paul Kruger they declared their independence. This led to a minor conflict known as the First Boer War (1880-1). The Afrikaaners defeated a British force at Majuba Hill (1881). Gladstone quickly came to the conclusion that the war was not worth fighting, and allowed the independence of the Boer republic, subject to British "suzerainty" (overlordship). This was just a face-saving formula, as it clearly meant nothing to Kruger.

Egypt was at this time run jointly by the British and the French. In 1882 a local uprising under Colonel Arabi was suppressed by British forces. Alexandria was bombarded from the sea, and Arabi and his army were defeated on land at Tel-el-Kebir by a force under General Wolseley. The French had opted not to join in, and were far from pleased at this outcome as the country was now effectively in British hands. South of Egypt in the Sudan, another insurrection broke out led by a religious adventurer styled the Mahdi. General "China" Gordon was sent to effect the peaceful withdrawal of the Egyptian garrisons in the country. However Gordon found himself besieged at Khartoum. An expedition to rescue him failed to get there in time, and Gordon was killed (1885). He would be avenged, but not until 1898.

Central Africa, though close enough to Europe, had resisted almost all penetration by explorers until the middle of the nineteenth century, when it was discovered that quinine could offer protection against malaria. The most famous explorers were Dr David Livingstone, Henry Stanley and Richard Burton, and gradually the valleys of the Nile, Zambezi and Congo were mapped out. In 1884 a Congress was held in Berlin to agree spheres of influence amongst the European nations now busy with the Scramble for Africa. Within twenty-five years, virtually the whole continent – with the notable exception of Abyssinia – had been colonised by one European country or another.

Local government underwent a dramatic transformation in the 1880s. The franchise for local elections was extended to all householders in 1880, and in 1882 the Municipal Corporations Act swept away the last restrictions on services which municipal bodies could provide. The result was that socialism at the municipal level preceded socialism at the national level by nearly 50 years. Local authorities of one sort or another took responsibility for roads and pavements, street lighting and cleaning, town gas, water supply and sewerage, schools, lunatic asylums, hospitals, parks, trams (in the 1890s), art galleries, libraries, workhouses, cemeteries and more – a far greater remit than they have today.

There was more electoral reform in 1884 with the Representation of the People Act, and the following year with the Redistribution Act. These extended the franchise to £10 householders in county constituencies, and redistributed seats once more. These acts effectively created one-member constituencies as the norm for Parliamentary representation, though many two-member constituencies remained.

Gladstone then yielded to Irish demands and created a bill to establish home rule. However, he could not get this passed, and only succeeded in splitting the Liberal party. So in 1885, Lord Salisbury came to power as the head of the Conservatives and Liberal Unionists. This marked the start of a period of Conservative/Unionist government which lasted, with the exception of the years 1892-6, until 1906. Irish home rule was taken off the government's agenda, though some minor Irish measures were passed. The most important act of the ministry was the 1888 Local Government Act, which created county councils and a council for Greater London. This put the rural areas and the outer London boroughs on the same footing as the towns had been since 1835.

Forster's Education Act of 1870 had made a big impact on the provision of elementary education, but the requirement still to pay the "school pence" was a barrier. This was removed by The Education Act of 1891, providing free elementary education.

In 1892, the Liberals returned to office. In 1894, having failed once again to enact Irish Home Rule, Gladstone retired as Prime Minister, handing over the reins to fellow Liberal Lord Roseberry. He was by this time in his eighty-fifth year, and had been Prime Minister four times with a total of 13 years in the job. However, the Irish problem scarcely went away. Outside Parliament, various extreme and violent Irish organizations were formed, including Sinn Fein and the Irish Republican Brotherhood, which fought for compete independence for Ireland. Roseberry himself achieved little and after his election defeat of 1896, he retired from public life amid a torrent of abuse. Salisbury returned to power.

In 1897-8 a revolt broke out amongst the Afridis of the north-west frontier in India. A large force had to be employed to suppress the rebellion. Almost immediately afterwards, in 1898, the government sent an expeditionary army into the Sudan under Kitchener. This followed repeated trouble from the Dervishes, supporters of the Mahdi and his successor the Khalifa, on the borders of Egypt. The Khalifa was defeated at the battle of Omdurman, eventually to be slain the following year. Winston Churchill gives a memorable account of both campaigns in his book *My Early Life* – he personally took part in the cavalry charge at Omdurman.

Apart from the Sudan, the British Empire was expanding fast in Africa. The Gold Coast had become a colony in 1874. In the 1890s Kenya, Uganda, Bechuanaland and Nyasaland were added, then Nigeria in 1901. Elsewhere new British territories included Upper

Burma, British New Guinea and North Borneo, and even Pacific islands as remote naval bases.

At the other end of Africa, gold had been discovered in large quantities in the Afrikaaner republic, the Transvaal. A flood of immigrants poured in, mainly of British origin, known as the Outlanders. The Boers refused these people any political rights, though they paid most of the taxes. The Prime Minister of the Cape Colony at this time was Cecil Rhodes, who had made a fortune from diamond mining in southern Africa. His company, the British South Africa Company, also obtained sovereign rights to Rhodesia, the territory to the north of the Transvaal. Under his direction, one Dr Jameson collected a few hundred policemen and set up a raid on Johannesburg in the Transvaal – the Jameson Raid. This was easily rebuffed by the Boers, still led by Paul Kruger.

In 1897 Sir Alfred Milner was made Lord High Commissioner in South Africa. He made it his business to foment trouble with the Boers, with the deliberate aim of taking control of the Transvaal and its gold wealth. Seeing the way the wind was blowing after the Jameson Raid, the Boers were already arming themselves with cannon and other weapons, and building forts. Before a British army could be embarked, the Transvaal and the other, hitherto peaceable Afrikaaner republic, the Orange Free State, invaded Natal in October 1899. The Boers were to provide tough opposition since they had grown up in the country as skilled horse riders and marksmen. They besieged a British force at Ladysmith and beat off a relieving army at the Battle of Spion Kop (1900). Other sieges were set up at Mafeking in the northern Cape, and Kimberley, the diamond capital.

The Salisbury government realised that it had completely underestimated the Boers, and 200,000 more men were sent to South Africa under Lord Roberts. Meanwhile there was widespread international criticism of British policy, correctly seen as a gold-grab. Nevertheless, all three sieges were relieved – with difficulty – in 1900. The British marched into Johannesburg and Pretoria, but the war was far from over. The Boers spilt up into small commandos or guerilla bands and caused endless problems. Eventually the British cleared the Boer women and children off the land, and put them into concentration camps, then scorched the earth, to remove support from the Boer riders. Once in the concentration camps, many died of epidemic diseases, notably typhus, incurring yet more international opprobrium. Large numbers of British and Empire soldiers were dying of the same disease. The war dragged on until 1902, when the Boers finally submitted by the

Treaty of Vereeniging. The terms of the peace were generous to the Boers, and within a few short years the political shape of southern Africa was transformed by the formation of the Union of South Africa – the Cape, Natal, the Orange Free State and the Transvaal – under one government in 1910. This government depended on close cooperation between the British settlers and the Afrikaaners. As it was in fact headed by the former Boers, Botha and Smuts, it may seem that the Boer War had been utterly futile. However, though costly, the war could have cost much more. It revealed the unexpected weakness of the British Army, which was thoroughly overhauled in the aftermath. Smuts was to become a leading figure on the side of the British in the Great War.

Meanwhile another colonial war had broken out in China, the Boxer Rebellion of 1898-1901. This was a popular, patriotic uprising against all Europeans, Americans and Japanese in China, targeting Chinese Christians in particular. The Ching dynasty, entering its final years, connived with the Boxers. Foreigners and Chinese Christians were slaughtered or driven back into their defended legations. An international task force was assembled from Britain, British India, Russia, the USA, Germany, France and Japan, suppressing the revolt with the capture of Peking. The result was yet another humiliating and "unequal" treaty forced upon the tottering Ching dynasty under the dowager Empress Cixi. The level of reparations was set at approximately 13,000 tons of silver.

Queen Victoria celebrated her sixtieth or diamond jubilee in 1897. She finally died in 1901, having reigned longer than any other British monarch - 64 years. In that time she had vastly increased the prestige of the monarchy after her shabby Hanoverian predecessors. Her life is thought to have been made miserable by the early loss of Albert, and she appeared to get rather too close to John Brown, her Scottish gillie, for the comfort of her family. In 1876, Disraeli had bestowed upon her the title Empress of India, and late in life she took this seriously, beginning to learn Urdu from an impressive Indian whom she called her Munshi. Once again, her family was scarcely pleased, and he was sent packing back to India when the old lady passed away. He was first obliged to hand over Victoria's letters to him to her unamused successor, Edward VII.

*   *   *   *

There were many eminent Victorians, remembered to this day. Certainly one of the cleverest was Michael Faraday (1791-1867), who rose from humble origins to unravel the mysteries of electricity and magnetism, paving the way in a very short time to the invention of the electric motor. Faraday was originally the assistant of Humphrey Davy (1778-1829), who had discovered a whole string of new elements including sodium and calcium when the technique of electrolysis first became known. The only eminent English chemist before Davy had been Joseph Priestley (1733-1804), who first isolated oxygen, though he did not fully realise what he had found. Later in the Victorian era lived the Scot James Clerk Maxwell (1831-79), who formulated the classical theory of electromagnetism. He was the first to demonstrate that the speed of light is always constant, no matter what the circumstances, a finding which led Einstein to formulate his theory of relativity. Another eminent Victorian scientist was also Scottish, William Thomson, Lord Kelvin (1824-1907) whose established one of the most fundamental principles in all science, the second law of thermodynamics.

The most famous Victorian engineer remembered today is Isambard Kingdom Brunel (1806-59), founder of the Great Western Railway and builder of the first propeller-driven iron steamship, the *Great Britain*.

In other fields, the Pre-Raphaelite artists founded their Brotherhood in 1848. The first members of the group were Dante Gabriel Rossetti (1828-82), John Millais (1829-96) and William Holman Hunt (1827-1910). Millais, whose family came from Jersey, was one of the finest technical painters the country ever produced. He was mortified to find one of his paintings – *Bubbles* – turned into a soap advert. Another great technical artist was Frederick Leighton (1830-96), painter of *Flaming June*, and now coming back somewhat into fashion.

In the cultural area, not to be forgotten are the comic operettas of W.S. Gilbert (1836-1911) and Arthur Sullivan (1842-1900), still performed all over the country until this day. There are eleven extant full-length operettas, and one shorter piece. After a few years the theatrical entrepreneur Richard D'Oyly Carte built a new theatre in London, the Savoy, especially for them. They include a string of hits such as *The Mikado* (1885), *HMS Pinafore* (1878), *The Pirates of Penzance* (1879) and *The Gondoliers* (1889).

The most famous writer of the age was Charles Dickens (1812-1870), creator of some of the most iconic characters in English literature, whose books have proved popular as TV dramatizations over many years. In the next generation came Sir Arthur Conan Doyle (1859-1930), whose stories of Sherlock Holmes remain perennially popular. His most famous book, *The Hound of the Baskervilles*, was serialized in the Strand magazine in 1901-2.

More influential than any of these over the longer term was Charles Darwin (1809-1882), whose seminal work *On the Origin of Species* appeared in 1859. This book marked the beginning of the replacement of a system of values based on religion by one based on scientific principles. Its publication represented the greatest blow organized religion ever received – and at that, all religions, not just Christianity. The book demonstrated that it was no longer necessary to invoke God as the Creator, because the diversity of nature could be explained by the evolution of all living things by the process of natural selection – the survival of the fittest. By implication, the life of mankind did not begin in 4004 BC with Adam and Eve in the Garden of Eden, but millions of years before that in the shape of an ancestor shared in common with the apes.

*   *   *   *

The Victorian period also saw the establishment of the People's Shop – the Co-op. The Co-operative movement was founded by a group of working men in Rochdale in 1844 when they opened a shop on Toad Lane in the town. Profits were distributed to members via a dividend. The movement spread rapidly and there were 805,000 members in England alone by 1889. The Co-op has remained a force in retailing through to the present day.

*   *   *   *

The abolition of taxes on newspapers, paper and advertisements between 1855 and 1861 led to the creation of a flourishing popular press in Britain. The main papers were the *Times*, the *Daily Telegraph*, the *Daily News* and the *Daily Chronicle*. All of these were aimed at the aristocracy and the upper echelons of the middle class. The real change came with the establishment of the *Daily Mail* by Alfred Harmsworth (later Lord Northcliffe) in 1892. Described by Lord Salisbury as "written by office boys for office boys", it was designed for a readership of the newly-educated masses and set new standards in sensational journalism and the size of its circulation.

In other respects, the world was changing fast at the end of the Victorian era, notably as a result of the spread of electricity. Electric street lighting appeared - the first street in the UK to have it was Mosley

Street, Newcastle (1879). The Nineties also saw the coming of the first electric trams, underground trains and motor cars. These had an immediate effect in facilitating the spread of the suburbs, especially around London.

Chapter 30 – Before the First World War

The golden age of the Industrial Revolution was over in Britain by the start of the new century, in some ways a pivotal date. Up until 1900 there had been a sense of all-round improvement lasting for half a century; the next half-century was to prove little short of disastrous. Protected by tariff barriers, new industries had been established overseas, particularly in Germany and the United States, shutting British goods out of these markets. The growing domestic prosperity of the previous half-century ground to a halt; living standards ceased to rise in the early part of the new century, and strikes and industrial disruption erupted on an unprecedented scale, culminating amongst the dockers, coal miners and railwaymen in 1910-12. Meanwhile the country depended on its old industries – particularly coal mining, iron and steel, textiles and shipbuilding – while newer industries including chemicals and electrical engineering gained ground abroad. Again, economic and social inequality on a scale scarcely seen before or since was the norm in Edwardian England. Two-thirds of the wealth of the country was owned by less than one percent of the population and by far the commonest employment for women was domestic service. In terms of life expectancy, two-thirds of the population would not live to reach the age of 60, and tuberculosis, smallpox and influenza were to remain great killers of otherwise healthy young people. As the new century got under way, unemployment was widespread. Continuing through from the 1890s into the 1920s, there were further waves of emigration, for example from the cotton mills of Lancashire to their newly built equivalents in New England. In the three years before the Great War, emigration reached a record level of 464,000 a year, though the proportion from England was lower than from Ireland, Scotland and Wales. There is no doubt that these people were leaving for a better life. When soldiers began to appear from Canada, Australia and New

Zealand, it was widely remarked how tall and fit they looked in comparison with the recruits from British towns.

Coming in the other direction was a flood of immigrants, over 200,000 between 1880 and 1900, many of them Jews driven out or frightened away from eastern Europe, and settling in large numbers in east London, Leeds and Manchester. They raised the problem of cheap or sweated labour, which upset the trade unions. In 1902 Arthur Balfour took over as Prime Minister from his uncle, Robert Salisbury (hence the expression "Bob's your uncle"). In 1905 his Conservative government passed the Aliens Act to restrict and control the immigration of foreign workers.

In these circumstances, and led by Joseph Chamberlain, demands grew at home for the end of free trade, which was now hurting the British economy. However the Liberals won the election of 1906, and they still supported free trade. This election marks a turning point in British political history, as for the first time 29 Labour members were elected under their own party banner. The movement had gained momentum after the formation of the Fabian Society of Sidney and Beatrice Webb in 1884 and the Independent Labour Party of Keir Hardie in 1893. The assault on inequality began immediately. Graduated estate duties ("death duties") had existed since 1894 but were much increased in scope in 1907. In 1906, the Trade Disputes Act was passed by the new government, reversing a legal ruling of 1901 when the Taff Valley Railway Company had successfully sued its striking railwaymen for damages. The act also confirmed the right of trade unions to "peaceful picketing" (if such a thing existed!).

From 1908 the Liberal prime minister was the Yorkshireman Herbert Asquith, known as "Squiffy" owing to his large consumption of alcohol, but the leading figure in the government was the original Welsh windbag, David Lloyd George, Chancellor of the Exchequer. It was under his impetus that the Liberal reforms of this era were enacted. First came non-contributory state pensions, provisions for which were made in the budget of 1908. These were limited in scope, as only people over 70 qualified. Labour exchanges were established to try to find work for the unemployed. In 1911 the National Insurance Act provided a vast contributory scheme for sickness and unemployment benefit, funded by national insurance payments. For decades afterwards, "going on the Lloyd George" meant living off a state benefit or pension.

All this – and an equally expensive program for the construction of new battleships, or Dreadnoughts – had to be funded by higher taxes, including what amounted to a wealth tax on the landowners who were only too well represented in the House of Lords. Lloyd George was not afraid to take them on: "A fully-equipped duke costs as much to keep up as two Dreadnoughts, and dukes are just as great a terror and last longer". After a terrific constitutional struggle and two separate elections in 1910, the Parliament Act came into force in 1911, severely restricting the power of the House of Lords. Henceforward it could not veto finance bills and could only delay other bills by up to two years. The maximum parliamentary term was also reduced from seven years to five.

The Liberals once again tried to resolve the Irish problem with a Home Rule Bill in 1912. This caused feelings to run very high, in both England and Ireland, as it would have forced the fiercely unionist population of Ulster into a united Ireland. The Ulstermen began to arm themselves for rebellion. Bonar Law, the Conservative leader, called on the Dublin regiments based at the Curragh to mutiny rather than coerce Ulster, but the British officers there were in any case ready to resign their commissions rather than fight their own side. The bill was rejected by the Lords, and so delayed for two years. It was then enacted as the Government of Ireland Act (1914), but the outbreak of war then put Irish affairs on hold.

It was also in these tumultuous years that the campaign to give women the vote – the suffragette movement – reached its crescendo. Led by the widow Emmeline Pankhurst and her daughters Christabel and Sylvia, a Manchester family, the Women's Social and Political Union generated a tremendous amount of publicity. In one famous incident, the suffragette Emily Davison died after throwing herself under the hooves of the king's horse, Anmer, in the Epsom Derby of 1913. Nothing was achieved before the Great War, but partly in recognition of the role women played in that war, a limited female franchise was established, based on a property qualification for women aged 30 and over, by the Representation of the Peoples Act of 1918. This act also created universal male adult suffrage.

Education expanded in the pre-war years. Compulsory education was extended to the age of 12 in 1899, and after 1900 this could be raised to 14 at the discretion of the local authority. Balfour's Education Act of 1902 replaced board-run schools with local education authorities. Meanwhile new universities were established at Leeds, Birmingham, Liverpool, Sheffield and Bristol in the years 1900-1909. The Cavendish Laboratory at Cambridge, operating just at the time when the mysteries of the subatomic world were first being revealed (following the discovery of radioactivity), employed a string of scientist with world-famous discoveries to their names. The best-known of these, Ernest Rutherford, made the greatest breakthrough since Democritus when he revealed the internal structure of the atom in 1911.

*   *   *   *

The years up to 1914 became dominated by preparations for what became the Great War. The menace posed by the energetic German Empire was obvious to both Britain and France, and so the two countries came together diplomatically, despite recent decades – if not centuries – of mutual suspicion, in the Entente Cordiale of 1904. This became the Triple Entente with the addition of Russia in 1907. This agreement reflects the change in the balance of power within Europe caused by the unifications of Germany and Italy and the rise of new states (and especially Serbia) from the shell of the Ottoman empire. Britain and France on the one hand, and Russia on the other, had been on opposite sides in the Crimean War, but this opposition needed to be adjusted in the light of modern realities. The Russians had long wished to become the dominant external power in the Christian Balkans, inhabited by fellow Slavs and Orthodox Christians – this concept is called Pan-Slavism.

On the other hand, the Austrians wanted to put the newly emergent regional power there, Serbia, in its place – under the Austrian thumb. (As Croatia was part of Austria-Hungary, Austria and Serbia shared a common border.) In fact, as the Ottoman Empire crumbled, the Russian and Austro-Hungarian Empires were also tottering. (Although they had all been been features of European polity for hundreds of years, in one form or another, this single war was to finish off all three.) Twenty-three different languages were spoken by units of the Austro-Hungarian army in the coming war, and the desire to fight for the empire was lukewarm at best. In fact the map of eastern Europe in 1914 contained very few countries, because so many modern states were part of the Austro-Hungarian empire. As well as Austria and Hungary these included Slovenia, Croatia, part of north-east Italy, the Czech Republic, Slovakia, a large part of modern Romania, the southern section of Poland, and an eastern province of what is now Russia (around Lvov). Poland itself had ceased to exist as a country by 1795, having been partitioned between Prussia, Austria and Russia.

The German Empire was much more homogeneous, though it did contain substantial minorities of Poles and Jews. Again, the ethnic map of eastern Europe in 1914 has changed. Large pockets of German settlement existed in what is now Poland, Romania and the Czech Republic. The settlers – mainly farmers and miners – had also found their way into the Dniepr Valley in the Ukraine, almost as far as Kiev, and even into Russia, where there was a considerable settlement on the Volga itself (around Saratov). The Germans had been encouraged to go to Russia at the time of Catherine the Great, who reigned in Russia from 1762 to 1796, and who was herself of German extraction. Many of these far-flung settlement had been in place for centuries and their people spoke German in outlandish, barely comprehensible dialects. Contiguous Germany itself – half as big again as post-1945 Germany – stretched along the entire southern coast of the Baltic Sea from Jutland to Koenigsberg (Kaliningrad). Beyond that, Germans dominated the area of what is now Latvia, Lithuania and Estonia. Germanic rule, settlement and influence had been extending eastward into Slavic territories for hundreds of years. Defeat in the wars of the twentieth century was to reverse this movement – to turn the clock back, literally by centuries.

The aim of Pan-German policy was to bring as much as possible of this huge territory into the German empire. In practice the Germans planned to assume control of a stack of client states in eastern Europe, from Finland on the Baltic to the Ukraine on the Black Sea. They were briefly to achieve these eastern ambitions in the Treaty of Brest-Litovsk of 1917, the provisions of which rapidly became obsolete. The British decision to go to war against the Germans must be seen in the context of the alternative – the creation of a German mega-state in central and eastern Europe.

In the spirit of Pan-Germanism, Germany elected to ally itself with the shaky Austrians, though its own empire was far from tottering - so why? The Germans feared the fate of Frederick II in the Seven Years War, when the Prussian king faced encirclement from a grand alliance of Austria, Saxony, France and Russia. Having the Austrians on side protected their southern flank, and meant putting another army in the field to face the Russians in the east. Germany was also allied to Turkey, where German army officers had been busy training Turkish troops. Turkey controlled the Dardanelles, and so the whole exit from the great rivers of eastern Europe – the Danube, Dniepr and Don. This would prove a great asset in weakening the Russians, who could not be supported in this theatre.

If Austria represented something of a liability as an ally for the Germans, the same could be said of Russia as an ally of France and

Britain. There had been repeated attempts at revolution in Russia, to replace the still-autocratic Tsardom with democracy, the latest in 1905, and the government was generally hated by its own people. The Russian army was equipped barely to mid-nineteenth century standards in terms of mechanization (none), artillery, automatic weapons and even army uniforms, boots and protective gear. It was by and large a peasant army. The Russia generals themselves entertained grave doubts. They knew that the traditional "peasant from Tambov" (a province of southern Russia) would fight to defend Tambov, but would he fight the Germans and Austrians in a quarrel over Poland or East Prussia? The prospect seemed uncertain, and indeed, proved to be so. What the Russians did have was manpower – lots of it. The Russian armies were to prove reasonably successful against the almost equally amateurish armies of Austria, but they were no match at all for the professional, ruthless, modern firepower of the Germans.

Preparations for the war took practical form in a naval arms race between Britain and Germany, with each side laying down battleship after battleship, the British in a massively expensive battle to stay ahead – an ambition which was never in doubt. As Winston Churchill later wrote, "The Admiralty had demanded six: the economists offered four: and we finally compromised on eight!" The Germans were driven on by their Emperor, Kaiser Wilhelm II, a man whose breech birth had left him with a withered left arm. Wilhelm fell under the influence of the Prussian military aristocracy and chose to ignore his more cautious counsellors. Although Germany did possess a parliament, the Reichstag, it had no power to restrain the emperor. Wilhelm – bombastic, impetuous and immature – had fanned tensions between Germany and Britain from the time he sacked his old Chancellor, Bismarck, and took personal control of his foreign policy in 1890.

The immediate cause of the war was the assassination of the heir to the throne of Austria, Archduke Franz Ferdinand, on 28 June 1914, by one Gavrilo Princip. He was one of a group of Bosnian Serb assassins, whose aim was to detach Croatia from Austria-Hungary to form a Greater Serbia or Yugoslavia. This event took place in Sarajevo, capital of Bosnia-Herzegovina, a province which had been transferred from Ottoman to Austrian rule at the Congress of Berlin in 1878 – part, in fact, of the Austrian scheme to take over the Balkans from the Turks. Austria sent Serbia a humiliating ultimatum which could only mean war, and the system of alliances then brought in Russia and France on the side of the Serbs, and Germany alongside Austria-Hungary and Turkey. Germany invaded France through Belgium which meant that

Britain was committed in two ways, through her guarantee of the Belgian frontiers, dating from 1839, and through the Triple Entente – but still she did not have to fight, and indeed the cabinet dithered. So why did she fight?

We can see that there were two likely scenarios for the war in France, both equally possible. The first was a quick German victory, as was achieved by the Prussians in 1870 and again by Hitler in 1940. Under this scenario, the British troops might easily have got their wish and returned home by Christmas, 1914, but as defeated refugees, as happened at Dunkirk in 1940. In the Second World War this ended the land war in the west, which could not be renewed for four years. In 1914 it is unlikely there would have been any renewal, especially as the Russians had collapsed by 1917. The second scenario was a long war of attrition, of uncertain outcome. Many influential people knew that this would be a terrible option, involving the whole country directly, mass slaughter and crippling expense. The model for this scenario was the American Civil War, where two subcontinental-sized foes battled it out over four years at enormous cost before the eventual annihilation of one. If Britain was going to be on the winning side, this was the only likely scenario. To the dismay of Kaiser Wilhelm, who knew full well that his fleet was far from ready to take on the might of the Royal Navy, the British chose to fight him. He had been convinced that the pacifists in the British cabinet would prevail. His haggard and utterly unnerved appearance in the early days of the war, as reported by those around him, was due to the realization that he had made a calamitous and irreversible misjudgment.

Nevertheless at the start of the land war, it was to be a close-run thing between scenario one and scenario two. The initial British Expeditionary force comprised only 100,000 men whilst Germany was mobilizing five million. Had the British Government under Asquith and his Foreign Secretary, Sir Edward Grey, not acted quickly in sending the British Expeditionary Force to fill a gap in the French defences in Flanders, the war in the west could have been over in weeks, leaving a hostile Germany as overwhelmingly the dominant power of Europe. This was the real reason for fighting. From the French point of view, the small immediate size of the BEF was less important than the token of things to come which it represented, and indeed Britain was eventually to commit a far larger army to a European war than it had ever done before. Moreover, it was that army that the Germans knew they had to beat to win the war, as the French were to take such a severe battering in the earlier campaigns.

Before the British government declared war, it consulted the dominions, which each promised support. Canada, Australia and New Zealand sent volunteer armies, South Africa invaded German South-West Africa and even the Irish came on board voluntarily. In the end Germany had to fight one and a quarter million men from the Dominions, showing that the Commonwealth had its uses! In fact the British Empire covered a quarter of the land area of the earth, and held a quarter of its population, so it was not to be underestimated. The British share of this, recorded in the census of 1911, was 42 million people (excluding southern Ireland). Nevertheless the task which lay ahead was daunting enough. "All over Europe, the lamps are going out. They will not be lit again in our time." Such was the view of Sir Edward Grey.

Chapter 31 – The First World War

In general terms, military tactics on the Western Front could not cope with advances in defensive technology. Barbed wire was a significant hindrance to massed infantry advances. Machine gun emplacements – small, dug in and almost impossible to knock out 100% with artillery – made crossing open ground suicidal. The artillery barrage, traditional precursor to any major advance, was much more powerful than it had been even as late as the 1870s, but it still had limited effectiveness against troops dug into deep trenches. Brand new weapons were introduced – poison gas, fighting aeroplanes, tanks and even Zeppelin bombers – but none could break the deadlock, though tanks did prove themselves late in the war. Introduced by the Germans but soon in use by both sides, poison gas proved lethal, if not decisive in battle. It soon became one of the most-feared and best-remembered horrors of the war. Its use was not repeated in the far more mobile conditions of the Second World War. By way of contrast, the military on both sides still relied heavily on horse transport, especially from the railhead. In this ancient-and-modern war, the British lost nearly half a million horses whilst requiring enormous volumes of motor vehicle fuel. Something as low-technology as the steel helmet was unavailable to any side until 1916. One enthusiast was Winston Churchill who wore one, he confided to his wife, "to protect my valuable cranium"!

Throughout 1915–17 on the Western Front, Britain and France suffered far more casualties than Germany, because of both the strategic and tactical decisions taken by either side. Knowing that their countries jointly had the greater manpower resources, the British and French commanders launched wave after wave of attacks and lost hundreds of thousands of men in the process. The Germans generals fought more conservatively, knowing that the manpower on their own side was limited. They were reluctant to launch major offensives and so lost far less men in forlorn "over the top" rushes of undefended human flesh against barbed wire and machine guns. So in terms of strategy, while the Germans only mounted a single main offensive in 1915-17 (at Verdun), the British and French made many attempts to break through German lines. Tactically, German commander Ludendorff's doctrine of "elastic defence" was well suited for trench warfare. This involved a lightly defended forward position and a more powerful main position farther back, beyond the first range of artillery fire, from which an immediate and powerful counter-offensive could be launched. In fact to this day the British generals have never shaken off their reputation as "donkeys". In a type of warfare which was new to all, their German counterparts seemed to learn the lessons of each major battle more quickly, and constantly applied these lessons in new forms of attack and defence.

The principal theatre of the war was the Western Front, and within that, Flanders, an area spreading across the far north of France into Belgium. Without actually being in England, the front could hardly have been closer – had it been safe to do so, the British soldiers could have caught a ferry to the war. The noise of the war could be heard in England. Ypres, where three major battles took place, and known to the British soldiers as "Wipers", lies barely twenty miles from the coast. From the English military point of view, communications were shortest to this point, so why fight further south, near the Swiss border, for example? If the British were there, the Germans had to be there too. So a selection of previously unheard-of villages and small towns suddenly became world-famous, and can never now return to obscurity.

In naval terms, the public on both sides expected a major battle to follow quickly after the declaration of war. However, neither navy was keen to start one. The Germans knew that they had the smaller navy, and would probably lose in any test of strength, leaving their coast vulnerable to British bombardment. Meanwhile, the British were aware that a naval defeat would be a disaster with the potential "to lose the war in an afternoon". In any case, the Royal Navy did not need to fight to implement its strategy, developed for the first time in this war. This was to take the traditional form of a blockade, but instead of the difficult and tiresome business of keeping station off a foreign port, the British Navy simply sought to control the two exits available to Germany – the English Channel and the North Sea between the Orkneys and the coast of Norway. To maintain this strategy the Grand Fleet was based at Scapa Flow, in the Orkneys. The two great battle fleets thus spent most of the war facing each other across the North Sea. This meant that the British strategy was implemented and the Central Powers

(Germany, Austria-Hungary and their allies) were gradually starved out of the war, while Germany's hard-won overseas colonies were left defenceless. Starting initially just against Germany, but soon expanded to include all neutral nations known to deal with the Germans, the naval blockade soon caused friction with the United States, which had a strong tradition of defending its maritime rights. Tensions faded as trade with the Allies was very good for business at home in the USA. In Germany, the blockade had a slow, but eventually major impact, resulting in shortages of many basic goods, including, by the end of the war, essentials such as foodstuffs, coal and horses.

The first maritime conflict was the Battle of Heligoland Bight (August 1914), which began as a British attempt to stop German patrols. The Germans lost three cruisers to no British losses. This defeat, just off their own coast, had a significant impact on the Germans, as henceforward they were reluctant to risk their big ships. However, they soon got their own back when a single U-boat sank three cruisers in the North Sea in September, 1914, a shocking setback for the Royal Navy. In the meantime, a German naval squadron led by the cruisers *Scharnhorst* and *Gneisenau* under Admiral von Spee was loose on the high seas. This caught and overwhelmed a small British squadron under Admiral Cradock off Valparaiso, Chile in November 1914. Hopelessly outgunned (but certainly aware of the fate of Admiral Byng), Cradock – who had disobeyed orders by leaving his slow battleship back in the Falklands – heroically chose to fight it out rather than run away. He went down with two cruisers in the battle of Coronel. Within a few weeks the Royal Navy had avenged him, sending both the *Scharnhorst* and the *Gneisenau* to the bottom at the battle of the Falklands (December 1914). There was one more early action, at the Dogger Bank in January 1915, when the Germans were lucky to escape with the loss of only one cruiser, the *Blucher*.

The main German answer to the naval blockade was submarine warfare. From early 1915, their submarines launched a sustained campaign against ships in British waters, although with limited effect. After the sinking of the British passenger liner *Lusitania* on 7 May 1915, off south-west Ireland, with the loss of 118 American citizens amongst others, Germany agreed not to attack liners or neutral merchant shipping, greatly reducing the impact of the submarines. The danger – and a very real one at that – was that this would bring the United States into the war on the side of the Allies.

On the Western Front, the German strategy for a war on two fronts against France and Russia was based on the Schlieffen Plan. This relied on the French to attack Germany at once in Alsace and Lorraine, the provinces taken from France by Prussia in 1871. The plan called for a massive German attack through Belgium into northern France, taking Paris and cutting off the French armies, thus winning the war quickly in the west before turning to deal with the slower Russian mobilization in the east. However, General von Moltke, the German commander, had tinkered with the plan, weakening the strength of the strike through Belgium and strengthening the southern army. Thus, when the French, as expected, launched their attack (Battle of Lorraine, August 1914), they were unable to make any progress, and were even soon in danger themselves. Another factor not properly considered in the plan was that Britain would join the war on the violation of Belgian neutrality. The advancing German troops soon discovered the British Expeditionary Force, a small but professional army. The Belgians had put up a stiff resistance to the German advance through their country, delaying the Germans by twelve days – enough to land the BEF in France. The two sides met at the battle of Mons (August 1914), where the British troops inflicted heavy casualties on the Germans before being forced to retreat. The French under Joffre counterattacked in the battle of the Marne. By the end of this battle, which included some troops carried to the battlefield by taxi from Paris, the German attack had failed – the "miracle of the Marne". Their army withdrew towards what would become the stable line of trench warfare for most of the war, and von Moltke was removed as commander. As the Schlieffen Plan had now failed and been abandoned, the Germans should have sought terms with the British and the French at this point and let the soldiers go home for Christmas. But they did not, and both sides suffered the consequences.

For the next few weeks, both sides took part in the Race to the Sea (September-November 1914), each hoping to outflank the other before the line of trenches reached the sea. The final German drive against the Channel Ports was halted by the BEF in the First Battle of Ypres (October-November 1914), which almost destroyed the BEF, but also prevented the Germans reaching the French ports. (Ostend and Zeebrugge, however, were in German hands, and were subsequently used as submarine bases.) The trenches now ran all the way from the Channel to the Swiss border. All mobility was gone from the war on the Western Front until 1918. Meanwhile a vast recruitment exercise was taking place at home. The face of Lord Kitchener, Secretary of State for War, glared down from the hoardings: "Your country needs you!" Volunteers came forward in hundreds of thousands, too many at once in fact to house in barracks, train or equip.

The year 1915 saw France and Britain desperate to penetrate the lines of trenches and resume manoeuvring. The British attempted a breakthrough at the battle of Neuve Chapelle, but were contained. Then at the Second Battle of Ypres (April-May 1915) the Germans introduced poisoned gas into the war, but despite the initial impact of the gas, made very little progress, having failed to provide sufficient support for their new weapon. For the rest of the year there were repeated attacks and counter-attacks, but the result was stalemate. The largest British offensive was the battle of Loos, which began on 25 September and cost 60,000 British casualties for negligible results.

Complaints about disorganization and poor supplies led to the formation of a coalition government in Britain in May, 1915. Inter-party hostilities were suspended for the duration of the war. The general election, due that year, was postponed. With Asquith still in charge, Lloyd George greatly enhanced his reputation by his running of a vast state enterprise, the Ministry of Munitions, on a scale quite unknown in any previous era. This was created in response to the shell crisis of 1915, when the failure of a British offensive was attributed by its commander to a lack of shells (this problem affected both sides at this stage of the war). In December, Field Marshal French was replaced by a dour Lowland Scot, General Sir Douglas Haig, as commander of the BEF.

Turkey joined the war on the side of the Central Powers on 29 October 1914. This had the immediate effect of denying the Allies any access to Russia via the Dardanelles, preventing them from providing material aid to their ally in this theatre. The Allies did not take Turkey seriously as a military power, and expected a quick collapse of the "sick man of Europe". They were to be disappointed. The Turkish war effort was commanded by Enver Pasha, war minister and generalissimo, only 32 in 1914. The Turkish part of the war was fought on several fronts, reflecting the size of the Ottoman Empire at this time. This included not only modern Turkey but parts of the Caucasus, Syria, the Lebanon, Palestine, Transjordan, Arabia and Mesopotamia (Iraq).

There was heavy fighting between the Turks and the Russians in the area around the Black Sea, and in the Caucasus. In 1915 the Turks committed the Armenian genocide. The Armenians, a subject people of the Ottoman Empire, had chosen to rebel, and the Turks responded with customary ferocity. By some estimates, one and a half million Armenians lost their lives. In the fighting itself the Russians advanced into Anatolia and at one point captured the important Turkish port of Trebizond.

Before the war, Italy had been part of the Triple Alliance with Germany and Austria. However, in 1914 Italy remained neutral, claiming that their alliance was only valid if Austria was attacked, and as Austria had herself started the war this did not count. Italy's demands were at the expense of Austria, which still controlled two provinces of northern Italy known as Trentino and South Tyrol (or Alto Adige), with a mixed population of German and Italian speakers, centred on the cities of Trento and Bolzano. Thus, on 23 May 1915 Italy joined the war on the side of the Allies. The entire Austro-Italian border was mountainous. The only possible areas for fighting were around the Trentino salient and to the east of it in the valley of the Izuno. With the Austrians happy to remain on the defensive, the Italians launched an attack on the Trentino salient as soon as war was declared, but encountered Austrian defences that stopped any further advance until very late in the war. The main Italian attacks thus came in the east, where a series of battles along the Izuno gained little ground at great cost.

Frustration at the stalemate on the Western Front led some home politicians, notably Winston Churchill, the First Lord of the Admiralty, to seek to open a new front somewhere which looked easier going - Turkey. This was to lead to Gallipoli, one of the great military disasters of the war. Control of the Dardanelles, the narrow sea lane connecting the Black Sea to the Mediterranean, was essential if the Allies were to get any aid to southern Russia. The initial Allied plan was to steam a fleet up the Dardanelles to Constantinople and force the passage at gunpoint. Troops could not be spared for the assault. This was attempted early in 1915, but had to be abandoned after three old battleships (one French and two British) were sunk by mines, and three others had suffered mine damage. A new plan was formed, this time a troop landing on the Gallipoli peninsular adjacent to the Dardanelles. The first landings were made on 25 April 1915, the bulk of the soldiers drawn from Australian and New Zealand regiments (ANZACS). However, by this time the Turks had reorganized, improving the defences of the area, and the ANZACS never got away from the landing beaches. By the end of the year it was clear that the plan had failed, and from November the withdrawal began, ending with the evacuation of the last 35,000 men on 8-9 January 1916. The Australians never quite forgave the English for involving them in the Gallipoli fiasco. Although the strategy had been agreed at cabinet level in London, someone had to take responsibility. That man was Winston Churchill, who resigned his post in the cabinet and went to fight on the Western

Front at Ploegsteert ("Plug Street"). Another casualty of the campaign was the war poet Rupert Brooke, who contracted sepsis after being bitten by a mosquito on his way to Gallipoli, and was buried in Skyros, Greece, thus getting his wish:

If I should die, think only this of me
That there's some corner of a foreign field
That is forever England

On the Eastern Front, the Germans under Hindenburg and Ludendorff inflicted heavy defeats on the Russians at Tannenberg, East Prussia, in August 1914, and in the same region at the Masurian Lakes. However the Russians defeated the Austrian army which was advancing into Poland. The Germans turned southward to assist their ally and pushed the Russians back at the battle of Lodz (September 1914). In 1915 the German advance continued into Poland where their army took Warsaw. 1916 saw the Russian counter-attack under General Brusilov. The Austrians were swamped once more and had to be reinforced by the Germans. By the end of the campaigning season, Brusilov had been forced back to his original lines with 1.4 million casualties.

In the Balkans, Austria invaded Serbia at the start of the war but her armies were soon forced to withdraw. A typhus epidemic then swept Serbia, causing serious weaknesses. However it was only when Bulgaria finally joined the war on the side of the Central Powers in October 1915 that a new attack on Serbia was launched. The Powers had a combined army of 600,000 men, twice as many as Serbia could mobilise, and by the end of November Serbia had been completely overrun. Serbia eventually had the worst war of any country, losing 1.1 million people, just over a quarter of its population. The Serbian army retreated to Salonika on the coast of Greece. The still-neutral Greece had allowed the Allies to land an army here to aid Serbia. Too few in number to break out, the Allied troops in Salonika settled down for a long period of inactivity facing the Bulgarians.

The year 1916 was dominated by two big battles on the Western Front. The town and fortress of Verdun, in French hands, formed a salient into the German lines. The Germans commander Falkenhayn decided to use Verdun to bleed the French dry of their reserves, and in 21 February began his assault on the fortress. Fighting continued throughout the year, but the French under General Petain held on. The fighting was bitter and very costly, with 542,000 French casualties and 434,000 German. By the time the battle ended, the French had regained almost all of the ground lost in the initial German attacks, while the German commander Falkenhayn had been replaced by the team of

Hindenburg and Ludendorff, riding high after their victories in the east, who decided to go on to the defensive in the west.

Right in the middle of the war, at Easter 1916, the Irish Volunteers staged a rebellion in Dublin and proclaimed a republic. The revolt was quickly suppressed. One of the conspirators, Roger Casement, who had been landed in Kerry by a German submarine with a consignment of rifles, was subsequently executed along with other ringleaders.

The summer of 1916 saw the only great naval engagement of the war, the Battle of Jutland (31 May - 1 June 1916). The German High Seas Fleet finally ventured out, with a plan to break the naval blockade. The first phase of the battle involved two smaller squadrons, the Germans under Hipper, the British under Beattie, but soon a full-scale battle ensued under the admirals Scheer and Jellicoe. In the end the Royal Navy Grand Fleet lost six capital ships, the Germans only two, but the German fleet had to run for home, only escaping under cover of darkness. The British maintained control of the North Sea, and with it the naval blockade of Germany.

While Verdun was eating at French strength, it fell to the British to launch the offensive that had been planned for 1916. Accordingly, after a week-long artillery bombardment, British infantry attacked the Germans along the Somme. In the initial assault on 1 July the British army suffered 19,000 killed and 41,000 wounded, still the greatest one-day loss in the history of the British army. The battle continued for four months. The human cost was both appalling and one-sided - the British and Commonwealth took 420,000 casualties (95,000 of them killed or missing), the French 195,000 and the Germans only 237,000. These are the worst losses in British military history. Hence it is this conflict more than any other that led to the British generals – in this case, Haig and Sir Henry Rawlinson – to be castigated as "donkeys in charge of lions". While the Allies only advanced eight miles during the entire battle, the Germans lost the cream of their experienced small unit officers (commissioned and non-commissioned). The troops lost in such conflicts had to be replaced somehow. One German cavalry officer, impressed by the British soldiers he had seen in 1915, was by 1916 complaining that British prisoners were "rickety, alcoholic, degenerate, ill-bred and poor to the last degree."

War had also flared up in the Middle East. One danger presented by the Turks was that they could disrupt Britain's oil supply from Persia (modern Iran) – at this point, the adjacent territory of Mesopotamia was a part of the Ottoman Empire. To prevent this, the British sent a force under General Nixon, drawn largely from India, to secure the head of the Persian gulf. By the end of November 1914 this had captured the port of Basra. This secured the pipeline. A force under Major-General Townshend was then sent up the Tigris, advancing to Kut-el-Amara, well over half way to Baghdad, where it defeated a Turkish army (battle of Kut, September 1915) and occupied the city. Townshend then continued upriver to Ctesiphon, where he was turned back by the Turks (November 1915). Obliged to retreat to Kut, he was soon besieged by the Turks (December-April 1916). After three attempts to relieve him had failed, he was forced to surrender, along with some 8,000 men.

A campaign in Palestine developed out of a desire to protect the Suez Canal, a vital artery of the British Empire. In January-February 1915 a Turkish army crossed the Sinai desert from Palestine, and even managed to cross the canal before being driven back across the desert by British forces coming out of Egypt.

The war also spread to Arabia. In June 1916, Hussein, grand Sharif of Mecca, proclaimed an Arab revolt against Ottoman rule. An attack on Mecca was quickly successful, but the Turkish garrison of Medina held out until the end of the war. The most famous individual to emerge from this theatre was T.E. Lawrence (of Arabia), a British officer who helped the Arabs to harass the Turks in Arabia, concentrating on sabotage attacks on the single-track Hejaz railway which stretched across the deserts from Damascus to Medina.

Two other countries joined the Allies in 1916, Portugal and Romania. Portuguese shipping was to suffer considerably at the hands of the U-boats, and by the end of 1916 Romania had been overrun by the armies of the Central Powers.

Such was the frustration with the conduct of the war and in particular the reverses of the Dardanelles, Gallipoli, the Somme, Kut and Jutland (hardly seen as a strategic triumph at the time), that Asquith was replaced as Prime Minister by Lloyd George in December, 1916. The motto of the one, "Wait and see", was replaced by that of the other, "Do it now!" Lloyd George brought great dynamism to the conduct of the war. He completely reorganized the decision-making process around a small War Cabinet. He set up the Ministry of National Service to commandeer manpower and direct it as required to the competing claims of civilian and military occupations. He brought the Dominion leaders into his counsels and kept them fully on his side – notably Jan Smuts, unattractively-named but a future Prime Minister of South Africa. In short he widely came to be regarded as the man who won the war.

One thing Lloyd George did not do was to change his military commander on the Western Front. Haig held on to the job, but for the wrong reason – Lloyd George could not find anyone better to replace him. In the face of Conservative opposition, however, he did find a role for the abandoned Winston Churchill, and a top job at that – Minister of Munitions.

By early 1917, the Germans were becoming desperate as the British blockade bit deeper. Believing that their submarines could bring Britain to her knees within months, Germany resumed full, unrestricted submarine warfare on 2 February. Then it was revealed that the German Foreign Secretary had sent a message, known as the Zimmerman telegram, to the government of Mexico, encouraging it to go to war against the United States. Sufficiently provoked by now, the USA declared war on Germany on 6 April 1917. The Allies took great encouragement from the accession of the Americans, but that would take time to have any effect. In the meanwhile, the submarines were causing havoc, sinking approximately one food-carrying ship in four. Nevertheless the U-boats had limited range. In the Second World War they were able to use bases on the Atlantic coast of France, an option not available in 1917.

Stubbornly refusing to form convoys, the Admiralty left British and Allied shipping scattered across the Atlantic, an easy target for the submarines, and losses were unsustainable: 540,000 tons sunk in February, 600,000 tons in March and 870,000 in April. Eventually, under the pressure of these losses, Lloyd George forced the convoy system upon the Admiralty. This proved to be effective, with escorts hunting down the submarines. It was combined with a huge campaign of mining that closed off the Channel and the gap between Scotland and Norway. By the end of 1917 the submarine menace was largely beaten.

The Germans began 1917 on the Western Front by falling back to a new defensive line, the Hindenburg Line, ironing out a salient in their front, and so making it shorter and easier to defend. They systematically laid waste to all land abandoned as they went, stabilizing on the new line by early April. In the meantime, the new French commander, General Nivelle – whose mother was English – planned an offensive that, he claimed, would win the war. This started with the Battle of Arras (9-15 April), a minor British victory, best known for the Battle of Vimy Ridge (9-13 April), a well-planned attack that saw the Canadian Corps fight together for the first time.

Nivelle then launched his main offensive (16-20 April). The Germans were fully aware of his plans, and the French attacks were a total failure, with 120,000 more casualties. By now the French soldiers had had enough, and between 29 April and 30 May widespread mutinies broke out, the men refusing to take part in any more offensive operations. Nivelle was replaced by Petain, successful at Verdun, who immediately set about improving ordinary conditions, such as home leave and railway canteens for the men.

Now Haig decided on an attack of his own. On 7 June, after exploding a mine that could be heard in London, the British took the Messines Ridge. This signalled the start of the Third Battle of Ypres (July-November 1917). The use of this medieval form of warfare was a sign of desperation. "It may not change history", said one officer in charge, "but it will certainly change geography". The offensive came to grief for two reasons. First, the long preparations and bombardment had given the Germans time to build up their defences in great depth. Second, in the terrain of Flanders, low lying and wet at the best of times, days of rain combined with the bombardment turned the battlefield into a swamp, impossible to cross at any speed on foot. Eventually, after the capture of Passchendaele, the British advance halted. The British had gained 5 miles at a cost of 300,000 casualties.

However, the year ended with the first signs of change at last. At the Battle of Cambrai (November 1917), Haig launched the first major tank assault of the war, with 358 of the newly-invented machines. There was no preliminary bombardment, and surprise was achieved. The tanks made a five-mile deep breakthrough along a six mile front, but there was inadequate support, and the Germans were able to seal the breach.

The disasters of the war had a dramatic effect in Russia, where the Tsarist government of Nicholas II collapsed in March, 1917, to be replaced by a provisional "bourgeois" government. This pledged to support the Allies, but there were two million desertions from the army in March and April alone. Meanwhile the Communists attempted to undermine the morale of the army. So the final midsummer Russian offensive on the Eastern Front failed. On 7 November the provisional government was in turn replaced when the Bolshevik Revolution brought Lenin and the Communists to power. The new government immediately sued for peace, signed at Brest-Litovsk, surrendering vast areas of land to the Germans and ending the war in the east. The Communist priority was to consolidate power at home – a major civil war was to follow – and worry about regaining Russia's peripheral provinces later.

The start of 1918 brought a new configuration to the war. The defeat of Russia in the autumn of 1917 meant that large numbers of battle-hardened German soldiers were now free to move to the western front, while for the Allies an increasing number of American troops were arriving in Europe. The Allied plan for the year was to stay on the defensive until American numbers built up sufficiently to permit an offensive. Ludendorff realised this, and saw that his best chance was a knockout blow early in 1918, before the Americans arrived in force. Reasoning that the French, whose heavy casualties earlier in the war had knocked the stuffing out of them, would probably collapse anyway, he aimed to take on the British, as they would keep fighting with or without the French. He selected a salient where the chances of a breakthrough were the highest. At the same time the problem with this approach was that he might indeed advance a long way, burning up resources but still not inflicting a fatal blow.

Between March and April the Germans finally broke through, struggling at first over land they had themselves devastated in 1917. They advanced sixty miles – an unprecedented distance on the Western Front – to within 45 miles of Paris, thoroughly alarming the Allies. However some felt that such an advance would spread out ever more thinly and then stop, as the water from a pail kicked over. The German troops were amazed at the luxury goods abandoned by the Allies, of a type which had long since disappeared from their own lines. Their men were seen driving cows, carrying hens under their arms and gorging on wine.

By July, the German attacks had indeed ground to a halt, and the mood in the German command was one of great despondency. The Americans now had an army a million strong on this front, seeming to many like a transfusion of blood into the pallid body of France, though as yet few had fired a shot in anger. Correspondingly, Ludendorff's breakout had cost his side a million men. Meanwhile, the Allies had finally put a combined command in place under the French Marshal Foch, improving coordination. The Allies now took the offensive and the final, swift end to the war – the Hundred Days – began to unfold. On 8 August, the battle of Amiens began, forcing the Germans back eight miles, in what Ludendorff called the "black day" for the German Army. There were many more black days to come.

In the fighting that followed, the Germans were pushed back to the Hindenburg line. In early October, the Allies were able to maintain pressure all along the front, taking the Hindenburg line, and forcing the Germans onto the retreat once more. Although this final stage of the war saw the greatest advances, it also saw some of the fiercest fighting. By now the Germans were in serious difficulties. At home revolution was in the air, while at the front resistance crumbled. There were mass surrenders with thousands of prisoners taken. The discussion of armistice terms took place from 15 October. On 9 November, Kaiser Wilhelm abdicated and retired to the Netherlands. The armistice finally was signed in a railway carriage at Compiegne on the morning of 11 November, when the ceasefire began at 11 am.

One week before the fighting ended on the Western Front, the war poet Wilfred Owen was killed there. In *Strange Meeting* he recounts how he descended into hell, to meet a stranger, but not just any stranger:

I am the enemy you killed, my friend.

I knew you in this dark; for so you frowned

Yesterday through me as you jabbed and killed.

The fighting had stopped short of the German border. This led to later claims that the German army was not really beaten and could have fought on had it not been "stabbed in the back" by socialist politicians at home – not a claim that any sensible German general would have sustained in November 1918. The Germans had stopped fighting to prevent useless casualties once the war was clearly lost. The American military commander, General Pershing, certainly did not wish to stop fighting – he would have preferred to push on, conquer Germany and obtain an unconditional surrender, fearing that anything short of absolute and visible victory would lead to a repeat of the problem in the next generation. In later years many – including Franklin D Roosevelt, the US President in the next war – came to agree with him. However the British and the French had seen quite enough slaughter by November 1918, and called a halt to it at the first opportunity.

In the Balkans, the front at Salonika stayed quiet until late in 1918. By this time, Bulgaria was in dire trouble, with food shortages affecting even the front line troops, and when the Allies attacked in September, the Bulgarian army collapsed. On 29 September 1918, Bulgaria signed an armistice.

Success also finally came to the Italians. In 1917 they made a significant advance, causing the Austrians to call on Germany for help. With the aid of German troops, the Austrians counter-attacked at Caporetto on the Izuno (October-November 1917), sweeping right back into the Trentino salient. The battle was a disaster for Italy, which lost half a million men, but the new line soon stabilised. In 1918 the Germans pulled their troops out of the front, expecting the Austrians to be able to deal with Italy on their own now that the Russian war had ended. The German soldiery in any case resented the repeated necessity to support the Austro-Hungarian Empire, saying it was like being shackled to a corpse. An Austrian summer offensive failed, and Italy launched her own attack, now aided by British and French troops, in October 1918. After initial resistance, the Austrian army collapsed, and the Italians made great progress. Austria signed an armistice on 3 November. Despite some successes on it, the Italian front had bled the Austro-Hungarian Empire dry, and within months the entire edifice had collapsed.

Meanwhile there had also been considerable improvements in Mesopotamia. In August, 1916, General Nixon was replaced by General Maude. By the end of 1916 he had rebuilt his force, and with 166,000 men started another advance up the Tigris. In February 1917 he won the second battle of Kut, and in March captured Baghdad. By the middle of November 1918, the northern oilfields around Mosul were also in British hands.

In Palestine, there had also been progress. Despite a strong Turkish defence, organised by General Falkenhayn, Jerusalem fell to Allenby's army in December 1917. There Allenby was obliged to halt, as his army was weakened to reinforce the Western Front, but in September 1918 he was able to launch another attack, defeating the Turks at Megiddo (September 1918). The resulting pursuit northwards was only ended by the Turkish surrender (30 October 1918).

In the adjacent theatre of Arabia, by 1918, the Arabs rebels had cut off Medina, and were able to play a part in General Allenby's final campaigns in Palestine and Syria, including the surrender of Damascus.

There had also been campaigns in the German colonial territories in Africa. Left unsupported because of the British domination of the high seas, the German colonists struggled. Togoland and the Cameroons were overrun relatively early in the war, as was South-West Africa. The German Colonel Paul von Lettow-Vorbeck however conducted a prolonged campaign in German East Africa (subsequently Tanganyika), latterly on a guerilla basis, and became a hero in Germany. (This theatre was made famous fictionally in film *The African Queen* starring Humphrey Bogart and Katherine Hepburn.)

So after stagnation and even defeat in the Balkans and the old Ottoman Empire, the British triumphed on every front. However, no one doubted that the war had been fought and won in its principal theatre, the Western Front. Here the British had taken on a first-rate adversary, confronted his main strength, and when the French had faltered, taken the leading part in the final victory.

*   *   *   *

The peace was never going to be a generous one for the Central Powers. Years of devastation, and the huge losses of life saw to that. The armistice agreement set the tone, and was in all but name a German surrender, with the Germans agreeing to evacuate all occupied territory and Alsace Lorraine, disarm, surrender their navy, and allow three occupied bridgeheads over the Rhine. When the Paris Peace Conference started on 18 January 1919, the mood was severe. Even the US President Woodrow Wilson, who had been seen as the voice of reason, had been hardened by American losses (117,000 war dead). He came armed with his "Fourteen Points" for post-war stability. One of these concerned the right of self-determination of formerly subject people, with particular reference to the Austro-Hungarian Empire. The French leader, Clemenceau, wanted to make sure Germany could never again threaten France. Lloyd George, who had already gained Britain's pre-war aims before the conference, wanted to ensure a stable and prosperous Europe to aid British recovery after the war. The overall result was to be the most comprehensive re-drawing of the map of Europe there had ever been.

The Treaty of Versailles (28 June 1919) has ever since been seen as harsh, but the German demands if they had won would have been more severe. Their war aims had included the reduction of Belgium and huge territories in northern and eastern Europe to the status of satellites of the German Empire, and the Royal Navy would have been replaced by the German fleet on the high seas. British African colonies – the "places in the sun" so beloved by Kaiser Wilhelm – were also on the shopping list. So, the main clauses of the treaty included German admission of war guilt; the loss of her overseas colonies; the return of Alsace-Lorraine to France; and the Saar to be held by France until a 1935 referendum (when the overwhelming vote was to return to Germany). Plebiscites or popular referendums were held in several territories so that the people themselves could decide their own nationality. The northern part of Schleswig returned to Denmark after just such a vote. The eastern part of Silesia went into the newly reformed Poland. So did the Baltic corridor of West Prussia and Posen, which Prussia had acquired to link East Prussia with contiguous Germany during the earlier partition of Poland. Despite these changes, Germany lost just thirteen percent of her land area, and remained easily the most powerful country in mainland Europe. There were no mass movements of population across borders, as happened after the Second World War. The population of Germany was after all overwhelmingly German, so taking away more territory would have put Germans into other states. In fact, considerable minorities of Germans remained outside Germany, including three million in Sudetenland, which became part of a new country, Czechoslovakia, constituting a quarter of its population. This was the seed of more trouble in the next generation.

Reparations for war damage were set at £13 billion, or 100,000 tons of pure gold. This was a totally unrealistic sum, only a fraction of which was ever paid. Finally Germany was virtually disarmed, allowed an army of only 100,000 men. The capital ships of the navy sailed to Scapa Flow, where they were scuttled by their own crews; so the German navy was reduced to a coastal defence force. There was to be no air force at all. This was a war that saw 9.7 million military dead, including 885,000 from the UK (of whom 50,000 came from Ireland), 1.4 million from France and two million from the German Empire. In the circumstances it is hardly surprising that the victors wished to make sure that Germany could never again threaten the peace of Europe. In this, clearly, they did not succeed. The exasperated French military commander, Marshal Foch, exclaimed at the time – "This is not a peace, but only a truce for twenty years!" How right he was. In fact the greatest weakness of the peace treaty was that there was no means of enforcing many its provisions without starting another war. It proved quite easy for Hitler to simply brush aside the restrictions on his armed forces during the Thirties.

If Germany lost relatively little territory in the peace, the same cannot be said of the Austro-Hungarian Empire. Austria and Hungary were separated and set up as small independent states. The northern and eastern territories of the old empire were either put back into Poland or into the newly-created country of Czechoslovakia, centred on the old kingdom of Bohemia. A large area of eastern Hungary was transferred to Romania. In the south, Croatia, Slovenia and Bosnia were detached and put into another newly-created country, Yugoslavia, the land of the south Slavs, along with Serbia and Montenegro.

On the Baltic, four new states were created from the Russian empire – Finland, Estonia, Latvia and Lithuania, the last three in reality little more than counties. The peacemakers thus created a buffer of states: Estonia, Latvia, Lithuania, Poland, Czechoslovakia and Yugoslavia, with the hope of containing German ambitions in the east. In the event, all of these states were to prove far too weak to resist the revival of German militarism and were quickly swept aside in the next war.

Italy gained the Trentino and South Tyrol provinces and so extended her territory to the watershed of the Alps, but was left frustrated in the

Adriatic, which she had hoped to dominate, by the inclusion of Croatia and Slovenia in Yugoslavia. This claim would again be renewed in the next conflict.

Britain neither sought nor obtained European territory from the peace, but it did take control over Palestine, Transjordan and Mesopotamia from the Ottoman Empire. Saudi Arabia was transferred from the Turkish to the British sphere of influence. From the German Empire came South-West Africa (ruled from South Africa for the next 75 years), Tanganyika and parts of Togoland and the Cameroons. Several German Pacific territories were transferred to Australia. These extentions to empire were termed mandates, rather than colonies, a distinction probably rather difficult to explain to a native of ex-German New Guinea.

By far the' most controversial of the British acquisitions were those in the Middle East, where promises of a fully independent Arab nation had been made. In fact these former Ottoman territories had been provisionally partitioned between Britain and France by the Sykes-Picot agreement of 1916, France obtaining Syria and the Lebanon. The Arabs felt betrayed and indeed Lawrence of Arabia resigned at the end of the war in indignation over the mistreatment of his Arab friends. Of these, however, Hussein eventually became King of Transjordan and his brother Faisal, King of Iraq – in fact, both British puppets. Saudi Arabia itself fell to the family of Ibn Saud.

Because Jewish settlement in the area had already begun, it was clear even then that Palestine would become the hornet's nest of competing Arab and Jewish claims which it has been ever since. Britain gained nothing but problems from the Palestinian mandate. By the Balfour Declaration of December, 1917, Britain supported in principle the Zionist idea of a Jewish homeland in Palestine, provided that it did not prejudice the rights of existing non-Jewish communities already living there. In fact it is difficult to see how it could possibly do otherwise. Britain did gain control of the main resource she wanted from Sykes-Picot, Mesopotamian oil, though a bumpy ride lay ahead in that country too. Of the other territorial gains, Tanganyika proved to be an expensive liability which Britain gratefully shook off in the era of African independence.

Nevertheless, it is quite clear that the First World War was all about empires – and about being on the winning side. Plebiscites and self-determination were for the losers. At the start of the war, Austria-Hungary had already placed a foothold in the old Ottoman Empire, in Bosnia, and was seeking greater influence in the Balkans, as was Russia

– neither empire saw itself as in terminal decline, though both collapsed. The Germans wanted an extension to their contiguous European empire, especially in the east, and would also have taken overseas colonies from Britain and France. As we have seen, the British and the French in turn took the opportunity to extend their empires at the expense of the Ottoman and German Empires. The French took their "lost provinces", Alsace and Lorraine, back in the fold, though they were originally German, and, particularly in the case of Alsace, remained Germanic in culture. Italy too had imperial ambitions, for though the province of Trentino had a majority of Italian speakers, South Tyrol was predominantly Austrian. Indeed in 1911 Italy had taken Libya from the Ottomans, and before long it would be carving out a larger empire in Abyssinia and the Horn of Africa. Empire was not an out-of-date concept in 1918 for the winners, only for the losers.

The League of Nations was established by the Treaty of Versailles under the inspiration of President Woodrow Wilson, the idea being to establish an international body which would be able to restrict future conflicts. It was never to be a success, partly because the US Senate refused to ratify it, leaving it very much in the hands of Britain and France only. By the end of the war a strong feeling of isolationism was developing in the USA, by which all foreign entanglements were distrusted. This policy was to prove misguided in the long run, but was very influential in 1919.

The Treaty of Versailles was much criticised at the time by the famous economist, J M Keynes, in his book *The Economic Consequences of the Peace*. His particular target was the reparations. He warned that condemning Germany to economic servitude for a generation would do nobody any good. The German industrial economy functioned as part of a larger machine, the western European economy, which could not work properly without it. The book sold well – especially in its German edition.

The feature of the First World War which marks it out from all other wars involving England is the level of casualties sustained amongst the combatants, so why was the war fought to a decisive result? When both sides realised the likely scale of the war, which was clear enough as early as the first Christmas in 1914, it would have seemed sensible to stop the conflict, but there was no political will to do so on either side. During the war various proposals were made for peace, including one from the Pope, but nothing could be agreed. The British and the Americans wanted "regime change" in Germany and a complete end to the dominance of Prussian militarism. So whilst the Germans may have been prepared to accept a return to the *status quo ante bellum*, the British and the Americans were not. Lloyd George himself dismissed any attempts at peace before the defeat of Germany – the general feeling being that the British and the French combined were strong enough to beat the Germans eventually. Indeed, though many blame Haig, Rawlinson and the rest of the Allied generals for the mass slaughter, they were only servants of elected politicians, Lloyd George included, who could have instructed them to follow a more cautious policy, or have replaced them. Indeed the elected politicians themselves were beholden to the electorate – and Lloyd George was re-elected after the war, with a large majority. The fact is that tensions between Britain and Germany had been building over many years, from the time Wilhelm II dismissed Bismarck and took personal control in 1890. One of the war aims of the British was to get rid of him. The feeling in Britain was that it was better to have this affair settled, as it was thought, once and for all, despite the tremendous cost. The war was fought on a totally different scale to any colonial conflict, or the Crimean War. Clearly this was a war that nobody wanted to lose – the consequences would be just too devastating.

Chapter 32 – The Inter-war Years

As the war was drawing to a close, another deadly peril appeared – an influenza epidemic known as the Spanish Flu. Lasting from June 1918 until December 1920, this swept right around the world. It is thought to have killed at least 50 million people – more than the war itself. Its main targets were healthy young adults rather than the aged and juveniles. Approximately 200,000 people died from the disease in Britain. Many soldiers who had escaped death in the war succumbed to this disease. One soldier who caught it was Robert Graves, who wrote a famous account of the war in his autobiography, *Goodbye to All That*, but he survived.

After the ravages of the war and the Spanish Flu, it may seem surprising that there was enough manpower available to resume full-scale war within twenty years. Nevertheless, that is what happened. During this period the population of Britain and other European countries had been expanding quickly, and large families were common. Many lost one boy to the war but still had several surviving sons, ready to create the next generation of servicemen.

A general election was called at the end of 1918 on a brand-new franchise. All males over the age of 21 were entitled to vote, as were women over the age of 30, subject to a property qualification of £5 rental value a year for themselves or their husbands. The size of the electorate doubled. In view of the fact that he was only the leader of a minority party, Lloyd George was anxious to keep the wartime coalition together and so himself in power. He and Bonar Law, the Conservative leader, issued an endorsement or "coupon" to their candidates so that they did not compete with one another. In what became known as the coupon (or khaki) election, the coalition of Conservatives and Lloyd George Liberals won 478 seats, of which 335 were Conservative. The Asquithian Liberals were reduced to a rump of 36 members, and the largest opposition party became Labour, with 59 seats, 58 of which were held by trades unionists. The complexion of the new House of Commons was not to everyone's taste: "A lot of hard-faced men who look as if they have done very well out of the war", in the words of Stanley Baldwin.

The war had not been quite so ruinous in its financial effects as might have been expected, as the accumulated savings of nineteenth-century Britain went part of the way to finance it. Nevertheless many expensive loans had been raised during the war. This financial policy – taxation only provided about 30% of wartime financial needs – proved highly inflationary in its impact, in that the post-war purchasing power of the pound was only about one third of its pre-war value. Inflation continued after the war so that the price index stood at 323 in March, 1920, up from 100 in July 1914. This inflation, however pernicious, did have the effect of reducing the burden of government debt in domestic war bonds.

The demobilisation of four million men took place within a year as the country freed itself from wartime controls and state-run business, and tried to return to normal conditions. Promising "Homes fit for Heroes", the government passed the Housing Act (1919) to provide finance for state-owned residential property (which later evolved into council housing). There was a brief and helpful economic boom in 1919 but very quickly, the pre-war pattern of labour strikes and disputes broke out again. A slump followed so that by 1921 there were 2.17 million unemployed. By the Unemployment Insurance Acts of 1920-2, basic benefits – "the dole" – were made non-contributory in the face of mass unemployment, breaking the original principal of national insurance. Meanwhile the Railways Act of 1921 replaced the wartime state-controlled system and brought into being the four great railway companies of the inter-war years: London, Midland and Scottish (LMS), London and North-Eastern (LNER), Great Western and Southern.

In Ireland the troubles resumed at the end of the war. Michael Collins and his Irish Republican Army set about boycotts, ambushes and assassinations. To counter the insurrection the British government created the Black and Tans, English ex-servicemen, so-called because of their khaki uniforms and black belts, who met terror with counter-terror. As Colonial Secretary, Winston Churchill played a leading role in bringing about a settlement over the "dreary steeples of Fermanagh and Tyrone" where not even the Great War could effect any change. He demanded an end to the fanatical quarrels which had driven Pitt from office and dragged down Gladstone in the summit of his career. Once it became clear that the Irish were to have their independence, a new civil war broke out between two Irish factions headed by Collins and Eamon De Valera respectively. Collins, whose party won more seats at the elections, was assassinated. By the end of 1922 the Irish Free State was finally established, independent of the United Kingdom, though the six counties of Ulster opted to stay within the UK.

There was also post-war unrest in India, where political concessions made to the Congress Party and its leader Mahatma Gandhi failed to satisfy the Indians. The troubles culminated in the Amritsar Massacre of 13 April 1919. After a mob had murdered four Europeans, the crowd was fired upon by soldiers under the command of one General Dyer. 379 people were killed and more than three times that number wounded. Gandhi's non-violent campaign had spiralled out of control; he himself was imprisoned in 1922.

In several areas, peace terms after the war took years to sort out. One such place was in the Eastern Mediterranean, where the borders between Greece and Turkey were not settled until 1923, with mass movements of people going either way. Part of this process was the Chanak crisis of 1922 – Chanak was a fort commanding the Dardanelles, occupied by British and French troops. Lloyd George threatened war with the new secular Turkish leader, Mustafa Kemal Ataturk, but lacking international support, backed down. The Australian Prime Minister told him that he could have as many troops as he wanted for a good cause, but none for a bad one.

1922 was the year of the foundation of the BBC, with John Reith as its general manger. The company was created under the aegis of the Post Office by six radio companies. In 1927 it was reconstituted as a non-commercial public corporation. At no time was it considered part of the government, and indeed it has always striven to maintain its independence. The BBC became immediately influential in forming public opinion as by 1926 there were two million radio sets in the country.

By the end of 1922 the majority Conservatives had tired of the Liberal Lloyd George, who was badly tarnished by corruption scandals. He resigned, to be replaced by the Canadian Scot, Andrew Bonar Law, one of Britain's forgotten prime ministers. In the election of November 1922, the Conservatives were returned to power, with 345 seats, while the Labour representation grew rapidly to 142 members. Within a few months, Bonar Law resigned, nominating as his replacement the mild and self-effacing Stanley Baldwin – much to the chagrin of his rival, Lord Curzon, the Foreign Secretary, thought to be too aristocratic to deal with trade unionists, troublesome Irishmen, Indian nationalists and the like. In December 1923, Baldwin went to the polls again, this time winning only 258 seats as against 159 for the reunited Liberals and 191 for Labour. A very small swing was grossly magnified in terms of parliamentary representation – to be reversed in the election of 1924. Under its Scottish leader, Ramsay MacDonald, illegitimate son of a farm labourer and a housemaid from Lossiemouth – a far cry indeed from Lord Curzon – Labour formed a minority government for the first time. However, the new administration lasted only nine months, and achieved little. Its main success was in tackling the housing shortage, providing subsidies for local authorities to build council houses on a large scale for the first time (Wheatley's Housing Act, 1924). The Conservatives returned to power at the end of 1924 after much-publicised Communist scares. From its earliest days the Labour Party had always disassociated itself from the minuscule Communist Party, but this did not stop a press campaign from tarring it with the red brush, assisted by a forgery – the Zinoviev or Red letter – allegedly from the Soviet Union, inciting the Communists of Britain to rebel.

So the Conservatives returned to power. One of the first actions of the new Chancellor of the Exchequer, Winston Churchill, who had returned to the Conservative fold after first crossing to the Liberals as long ago as 1904, was to return the pound to the gold standard at its pre-war parity. Effectively, this set sterling at too high a rate, causing hardship in industry and leading to the General Strike of 1926. However it had also been the intention of the outgoing Labour Chancellor, Philip Snowden, to do the same thing.

In 1925 the government signed the Locarno Treaties with Germany, France and Italy, essentially bringing Germany back into the fold. If inflation had been a serious problem in Britain, it had completely run out of control in Germany under the Weimar Republic (1919-33), reaching a peak in 1923. Inflation became a deliberate policy of the Weimar authorities, as it reduced the value of German war bonds ultimately to zero. This meant that Germany had in effect reduced its national debt to pre-war levels by 1922, when Britain was still servicing $34 billion of debts built up during the war. The price in the ruination and subsequent cynicism of the middle classes was to create a revolutionary change in the German political system – the Nazi party was established in these years, just one of several competing groups aimed at ridding Germany of its democracy. (The main basis of Nazi support was to be the peasantry and the middle classes – the industrial workers tended to favour the socialists and the communists.) 1923 a brand new currency, the Rentenmark, had to be introduced. In 1924, under the Dawes Plan, Germany took out American loans to try to get its economy in order and meet its bill for reparations. Meanwhile in

Italy the first Fascist dictator, Benito Mussolini, had come to power by a coup d'état in 1922, and was planning great things for his country.

The great event of 1926 was the General Strike, lasting just nine days, from 3 May. A million coal miners were already on a strike of their own, and the Trades Union Congress called out a million more men in sympathy. Apart from a government paper, the British Gazette, the press disappeared, as did regular public transport. However the government was ready. Volunteers ran public transport vehicles, the mood of the country was surprisingly upbeat, strikers and the public got along well and in short, the very idea of a worker's revolution in Britain disappeared in just nine days. By this time there were a million and a half private motor vehicles on the roads so the strikes by public transport workers had a limited effect. After the strike collapsed, the coal miners hung on for another six months, but eventually were obliged to return to work on humiliating terms – no national agreements, no shorter hours, no more money. In direct response to the General Strike, in 1927 the government passed the Trades Disputes and Trade Union Act, outlawing sympathy strikes and the use of union funds for political purposes.

The year 1928 saw the signing of the Kelloggs-Briand Pact for the renunciation of war. Idealistic and unrealistic, it was brushed aside in the events of the thirties.

In 1929 there was another general election, based on the 1928 franchise which now included all women over the age of 21, thus including the "flappers". The election returned a new minority Labour Government, again under Ramsay MacDonald as Prime Minister. Determined to be moderate and respectable, it pleased few before collapsing after two years in the face of the worst economic storm of the century, the Great Depression. This began in earnest with the Wall Street crash at the end of October, 1929. The unemployment situation in Britain was already serious, as the number of insured unemployed never dipped below a million throughout the twenties. The crash had been preceded by a stock market bubble, and was followed by a collapse in credit availability, broken banks and hastily-erected trade barriers (which exacerbated the problem) around the world. American loans to Germany, on which so much of the recovery of that country, and so of Europe as a whole, had relied, suddenly dried up. In Germany the number of registered unemployed rose from two to six million by 1932, and in Great Britain to three and three-quarter million in the same period. No one really knew how to solve the problem. There were half-hearted attempts at schemes of public works to mop up unemployment, and also cuts in the dole and means-testing to restrict it.

In domestic politics, Ramsay MacDonald, like his opposite number Baldwin, essentially a moderate, battled his way through the storm. Baldwin himself came under attack from the two great press barons of the day, Lords Beaverbrook and Rothermere, who wanted to establish a tariff wall round the British Empire. They tried to bring Baldwin down; he famously responded that all they wanted was power without responsibility, and saw them off.

By August 1931 the economic situation had become so dire that normal politics were abandoned and a National Government was formed. MacDonald remained as Prime Minister, but now the leading Conservatives and Liberals joined his cabinet. This development was not acceptable to most of MacDonald's Labour colleagues, who subsequently abandoned him to the Conservatives, claiming he was far too fond of hob-nobbing with duchesses. The first important action of the new government was to take sterling off the gold standard. A general election was then called (October, 1931) at which Nationalist candidates won 554 out of 615 seats. This meant that the extremes of left and right were excluded from office, and in fact within the Conservative party favoured the up-and-coming Neville Chamberlain against his rival, Winston Churchill. He was left smouldering on the back benches, unable to contemplate any of the moves towards independence for India being promoted by his more centrist colleagues.

There was much debate in these times about the status of the Dominions, that is, South Africa, Canada, Australia and New Zealand. Their constitutional position was formalised in the Statute of Westminster of 1931, which recognised the independence of their governments within the Commonwealth. Their only formal link was a Governor-General, representing the King, not the Prime Minister. India was induced to aspire to dominion status. Gandhi remained at the forefront of Indian politics. In 1930 he undertook his famous Salt Satyagraha, a march of 240 miles from Ahmadabad to the sea to obtain salt without paying tax. He was regarded as a semi-divine being by some and as a charlatan self-publicist by others, notably Churchill, who called him "a seditious middle-temple lawyer, now posing half-naked as a fakir". Closer to home, the Irish under De Valera came to reject dominion status, opting instead for complete and absolute independence by 1937.

In 1932 the Chancellor Neville Chamberlain brought in the Import Duties Act, which imposed a ten percent duty on most goods from outside the Commonwealth. Free trade was finally dead, killed off by the vicious economic circumstances of the time, in favour of imperial preference. The economy began to recover. Unemployment had dropped below two million by July, 1935. The index of production, from a baseline of 100 in 1929, fell to 84 in 1931, then rose to 93 in 1933 and 110 in 1935 – so it is a myth that recovery only came with renewed expenditure on rearmament. In fact the biggest boost came from a housing boom, and the new industries which were flourishing at the time – motor cars, aircraft, chemicals, synthetic textiles, radio and even film-making. However, the new prosperity was very unevenly spread across the country. Conditions remained dire in the old industrial areas, notably Clydeside, the Tyne and Tees, the Welsh Valleys and the Lancashire cotton towns – the "depressed areas" – whilst in the south-east, new suburban construction and new industry flourished. In 1934 the government passed the Special Areas Act aimed at encouraging workers to move from deprived places to areas where there were opportunities, and to encourage new industries in the depressed areas. In fact many workers did move from Wales into the expanding motor industries in Birmingham, Coventry and Oxford. The administration of the dole was meanwhile transferred to new Unemployment Assistance Board, which quickly acquired a bad reputation for mean-spiritedness amongst the unemployed, and gained the government no credit from the large sums eventually expended. As late as 1936 the men from the Tyne launched the Jarrow March, all the way to London, to protest against poverty and unemployment, famously having to eat their boots along the way, but they got nothing for their trouble but the rail fare home. It was a poor comparison with the United States, which had found an altogether more dynamic and purposeful leader than Britain possessed in Franklin D Roosevelt, who came to office in 1933 pledging a New Deal and in fact a new plan for the poor.

Meanwhile events took an ominous turn abroad. The devastating unemployment in Germany played straight into the hands of Adolf Hitler's National Socialists. As leader of the largest party in the Reichstag (though with only 32% of votes cast), Hitler was nominated as Chancellor by President Hindenburg (hero of Tannenberg) in January 1933, despite the fact that Hindenburg considered him a much more suitable for a job as a postmaster. Hitler immediately dismantled democracy in Germany – kicking the ladder away underneath him – and established a Fascist and anti-Semitic dictatorship with its dreadful paraphernalia of brown-shirted hooligan storm troopers, the secret state police (SS) or Gestapo (under Heinrich Himmler), mass rallies and hideous demagogy.   Nevertheless Hitler very quickly reduced unemployment in Germany, notably by public works, including the construction of an impressive series of motorways (the first of which was not completed in Britain until 1959). He also immediately speeded up the illegal rearmaments program which had already started in Germany. In Britain, Sir Oswald Moseley quit the Conservative party to create a local copy of the Nazis, the British Union of Fascists.

In an early foretaste of things to come, Japan attacked Manchuria from its colony of Korea in 1931. Despite international attempts to stop the conflict, Japan then invaded mainland China itself in 1933, a conflict which was later resumed in 1937 with the appalling Rape of Nanking. In 1935, Italy attacked Abyssinia, a fellow-member of the League of Nations, with the clear aim of establishing a new Roman Empire over a vast area of north-eastern Africa. The British and the French, in the Hoare-Laval Pact of 1935, agreed to leave Mussolini alone. The pact was soon discredited, and Hoare replaced as Foreign Secretary by Anthony Eden, but still the government did nothing. Heile Selassie, Emperor of the Abyssinians, was soon forced into a dignified exile.

In another quarter, the Communist government of the Soviet Union, which had at first attracted widespread interest and support in western Europe, had now fallen into the hands of another sinister dictator, Joseph Stalin. The enforced collectivization of agriculture in the early thirties led to widespread starvation, especially in the Ukraine, seen by Stalin as too rebellious and independent-minded a province. Modern estimates put the death toll in the enforced Ukrainian famine at seven million. Following the great famine, the Soviet Union then underwent another almighty upheaval, the Great Purge (1936-8), a campaign of repression aimed to stamp out all opposition to Stalin himself in the Communist Party, the government and the army. Millions were sent to the gulag concentration camps in the frozen northern and eastern parts of the country. All the evil instruments of a totalitarian police state were used – informers, surveillance, accusations of sabotage followed by imprisonment, show trials and arbitrary executions. It became apparent that British liberal sympathies with the Soviet regime were badly misplaced.

In contrast, the relatively mild evolution of India towards full independence was consolidated by the Government of India Act of 1935, allowing greater local autonomy. From this point onwards – interrupted by the war – the main impetus of British policy in India was for a peaceful transition to independence. All parties were aware of the dangerous potential for civil war whenever the British were to leave.

MacDonald, now ailing, was replaced as Prime Minister by Baldwin in June 1935, and a general election was called in November. The National Government won a large majority with 432 seats. By this time Baldwin was coming under fire for failing to take on the foreign dictators, and to re-arm the country. He responded that his pro-rearmament Nationalist candidate at the Fulham by-election of October 1933 had been heavily defeated by a pacifist Labour candidate. A majority of 14,521 had turned into a defeat by 4,480. Neither the public nor the Opposition wanted anything to do with rearmament. In 1933 the Oxford Union had passed a motion that "In no circumstances will this House fight for its King and country". The popular radio preacher Canon Dick Sheppard founded the Peace Pledge Union in 1934 and very quickly had 80,000 members. In the circumstances, Baldwin had waited until 1935 to hold an election, when the public at large was beginning to recognise the unpalatable truth that collective security (i.e. the League of Nations) was of little use without military power behind it.

By the end of 1935, reality was also dawning in Opposition politics. The Labour Party ditched its pacifist leader, George Lansbury, in favour of Clement Attlee. He was hardly an inspiring choice, being a very modest man, but so many Labour men had lost their parliamentary seats, including the favorite to succeed Lansbury, the Londoner Herbert Morrison, that the field was narrow. One trade unionist who made a great impression in the thirties, Ernest Bevin, a former lorry driver from Somerset with an unknown father, and head of Britain's largest trade union, the Transport and General Workers, allied with Attlee against the future machinations of Morrison to take over the leadership.

In March, 1936 Hitler defied the terms of the Treaty of Versailles once more when he reoccupied the demilitarized zone of the Rhineland, effectively destroying the security of both Britain and France, neither of which intervened. The "wait and see" and "hope for the best" attitude of Baldwin and his cabinet was certainly exasperating to Churchill and his supporters, but as the only other options were rearmament and probably war, the country as a whole still preferred to turn a blind eye. In the same year, Germany came to agreements with both Italy and Japan concerning future conflicts – the "Axis" powers were preparing for action.

Also in 1936, a civil war broke out in Spain. Nothing illustrated the ineptitude and ambivalence of the British and French governments better. A Republican victory at the general election in Spain was met with an armed rebellion by the right-wing and military Nationalists. Before long the Germans and Italians were sending aid, and indeed the Germans used the conflict to test their new warplanes and train their pilots. The British and French insisted on non-intervention whilst their future opponents intervened so much that they tipped the scales in favour of the Nationalists. The Soviet Union did support the Republican side, but at the cost of ruthless Communist control when most of the Republicans were not Communists. The conflict lasted until 1939. It included the infamous bombing of the Basque town of Guernica by German aircraft, and the recruitment of the International Brigade, drawn from supporters all over the world, to fight for the Republicans. However victory went to the Hitler-sponsored Fascist, General Franco. Nevertheless the war had one useful long-term effect. It so badly damaged Spain, set back for a generation, that Franco kept the country out of the Second World War. Had he intervened when he saw that the going was good – as did his fellow Fascist dictator, Mussolini – Gibraltar would have been threatened, and Gibraltar was the geopolitical king-pin of the western oceans.

Edward VIII succeeded his father George V (1910-36) as King at the beginning of 1936, but was destined to remain in the job for less than a year. He at once declared his intention to marry an American, Mrs Wallis Simpson, already divorced once and about to be divorced again. As the monarch and his consort were supposed to represent the very epitome of moral rectitude and family life, this was too much for Baldwin, who – in this unimportant matter – for once acted decisively, obliging Edward to abdicate, as Edward would not back down. So the new king retired to France with the title Duke of Windsor, to be succeeded by his reluctant brother, George VI, and his wife Elizabeth, who really did represent the kind of model family required for the job.

Baldwin continued in office for two years, until May, 1937. His appointment of Sir Thomas Inskip (up to now known mainly for his defence of the old Book of Common Prayer) as Minister for the Coordination of Defence caused dismay, as the man who should have done the job, Winston Churchill, languished on the back benches. Baldwin was succeeded by Neville Chamberlain, a former Mayor of Birmingham and a member of one of the most important political families of the age, a far more vigorous man whose judgment turned out to be distinctly lacking. It was a bad omen when early in his prime ministerial career his attempt to appease Mussolini caused the resignation of his Foreign Secretary, Anthony Eden.

In March 1938 Hitler marched into his home country, Austria, and declared the Anschluss or political union with Germany. This was only a prelude to further expansion, as he then made menacing noises concerning Czechoslovakia, with its population of three million Sudeten Germans under Czech rule. The Pan-German-style demands for the inclusion of German speakers within the mother country, first in the Rhineland, then in Austria, now in Sudetenland, did not seem unreasonable to many, if only Hitler had stopped there. In the latter two cases, it would have been very difficult to prevent him anyway. Many doubted that he would stop, but Chamberlain opted for appeasement, which to him meant the sacrifice of the Sudetenland by Czechoslovakia. He did not want to be "digging trenches and trying on gas masks here because of a quarrel in a faraway country between people of whom we know nothing". Hitler in turn claimed only to want Sudeten Germans, and "not one Czech". Chamberlain returned from meeting Hitler in Munich in September 1938 proclaiming "Peace in our time", having conceded the German occupation of the Sudentland, and with it most of the significant motor and armaments industries of Czechoslovakia. There was a huge collective sigh of relief in Britain, but Churchill was scornful.

Six months later, in March, 1939 Hitler's troops marched into Prague. The Czech part of Czechoslovakia was subsumed into Germany, Slovakia was given a nominal independence and thirty-three Czechoslovak divisions (a division representing about 15,000 men) were eliminated from the Allied side in any future armed conflict. Chamberlain was humiliated. Hitler had already absorbed two of the key heartlands of the old Austro-Hungarian Empire at virtually no cost. Shortly afterwards, Britain guaranteed the frontiers of Poland – expected to be the next target of German aggression.

In what seemed to be the most important area – battleships – Britain had kept ahead of Germany in the arms race before the First World War. Now it was very different, because in the new era of mechanized warfare, and especially of tanks and military aircraft, she was a long way behind. In 1938 Germany spent £1,710 million or a quarter of her national income on armaments. The UK spent £358 million, 7% of national income, and this was more than France was spending. The apathy of the thirties generation of politicians is striking in comparison to their predecessors. Only after Munich did rearmament accelerate. 2,827 planes were produced in 1938, 7,940 in 1939.

Diplomatic shocks were not in short supply in this rapidly evolving scenario, and the next was the Nazi-Soviet Non-Aggression Pact of

August, 1939, also known as the Ribbentrop-Molotov Pact. This was in fact a carve-up of the tier of northern and eastern European states created by the Treaty of Versailles, including Poland itself, between the two powers. Despite being diametrically opposed in the political sense, the Russians had struck a Faustian bargain with Hitler – in fact their version of the Munich agreement – to buy peace (for now) and time. For Germany, where the fear of war of two fronts remained very strong, the pact secured its eastern frontier. The pact was the immediate precursor of war, which began when Germany attacked Poland on 1 September. Hostilities with Britain and France followed two days later.

Given that up to this point the German Nazis and the Russian Communists had seen themselves as mortal enemies, it might be useful at this point to consider the differences between the two, as there are certainly many similarities. Both ran totalitarian states, under dictators without any form of parliament. In both countries the rule of law was abolished for many groups of citizens. Each discriminated against its internal enemies by constructing concentration camps where they were eventually liquidated. However, the Soviets simply abolished their monarchy and aristocracy completely, driving those into exile that they could not kill first. The middle classes were deliberately impoverished in that doctors, teachers and industrial managers earned no more than factory workers. In Germany this did not happen – the Nazi party was "socialist" in name only. Old industrial families such as the Krupps arms manufacturers continued to prosper. There was no attempt at an artificial levelling of society. The German army, despite the presence of a politicized corps, the SS, remained a professional body run by trained officers – there was no purge on political grounds. On the other hand the Nazis were overtly racialist and eventually set about murdering people it did not consider to be German enough, notably of course the Jews, who had been intermarrying with Europeans, including Germans, for centuries, and also gypsies and political opponents, especially the Communists themselves. The Soviets were not overtly racialist and indeed the Red Army included many ethnic groups from Soviet Asia. The Jews hardly had a good time in the USSR either, many being sent to Siberia, but in general they survived the coming war.

Chapter 33 – The Second World War

What became known as the Second World War was in fact two wars, European and Asian. There was very little contact between the main Axis allies, Germany and Italy in Europe and Japan in Asia. The second or Asian war may never have spread outside China but for the early success of the Axis powers in the European war. This left the Asian possessions of France, Britain and the Netherlands under-protected and the Japanese sought to take advantage.

In the twenty years from the end of the First World War, military technology had advanced rapidly, to the point where the decisive weapons in some theatres – including the aircraft carrier and the atom bomb – had been completely unknown in the previous conflict. The German concept of *Blitzkrieg* or lightning war, an all-mechanized fast assault of tanks, aircraft and motorized infantry and artillery, moving so quickly that it could break through and turn a flank before the enemy could reorganize to face it, had been developed by the strategists. There were vital developments in radar and sonar, new weapons including dive bombers and heavy bombers, and even the first unmanned aircraft, the V1 flying bomb and the V2 rocket. Also new were multiple rocket launchers, including the Russian Katyushas known to the Germans as "Stalin's organs". Nevertheless, in its main theatre, the Eastern Front, the war, if not something that Napoleon would fully recognise, was still very much fought out between huge armies backed by heavy artillery, as it had been on the Western Front in the previous conflict. Also, there was a problem with U-boats, in that German submarine technology had barely changed from the days of the First World War. The limitations of these relatively primitive machines, able to dive deep and stay out of trouble for relatively short periods only, were ultimately to be their undoing. The Americans had developed much larger and more powerful submarines, but they were not critical to the success of the American war strategy, as the U-boats were to the German. Of all the new weapons, the heavy bombers were to prove the greatest disappointment in terms of strategic power. Air superiority could be devastating, but only where there was little opposition. Faced with concentrated anti-aircraft fire, barrage balloons and fighter attacks, the bombers often released their loads high and off-target. One load of bombs dropped on Hamburg succeeded only in flattening a field of rhubarb, causing the locals to comment that the British were trying to starve them out.

In the first month of the European conflict, the German and Russian armies swept aside the horse-era Polish forces and met half-way across Poland at Brest-Litovsk, duly dividing the country between them. Poland, like Serbia in the First World War, was the first country to be invaded and suffered eventually more than any other as it was overrun first from both sides, then from the west, then from the east. Russia also took Estonia, Latvia and Lithuania and set about making war on Finland, its province until 1918. The tiny Finnish army delivered a serious check to the Red Army, leaving many to doubt its real value after the Stalinist purges of the thirties, but the Finns were before long obliged to concede their eastern province, Karelia.

When war began, Chamberlain, though badly tainted by Munich, was still Prime Minister, and he reconstituted his cabinet, bringing back both Churchill (at the Admiralty once more) and Anthony Eden. Churchill was to have an exciting start at the Admiralty. In September the aircraft carrier *Courageous* was sunk by a submarine, to be shortly followed by an old battleship, the *Royal Oak*, sunk by another U-boat which had penetrated the leaky barriers of Scapa Flow. The U-boat captain, Lieutenant Prien, became an overnight superstar in Germany (he went down with his submarine in 1941). Then in December came the Battle of the River Plate, in which one of Germany's few capital ships, the pocket battleship *Admiral Graf Spee*, was trapped by British ships off Montevideo in Uruguay and scuttled by her captain.

As the Germans consolidated in the east and built up their forces, at first there was no action on the western front, in what came to be known as the phony war. In early April Chamberlain chortled that Hitler had "missed the bus". Plans were then laid for Britain to seize Narvik, the ice-free port and railhead for Swedish iron ore on the coast of Norway, in April 1940. The Germans got there first, invading both Denmark and Norway. Chamberlain was howled down in the Commons for the fiasco, amid cries of "missed the bus". The next day, May 10 1940, Germany invaded Belgium, Holland and France. Under proposals for a new wartime coalition of all parties, Labour refused to support

Chamberlain. The choice of the next Prime Minister then fell between the dovish Foreign Secretary, Lord Halifax, and the distinctly hawkish Winston Churchill. By some mysterious and later much-discussed process, Chamberlain was replaced by Churchill (and died six months later). Morale rose nationwide – "Winston is back"!

By this time 65 years old and highly experienced in both politics and war, Churchill had much enhanced his reputation by his prescient criticism of the pre-war failure to match Germany in warplane production, and by his prediction that the Munich agreement would soon collapse. He himself offered "nothing but blood, toil, tears and sweat". His historic radio broadcasts were soon rolling out across the land, inspiring confidence and fortitude alike. He gathered around himself a small War Cabinet, before long including his deputy, the Labour leader Clement Attlee, the press baron Lord Beaverbrook (Minister of Air Production), Ernest Bevin (Minister of Labour and National Service) and the Liberal leader Sir Archibald Sinclair (Secretary of State for Air). (Another member until 1943 was the Labour man Arthur Greenwood, said to have had a lifelong fight with the bottle, in which the bottle won every round. Such were the times.)

There was a rapid and rude awakening from the eerie silence of the phony war as the German *Blitzkrieg* fell with astonishing speed upon France in May 1940. The British Expeditionary Force was swept aside and forced to make for Dunkirk on the coast, to be largely repatriated by a flotilla of over 800 ships, large and small, three-quarters of them private, leaving its artillery, tanks and transport behind. 224,000 British and 140,000 French troops escaped (most of the French troops were soon repatriated into Brittany). This was far more than expected – most of the BEF – and so came to be regarded as a proud achievement. One thing which helped was that the bombs from the terrifying Junkers JU-87 Stuka dive-bombers made little impact when dropped on sand. Notably, aware of the huge losses in the First World War, the British authorities were much more careful with manpower in the Second. In the First World War these men may well have been left to fight and die as part of a policy of "attrition".

Churchill obtained the impression that there was little fight in the French. They were not about to repeat their experiences of 1914-18. Flying to France to in the hope of rallying their leaders, he was met by a rueful General Weygand, who commented that England had "rather a good anti-tank ditch". Churchill brought bad news. Despite French pleas, the War Cabinet had decided to retain Britain's best air squadrons at home, sensing that they would soon be needed there, rather than risk them in the forlorn battle for France, which indeed surrendered after only six weeks – a sensational result for Germany. The war on the western front was over, for now.

Churchill was suitably defiant: "We shall defend our island, whatever the cost may be. We shall fight on the beaches, we shall fight on the landing grounds, we shall fight in the fields and in the streets, we shall fight in the hills; we shall never surrender!"

Under Marshal Petain a pro-Nazi French government was formed at Vichy, controlling the southern part of France and the many French colonies. The French Mediterranean fleet at Oran (Mers El-Kebir), Algeria, refusing to accept any British proposal to keep it out of Germany's hands, was attacked at anchor by the Royal Navy with the loss of three battleships, an event which demonstrated to the world (and in particular to President Roosevelt) that the ruthless British meant business in this war. After this event, elements within the Vichy Government, notably the rabidly anti-English Pierre Laval and Admiral Darlan, would have preferred an actual declaration of war by France against England. As it was, and as the French prefer to forget, the Vichy government became the effective allies of the Germans. The British were to find themselves fighting the colonial French, notably in Syria and at Dakar in Senegal.

The stage was now set for Operation Sea Lion, the German invasion plan for Britain. This required the establishment of air superiority over the Channel. On 10 July the first regular heavy bombing raids on southern England began, concentrating first on the ports, then on airfields and London. By this time the RAF had equipped itself with high-quality fighters, notably the Spitfire and the Hurricane, and was aided by radar which could direct these aircraft to the incoming bombers (much to the amazement of the German aircrew). Churchill was ready for the Luftwaffe:

"The whole fury and might of the enemy must very soon be turned on us.....Let us therefore brace ourselves to our duties and so bear ourselves that if the British Empire and its Commonwealth last for a thousand years, men will still say, this was their finest hour!"

The Stukas of the *Blitzkrieg* proved too slow and were easily knocked out, as were the unwieldy twin-engine Messerschmitt 110s. The Messerschmitt 109 fighter, BMW of the skies, was another matter, but with new home production coming on stream, the RAF held on. Its pilot losses were much less than those of the Luftwaffe because many who were shot down parachuted to safety, while their German equivalents were captured or drowned. By 17 September the Luftwaffe had sustained losses it could not maintain, and a new strategy of the indiscriminate bombing of British cities was adopted. In popular myth, the Battle of Britain had been won by a couple of thousand pilots. "Never in the field of human conflict was so much owed to so few," according to Churchill, but was he right? No, he was not, because the years of preparation, the tremendous armada, the complete naval and air superiority, the floating harbours, and the undersea pipelines which it took to cross the Channel the other way in 1944 were simply not there. The Germans had absolutely no specialized landing craft of the type which were later regarded as essential by the Allies in Italy and on D-Day. They hoped to get their army, all its heavy artillery, tanks, lorries and all other supplies across the Channel on Rhine barges towed by tugs, motor boats, fishing vessels and a limited number of warships unequipped for army transport. It was never going to work, and the German Navy knew it. Hitler came no closer to an invasion of England than had Napoleon in 1804. Moreover, success in the Battle of Britain was due not only to fighter pilots, but also to all the ground crews which supported them, and just as much to the aircraft factories which were able to replace the fighters as fast as they were shot down. Behind these, too, lay a supply chain of engineering, steel, armaments and even tyre companies.

However, Hitler's new strategy was scarcely more comfortable for Britain, as for the first time its citizens came under direct fire in the London Blitz, which lasted from September 1940 until the middle of the following May, including one stretch of 68 consecutive nights. Other targets including Coventry, Liverpool, Glasgow, Bristol, Southampton and Hull were also badly affected. Over a million homes were destroyed or damaged in London alone, and 40,000 civilians were killed, half of them in London. However, precautions had been taken, including the construction of air raid shelters and the use of underground railway stations for that purpose, the evacuation of children and others who could be spared to the countryside, and the relocation of some industries to rural areas. The losses could have been greater. Also, in the end, only sixteen towns and cities were affected by bombing in the Blitz. Other towns were later affected by much smaller scale raiding, including the "Baedeker raids" on Bath, York, Canterbury Exeter and Norwich (made in retaliation for the bombing of Luebeck) and other smaller centres. Yet more were on the receiving end of jettisoned bombs, but damage was relatively slight. Large areas of the country were barely touched. In strategic terms, bad as if felt at the time, it was another hopeless campaign by the Germans.

In the spring of 1940, Italy attacked and occupied Albania while remaining at peace with Britain. Seeing his opportunity, Mussolini declared war on Britain and France in June 1940, taking the province of Nice from France. In September his Marshal Graziani launched an attack on the British protectorate of Egypt from Libya. Mussolini's plan, absurd though it may now seem, was to take the Suez Canal for Italy. However, he had a problem. The Italian soldiery was not as keen to fight for the glory of Italy as he was. General Wavell counter-attacked and took 130,000 prisoners with very few losses to his own forces. Wavell then withdrew from the Libyan deserts back into Egypt, leaving a small Australian garrison at Tobruk. From Kenya and Sudan, two British columns advanced northwards and took Eritrea, Italian Somaliland and Abyssinia by May 1941. In November 1940 a British air attack from the carrier *Illustrious* on the Italian mainland naval base at Taranto knocked out three Italian battleships, and further attacks inflicted heavy losses on the Italian fleet at Cape Matapan in southern Greece (March 1941). Italy also suffered reverses in its attempt to conquer Greece and so dominate the Adriatic. Only when substantially reinforced by the Germans (as Austria had been in the previous war) did the Italians take Greece and its islands, including Crete. British troops once again had to be hastily evacuated, or were taken prisoner.

German submarines again posed a terrible problem to British, Allied and neutral shipping from the earliest days of the war. The limitations of U-boat technology were far from obvious in 1940 and 1941. By the end of 1941, 9 million tones of shipping had been sunk by U-boats in the "Battle of the Atlantic" – hundreds of ships had gone down. In order to combat the threat, Churchill negotiated a desperate deal with Roosevelt to exchange a number of important military and naval bases in the West Indies, Newfoundland and Bermuda for "fifty of your oldest destroyers". Meanwhile Joseph Kennedy, US Ambassador in London, reported that the surrender of Britain was "inevitable". Roosevelt wanted to help but Congress was very isolationist in outlook. It did however pass the Lend-Lease Act in March, 1941, which meant that very large deliveries of ships, aircraft and other war material could be made from the USA, on very favorable terms – to be returned unless destroyed.

In May 1941 the mighty German battleship *Bismarck* was let loose into the Atlantic, accompanied by the battle cruiser *Prinz Eugen*. The Royal Navy gave chase with its newest and best ships, the battle cruiser *Hood* and the battleship *Prince of Wales*. The *Hood* was sunk and the *Bismarck* escaped, but not for long. Pursued by a flotilla of Royal Navy craft, she was immobilized by a torpedo fired from a biplane, a Fairey Swordfish launched from the carrier *Ark Royal*, and eventually went down.

By this time Hitler had new allies in Europe – Hungary, Romania and Bulgaria, the first two of which were to send considerable forces to the Eastern Front. Romania was particularly valuable as it did have its own oil supplies. Having first conquered Yugoslavia, Hitler changed the whole complexion of the war overnight on 22 June 1941 when he invaded the USSR under Operation Barbarossa. Many in Britain expected the Soviet Union to collapse within weeks, but not Churchill, who was jubilant. After all, Hitler had committed a fundamental strategic error, opening a new front before closing the old one – an error Japan was later to repeat. Within Germany, there were also grave doubts. The permanent head of the German Foreign Office, Weizsacker, said he would support the invasion if only every Russian city reduced to ashes were as valuable as a sunken British warship! Germany would only meet passive resistance in conquered Russian territories and lose economically, while at the same time encouraging England.

The German army advanced very rapidly by 600 miles into Russia. Churchill, who had real evidence from train movements, had tried desperately to warn Stalin of the coming invasion, but his telegrams had been brushed aside as British propaganda. A large part of the Soviet air force – hundreds of aircraft – was simply destroyed on the ground. In the first two months of the campaign, four million Russians soldiers were killed or captured, including over 650,000 each in two huge encirclements in the south of Russia. At Katyn, near Smolensk in western Russia, the German army found mass graves. Here 22,000 Polish officers – in fact the officer corps of the Polish army which had fallen into Russian hands – had been massacred by the NKVD, the Russian secret police.

By the end of the summer, however, Barbarossa was in trouble. The offensives became bogged down in the mud as resistance intensified. None of its three major targets – Leningrad, Moscow and the oilfields of the Caucasus – were taken. On 5 December came the first Russian counter-attack, driving the Germans away from Moscow and back the way they had come. Then the dreadful first winter in Russia took a terrible toll. The Russian soldiers for once were much better equipped, with winter clothing and heaters for both themselves and their machines. Their army cooks knew how to keep the men warm, melting blocks of margarine in the soup. The German commanders had hoped to conclude the campaign before winter set in, and when they failed to do so, their men and their machines froze. Frostbite became a major factor in German losses. Barbarossa had failed, and as in the First World War when the Schlieffen Plan also failed, the Germans should have made peace.

So what went wrong with Barbarossa? Everyone recognised that the German army was a supreme fighting machine, a fact not disputed to this day. However, the German military planners made the serious mistake of regarding the Soviet Union as a rather larger version of France, instead of a country on a subcontinental scale. It is 3300 miles overland from Berlin to Baku in the Caucasus. This huge distance required an equally huge amount of fuel for motorized troops, and left enormously long lines of communication wide open to partisan attacks. The Soviet Union also had a population of 190 million, compared to 41 million in France. It could replace even four million soldiers with four million more, and then do it again. Above all, every German soldier soon found out that the "Popovs" (Russian soldiers) were fanatically brave and patriotic. The peasant from Tambov from the First World War was now fighting for Tambov, not for East Prussia. In turn, the Russians had learned their lessons from the disasters of the First World War. Even in 1941 they had a great tank, the T34, which was very difficult to knock out and cheap to manufacture. The Germans eventually produced a T34 killer, the Tiger, but it was over-engineered, and so expensive to produce and difficult to repair. Had they taken notice, the Germans might have guessed more about the quality of the Russian army from the two sharp defeats suffered at its hands by the Japanese on the borders of Manchuria in 1938 and 1939, but they did not. They thought the Blitzkrieg was invincible, when it only worked in certain conditions. The network of minor metalled roads which supported it in France was replaced by rutted mud in Russia.

In the Pacific the Japanese could no longer sustain their impatience in view of the tempting prizes available and practically undefended. particular the oilfields of the Dutch East Indies, Holland being under German occupation since 1940. Also very desirable were the tin and rubber of Malaya, and the oil of Borneo and Brunei, all British territories. Their first move was the occupation of French Indo-China by the end of July 1941. This left them poised to strike at Malaya, the American Philippines and the Dutch East Indies. President Roosevelt told the Japanese to get out, and to add teeth to this demand, immediately froze all Japanese assets in the USA, bringing trade between the two countries to a standstill. The British and the exiled

Dutch governments immediately followed suit with similar actions. The adherence of the Dutch meant that Japan was deprived at a stroke of her vital oil supplies and would not long be able to sustain her position in China. If the USA wanted war, this was a very good way to go about it. Nevertheless no sane government would have taken on the overwhelming military potential of the USA, so how sane were the Japanese? Like Kaiser Wilhelm in the First World War, the Emperor Hirohito had fallen under the influence of the militarists in his government, led by the Prime Minister, General Tojo, and this led him to the most disastrous miscalculation in Japanese history. True, the Japanese had taken on and beaten the Russian Empire, in 1905, but there was no serious comparison between the semi-decrepit Russia of 1905 and the vigorous USA of 1941. The productive military capacity of the USA was barely touched by that date, yet already 25% of the Japanese economy was given over to war manufacture. The extent of the miscalculation can be measured by the length of the war. Germany aimed to harness the productive capacity of the Ukrainian wheatfields and the oil of the Caucasus, and had she done so, would have proved a far more dangerous enemy than Japan – and even then took six years to beat, against the combined forces of Britain, France, the USA and Russia. Therefore the defeat of Germany was given first priority by the USA. Despite this, the Japanese war lasted only three and a half years. Also, the Japanese undertook a new war when it had been unable to finish off the Chinese. In China it dominated the coast, but the Chinese government withdrew beyond the mountains into Szechuan, and kept fighting. This was indeed frustrating for the Japanese, for no matter how badly armed and equipped they were, and how often they were beaten, the Chinese always managed to produce another army.

The Japanese leaders might have reckoned on the isolationist policy of the majority in the US Congress, unwilling to fight any major war. If so, they did the one thing that was capable of shaking Congress out of its indifference by making a direct and unprovoked attack on the American navy. Without making any declaration of war a Japanese fleet under Admiral Nagumo attacked the US Pacific fleet in its naval base at Pearl Harbour, Oahu, Hawaii from its aircraft carriers on 7 December 1941. 353 combat aircraft managed to sink four battleships (two of which were later refloated) and damage four others. Many cruisers, destroyers and other warships were also sunk or damaged, but crucially, a number of capital ships including three aircraft carriers were not involved – these had already been sent to sea as a routine precautionary measure. There followed an immediate declaration of war from the United States, and naturally, much quiet satisfaction in Britain, where it was obvious that no matter how hard the road ahead, ultimate victory could scarcely be doubted. That the road immediately ahead would indeed be hard was clear enough to Churchill, who feared the worst from this phase of the war, and was not to be disappointed. Within days, Germany declared war on the USA in order to begin unrestricted submarine warfare on her Atlantic shipping.

Simultaneously with the move on Pearl Harbour, Japanese forces were fanning out in the direction of Hong Kong, Malaya, the Philippines and the Dutch East Indies. Landings took place in the north-east of Malaya. The Japanese army, including battle-hardened troops from China, yet riding bicycles, headed south, flushing out British positions as they went. British prestige in Malaya never recovered. Two battleships sent to Singapore as a warning to the Japanese, the new *Prince of Wales* (fresh from its encounter with the *Bismarck*) and the *Repulse*, were caught without any air cover off the coast of Malaya and sunk by Japanese torpedo planes. In February 1942 Britain suffered its worst-ever military defeat with the ignominious surrender of Singapore, and that to an inferior force of Japanese, who had the advantage of complete air superiority. 80,000 British, Australian and Indian troops, most of whom had never fired a shot in anger a month before the surrender, were taken prisoner. Another 50,000 had suffered the same fate in the retreat through Malaya. Of these losses, half were Indian troops. (Note that actual casualties were much worse on the Somme in the First World War.) Had they known what treatment to expect from the Japanese, they would certainly have fought much more tenaciously and conserved their ammunition much more carefully. The British troops were running out of ammunition, but so were the Japanese. The Dutch East Indies also rapidly succumbed, while the Americans endured similar disasters in the Philippines two months later. Encountering very limited opposition, the Japanese also overran Burma and many Pacific islands over a vast area.

As early as May, 1942, however, the tide began to turn. At the Battle of the Coral Sea, a Japanese attack on Port Moresby, New Guinea was halted by the US Navy. Only a month later, in probably the most bizarre and stirring naval battle ever fought, the Americans under Admirals Spruance and Fletcher sank four large Japanese aircraft carriers under Nagumo for the loss of one of their own, the *Yorktown*. The opposing fleets never sighted each other.

Another combat theatre in a totally different environment was the Sahara Desert. Here Italians forces, buttressed by German troops and panzer (tank) divisions under Ernst Rommel, and based in the Italian colony of Libya, took on the British and Commonwealth army coming out of Egypt. Because the terrain was indeed largely desert, the side which won a battle could then advance hundreds of miles until hit by supply problems. The retreating side would then gain the advantage as its own supply lines shortened. The Axis side suffered repeated problems, sometimes overcome, in obtaining seaborne supplies from Italy, as the British-held island fortress of Malta lay directly on the route. Malta suffered far more bombing than any British city apart from London as at times ceased to function as a base. Two capital ships, the old battleship *Barham* and the carrier *Ark Royal*, were lost in this theatre. Rommel himself ("Desert Fox") acquired a reputation as a superman for his sudden and daring charges through British lines, but suffered as resources – especially aircraft – were withdrawn to the Eastern Front. Also the British, who had slow but reliable sources of supply via the Cape of Good Hope, targeted his arriving fuel tankers. The low point in this conflict for the British was the fall of Tobruk in June, 1942, another disaster in the downward spiral from Singapore. Only four months later, however, in October 1942, the 8th army under General Montgomery finally beat Rommel at El Alamein, only sixty miles from Alexandria, and began an unstoppable march right back through Libya, past Tobruk and on to Tripoli. There is no doubt that the selection of Montgomery at this point was an inspired if fortuitous choice. Until he arrived in charge, every man at the front had an eye on his seat in a wagon for the retreat back to Cairo. Churchill commented that before Alamein, the British never won a battle, and after it never lost one.

The Germans continued their advance across southern Russia in 1942, but the Russians were learning from their previous mistakes. Stalin had refused to contemplate retreats in 1941 and this had cost him huge losses in German encirclements. Now that his troops were allowed to withdraw and regroup, German encirclements took a lot more land but few prisoners. Meanwhile, much of the Russian plant and machinery for wartime manufacture had been withdrawn east of the Urals, so that when the Germans overran the industrial areas of the Don basin, Russian war production was not seriously affected. Moreover, war material from Britain and the USA, eventually delivered in huge quantities, was beginning to make a difference. In one last great eastward surge the German 6th army reached Stalingrad on the River

Volga in August, 1942. Its lines of communication back to Germany were now hopelessly overstretched and guarded by reluctant divisions from Italy and Romania. In November the Russians struck at this weak link, cutting off General Paulus and 200,000 men in Stalingrad. By February 1943 the half that were left surrendered. Very few ever returned to Germany, itself now staring defeat in the face.

November 1942 was the worst month of the war for sinkings by U-boat attacks. After that point the situation was gradually retrieved with better radar, sonar and depth charges, and more and better convoy defences. One particularly important breakthrough was made when the German naval code, Enigma, was (temporarily) cracked. Another breakthrough was the closure of the "air gap" in the middle of the Atlantic. This required the development of very long-range aircraft which could allow the whole ocean to be patrolled, so not allowing the U-boats to wait unmolested in the "gap". Nevertheless the success of the U-boats probably delayed D-Day from 1943 to 1944, so lengthening the war. If, instead of spending money on fancy weaponry such as the V2 rocket, the Germans had put more resources into the simple U-boat, they could have further extended the war.

The Germans made one last great attempt at encirclement in southern Russia in the summer of 1943, at Kursk, in a gigantic battle of tanks and aircraft. This time the Russians were ready and the Germans were beaten back. From this point onwards, they faced a steady retreat all the way back to East Prussia, then to Berlin itself. In other theatres, 1943 was also a turning point. After the German invasion of Russia, Stalin repeatedly and stridently demanded that Churchill open a western front in France, preferably in 1942. Churchill and his army advisers refused, wishing to attempt a Channel crossing only from a position of overwhelming armed superiority. Any other approach risked great losses, the memories of the First World War again reverberating. Far better to give Stalin all the war material he needed and let the Germans exhaust themselves against the Russians in the east. There were many British-American conferences to decide priorities, but it was always the Americans who pushed for an early western front. The British preferred to strengthen the North African campaign, which was after all drawing off considerable German forces. The aim here was to clean up in North Africa, clear the Mediterranean of hostile shipping, then attack Western Europe through its "soft underbelly" – Italy. This is what happened, and a western front was only opened in France fully two years after Stalin had requested it.

The Pacific was emerging as a major battle zone for the first and only time in its history. The Asian/Pacific war was a conflict in which the respective navies played a leading role in the combat itself. As in the First World War, previously unknown and remote places – in this case Pacific Islands – suddenly became world news, never again able to sink into obscurity. The Japanese had established a far-flung perimeter of defended island bases designed to protect their conquests – and in particular the Dutch East Indies – within the "Greater East Asia Co-Prosperity Sphere". This was just another word for the (temporary) Japanese empire, the idea being that the conquered Asians themselves would join in the enterprise in solidarity with the Japanese. However, the vast majority did not see the Japanese as liberators, but as another set of imperialists.

The American strategy was unavoidably island-hopping, winkling out the ferociously tenacious Japanese as they went. Very few Japanese soldiers surrendered, preferring death to captivity. Extremely well dug in, and well supplied with both food and ammunition, they really did fight to the last man. It was normally necessary to flush the last of them out of their warrens with grenades and flame throwers, and even then, they came out shooting. The first major battle was at Guadalcanal in the Solomon Islands. The American invasion started in August 1942 and the island was not cleared of the Japanese until February, 1943.

In Operation Torch, American forces under Eisenhower landed in French North Africa. Marching east, they combined with the Eighth Army marching west to clear Tunisia, taking 150,000 German and 90,000 Italian prisoners in May, 1943. Hitler as usual had sent orders to fight to the last man and the last round. The Axis troops sensibly obeyed orders and fired off their ammunition into the sky. The German decision to defend Tunis, given the time as many American troops actually landed on the Atlantic coast of Morocco, had given the Allies a much bigger bag than they might have expected. From here the combined army crossed to Sicily. Mussolini was overthrown in July and eventually executed by Italian partisans. In September 1943 the Allied army crossed to mainland Italy where the government agreed to an armistice and the Italian withdrawal from the war. The Italian forces were promptly disarmed by the Germans, who continued fighting tenaciously in a slow withdrawal northwards across rugged, mountainous and easily defended terrain. To Hitler's pleasure and Churchill's frustration, the Allied landings were contained at Salerno as the Germans occupied their fortified "Winter Line", causing the Italian war to spill over into another year, 1944. Hoping to cut German communications behind them, an Allied force was then landed a long way up the coast at Anzio, south of Rome. This was far too slow in getting off the beach and so became trapped there as the Germans reinforced. Churchill complained that "instead of hurling a wild cat on the shore, all we got was a beached whale". The main force, gradually moving north past the defended line at Monte Cassino, reached Rome – not defended by the Germans – only on 4 June 1944. The crawl through southern Italy, though tactically disappointing, was however strategically successful, partly because it threatened the Balkans. There were 34 German divisions in Italy and another forty inferior German or German-controlled divisions in the Balkans on D-Day, 6 June.

The war in the air had developed into a strategic offensive of carpet bombing by massive fleets of Allied bombers. In July 1943 Hamburg became the first city to be engulfed in a firestorm, where so many incendiary bombs were dropped that the massive blaze became fanned by hurricane-speed winds, and loss of life was many times the usual level – in this case, 42,000 people were killed. The American air force based in Britain preferred raids on specified targets, particularly oil facilities, but in practice the results were often little different. The life of bomber crew was very dangerous, even in the best British bomber, the Lancaster, which had two gun turrets. The RAF scheduled tours of thirty flights, followed by second tours of twenty. In most of the earlier raids the loss rate exceeded five per cent, or one plane in twenty, so that a bomber crew had little hope of finishing one tour, never mind two. The loss rates dropped with the introduction of the long-range Mustang fighter towards the end of 1943, as this could beat off the Luftwaffe.

Between 1943 and 1944 the Russians under Marshal Zhukov pushed their front westwards by as much as 600 miles, retaking the Ukraine, entering Romania, crossing the pre-war Polish frontier and finally breaking the siege of Leningrad after two and a half years. The four- and six-wheel drive American trucks used by the Red Army were serviceable in the mud and allowed greater freedom of movement than the Germans possessed.

Between March and April 1944, the seemingly unstoppable advance of Japanese forces through British territory in Asia was finally halted. After a miserable retreat through the steaming, pestilential jungles of northern Burma, which Churchill regarded as the very worst place to fight the Japanese, the British had regrouped and rearmed in great numbers in India. The Fourteenth Army, including many Indian and even African troops, under General Slim, was ready to face the Japanese. The two sides met in two tremendous battles in the north-east border state of India, Manipur, at Imphal and Kohima. The results were decisive victories for Slim. This theatre is noted for the behind-enemy-lines heroics of the Chindits under their charismatic General, Orde Wingate. However, given that the British knew full well that the independence of both India and Burma would follow at the end of the war, it can be difficult to see why such large resources were committed in this theatre. In a way it is similar to North Africa – it was just a suitable place to engage the enemy, and the enemy has to be taken on and beaten somewhere if the war is to be won. All the better if in that place, the enemy's supply lines are stretched to the limit, and British supply lines, if slow, are not. As it was, the two battles cost the Japanese 55,000 casualties, including 13,500 dead – up to that date, the greatest losses in Japanese military history. British/Indian losses were only a third of these. The British were able to begin the liberation of Burma. By the end of the campaign in 1945, the Fourteenth Army comprised half a million men.

The American assault upon Saipan in the Mariannas led to one of the greatest naval battles in history, the Battle of the Philippine Sea, in June 1944. By this time the Japanese were running short of experienced pilots. The Americans were not, and their pilots were both elaborately trained and frequently exercised. Also, the American ships carried much better defensive armour than their Japanese equivalents. Japanese radar, elementary and little used, bore no relation to the by-now sophisticated American version. Though roughly equal in fighting strength, when the two forces met in the battle, the result was the "Great Mariannas Turkey Shoot". The Japanese aircraft carrier force was reduced to a shadow. On 20 October 1944, in another huge naval battle at Leyte Bay in the Philippines, the same thing happened again. The Japanese forces were annihilated and went a long way to proving the British First World War maxim that only the Royal Navy – or in this case the Japanese navy – had the capacity to lose the war in an afternoon. The Philippines were subsequently reconquered by the Americans under General MacArthur after much bitter fighting.

D-Day on the western front finally arrived on 6 June 1944 when, after two years of planning and preparation, the Allies landed on the Normandy beaches, code-named Utah, Omaha, Juno, Gold and Sword, in the largest amphibious operation in world history. By the end of August a British and Commonwealth army of 830,000 men and American one of 1.22 million had been transferred to France. Everything depended on the availability of specialized landing craft, especially the LST (Landing Ship, Tank), capable of carrying military vehicles. There was competition for the limited numbers of these available from other theatres including the Pacific, Italy and the south of France. The Allies had built up massive air force and naval support and despite some problems, most notably on Omaha beach, there was to be no repeat of the Anzio fiasco. The Germans, fully expecting an invasion somewhere along the coast, had build extensive fortifications – the "Atlantic Wall" with pill boxes, mines and barbed wire. Many experienced divisions were moved from the Eastern Front and held in reserve, ready to meet the blow, wherever it fell. However, naval bombardment of coastal positions and an extensive bombing campaign to disrupt communications within France had an effect. One German division took longer to reach Normandy from Paris than it had from the Eastern front.

The Allies could not rely on beach landings for long and had built floating harbours or Mulberries which were towed across the Channel. The Americans were soon in charge of the port of Cherbourg. There were then major battles as they moved inland, notably around Caen and Falaise to the south of it. A Hitler-inspired dash to cut the Allied armies in two at Avranches at the base of the Cotentin peninsula failed. In the midst of all this, an attempt was made on Hitler's life on 20 July, led by Colonel von Stauffenberg with the support of other high-ranking army officers. Unfortunately for all parties except the intended victim, the bomb exploded in Hitler's Wolf's Lair in East Prussia, but failed to kill Hitler. There followed a witch-hunt under the Gestapo. One of the people implicated was Ernst Rommel. He committed suicide in October, aged 52.

In the meantime a second invasion force under the American General Patton landed in the south of France on 15 August, securing the port of Marseilles. Churchill and his advisers considered this operation a waste of time, as there was no German army to oppose Patton, but the possession of Marseilles did prove useful. On 25 August the Allies secured Paris undamaged after the local German commander withdrew, ignoring Hitler's demand to defend the city until it was reduced to rubble. The northern Allied armies, under the insufferable Montgomery and the American Bradley, moved eastward. Overall command rested with Eisenhower, who chose to secure ports rather than let Montgomery charge into Germany without a solid supply line. Antwerp was taken early in September and the Allies headed for the Rhine. The northernmost army under Montgomery then made a bold move, attempting to take the Rhine bridge at Arnhem in Holland with parachuted troops and equipment – Operation Market Garden. These men had the misfortune to land practically on top of two Panzer divisions sent there to re-equip, and were annihilated. This episode is documented in the book and film, *A Bridge Too Far*.

In the east the Russian summer offensive starting in June 1944 was equally successful, inflicting the biggest defeat of the war on the German army and reaching the outskirts of Warsaw. Altogether between June and September the Germans lost one and a quarter million men, two-thirds to the Red army, and fleets of British and American bombers roamed freely over Germany. At this point, the war should have ended, but it was destined to be fought to the bitter end, partly because Hitler had some initiatives left. One of these was the V1 flying bomb or "Doodlebug" which certainly caused havoc, if no serious military damage, on civilian targets in London and Antwerp. However, it was slow enough to intercept. By the end of the bombing campaign, which lasted from June 1944 until March 1945, three-quarters of those crossing the Channel were shot down. Next came the V2 rocket, of vastly superior technology, travelling at 3,600 miles per hour (and so arriving in England in minutes from the launch base at Peenemunde). There was no defence against V2s, but they were expensive to produce and as inaccurate as the V1, so once again the initiative was a strategic failure. The same applied to jet-propelled aircraft, first used on the German side in numbers only in March 1945. Again, the German Navy under Admiral Doenitz finally acquired better submarines, the types XXI and XXIII, able to stay under water for long periods. Bombing disrupted production and the initiative came too late in the war to have much effect. That the development of better U-boats was an urgent priority can be seen from the statistics. Eventually the casualty rate amongst U-boat crews was to be the highest of any form of combatant in any war. Of 40,000 men who passed through U-boat training, 30,000 were killed and 5,000 taken prisoner.

Hitler's main hope rested on a counter-offensive in the west, which duly began on 16 December in the Ardennes – the Battle of the Bulge, whose objective was the recapture of Antwerp. However the weak American line was rapidly reinforced, the road junction of Bastogne was held, and the Germans were soon unable to move during the day because of Allied air superiority. This sudden surge certainly shook up the Allies, but it had failed by Christmas 1944.

The pattern was continued early the following year when the Russians rapidly took Romania, Bulgaria, East Prussia and Warsaw, advancing to the River Oder. The western Allies crossed the Rhine in numbers. Greece was abandoned.

The air campaign reached its dreadful crescendo in February, 1945 with the carpet bombing of Dresden, an ancient city associated with beautiful architecture, the arts and fine china. It was crowded with refugees from the east and soldiers and equipment going to and from the Eastern Front. Until now beyond the range of the big bombers, its centre was literally flattened with thousands of casualties – no one really knows how many, but certainly at least 25,000. Coming at this late stage of the war, only three months before the German surrender, the raid has attracted criticism to this day. The leader of Bomber Command, Sir Arthur "Bomber" Harris, claimed that before the raid Dresden was a major military, industrial and communications centre, and after it, it was none of these things. Both he and Churchill are quoted as saying that "He who sows the wind shall reap the whirlwind". However, after Dresden, even Churchill advised Harris to be more selective in choosing targets. Of course, by this stage, the Germans had lost the war in all but name, and could have surrendered on no worse terms than they eventually did, thus sparing their cities and their citizens, as happened at the end of the First World War. But in that war, Hitler, who stood to lose everything, including of course his life, was not in charge.

The Allies now advanced upon the bomb-shattered Berlin from east and west. By this time there was also perceived an urgent need for the western Allies to occupy as much territory as possible, something which the commander, Eisenhower, failed to appreciate. He restrained Patton from a race to Prague, which he could easily have won, so condemning Czechoslovakia to 45 years of Soviet domination. Meanwhile the German army increasingly fought for only one thing, the right to surrender to the British or the Americans rather than the Soviets. As the Allies closer in, one of Hitler's aides joked that it would soon be possible to take a tram from the western to the eastern fronts. On 30 April, Hitler killed himself in his bunker in Berlin. The end finally came on 8 May after earlier local surrenders.

The war in Asia and the Pacific was also approaching its denouement. In February 1945 American forces landed on the small island of Iwo Jima, intending it for use as a forward base for bombing raids to Japan. Famous for the photograph of American servicemen raising the Stars And Stripes, another ferocious conflict ensued. Next on the list, in April, was Okinawa, largest of the Ryuku Islands which form an arc running southwards from Japan itself. A British naval squadron sailed in support of the US Navy. Japanese ancillary staff and their families threw themselves off the cliffs to avoid capture. By this time the Japanese had developed a new and devastating tactic – Kamikaze aircraft. Steered directly into enemy shipping by their pilots with no idea of simply dropping torpedoes and flying home, they were very difficult to stop. They hit 182 ships at Okinawa, sinking 25. The Japanese fought with ever greater intensity, inflicting heavy losses, and it was clear that a frontal invasion on Japan itself must cost the lives of hundreds of thousands of American servicemen, to say nothing of Japanese civilians, already suffering from intensive bombing, and soldiers. This was one of the main justifications for using a new and terrible weapon developed in the course of the war, the atom bomb.

The British had realised the potential of uranium as a source of massive energy on a scale altogether different from conventional explosives. However the huge investment such as only the Americans could provide – in fact $2 billion – was required to develop the bomb, and now they wanted a bang for their bucks. The first bomb was ready for use by August 1945. Roosevelt had died on 12 April, 1945, to be replaced as President by Harry S Truman. Given the alternative, he authorized the bombing of Hiroshima on 6 August 1945. When "Little Boy" fell through the skies, at least 70,000 people were killed outright. Only three days later, a second bomb, "Fat Man", was dropped on Nagasaki, with similar results. In between those two dates, on 8 August, the Japanese suffered another blow when the Soviet Union declared war and immediately took over the northern Japanese island of Sakhalin, previously shared between the two countries. The Japanese, who had hoped to bring in the Soviet Union on their own side, had nowhere to turn, and surrendered on 15 August. Emperor Hirohito broadcast the news to the Japanese people: "The war situation has developed not necessarily to Japan's advantage"!

The outlines of the peace were established at a conference held at Potsdam, near Berlin in the summer of 1945. While this was taking place, a general election was held in Britain which returned a large majority for Labour and its leader Clement Attlee. The social mixing process which had taken place in the war had gone a long way to foster sympathy for Socialist beliefs, and the Conservatives were blamed for getting Britain into war in the first place. A stunned Churchill went into opposition to lick his wounds. His wife Clementine suggested that perhaps the defeat was a blessing in disguise. Churchill retorted that in this particular case, the blessings were very well disguised! Attlee took his place at Potsdam.

The post-war world had already been divided into spheres of influence at the conference held at Yalta in the Crimea in February,

1945, with Churchill, Roosevelt and Stalin (called "Uncle Joe" privately by the other two, much to his chagrin when he found out) all present. Now faced with the reality of Soviet troops on the ground, the whole of eastern Europe fell into the Soviet sphere, with new Communist governments in Hungary, Czechoslovakia, Poland, Bulgaria, Romania, East Germany, Albania and Yugoslavia, the latter two outside direct Soviet control. Greece and Austria were eventually rescued from the clutches of the Russians and Communists. The position of Poland was particularly distressing to Churchill, but there was nothing he could do. Estonia, Latvia and Lithuania were absorbed into the Soviet Union once more. Poland itself was shifted two hundred kilometers to the west, conceding a large strip of territory to the Soviets, and taking a similarly-sized slice of eastern Germany for itself. The ancient Polish city of Lvov became a Russian city, and the ancient German city of Breslau became Polish Wroclaw. The old German Baltic ports of Stettin and Danzig became Polish, and Koenigsberg became a Russian enclave, Kaliningrad. Germany shrank in size by about a quarter compared to its 1937 borders. German populations living east of the new border were physically moved into the new Germany. As Churchill was to put it in a speech in Fulton, Missouri in 1946, "From Stettin in the Baltic to Trieste in the Adriatic, an iron curtain has descended across the continent".

The post-war settlement also included the establishment of the United Nations and a number of other multi-national bodies. As it had now learnt that isolationism comes at a price, the UN was set up under the aegis of the USA, and headquartered there. Its distinguishing feature was the Security Council, consisting of five permanent members countries - the USA, the Soviet Union, Britain, France and China, each of which had the power of veto, and other member countries elected on a temporary basis.

Shortly after the end of the war, Britain conceded the independence of India, Pakistan and Burma so the British Empire, if not reduced in size by the war, was on the verge of dismemberment. The war itself had set the country into debt for decades. Germany had been vanquished and Hitler and the Nazis annihilated – the original war aims – but at a heavy price. The war had also led to 256,000 military and 60,000 civilian deaths. The first figure is much less than in the First World War, partly reflecting the care taken to conserve lives by the authorities. By contrast, Germany suffered more than five million military deaths.

As the war was ending the Allied armies found concentration camps containing emaciated Jews, piles of dead bodies, gas ovens and all the ghastly paraphernalia of the Holocaust. Only then did the full extent of the Nazi drive to exterminate any Jewish population that it found became clear. This was racial murder on a truly industrial scale. The executions of men, women and children had started long before the gas ovens were constructed, but had proved too distressing – for the Gestapo, not the victims! A series of death camps was found in the east, at Buchenwald, Auschwitz and elsewhere. It is estimated that six million Jews lost their lives in the "final solution" to the Jewish problem. A conference at Wannsee in Berlin in January 1942 had settled their fate.

Rules were put in place to decide which person was Jewish, and which was not. A Jewish population had been resident in northern and eastern Europe for centuries and had widely interbred with the indigenous people, to the extent that many so-called Jewish people were physically little distinguishable from their European neighbours. Many were descendants of mixed marriages. A proportion of the Jews had even converted to Christianity, though for the Nazis, this did not count.

In some ways the Jews of Germany itself were the lucky ones, as they were only too well aware of the danger posed by the Nazis. Approximately 300,000 of a population of half a million fled into exile before the war started - England itself received a substantial influx. The Jewish populations of the invaded countries had no such opportunity, and were rounded up and sent to concentration camps as soon as was practicable by the Nazis. In particular, the 60,000 Jews in Hungary were incarcerated at the last minute, even as the German defences were collapsing in the east, to be liquidated while there was still time left.

The Jews were not the only ones to suffer in this way. Any enemy of the Nazis could fall victim to the Gestapo. Gypsies, homosexuals, people with physical disabilities, political opponents, Russian and Polish civilians and prisoners of war, and partisans and their supporters everywhere were all executed mercilessly. In some cases this was thuggery of the worst type – stealing property by murdering its owners. Also, on the Eastern Front, the Germans did not fight the war by the rules of the Geneva Convention, as they generally did in the west.

Hitler wanted *Lebensraum* – living space – for German people. If that meant eliminating Slavic villagers, so be it. It is estimated that as many as 17 million non-combatants were executed by the Nazis. When the Soviets swept back, they took their revenge, raping women, executing collaborators and herding starving ethnic Germans in front of their tanks, back across the new border, the Oder-Neisse Line.

*   *   *   *

The Second World War did not have to end the way it did. What if Hitler had decided to consolidate his gains in Europe instead of invading the Soviet Union? It would have been very difficult to get him out. In not dissimilar circumstances, the French Revolutionary and Napoleonic Wars lasted 23 years. However, Hitler's government was fundamentally unstable – every year he wanted something more. He could not relax and consolidate when his real target all along was the Soviet Union. Similarly, what if the Japanese had climbed down in 1941? By any sensible calculation, they should have come to some kind of agreement with the USA. If they had pulled out of French Indochina and even China itself, they would have still held on to Manchuria and Korea, which they lost in the end. Had that happened it is perfectly possible that the USA would never have joined the war against Germany. Britain may have then had to give up the war for the old-fashioned reason – that they had run out of money to fight it. If that had happened, it is unlikely that the peace would have lasted very long. In the manner of the repeated French wars between 1692 and 1815, the war could have been fought out over generations, sea power against land power, with no final resolution in all this period. In that case, the baby boom generation of children which appeared after the Second World War would have faced a more difficult future than they did.

*   *   *   *

Domestic affairs had not stood entirely still during the war. The Beveridge Report was published in 1942, aiming to address the five great evils in society: squalor, ignorance, want, idleness and disease. It formed the basis of the post-war "Welfare State", including the expansion of national insurance and the creation of the National Health Service. Also, Butler's Education Act of 1944 remodelled secondary education, creating the tripartite system of grammar, technical and secondary modern schools.

*　　　　*　　　　*　　　　*

One of the greatest breakthroughs ever achieved in medicine took place in Britain before and during the war. Penicillin was first isolated and described in a scientific paper by the Scot Alexander Fleming in 1928. Fleming was fully aware of its antibiotic properties, but lacking the training in biochemistry and unable to produce significant quantities of the drug, he moved on to other work. The baton was picked up in 1939 at Oxford by the Australian Howard Florey and émigré German Jew Ernst Chaim, but having made some progress, they found the drug impossible to synthesise. What little quantities they were able to produce showed the seemingly magical properties of the drug to cure mice dying of infections. Work on this project, vital for dealing with infections, especially in the military, passed to the USA. Here it was found that the best source of supply was a mould which grew on cantaloupe melons in Peoria, Illinois. Soon millions of melons were grown and allowed to go mouldy. A fermentation process based on corn was developed. By the time of D-Day, 2.3 million doses of penicillin were available for the troop landings, many of them prepared by the drug company Glaxo in England.

The chemical structure of penicillin was finally determined by the Englishwoman Dorothy Hodgkin in 1945. Fleming, good at publicity but having done no work on the development of the drug, received the credit for its discovery, and a Nobel Prize. These prizes also went to Florey, Chaim and Hodgkin.

*　　　　*　　　　*　　　　*

The end of the war saw an important wave of immigration into Britain of refugees from Soviet-controlled territories, mainly from Poland and the Ukraine. An estimated 120,000 Poles arrived during and after the war. This population, mostly of younger men, proved useful in replacing the men lost in the fighting.

Chapter 34 – Post-War Britain 1945-64

After the war a wave of communism and socialism swept around the world, partly as a result of admiration for the evidently successful Soviet communists during the conflict. This affected Britain, France, Italy, Greece, all of eastern Europe and eventually (by 1949) China. The British share of this was a Labour victory in the 1945 election, when Attlee secured a massive majority, with 393 seats for Labour against 197 for the Conservatives. Churchill had fought a campaign warning of a "Socialist Gestapo" which did not go down well. Nevertheless this was to be a real socialist government, which was to make other Labour administrations look pale pink by comparison.

The new government faced a grim period of reconstruction under straitened financial circumstances, and the period is remembered by one characteristic word, "austerity". There was an immediate shortage of dollars to pay for imports following the abrupt end of Lend-Lease in 1945, to the extent that J M Keynes was dispatched to Washington to negotiate a new loan on favorable terms, which, after much moral persuasion, he eventually did. A condition was that sterling was to return to its pre-war dollar parity, which was harmful to resumed growth and could not long be sustained. Much of the rest of western Europe was in fact in a similar position, so the specifically British loan was extended in 1947 by the Marshall Plan. This was a system of loans to European governments favored by the USA (thus excluding the Soviets and their satellites), administered by a new body, the Organization for European Economic Cooperation.

The great problem for Britain was that it still had many expensive overseas colonial and defensive commitments, to which was added a brand new one, a large permanent army on the Rhine. After the war, Germany was divided into four zones, which soon became two, West and East Germany. The western European countries and the USA on the one hand and the newly expanded Soviet empire on the other were almost immediately at one another's throats as the "Cold War" began. This entailed the maintenance of a large army and air force in West

Germany, spending foreign currency and in the long term greatly assisting the postwar German "economic miracle", but continuing to impoverish the British economy.

Ernest Bevin, wartime Minister of Labour, became the Foreign Secretary in 1945. He had to steer a course between three competing priorities – the "Atlantic Alliance" – that is, the alliance with the USA; closer integration with the evolving Commonwealth; and closer integration with western Europe. The Atlantic Alliance eventually took precedence, with the signature of the North Atlantic Treaty in 1949, leading to the formation of the North Atlantic Treaty Organization (NATO) as an alliance against the spread of communism. The USA was gradually changing its view of Britain. At first seen as a country at odds with the USA in its determination to pursue its own imperial destiny, it soon came to be viewed as an important base (literally an air base) against the much more dangerous Soviet empire. At the bottom of the list of the Labour government's foreign priorities was European integration. The first step towards this was made by France, Germany, Italy and the Benelux countries with the formation of the European Coal and Steel Community, a common market for these commodities and usually considered the forerunner of the European Economic Community, details of which were finalized in 1951. Britain kept out.

Nevertheless immediate steps were taken to implement pre-war promises. By 1947, independence had been granted to India, Pakistan, and Ceylon and by 1948 to Burma. Lord Mountbatten was sent to India to bang heads together. This resulted in the division of the subcontinent into two countries, the predominantly Hindu India and the Muslim Pakistan (the eastern part of which separated to become Bangla Desh in 1971). Although Indian independence was established with much bloodshed as mass movements of population took place across the new borders, it was generally thought that given the size of the problems and the size of the population, things could have been much worse. In Palestine, the British were equally determined to get out, and leave the competing Israeli Zionists and Arab nationalists sort things out for themselves. This they did, and after a brief war the state of Israel was established in 1948.

Domestically, the new government had a Soviet-style five year plan. One aim of this was the nationalization of the "commanding heights of the economy", including the coal mining, gas and electricity industries, the railways and road and water-born haulage. An act was also passed to nationalise the iron and steel industries, but this was not implemented. In practice, the nationalised concerns were largely run by the same people as before, and their employees felt none of the expected sense of "ownership". Housing Acts were passed in 1946 and 1949 to vastly increase the scope of council housing, and standardized housing often of the most incongruous design began to appear in even the smallest villages. In 1947 came the Town and Country Planning Act, establishing local and regional planning all over the country, with new green belts around each major city and conurbation, and new towns beyond them. This act put a stop to the unsightly ribbon development which had taken place along all main roads before the war. The National Health Service was set up in 1948 under the Minister of Health, Aneurin Bevan (the son of a Welsh coal miner) following an act of parliament in 1946. Its main and abiding attribute is the provision of medical care free at the point of delivery. It has been so popular and so successful that no political party has dared to tamper with its fundamental structure ever since. The chief architect of much of this legislation was Herbert Morrison, who as Lord President of the Council was responsible for most domestic issues. Another personality of note was the Chancellor of the Exchequer (from 1947), Sir Stafford Cripps, the epitome of post-war austerity, who was a very severe aristocratic socialist – "Fish and Cripps". It is thought that most of Attlee's cabinet considered themselves intellectually superior to Attlee himself, but the Prime Minister, with his mixture of tact, his ability to delegate and his obvious integrity, was a great success.

There was obviously much to do in the physical reconstruction of the country – there was a building boom – and the government had no trouble in maintaining full employment, one of its key election pledges. Yet despite the many achievements of the Attlee government, it was not popular, because no one wanted a continuation of wartime deprivation, and that is what they got. Food rationing had been established very successfully during the war to provide a basic but adequate diet for all, along with rationing for clothing and petrol. After the end of the war, food rationing was continued right through until the last of it was abolished in 1954. It was even extended to new items including bread and potatoes. Sir Stafford Cripps kept taxation high, at wartime levels.

Then in 1947 the country was struck by the most appalling winter in living memory, with most of it under a thick cover of snow and ice for three months or more. February of that year was thought to be the coldest in 300 years. Snow drifted up to thirty feet high and would not melt. Roads and railways were blocked all over the country, in many cases for weeks. Scotland was cut off. Coal stocks froze at the pit heads and could not be moved; power lines came down. By terrible bad luck, January 1 1947 was the date of the nationalization of the coal and electricity industries. The minister in charge, the extreme socialist Manny Shinwell, promised that there would be no power cuts, but these had to be introduced very quickly. Factories across the country had to close down immediately, leaving two million people idle. The nation froze and with thousands of wartime restrictions still in place and little to buy in the shops, the people were utterly miserable.

To try to relieve economic pressure, sterling was devalued in September 1949 from $4.03 to the pound to $2.80. This established Labour's reputation as the party of devaluation – not a good reputation to have – and was to be repeated by the Wilson government in the sixties. Such devaluations always lead to short-term inflation.

By the time of the next election in February 1950, patience was wearing thin. Labour still came out ahead, winning 315 seats to the Conservative's 298, but its leaders were growing old and tired, and in some cases dying. In the summer of that year a new war broke out in Korea, setting the West against the communists in armed conflict for the first time – one of the many instances when the Cold War became hot. British forces including national servicemen were drawn in to support the Americans. The conflict see-sawed wildly as each side poured in resources until a reversion to the *status quo ante bellum* – the 38th parallel between North and South Korea – was agreed in 1953. The new Chancellor of the Exchequer, Hugh Gaitskell, was faced with a "guns or butter" decision. Opting for rearmament – guns – he imposed charges on previously free items available from the NHS, spectacles and dentures. Aneurin Bevan and Harold Wilson resigned in principle. (By this means, Wilson positioned himself on the left of the Labour party.) The government staggered on until the election of September 1951, when the Conservatives returned to power with 321 seats to Labor's 295 (the Liberals were reduced to a low of only six seats). Labour actually polled slightly more votes than the Conservatives, but Winston Churchill was back in power.

One phenomenon of this era was the baby boom, when millions of demobbed ex-servicemen went home, married their sweethearts and immediately set about producing long-delayed families. By the late forties nearly 900,000 babies were being born each year. This generation of children was to work its way through the education system, creating unprecedented competition for the best places during the sixties.

*　　　　*　　　　*　　　　*

Churchill was seventy-six years old when he became Prime Minister for the second time – and in fact it was the first time he had ever been elected to the office directly. His age told upon his administration as he became increasingly less coherent, though still, according to one visitor, oozing power. In 1953 he had a stroke, but carried on, much to the frustration of Anthony Eden, who had been his heir-in-waiting ever since 1940. However, with a majority of only sixteen, it was not practical to undertake the repeal of the major legislation enacted under the previous administration. In particular, the NHS was left to bed down. The nationalization of the iron and steel industry was withdrawn and road haulage was denationalized. Otherwise the country was left without major upheavals as prosperity slowly returned. Economic policy under the Chancellor, R A Butler, was so similar to that of his predecessor, Gaitskell, that it became known as Butskellism. One outstandingly successful minister was Harold Macmillan, in charge of Housing, who exceeded the promised target of 300,000 new houses a year.

In 1952 King George VI died unexpectedly, to be replaced by his daughter, Elizabeth II, who was only 25 years old. Her grand coronation in 1953 provided an early memory for the baby-boomers, and hopes were raised of a new and prosperous Elizabethan age.

*   *   *   *

A great scientific breakthrough was made in Britain in 1953 with the discovery of the double helix structure of DNA (deoxyribonucleic acid), finally pinned down as the mechanism of heredity. This was the work of a freelance team at Cambridge, Francis Crick and the American James Watson. For their discoveries they relied upon an X-ray diffraction image produced at London University by Rosalind Franklin. Their paper in *Nature* was supported by other evidence from Professor Maurice Wilkins. Crick, Watson and Wilkins shared a Nobel prize. As these prizes could only be awarded to living recipients, Franklin missed out, as she had died before the award was made.

*   *   *   *

In 1955 Churchill finally retired (he was to die in 1965, aged 91) and Sir Anthony Eden became Prime Minister in an administration not unlike that of Neville Chamberlain. Seeing the Labour Party in schism between its two wings, he called an election and won a majority for the Conservatives of sixty seats. The great issues of the day were all in foreign policy. In 1955 there was an outbreak of terrorism in the colony and military/naval base of Cyprus, divided ethnically between Greeks and Turks. The Greeks under Archbishop Makarios sought *enosis* or political union with Greece. This dispute was to run for many years. Meanwhile there was further terrorism in Kenya, perpetrated by the largest tribe, the Kikuyu, and known as the Mau Mau. From 1952 until 1956 large numbers of British troops were required to protect the European and defenceless African populations. Allegations of British brutality reverberate to this day.

However a much bigger issue surfaced in 1956. In 1955 Colonel Gamel Abdel Nasser seized power in a revolution in Egypt. By agreement with him, Britain began evacuating her military base at Suez in favour of the one in Cyprus. Nasser then formulated a grand project, the construction of a high dam at Aswan to regulate the flow of the Nile and provide hydro-electric power. He negotiated a loan of $56 million from the USA for the project, with a British contribution of $14 million. When the Egyptian ambassador hinted to the American Secretary of State, John Foster Dulles, that the Russians might step in to help if the Americans did not, Dulles promptly withdrew the offer. Nasser retaliated by nationalising the Suez Canal in 1956. Eden, in secret collusion with the French and the Israelis – he did not even inform his own cabinet what he was doing, in the manner of Chamberlain at Munich – planned an invasion to seize the canal back for its rightful owners. Troops were landed and Port Said was taken in November, 1956, causing an international outcry, in the USA, the Arab world, the Commonwealth and amongst the Opposition at home. Britain's gold and currency reserves plummeted as sterling was sold around the world, notably by the US Treasury. Oil ran short and rationing was introduced at the petrol stations. Emergency oil supplies were needed which would have to be paid for in dollars. The Americans refused the dollar loan needed to pay for the oil. Panicking, Eden withdrew the British troops, much to the chagrin of the French and the Israelis. Meanwhile Nasser sank ships filled with concrete in the canal itself, putting it out of use for a long time.

The hostility of the Americans under President Eisenhower and the rabidly anti-British Dulles had brought humiliation on Eden. They were piqued that he had taken decisive action without obtaining their permission first, and sought to teach him a lesson about the modern realities of international power. Their view was that Britain and France were up to their old colonial tricks again, when in fact Dulles was trying to turf them out of the oil-rich Middle East in favour of the Americans themselves. Eisenhower and Dulles were wrong, and the USA paid for their folly in the end. Eisenhower, one of the most stupid Presidents in history, later admitted that Suez was his greatest mistake, as did Dulles. After all, the British and the French were not trying to crush Egyptian independence, but to retake a valuable strategic asset which belonged to them and had been seized without compensation. In supporting Nasser and driving out Eden, they had both encouraged Arab nationalism and the seizure of foreign-owned local assets (including, of course, American-owned oil assets) by home-grown nationalist governments. Both these problems were to return to haunt the Americans over many years to come. Also they alienated not only Britain, but France, driven henceforward into the Franco-German axis which persists to this day.

Meanwhile the closure of the Suez Canal did not cause serious disruption in oil supplies. Tankers simply too large to use the canal were already being built to go the long way round from the oilfields of the Middle East. The crisis did however bring down Eden, who became ill and resigned as Prime Minister in January, 1957. Like the later Gordon Brown, having waited so long to become Prime Minister, he had crashed out of the job in a very short time – twenty months. Asked if he would have attacked Egypt, Churchill said "I would never have dared, and if I had dared, I would never have dared stop." This was Eden's problem – he should have sorted the matter out with the Americans first, or failing that, have stuck to his guns and defied them. For in this episode, so soon after the end of the Korean War, they had become – briefly – the enemy.

Eden was replaced by the suave Harold Macmillan, a successful businessman and publisher who liked to project an image of unflappability – just what was needed in the circumstances. He was to have a successful run of over six years in power, from January 1957 until October, 1963, a time when the country was becoming steadily more prosperous. Nevertheless it was far from easy going. In 1957 there were more strikes than there had ever been, with the loss of 8.41 million working days. Balance of payments problems were persistent and seemingly incurable in the longer term, the root cause being the sustained high level of overseas defence expenditure. "Stop-go" economics became a feature of the period, with interest rates and taxes first raised, then relaxed before the brakes were slammed on again. The offices of Chancellor of the Exchequer and Minster of Defence changed hands with bewildering speed, while Macmillan himself sailed blithely on. His own motto was famously "You've never had it so good" as households stocked up on washing machines, fridges, televisions (the commercial Independent Television Authority had been established in 1954), motor cars, radios and all the paraphernalia of the new consumerism. Britain became the "affluent society", though some would call it the land of hire-purchase and bingo. The working trade unionist, however, said "I'm all right Jack", and if he was not quite all right enough, he went on strike.

After the USA and the Soviet Union, Britain became the third country to test an independently-produced atom bomb as early as 1952. The first weapons were designed to be dropped from aircraft, but this delivery system was soon made obsolete with the development of long-range and accurate rocket systems. After the failure of the home-grown Blue Sky missile, there were many negotiations with the Americans to supply an advanced delivery system (notably Skybolt), before it was agreed to purchase the American Polaris missiles in 1962. Atomic weaponry and the delivery systems for it were a highly expensive luxury for the straitened British economy of the fifties – one in which Germany and Japan, major industrial competitors, could not and did not indulge. More than any other single policy, this demonstrated Britain living beyond her means (but if Britain was doing this, the Soviet Union was living way beyond hers). Also the question remained – just how independent was the British nuclear deterrent of the Americans?

There was in fact strong opposition within the UK to the nuclear deterrent, taking formal shape in the Campaign for Nuclear Disarmament (CND), created in 1957 and organizing annual marches to the Atomic Weapons Establishment at Aldermaston. However, the CND objected to nuclear weapons mainly on moral rather than economic grounds, and its supporters were typically seen as duffle-coat wearing beatniks, anti-establishment figures, liberal intellectuals and creeping Jesus types. Within the Labour Party there was a strong faction in favour of unilateral nuclear disarmament – ditching the weapons even if other nations kept them. A resolution was passed in favour at the 1960 Labour Party conference, despite the earlier pleas of Aneurin Bevan not to send the British Foreign Secretary "naked into the conference chamber."

In 1957 the European Economic Community was established by the Treaty of Rome. This included just six countries – West Germany, France, Italy and the three Benelux states. Still distrusting their old continental enemies, Britain formed a rival group in 1960, the European

Free Trade Association, consisting of Austria, Denmark, Norway, Portugal, Sweden, Switzerland and the UK itself.

At the general election of 1959 the Conservatives were returned with a majority of over a hundred seats. One of the most important policy areas at this time concerned the Commonwealth. Macmillan himself famously stated the case in a speech given in Cape Town in 1960: "The wind of change is blowing through this continent. Whether we like it or not, this growth of national consciousness is a political fact." The British colonies in Africa and elsewhere, following the example of India in 1947, sought their independence. First to go were Malaya and Ghana (formerly the Gold Coast) in 1957. Nigeria, easily the largest of the African colonies, followed in 1960, Jamaica and Trinidad and Tobago in 1962, Kenya in 1963 and Malta in 1964. By 1966 all former colonies of any size had been decolonised, with the exception of Hong Kong, and also of Southern Rhodesia, where the white colonists made a unilateral declaration of independence in 1965. With very few exceptions, the new countries joined the Commonwealth as independent members. Heading the other way was South Africa, which turned itself from a dominion into a completely independent republic in 1961 and duly left the Commonwealth. Having established the policy of apartheid to keep its white and black populations separate, it wanted nothing to do with the Commonwealth, where it could expect nothing but abuse.

The fact is that colonialism had simply gone out of fashion. Unless they had valuable mineral deposits, the colonies generally cost more to administer than they earned in revenues. India (and particularly the Indian army) had certainly provided jobs for otherwise difficult-to-employ sons of aristocrats, and everywhere the infrastructure of the colonial civil service provided opportunities for home graduates and others, but the mass of the British people scarcely felt the benefit of an empire that had covered a quarter of the world. Other countries, notably in Scandinavia, had no empires but seemed just as prosperous as Britain, if not more so. The important businesses within the old empire, for example the copper mines of Zambia, remained the property of the original owners, though many were nationalised before long.

From the middle of the 1950s until 1962 there was a massive wave of immigration into Britain from the Commonwealth, most notably from the West Indies – peaking at over 50,000 a year – India, Pakistan and Hong Kong. No referendum was ever offered to ask the people what they thought of this phenomenon, the start of the greatest change to the racial composition of the British population there has ever been.

The new populations concentrated very heavily in certain regions, notably London, the West and East Midlands and the textile towns of Lancashire and Yorkshire, where industrial and service jobs were proving difficult to fill; large areas such as the West Country and East Anglia were virtually unaffected. By 1962 concern – especially in the form of complaints to local MPs – had risen to the extent that a new quota system was introduced in the Commonwealth Immigration Act. This itself stimulated a massive last-minute influx of newcomers aiming to "beat the ban".

Selwyn Lloyd was Chancellor between 1960 and 1962, instituting a "pay pause", a limit on pay increases to 2.5% which initiated a wave of strikes. The dock workers barged through it and came away with an increase amounting to 9%. The government also created two new bodies, the National Economic Development Council ("Neddy") for economic planning, and the National Incomes Commission, to help to formulate an "incomes policy" – signs of things to come. Neddy remained influential until 1979.

Following a report by Dr Richard Beeching published in 1963, drastic cuts were made to the loss-making railway system. Over the next decade, 4000 miles of track were taken out of the network, and 3000 stations were closed. The "Beeching Axe" was only part of a longer-term contraction as the total railway mileage shrank from 21,000 in 1950 to 12,000 by 1975.

By 1963 things had started to go wrong for Macmillan. The safe Tory seat of Orpington was lost to the Liberals in a by-election in October 1962. In the hope that joining it would boost the economy, the government finally decided to apply for membership of the European Economic Community. As unemployment had risen to the unheard-of postwar total of 810,000, some kind of structural action was seen as necessary to bring it down. In January 1963, the application was vetoed by one man, President De Gaulle of France, despite the fact that the other five members favoured it. De Gaulle feared that Britain was too closely tied into its "special relationship" with the United States, now repaired after the disasters of Suez.

In June of 1963 another blow fell when John Profumo, Minister of War, was obliged to resign amidst the most lurid scandal involving a glamorous prostitute, Christine Keeler. Another of her clients was a Russian military attaché. As the nation's press wallowed in the details, others were dragged in. One of them was Lord Astor, who denied having sex with Keeler's friend, Mandy Rice-Davis, in court. "Well he would say that, wouldn't he?" she replied. The country nodded its head in agreement. It was all too much for Macmillan. Like Eden before him, he was struck down by illness – he thought he was dying of prostate cancer, but in fact lived on until 1986! He resigned in October 1963.

By the mysterious backroom processes of the day, a new leader was found, the Foreign Secretary, Lord Home, a peer of the realm. He was obliged to resign his peerage and enter the Commons as Sir Alec Douglas-Home, but no one doubted that he was an aristocrat. R A Butler, who had nearly succeeded in 1957, was passed over once more. Just as the era of televised politics was dawning, Douglas-Home, with his boney head, was perhaps not the best choice. His problems were two – firstly, that there was a widespread feeling that the country was due for a change – and this is a very difficult feeling for a politician to counteract. Secondly, he found himself up against a formidable opponent, who came across well enough on TV – Harold Wilson.

In the election of October 1964, Douglas-Home in fact did much better than expected, retrieving a disastrous position in the opinion polls. Nevertheless Labour won with an overall majority of just four seats. For the Conservatives, defeat meant the end of Douglas-Home as leader, though he stayed in front bench politics. After a direct election by Conservative MPs, he was replaced by the bachelor Edward Heath, a fanatic pro-European, musician, sailor and like the new Prime Minister a former grammar school boy. The ex-Chancellor Reggie Maudling came a close second, and trailing in a distant third, Enoch Powell. This last was going to have to find another way to make his name.

Chapter 35 – Post-War Britain 1964-79

After the retirement of Attlee in December 1955, Hugh Gaitskell became leader of the Labour Party. Indulging in one of its wild swings to the left, the party tore itself apart over two issues, Clause Four of its constitution, which committed it to wholesale nationalization, and unilateral nuclear disarmament. Gaitskell, on the right of the party, opposed both, and reversed a decision in favour of the latter. However he died of a lupus infection in January 1963 – conspiracy theorists say the victim of the Russian KGB. His replacement was Harold Wilson, a Yorkshireman and ex-Oxford don with a signature pipe. Pugnacious and very sharp at Prime Minister's Question Time and genial enough on TV ("Thirteen years of Tory misrule!"), he ran rings round both Douglas-Home and his successor, Edward Heath. Emerging from the left of the Labour Party, he changed his politics to suit the circumstances.

He had made a good impression as a potential modernizer. In a speech in 1963 he famously said: "The Britain that is going to be forged in the white heat of this revolution will be no place for restrictive practices or for outdated methods on either side of industry." Now he was in power, but what could he do about those restrictive practices? One of his first appointments was to make the Birmingham trade union dinosaur Frank Cousins Minister of Technology so the omens were not good. Nevertheless at the age of only 48, Wilson had a great future in front of him. His stated aim was to make Labour the "natural" party of government. Though he was never even to come close to achieving this objective, for a time it looked as if he may succeed.

Wilson was the first of a new breed of Prime Minister. His Labour predecessors, Attlee and Gaitskell, were both ex-public schoolboys, and could claim to be gentlemen; Wilson emerged from the meritocratic grammar school system, and could not. There was something inherently shabby about him, and especially his entourage. This included Marcia Williams, later Lady Falkender, his private secretary from as early as 1956, then his political secretary when prime minister. Her tantrums became notorious and there were rumours that Wilson only tolerated her for fear of blackmail. Accusations about an early affair between the two eventually brought about a libel case in which the BBC paid £75,000 to Falkender. Another of the dismal group was Joe Haines, Wilson's press secretary, part-time speech writer and later journalist on the Daily Mirror. A further close associate was the deputy leader of the Labour party, George Brown, arguably one of the least respectable politicians of the century, who was born on a council estate in Lambeth and had left school at 15.

It was certainly the custom in these times for any government approaching an election to bribe the electorate with tax reductions and increased benefits, and 1964 was no exception, to the extent that Maudling apologised to the incoming Chancellor Jim Callaghan for leaving such a mess behind. Callaghan was indeed to have some sleepless nights ahead of him as the economy lurched to the edge of disaster from his first day in office. In charge of economic planning at the newly created Department of Economic Affairs was George Brown, who frequently appeared drunk on TV. His new department never managed to wrench much power from the Treasury. Brown repeatedly threatened to resign when piqued, finally doing so in 1968, to lose his seat in the 1970 election and disappear from public life. Callaghan, the epitome of common sense, was to prove more durable.

In the short term, the Wilson government was blessed with good fortune as balance of payments problems eased, confidence in sterling returned and unemployment fell to a record low. Quick to take advantage while the going was good, Wilson called another election in March 1966 and was rewarded with an overall majority of 97 seats.

During the sixties and seventies four separate, sustained efforts were made to try to keep wages increases and so inflation down, either by a statutory incomes policy or by agreement with the Trades Union Congress. This would work well enough for two or even three years, with wages increases held below the rate of inflation, before the dam burst with large wage increases all round, far ahead of the rate of inflation. This is what now happened to the Wilson administration. A Prices and Incomes Board was set up in 1964 and reinforced with a statutory (as opposed to voluntary) incomes policy in 1966. It worked reasonably well at first but had to be abandoned in the face of trade union opposition. In 1969-70 there was a wages explosion with average earnings increasing by 13%. It seemed impossible to maintain three balls in the air – low inflation, a balance of payments which balanced, and full employment. In the sixties and seventies low inflation was sacrificed; under Thatcher in the eighties, low unemployment.

The balance of payment issue would not clear up. Pressure built up on sterling and eventually in 1967 Wilson was obliged to concede what he had fought since gaining office, a second devaluation by a Labour government in twenty years. The dollar rate was reduced by 14.3% from 2.80 to 2.40. Wilson assured his bemused (if not stunned) TV audience that this would make no difference to the value of the pound in their pockets. Of course the devaluation caused an immediate surge in inflation because of the increased cost of imported goods. Jim Callaghan came to the end of his disastrous career as Chancellor, but did not give up, changing places with the Home Secretary, Roy Jenkins. To general relief, devaluation then did work over the next three years as exports surged and the balance of payments swung positive.

Also in 1967, an old Labour policy was finally enacted with the nationalization of British Steel. It was to stay in the public sector until 1988.

The permissive society was born in the sixties, ushered in by a raft of liberal reforms, many while Roy Jenkins was Home Secretary. Following the Obscene Publications Act of 1959 and the abolition of the Lord Chamberlain's role as censor in 1968, books and films became much more sexually explicit. After a court case, Penguin Books was allowed to publish an unexpurgated paperback edition of just such a book, *Lady Chatterley's Lover*, by D H Lawrence. The public formed queues to buy it, and were only allowed one copy each. Again, after a long campaign by Labour MP Sydney Silverman, the death penalty was suspended in 1965. Homosexual acts between consenting male adults were legalized in 1967. (They had never been illegal between female adults, allegedly because Queen Victoria refused to believe that they existed.) Abortion was legalized in the same year. Divorce law was liberalized in 1969, allowing divorce after two years of separation if both parties consented, and otherwise after five years. The number of abortions and divorces immediately rocketed. Not the subject of legislation, the availability of the contraceptive pill to unmarried women from the later sixties brought about a veritable sexual revolution.

A second attempt was made to join the EEC in 1967 but this again met with a rebuff from President De Gaulle, who said it was hard enough to keep five other countries in line with the interests of France without admitting another cock amongst the hens.

The defence policy of maintaining a military presence "east of Suez" proved unaffordable and eventually had to be abandoned, another step down from old imperial Britain. Having divested herself of her colonies, notably Singapore and Malaya, Britain had far fewer interests to protect in the Orient, so this withdrawal was only realistic. If colonies wanted independence, they would also have to make their own arrangements for their defence. One of the main stepping stones along the way to the Orient, Aden, was given its independence in 1967.

In Africa the white Rhodesians cocked a snook at Wilson by declaring independence unilaterally in 1965. Wilson met the Rhodesian leader Ian Smith twice on board ships of the Royal Navy, *HMS Tiger* and *HMS Fearless*, but made no progress. Wilson made it clear he would not fight – and in any case how could he? – Rhodesia was landlocked and far away, and the armed forces would not fight their own kind. Instead he imposed economic sanctions. As however Rhodesia's neighbours, South Africa and Mozambique (a Portuguese colony) both supported Smith, the sanctions were useless. Smith made a complete fool of Wilson, but nemesis was to pursue him in the seventies when the black Rhodesians armed themselves.

After many years, the troubles returned to Northern Ireland in 1968. The province contained a million Protestants and half a million Catholics, and so was ruled entirely by the Protestants, who gave preference to their own kind, especially in jobs and housing. The Catholics rebelled. The situation ran so quickly out of control, with riots and bloodshed, notably in the two largest cities, Belfast and Londonderry, that troops had to be sent in. Over the next generation and more, English politicians just wanted a quiet life in Ireland, and tried to obtain it, but this problem would not go away.

British policy in its African colonies had allowed the immigration of a large number of Asians as indentured workers. Their descendants, thought to number up to half a million people, became traders, and every town of any size in old British areas of southern and eastern Africa had its own Indian ghetto, or Indiatown. When independence arrived these African Indians were offered the option of British passports, which most of them took. As far as the new governments of Africa were concerned, these "British" Indians were not necessarily desirable citizens. In 1967, the government of Kenya took action to force them out, and they began arriving in Britain by the planeload. Thoroughly alarmed, Home Secretary James Callaghan produced a new Commonwealth Immigration Act in 1968 to restrict entry to small quotas, but there was little he could do faced with mass expulsions from

Africa. The Kenya episode was replayed from Uganda in 1971 when 28,000 Asians were expelled in a few weeks, each of them arriving with little more than a suitcase of clothes.

It was against this background that in April, 1968, the former Conservative cabinet minister Enoch Powell burst into the political spotlight. His own constituency – Wolverhampton SW – was heavily affected by West Indian immigration. His constituents were complaining about the impact on housing and jobs, and so he made the first of a series of highly inflammatory anti-immigration speeches predicting "rivers of blood" in the streets of Britain's cities. The silent majority actually agreed with Powell, and the tabloids loved it, but the vocal minority did not, and they attended mass demonstrations all over the country. The liberal establishment – including the Labour government – scoffed at Powell, but he was a clever, articulate and thoroughly respectable man. Unlike for example Sir Oswald Moseley, he was not so easy to dismiss. He commanded mass support in the country and though he lost his cause in the end – as did the anti-pornography campaigner, Mary Whitehouse – there remain many to this day who think both were right all along.

Wilson's aim to control the troublesome trade union movement was another initiative to end in tears. With his encouragement the Employment Secretary, Barbara Castle, produced a white paper, *In Place of Strife,* in 1969. This proposed a cooling-off period for unofficial strikes and fines for non-compliance, but it was vetoed by the cabinet itself as it seemed to undermine the very foundation of the Labour party, its alliance with the trade unions.

As the economic winds seemed favorable and the balance of payments went into surplus, Wilson decided once more to take his chance, calling an early election in June 1970. Opinion polls predicted a clear victory for Labour. However in the only poll that mattered, the Conservatives under Edward Heath were returned to power with an overall majority of thirty seats. A poor final set of trade figures was blamed, but Wilson would be back.

Edward Heath was the second in the sequence of ex-grammar school students, in his case from Kent, to become Prime Minister. Probably a suppressed homosexual, he never married, but loved the company of young people on his yacht, the *Morning Cloud.* Heath had been an organ scholar at Oxford and a major in the artillery in France after D-Day. What he saw there convinced him that a way must be found to prevent any repeat of European war, and for him that way was British membership of the EEC. He was to preside over the most chaotic

386

government of the second half of the twentieth century, but he was unlucky, just as his Tory successor Margaret Thatcher was lucky. The Heath government coincided with the Yom Kippur War between the Arabs and the Israelis in October 1973, after which the price of crude oil quadrupled. Thatcher's period in power, in contrast, was the time when Britain became self-sufficient in oil as developments in the North Sea came on stream.

Heath came to power on the back of a radical free-market manifesto created at the Selsdon Park Hotel in 1970, hence the phrase "Selsdon man". Public expenditure would be brought down and market forces were to rule. The Prices and Incomes Board was abolished as an example of socialist interference. However as early as 1971 the Upper Clyde Shipbuilders and Rolls Royce had to be saved from bankruptcy by public money, being considered too important to be allowed to fail – hardly the operation of free market forces. In the same year a National Industrial Relations Court was established by the Industrial Relations Act to arbitrate in industrial disputes, but trade union intransigence soon saw it off.

Another aspect of old Britain disappeared in February, 1971 when the currency was decimalized. 240 old pence were replaced by 100 new pence and the shilling, florin, half-crown and ten-shilling note all became history.

Heath was quick to reopen negotiations to join the EEC and by the summer of 1971, agreement had been reached. In practice, everything depended on the attitude of the French president, and De Gaulle had by now been replaced by the much more amenable Georges Pompidou, so Heath found himself pushing against an open door. The UK formally joined the EEC on 1 January 1973, along with Ireland and Denmark. This decision was by no means universally popular in the country, however, and there were many opposed to it in both main political parties. Wilson decided to make political capital by saying that he agreed with membership in principle, but not on the terms as negotiated by Heath, though in fact, he would have been happy to accept those same terms back in 1967.

Events in Northern Ireland went from bad to worse. British troops, at first seen as the protectors of the Catholics against the Unionist majority, soon came to be regarded by the Catholics as the tool of their oppressors. There was a serious incident in the Catholic Lower Falls area of Belfast in June 1970, when four civilians were killed, followed by a much worse one in Londonderry on 30 January 1972 when paratroopers opened fire on a Catholic crowd, killing thirteen of them –

"Bloody Sunday". The Provisional Irish Republican Army, formed in 1969, went on the offensive. Altogether there were 467 violent deaths in Ulster in 1972 in an unstoppable spiral of vengeance killings. For the rest of Britain, Northern Irish politics was both alien and baffling, because democracy simply did not function – despite one man, one vote – when there was never a change in power between parties. The Ulster government at Stormont was always dominated by Unionists.' However it was clear enough that the soldiers from the mainland were being shot on Irish streets. The Conservative representative, William Whitelaw, got heads together and fashioned a power-sharing agreement at Sunningdale, but it lasted only a few months.

In February 1972 the National Union of Mineworkers under Joe Gormley launched a strike. Organized by the up-and-coming Yorkshire miner, Arthur Scargill, this featured truly terrifying picketing at the Saltley coke depot, and won a pay award of 30 per cent for the miners. This led to a complete U-turn by the Heath administration when it announced a statutory prices and incomes policy. This worked reasonably well over its first year, but then came the Yom Kippur War, where the Arab oil suppliers deliberately raised prices for political reasons. In a straight attempt at class warfare, the NUM went on the warpath once again, declaring an overtime ban in November 1973. Heath retaliated in the most astonishing way, decreeing a three-day working week for British industry to conserve the nation's dwindling energy supplies. This was a radical move indeed, but surprisingly, production dropped much less than expected, as productivity rose to previously unknown levels during the three busy days!

During this period the Conservatives passed the Local Government Act of 1974, which completely reorganized the boundaries of local government. Some names which had existed for centuries disappeared from the map, including the counties of Rutland and Middlesex. Metropolitan boroughs appeared which included the whole areas around major towns and cities which were formally separately administered. Brand new counties such as Humberside and Teesside appeared.

Meanwhile the miners were not finished yet and declared a full-scale strike in February, 1974. Heath decided to call their bluff and sought a popular mandate to crush them in a general election. His general theme was "Who runs the country? Elected representatives or the class warriors from the NUM?" If Heath had made a better job of running the country up to that point, he might have won the election, but the public was not impressed, and he lost, though by a tiny margin (the Conservatives gained the greatest number of votes). Labour had 301 seats to the Conservatives 297 and so formed a minority government, relying on the support of the small parties. Their own share of the vote was less than at any election since 1931. The Liberals had won a fifth of the votes, but this did not translate into seats. Heath had made a great mistake. If he had shown resourcefulness and courage in facing up to the miners – and he had another year left to do so – he could have succeeded. Calling an election a year early was simply the wrong tactic; it showed poor judgment.

So Harold Wilson resumed in office. Hoping for a better result, he called another election after only six months, which gave him a wafer-thin overall majority of three seats. This was soon eroded by reverses at by-elections, so Labour still had to rely on the support of minor parties, most notably the Liberals in the Lib-Lab pact which lasted until the end of 1978. The Labour victory in October 1974 doomed Edward Heath. Though he retained much grass-roots support, as far as his fellow Conservative MPs were concerned he was a loser, and had indeed lost three elections out of four. Leadership elections were held, in which the expected winner, William Whitelaw, graciously stood aside in the first round to give Heath his chance. But the winner of the first ballot, former Minister of Education Margaret Thatcher, a true blue and dyed-in-the wool Conservative, had by then built up such a head of steam that she was unstoppable in the second ballot, and became leader, and effectively prime minister-in-waiting.

The new government pinned its hopes on finding a solution to the country's economic problems on the Social Contract with the trade unions, broadly an agreement by the unions to exercise restraint in pay claims in return for the abolition of anti-union legislation and statutory incomes policy, plus better pensions and redistributive taxes. The Industrial Relations Act of 1971 was effectively repealed and a new body was created to mediate in disputes, the Advisory, Conciliation and Arbitration Service (ACAS). Needless to say, the unions failed to deliver on their side of the bargain, as the TUC could not control individual unions. Inflation was running at 16% in 1974, partly due to the reckless increase in the money supply which had taken place under the Conservative Chancellor Anthony Barber. The pound, a floating currency since the abandonment of the fixed-rate Bretton Woods system in 1971, came under pressure. The inflation rate for 1975 reached a record level, 25.2%. (High rates of inflation were by no means confined to the UK in this period – the equivalent rate in the USA in 1975 was 9.5% and in France 14%.) By July 1975 it was perfectly clear to all parties that something must be done, so another round of pay restraint was begun with a £6 increase for all workers except those earning £8,500 or more, who got nothing. The following year, 1976, the limit was set at 4%. The rate of inflation fell, at the cost of a cut in real wages all round.

Carrying out Wilson's policy of renegotiating the terms of entry into the EEC, the foreign secretary James Callaghan agreed a few minor changes and a referendum took place in June, 1975. Despite all the ballyhoo from anti-Marketeers, this returned a majority of two to one in favour of remaining in the EEC, and put an end to all further serious discussion about leaving it. Not, however, that the British liked what they found there – in particular the wasteful farm support program which regularly produced unsold "lakes" of wine or milk and "mountains" of butter. By 1978 they were horrified to find that despite being one of the poorer members on a per-capita income basis (ahead of Italy and Ireland), Britain was by far the largest contributor to the budget – a problem Margaret Thatcher would later address. Adopting something of a dog-in-a-manger attitude throughout the later seventies, the UK opposed the introduction of the tachograph, a device which measured the speed and distance travelled by lorries – because it would upset the Transport and General Workers Union – and refused to join the European Monetary System, forerunner of the euro.

Northern Ireland continued to pose apparently insoluble problems. As early as May 1974 there was what amounted to a general strike by Protestant workers against the power-sharing executive of Brian Faulkner, organized by the Ulster Workers' Council, a body which had strong links with Protestant paramilitaries. Intimidation was widespread; the army did nothing; and the power-sharing executive collapsed. The IRA bombing campaign then spread to the mainland. 21 people were killed and 184 injured in the Birmingham pub bombing of 21 November 1974, alienating public opinion in England against all things Irish. In order to try to put a stop to the violence the Prevention of Terrorism Act was rushed through Parliament only eight days later, allowing for internment in Northern Ireland – imprisonment without trial in the Maze prison. Membership of either the Provisional IRA or of the Protestant paramilitary groups was made a punishable offence carrying a maximum ten-year prison sentence. The new act brought some respite as the main suspects were rounded up and interned. The problem scarcely went away in Ireland itself. In 1979 18 soldiers were killed in a bomb blast, and the aged Earl of Mountbatten, a relative of the queen, was assassinated whilst on holiday in Ireland.

In March 1976, Harold Wilson mysteriously resigned, aged only 60. This event has been much discussed, but it could be that he had had enough of Lady Falkender (Maria Williams). His resignation honours list was claimed by Joe Haines to have been written out by Falkender herself on lavender notepaper – hence its name, the Lavender List. In any event, Wilson was replaced by the reassuring if doomed figure of James Callaghan, a trade unionist from the Inland Revenue originally from Portsmouth. Denis Healey, appointed Chancellor by Wilson, continued in post.

During 1976 there was a run on the pound, which fell in value from $2 in January to $1.60 by October. In an atmosphere of crisis, the workers at Ford Motors went on strike. Unemployment rocketed and went on to reach 1.6 million in 1977, an unheard-of figure in post-war Britain. Healey was told to stay away from the Labour Party conference in Blackpool (he went anyway). In a humiliating intervention for any Chancellor, the International Monetary Fund was called in and agreed to a new loan, with stringent conditions attached. However, pay restraint was by this time beginning to reduce to rate of inflation, which fell to 8.2% by 1978. In fact only half the IMF loan was ever used, and that was quickly paid back.

Callaghan managed to impose a pay limit increase of 10% in 1977. In the pay round of 1978-9, he then made a disastrous mistake. Rates had been successfully held down for three years, and he now set a figure of only 5%. Given the falls in real wages which had taken place, it was obvious to the man in the street that this was never going to work. It did not work. There followed the "winter of discontent" as lorry drivers, grave diggers, sewage workers, ambulancemen and hospital workers, amongst others, went on strike.

The shaky government was, however, eventually brought down by quite another issue - devolution, by which separate directly elected assemblies for Scotland and Wales were proposed. In the general election of October 1974, the Scottish National Party won eleven seats and took over 30% of the Scottish vote. In Wales Plaid Cymru, the Welsh nationalist party, also won a seat. In order to stay in power, Labour agreed to promote devolution and the Scotland and Wales Bills were passed by Parliament in 1977-8. One condition was that the legislation then had to be approved by referenda in Scotland and Wales. A clause was inserted by anti-devolutionists to the effect that 40% of the electorate had to approve, no matter how many actually voted. Referenda were duly held in March, 1979. In Wales the referendum was rejected by a huge majority; in Scotland 51.6 voted in favour of devolution, but as this represented barely a third of the electorate, the issue was then resolved in favour of the anti-devolutionists. The SNP immediately deserted the government in Parliament. Without their support, the government lost a vote of confidence by a single vote. At the ensuing general election of May 1979, the Conservatives under Margaret Thatcher were returned with a majority of 43 seats. The SNP had hardly covered itself in glory and its 11 seats were reduced to two.

Three figures stand out from the riotous seventies – the Communist demagogue Arthur Scargill, leader of the Yorkshire miners and later of the NUM; the Reverend Ian Paisley, another highly effective demagogue and Protestant bigot from Ulster; and "Red" Derek Robinson, shop steward and convener at the British Leyland car plant at Longbridge, another Communist and a man who would call a strike over the most trivial demarcation dispute, pay differential or slight from management and whose only ambition was to wreck the company for which he "worked". The plague of strikes across industry – "British disease" – caused the UK to slip down the international prosperity league. All three men would lead their followers to disaster, and in the case of Paisley, verily into the valley of death. There scarcely seemed an evening from 1972 onwards that did not feature an Irish funeral on the ten o'clock news. Here is an example of the Paisley style, addressed to a Catholic priest visiting Northern Ireland in as early as 1958: "Priest Murphy, speak for your own bloodthirsty, persecuting, intolerant, blaspheming, political-religious papacy, but do not pretend to be the spokesman of free Ulster men. You are not in the south of Ireland. Go back to your priestly intolerance, your blasphemous masses, back to your beads, holy water, holy smoke and stink; and remember we are the *sons of martyrs* whom your church butchered, and we know your church to be the *mother of harlots* and the abomination of the earth!"

During the course of the seventies, the imbroglio of Rhodesia gradually unfolded. In 1965 Southern Rhodesia (simply Rhodesia after UDI in that year) contained about a quarter of a million whites, many of them British ex-servicemen, and four and a half million blacks. Many of the Europeans were relatively recent immigrants, and indeed the country was only colonised after 1890. The proportion of whites was far higher than in Northern Rhodesia, which became Zambia and which seemed in no hurry to remove its white population. There was no apartheid in Southern Rhodesia and little sign of unrest amongst the black population, which, by African standards was doing well. By contrast, in South Africa there were four million whites, perhaps one-fifth of the population in 1965, some of whose families had been there for centuries, and certainly since 1650. Here the system of apartheid was rigidly enforced.

The white Rhodesians had quickly figured out that they could ignore the British Government. Heath's foreign secretary, Douglas-Home, tried to reach an agreement, but failed. However, circumstances changed. In practice Rhodesia was heavily dependent for its trade with the outside world on the port of Beira, in Mozambique, to which it had a direct railway connection. That route became unavailable after the independence of Mozambique under its new leader, Samora Machel, in 1975. Black Rhodesians received arms from Mozambique and began to infest the bush, carrying out terrorist attacks on isolated white farms, of which there were many. The South African government became nervous that the freedom fighting would spread southwards into South Africa itself, and urged a settlement on Ian Smith.

Recognising that some sort of transfer of power to the blacks was inevitable, the Smith government representatives arrived at a conference held in Geneva in 1976 ready to make concessions, but no agreement could be reached with the most militant group, the Patriotic Front of Robert Mugabe and Joshua Nkomo. Ian Smith then did his own deal with the more moderate blacks, elections were held, and Archbishop Muzorewa became the first black President of what now became Zimbabwe in 1978. This man was regarded as a mere stooge by the Patriotic Front and the new government failed to gain international recognition. So it was that the problem was passed on to the Tories in 1979. The new Foreign Secretary, Lord Carrington, and his envoy Lord Soames finally implemented an agreement in 1979 which led to the international recognition of Zimbabwe in 1980. Very influential in this process was Samora Machel, President of Mozambique, who persuaded Mugabe to tone down his Marxist rhetoric.

In fact, Margaret Thatcher had simply wanted the matter cleared up as quickly as possible, and so handed power to the radical Patriotic Front – probably not something that Douglas-Home would have done. The result was that Zimbabwe ended up with the very worst type of government possible. Mugabe, who came from the majority Shona tribe (centred on Harare) quickly got rid of the more reasonable Nkomo, who was from the Matabele tribe (centred on Bulawayo). Though careful and moderate at first, Mugabe soon became a typical African dictator (notably after the death of Samora Machel in 1986). The white population was gradually forced out. Eventually even agriculture failed, famines set in and a large proportion of the population fled starving to South Africa. Thatcher would say that the native

Zimbabweans voted for Mugabe, so had only themselves to blame, but the result was a poor deal for whites and blacks. In general the post-colonial governments of Africa and the Indian subcontinent were blatantly racialist and seemed only to want indigenous people, while at the same time the developed western countries were becoming increasingly multi-racial. As a result the post-colonial governments effectively de-skilled their workforces, failed to develop economically and in some cases went backwards. Zimbabwe was an extreme version of this. As one Zambian put it, Zimbabwe got rid of its white people too quickly.

Chapter 36 – Post-War Britain 1979 - 2010

Margaret Thatcher was the daughter of a grocer from Grantham in Lincolnshire. Taking a degree in chemistry from Oxford, she became first an industrial chemist, then a tax barrister, but soon she was rising in the ranks of the Conservative party. She married Denis Thatcher, a divorcee and executive at Burmah Oil; the couple produced twins. During her time as Heath's Minister of Education, she famously abolished free school milk, earning the soubriquet "Margaret Thatcher, milk snatcher". The lesson she learnt from this episode was to measure the political cost of her decisions against the actual money saved, which in the case of school milk was trivial. In 1977 she gave an anti-communist speech which caused the Russians to call her the "Iron Lady", a new title which delighted her. Another famous description came from President Mitterrand of France: "The eyes of Caligula and the mouth of Marilyn Monroe."

Her first cabinet was composed of senior Tories, most of whom she despised as "wets", Heathite consensus-seekers; Thatcher was not interested in consensus politics. One of these was Jim Prior, Employment Secretary, who introduced a bill to ban the closed shop (whereby all workers at a place of business were obliged to join a trade union) and secondary picketing. The new Chancellor, Sir Geoffrey Howe, immediately cut income tax, reducing the top rate from the ruinous 83% bequeathed from Healey to 60%, and the standard rate from 33% to 30%. To pay for this, VAT (value added tax, paid by all and levied on most non-food goods and services) was raised from 8% to 15%. Not quite knowing what would happen, but hoping for the best, Howe also released all controls on foreign exchange.

Thatcher's aim was to control the money supply, following the ideas of the American economist Milton Friedman. However the money supply increased by 19% in 1980-1. Meanwhile British Leyland had to be rescued with a government bailout, inflation hit 22% and unemployment rose by 800,000. Large swathes of industry were closed down, leaving piles of red brick rubble at former metal-bashers all over the West Midlands. This was not what was supposed to happen, and the Tory left expressed alarm. Thatcher, far more determined than anyone realised, was dismissive: "You turn if you want to. The lady's not for turning." Much of the problem was in fact due to the new status of sterling as a petro-currency. Its rate against the dollar soared to $2 to the pound, a ruinous rate for home manufacturers. Britain had become fully self-sufficient in oil by 1980, and the revenues from it represented a tremendous boost to the Treasury throughout the decade and beyond. What was left of manufacturing industry became more automated and productivity within it increased ("leaner and fitter"), but oil money had to be used to pay for this restructuring and the unemployment it caused.

By 1981 unemployment had risen to 2.7 million, and was heading for three million, but Howe introduced another deflationary budget, taking more money out of the economy. 364 prominent economists wrote to the *Times* to denounce this policy. Shortly afterwards rioting and arson broke out in Southall in London, then at Toxteth in Liverpool and Moss Side in Manchester. Michael Heseltine, nicknamed "Tarzan" and the darling of the Tory party conference, now Environment Secretary, was dispatched to Liverpool to try to sort out the mess. He did his best, staying with the job for over a year. Meanwhile Thatcher gradually weeded out the wets from her cabinet, replacing them one at a time with like-minded thinkers such as Norman Tebbit (the "Chingford Skinhead") and Nigel Lawson. Len Murray and other trade union leaders, used to spending much of their time consuming sandwiches at 10 Downing Street, found the door firmly shut. In Europe, the German Chancellor Helmut Schmidt and the French President Valery Giscard d'Estaing soon found themselves subjected to the Thatcherite hair dryer. She would not back down or go home until she won a substantial rebate on the UK contribution the EEC budget, which she duly obtained.

Opposition politics came to Thatcher's rescue. Having lost power under right-wing Labour men, the grass roots wanted a left-wing leadership ready to take over when Thatcher was inevitably slung out. Trotskyites from a group called the Militant Tendency had infiltrated the Labour branches and exercised disproportionate influence. Following the resignation of Callaghan in 1980, Michael Foot was made the new leader. Though certainly left-wing, he was a most unlikely choice – shambolic, bookish, upper middle-class and once criticised for attending Remembrance Day at the Cenotaph wearing a duffle coat.

His deputy was Denis Healey, who only just beat off a challenge from a man who had adopted extreme left-wing views, Tony Benn. In disgust at this behaviour, the senior Labour politicians Roy Jenkins, Shirley Williams, David Owen and Bill Rodgers (the Gang of Four) split off and formed the Social Democratic Party. After a couple of by-election victories the new party was soon in the lead at the opinion polls, with the Conservatives languishing in third place.

Everything changed in March 1982 when forces from Argentina invaded first the uninhabited island of South Georgia, then the British colony of the Falkland Islands in the South Atlantic. Containing only 1800 British settlers and defended by just 80 marines, the last British warship had been withdrawn and the Argentines under General Galtieri saw their chance. The failure to anticipate this move led to the resignation of Lord Carrington, Foreign Secretary. Thatcher ordered the Royal Navy to assemble a task force, and refused to listen to any of the many increasingly frantic attempts at mediation from the USA and elsewhere. The Falklands were going to be re-taken and nothing else would do. In Parliament, Enoch Powell, in reference to the Iron Lady, said we would soon find out from which metal she was made.

As with Oran in the Second World War, the first sign that Britain really did mean business was the controversial sinking of the well-armed Argentinean cruiser, the *Belgrano*, by a British submarine, outside the military exclusion zone but looking for trouble. By 18 May British forces had made a successful landing in the bay of San Carlos in East Falkland. Coming under heavy pressure from Argentine aircraft armed with the French-made Exocet missiles, naval losses began to mount, causing great alarm to the British public, which began to watch the TV news from behind the sofa. Four warships were sunk in quick succession, the destroyers *HMS Sheffield* and *HMS Coventry*, and the frigates *HMS Ardent* and *HMS Antelope*, plus the transport ship *Atlantic Conveyor*, which was carrying the task force's supply of Chinook helicopters. The luxury liner *Queen Elizabeth 2*, requisitioned as a troop carrier and carrying 3000 soldiers, was nearby and under threat. This was the worst moment for Thatcher. More losses seemed imminent and would have been realised had the Argentinean pilots flown higher. Forced down by Harrier jets, they released their Exocets too late for their fuses to arm. Thirteen missiles hit British ships but failed to explode. There were then more hits on shipping, to the small landing ships *Sir Galahad* and *Sir Tristram* and the destroyer *HMS Glamorgan*, with many aboard suffering burns. Nevertheless the men got ashore and fought their way past Goose Green and on to retake the capital, Port Stanley. The Argentinean land forces surrendered. The war had cost 900 casualties (one for every two islanders), more than two-thirds of them Argentinean, and 321 from the *Belgrano* alone.

Victory had been obtained, but was it worth it? Neglected as they had been, the Falkland Islands have a strategic position. There are only two sea routes between the Atlantic and Pacific, via the Panama Canal and via the tip of South America. The Panama Canal cannot in any case take the largest ships, and has capacity constraints. Forces based in the Falklands are in a position to command the southern route. Also oil has been found in the seabed around the islands - Port Stanley is no longer the quiet backwater it used to be. In any event, Enoch Powell was delighted with the outcome. He reported that the metal under test "consisted of ferrous matter of the highest quality, and that it is of exceptional tensile strength, is highly resistant to wear and tear and to stress, and may be used to advantage for all national purposes."

The nation agreed; Thatcher had turned the tide of decline abroad, and would soon do so at home. Unemployment may have reached three million and taxes had risen sharply, but inflation was on the way down. In the election of May 1983, though the Conservatives polled fewer votes than in 1979, they won a majority of 144 seats. Thatcher was indeed fortunate; the Alliance between the SDP and the Liberals took nearly a quarter of the popular vote, but it was spread too thinly, and only yielded 23 seats, with a meagre six for the SDP. The Labour Party manifesto as approved by Michael Foot was accurately described as "the longest suicide note in history".

Having dealt with the enemy without, Thatcher now turned to the enemy within. Arthur Scargill, now President of the National Union of Mineworkers, had been itching for a fight. The NUM presented a large pay demand when Thatcher first took office, but knowing she was not ready, she bought the miners off. The reason she was not ready was that there was insufficient coal stockpiled at the power stations. By 1984, stocks had been building up for over two years. Thatcher then appointed the Scots-born American Ian MacGregor as head of the National Coal Board with a remit to close uneconomic pits and lop 64,000 jobs out of a total of 202,000. MacGregor had already carried out a similar exercise at British Steel where 65,000 jobs had been cut, so Scargill knew exactly where he stood. He relished the prospect of a fight, particularly over pit closures, which were a much more emotive issue than pay deals.

Early regional ballots failed to produce a majority in favour of strike action, so Scargill decided upon a strategy of rolling local strikes, merely approved by his national executive – there was no national ballot. Soon four miners out of five had been called out on strike by this unconstitutional trick on the part of Scargill. However he had two problems – firstly, other unions failed to come out in support, so there would be no repeat of the General Strike of 1926. Secondly the Nottinghamshire miners refused to join the strike. This duly began in March 1984. The new Labour leader, Neil Kinnock (who had replaced Michael Foot in 1983), son of a Welsh miner, expressed disbelief that a coal strike had been started in the spring, when demand was falling off.

Violent pickets appeared at working mines and strategic sites, most famously at the Orgeave coking plant near Rotherham and the Saltley coke depot in Birmingham. The police, trained in the use of riot gear after the disturbances of the previous years, were also ready, and confronted the pickets with determined horse and baton charges of their own. It is thought that there were 10,000 miners against a similar number of police at Orgreave where the titanic, violent clashes were watched on TV by the appalled public. There could be no doubt about Scargill's motive (he claimed he would rather see the miners dig out mud than close a pit). He called the Welsh miners' leader, Dai Francis, to ask for pickets to come to Saltley. Francis asked when they would be needed:

"Tomorrow, Saturday."

Francis: "Er.... But Wales are playing Scotland at Cardiff Arms Park on Saturday!"

Scargill: "But Dai, the working class are playing the ruling class at Saltley."

At the Conservative party conference in Brighton in the middle of the strike, the IRA made a considerably more impressive attempt than Guy Fawkes to blow up the Prime Minister at the Grand Hotel. Five people were killed and several more seriously injured, including Norman Tebbit and his wife, but Thatcher was unharmed. The IRA struck close to home again when they later blew up Ian Gow, her personal friend.

Gradually as the miners' strike wore on, the Scargill rhetoric began to fall on deaf ears in the mining community, well aware that it had never been offered a ballot. Workers drifted back in increasing numbers. The strike finally ended on 3 March 1985, almost a year after it had begun, with the miners utterly defeated. From that point onwards the coal mining industry was run down, more quickly and with less sympathy from the government than would have been the case without the strike.

399

The next storm – or at least squall – to erupt concerned the helicopter manufacturer, Westland, based in Yeovil, which was seeking a foreign alliance to help it survive. It favoured a takeover by the American company Sikorsky, maker of the Black Hawk helicopter, but a European consortium was also interested. The issue split Thatcher from the other big cat in her cabinet, Michael Heseltine, Minister of Defence. Thatcher favoured the American takeover, but Heseltine, quite reasonably not wanting to let a strategic defence industry go to the Americans, opted for the other party. Two themes emerged – pro-Europeans against anti-Europeans, a split which was to seriously damage the Conservatives in the next decade, and also Thatcher's dictatorial and sometimes questionable methods. She sought to undermine Heseltine by seeking advice against him from the Attorney General, the government's legal officer. This private advice was then leaked to the press by a junior official in the Department of Trade and Industry, which was headed by Leon Brittan. It was suspected that her own direct boss, the Prime Minister's press secretary and all-round attack dog Bernard Ingham was involved. Furious at attempts to both gag and undermine him, Heseltine walked out of the cabinet in disgust and resigned from the government. Thatcher was badly rattled and feared it might be her turn next. Heseltine was a serious rival who would ultimately challenge her for her job. In the event, Leon Brittan was made a scapegoat and obliged to resign, though he seemed little more than an innocent bystander; so the Westland affair had cost two cabinet ministers their jobs.

Chancellors Geoffrey Howe and Nigel Lawson (from 1983) found a brand new and extremely lucrative means of raising funds – privatisation. This proved such a popular idea that it spread around the world. During the eighties, £29 billion was raised from the sale of land and businesses, and £18 billion from the sale of council homes to 1.14 million tenants. The purpose was not only to raise money, and so reduce borrowing and taxes, but also to give the public at large a bigger stake in society, and make them more likely to vote Conservative – the "property-owning democracy". The first big sale was 52% of British Telecom, which raised £3.9 billion in 1984 – two million people bought shares, doubling the number of shareowners nationwide in a single day. Next was the largest privatisation of all, British Gas, which raised £5.4 billion. British Airways, British Steel, Rolls Royce and all the major electricity and water companies were to follow. Council homes were sold at discounts of between 33% and 50% of their market value, according to length of tenancy. The proportion of owner-occupied homes rose from 55% in 1979 to 67% ten years later.

As well as all these, some entities not actually owned by the government were also privatized, including the Trustee Savings Bank. All the largest building societies including the Abbey National, the Halifax, the Bradford and Bingley, the Alliance and Leicester and Northern Rock were also "demutualised" or handed over to their members as shareholders. All this had a tremendous impact – total personal wealth rose by 80% during the eighties (additionally fuelled by a housing boom later in the decade). The political impact was that "old" Labour was never reelected after the privatizations, which were in their way the very reverse of Clause Four nationalization.

Meanwhile, Thatcher had had enough of "loony left" local councils. By the Local Government Act of 1985, the county councils of the metropolitan counties (all the major conurbations including Greater London) were abolished and their powers transferred to the boroughs. At the same time Thatcher began to transfer power away from locally elected bodies, including those which ran hospitals and schools, to appointed nominees, whose politics were less likely to be of the militant Trotskyite variety. All this had little effect on her popularity. Despite the ballyhoo and the slick election campaign conducted by Neil Kinnock for Labour, and the double act "two Davids" – Steel (Liberal) and Owen (SDP) – of the Alliance, the Tories romped home in the 1987 election with a majority of 101 seats.

After the strikes and industrial devastation of the seventies and early eighties, something encouraging began to happen in the British motor industry. The Japanese manufacturer Nissan opened what was to become a very large factory at Sunderland in 1986, to be followed by Peugeot (at Ryton, Coventry), Honda (Swindon), Toyota (Derby) and BMW (Oxford). The three Japanese companies all set up brand new facilities, each deliberately sited well away from the traditional union-dominated West Midlands.

In her third term Thatcher, now variously known as the Leaderene, She Who Must Be Obeyed and the Great She-Elephant, became increasing arrogant. She drifted further and further away from her old friends, notably her two Chancellors, Howe (now Foreign Secretary) and Lawson. They urged a policy of closer integration with the EEC, and for the UK to join the ERM (European Exchange Rate Mechanism). This tied the exchange rates of the various independent European currencies together in close bands. The idea was to link sterling to the West German Deutschmark, which was policed by the fearsome

Bundesbank, the central bank which – never forgetting the days of the Weimar Republic – was the least tolerant of inflation in Europe. In the meantime the sinister French Socialist, Jacques Delors, was advancing his project of ever closer European union. This was supported by Howe. Thatcher wanted nothing to do with either the ERM or European union, and said as much in her speech at Bruges in 1990. At the same time she started rather publicly taking the advice of the economist Sir Alan Walters, putting Lawson in an ignominious position. Howe was demoted to Leader of the House of Commons and replaced by the up-and-coming John Major, Chief Secretary of the Treasury. In this job, Major looked as if he was wearing on overcoat several sizes too large, but he was having an exciting time. After only three months in the job he became Chancellor in October 1990 – Lawson had had enough of Sir Alan Walters, and resigned.

However, Lawson had also lost credibility in the country. A brilliant Chancellor from 1983 onwards, he had not only cut income taxes but abolished other taxes completely. Inflation and unemployment had fallen. However, in the later eighties he had presided over a massive expansion of credit, the Lawson boom. Banks had muscled into the mortgage business and so he had allowed traditional building societies to borrow funds on the money markets to compete; previously they had only their depositor's money to lend. Suddenly mortgages became very easy to obtain. House prices doubled, then continued rising. Also on Lawson's watch, the City of London had been deregulated. The little old firms of jobbers and brokers were swept away as huge international investment banks moved into shiny palaces. Computerized share-dealing (SEAQ) was introduced in the Big Bang of October, 1987. London, far from fading away as a rival financial centre in favour of New York (in the manner of the imperial Royal Navy) grew to rival it in importance, and became a major earner of foreign exchange.

However by the start of 1990, there was a sudden and eerie silence in the economy. Nationwide, telephones stopped ringing. The boom was over. Between February 1988 and August 1990 the inflation rate increased from 3.3% to 10.6%. The Bank of England base rate, consistently high in the late eighties, reached 14%. Unemployment would inevitably rocket. Lawson certainly had a row with Thatcher, but he was doomed anyway.

These events took place against a background of a massive reconfiguration in eastern Europe. The Berlin Wall fell in November, 1989. West and East Germany were reunited by October 1990 (an event certainly not celebrated by Thatcher, who liked the Berlin Wall). The Cold War was over and all the former Soviet-dominated states in eastern Europe became free countries after 45 years. By December, 1991, the Soviet Union itself had collapsed into its constituent, now independent republics.

Thatcher outlasted Lawson by barely a month, but it was none of the above issues which brought her career as Prime Minister to an end. That issue was local authority finance – the poll tax. Here the problem was that the domestic rates – local authority taxes – were paid only by 14 million householders, whereas the local authority franchise included all adults, many of whom could vote for whatever extravagant program was on offer by "loony left" councillors without concerning themselves about paying the bill. The idea of the poll tax was that everyone should pay, and everyone should pay the same. Rates were based on the value of domestic property, and so were a progressive form of taxation – the more expensive the property, the bigger the rate. The poll tax was flat rate, and so regressive; no matter what the payer's income, he would have to find the money for the tax. The idea greatly appealed to Thatcher, who thought it would teach the idlers and scroungers a lesson. However as it would mean a brand new tax for 20 million people, and as 80% of people would pay more than they did before, it did not take a genius to realise that there would be a problem. Nigel Lawson advised that the poll tax would be "completely unworkable and politically catastrophic". Out of office for four years, Michael Heseltine nodded gravely as panicked MPs queued up to share their concerns, sharpening his claws ready for the inevitable attack.

The manner of Thatcher's departure was suitably dramatic. Firstly she was criticised in Parliament by Sir Geoffrey Howe, her loyal supporter whom she had repeatedly humiliated in public. Heseltine announced that he would challenge her for the leadership of the Conservative party and a ballot was called. While the first round of voting was taking place, Thatcher foolishly attended a meeting in Paris. Under the rules of the ballot, though she beat Heseltine by four votes, this was not enough to avoid a second ballot. Loyal cabinet ministers who had kept their names out of the first ballot could now stand. Back in London, Thatcher interviewed her cabinet, one by one. It was clear that few would support her in a second ballot – if she stood, she would be humiliated. She was finished as Prime Minister and left office within days, her great British revolution over. At the second ballot the dark horse, John Major, easily beat Heseltine – who clearly was not as popular as he thought he was – for the leadership, with Douglas Hurd coming in a respectable third.

*   *   *   *

John Major never went to university. He had a reasonably prosperous start in life but his father, a former showman, ran a business making garden gnomes and this collapsed in 1955 when Major was twelve. The family moved from suburbia into a flat in one of London's poorest areas, Brixton. Leaving school at 16, Major struggled for both work and motivation before finally getting a decent job in a bank. Joining the Conservative party, he found new energy. Elected MP for a safe seat, Huntingdon, he rose "without trace", suddenly emerging as Foreign Secretary shortly before the fall of Thatcher, a position he held for just 94 days. He became Prime Minister at the age of only 47. Deep down, however, he was an old-fashioned workaholic, as Thatcher had been. Nevertheless when the chips were down, as they often were, Tory MPs wondered how they had managed to elect such a poorly educated and third-rate leader, a "grey" man. Yet Major held off his critics inside and outside of the party and remained Prime Minister for seven years, longer than Macmillan.

Major's first business was to get rid of the poll tax, replaced by the Council Tax, a very similar system to the old rates and based on the value of domestic property. Otherwise he inherited a perilous situation from Thatcher as a serious recession was just getting started, particularly affecting white-collar workers, with its worst effects in the south of the country. Unemployment was heading towards two million, and a new phrase entered the national vocabulary – "negative equity". 1.8 million people found that their homes were worth less than the amount they had borrowed to pay for them. 75,000 homes were repossessed in 1991 alone. Prices fell by 25% in the worst-affected area over four years – in fact by 40% or more if adjusted for inflation. Major's situation was perilous in another way. In February 1991, he and his war cabinet were sitting in 10 Downing Street when it was hit by IRA mortar bombs; no one was killed.

A war cabinet was required because the Iraqi dictator Saddam Hussein had invaded the oil-rich city state of Kuwait the previous year. After six months of planning, the Americans and their allies, including British forces, struck back on 17 January 1991 in what became known as the First Gulf War. After a campaign of only six weeks, Saddam's

404

Revolutionary Guard was smashed and all Iraqi forces retreated out of Kuwait.

In the winter of 1991-2, Major and his Chancellor Norman Lamont went to Maastricht in Holland to negotiate the eponymous Treaty, the next stage in the grand Delors road map towards European Union. They obtained agreement to opt out of the coming European single currency. The "Social Chapter" obliging Britain to follow French practices of enormously expensive employer "social charges" at the workplace was dropped from the treaty at British insistence. Despite these gains, Major only secured the ratification of the Maastricht treaty after an enormous expenditure of time and effort in Parliament. A group of his own MPs united with Labour anti-marketeers to obstruct his every step. Yet in the end, the only thing which mattered about Maastricht was the single currency, and Britain had opted out of that from the outset. In any case the Maastricht Treaty was rejected by referenda in Holland and France.

Major was obliged to call a general election in 1992 as the five-year parliamentary term expired, and he must have done so with trepidation, but the campaign swung unexpectedly his way. The public warmed to this obviously rather shy man getting on his soap box with a megaphone. His Chancellor, Lamont, promised a cut of five pence in the pound from the bottom rate of income tax. His opposite number, John Smith, had costed the Labour program, and planned tax rises. More than any other factor, the public had never learned to trust the Labour leader, Neil Kinnock. In the event on 9 April 1992 the Conservatives won 14 million votes, more than any other party in British history, though through the vagaries of the electoral system, this translated into an overall majority of just 21 seats. After the election, Kinnock stood down as Labour leader, to be replaced by the Scottish lawyer John Smith. He in turn assigned leading roles to his up-and-coming young stars, Tony Blair (shadow Home Secretary) and Gordon Brown (shadow Chancellor), but was himself destined to die of a heart attack in 1994.

Within months Major came to the main crisis of his premiership. Sterling was part of the ERM, the Exchange Rate Mechanism. It was also Major's foreign policy to move "ever closer to the heart of Europe", something intensely disliked by his back seat driver, Thatcher. The policy was working – inflation was down to 3.7% in the UK. However, the US dollar came under selling pressure, fell and dragged sterling down with it. A run on the Italian lira forced it out of the ERM. The mark rose further as those who sold dollars and sterling bought it. Major begged Chancellor Kohl of Germany to reduce his interest rates, but he refused. The speculators, led by the Hungarian-born American George Soros, saw a one-way bet, sold sterling short and bought more marks. The situation became unsustainable. The Bank of England base rate had already been raised to 10%. On the morning of Black Wednesday, 16 September 1992, Lamont put up interest rates to 12%, then later the same day to 15%, but it made no difference. Sterling crashed out of the ERM on the most humiliating day in British politics since the IMF crisis of September 1976.

Interest rates were immediately reduced and the economy began to recover. A lower rate for sterling was in fact just what was required. To the public, it looked like chaos, but Black Wednesday was eventually rechristened White Wednesday by some economists. The long-term political effect was that nobody in the British Treasury, having been let down so badly by the Germans, would ever again give power over sterling to foreigners. The future euro single currency project was permanently off the agenda. Lamont himself was badly damaged by the crisis and was sacked six months later, but Major held on.

In 1993 the government set about the privatisation of what remained of British Coal, most of it sold off in one piece to RJB Mining, subsequently renamed UK Coal. British Rail was also sold off in the messiest and least successful privatization of them all. The Railways Act of 1993 led to the creation of a host of operating companies. The infrastructure – track, signalling and stations – was sold off to a consortium, Railtrack. Complaints about the poor service on the railways, far from diminishing, vastly increased. Meanwhile Major tried to make a reality of his "Citizen's Charter", which set out to improve public services and make the whole of the administration of the country accountable and citizen-friendly. It meant nothing to most of the population, but the first league tables for school and police force performance began to appear. Major also tried to bang heads together in Northern Ireland, with (at last) some success. A new generation had grown up in Ulster which preferred to put the past behind it. Though the ultimate closure of this issue is normally attributed to Tony Blair in the next administration, the number of killings dropped from 84 in 1993 to nine in 1995.

*   *   *   *

When John Smith died in 1994, Labour needed a new leader. The earlier favorite, Gordon Brown, son of a Scottish Presbyterian minister ("son of the manse"), had by this time been overtaken by Tony Blair, who certainly sounded English enough, though his father had been a Scottish lecturer in law at Durham University. Blair himself grew up partly in Scotland and also Australia, and attended secondary school at Fettes, a private institution in Edinburgh, before going up to Oxford and then studying for the bar. Outgoing, bright, Christian, sincere by political standards, and full of enthusiasm, he made a sharp contrast with the dour Scot, Brown (said to have a volcanic temper in private). There was a sense that Blair was a man who would succeed in whatever career he chose. Some questioned his commitment to Labour, noting that the Conservative party was already full of aspiring young lawyer-MPs – and indeed in general outlook Blair could just as well have been a leftist Conservative. It is thought that the real socialist was Blair's wife, Cherie, another London lawyer but the daughter of a soap opera star, Tony Booth from *Coronation Street*, who had left a number of one-parent families scattered across the north of England, including hers, on Merseyside.

In any event Brown undertook to stand aside in the election for Labour leader in an agreement finalized at the Granta restaurant in London. In exchange Blair agreed to give Brown a very large say in domestic policy, and not to stay in office forever – but who knew exactly for how long? After Black Wednesday Major was already stricken, so the agreements made with Brown were to have great significance. At the leadership election Blair romped home ahead of John Prescott, the trade union candidate. One of Blair's first acts was to remove the infamous Clause Four (the commitment to nationalization) from Labour's agenda – something which John Smith had had no intention of doing – and so in one fell swoop moving the party firmly to the right, under the name "New Labour". Old Labour was gone, probably forever, as an electable organization.

By 1997 it was getting increasingly difficult for the electorate to tell Labour and the Conservatives apart in policy terms. However Major's administration had been mired in sleaze and scandal, and the Prime Minister was faced by that almost unstoppable force, the feeling that the country wad due for a change. In the general election which was held in May, Labour took 419 seats, an enormous majority, giving Blair *carte blanche* to do as he wished for the next five years. However Labour had actually polled far less votes than Major in 1992; but the turnout was low, only 71% - the Conservative voters had stayed at home.

Only two months after the election, the curtain came down on the British colony of Hong Kong, transferred to China when the British lease on the territory expired. China could have taken the territory for itself much sooner – as India took Goa from Portugal soon after independence – but had preferred to keep open its letterbox to the world.

The next great event was a sad one, the death of Diana, divorced wife of Charles, Prince of Wales and heir to the throne, in a car crash in Paris on 31 August 1997, aged 36. Charles was not popular – very much because of his attitude to his former wife – but Diana was hugely so, and her funeral was attended by a great national outpouring of grief.

A better story was the all-but final resolution of the Troubles in Northern Ireland. The polar opposites, Gerry Adams and Martin McGuinness of the Catholic Sinn Fein and the Protestants under David Trimble, John Hume and the indestructible Rev Ian Paisley, finally buried the hatchet with a power-sharing agreement implemented in 1998.

From the outset of his tenure as Chancellor, Gordon Brown was determined to establish for Labour a reputation for the sound management of the economy – "Prudence" became his favorite girl. This was a backlash against the disasters which had occurred under previous Labour governments, the devaluations of 1949 and 1967 and the IMF visitation of 1976. Brown announced that he would stick to the spending plans which had been announced by the outgoing Chancellor, Kenneth Clark. He also astonished the City scribblers by transferring the control of interest rates to the Bank of England. Too many previous Chancellors had been tempted to reduce rates ahead of elections for political reasons, whatever the economic circumstances. Secondly, in what was portrayed as little more than a technical adjustment, Brown stopped the tax credit on share dividends payable to pension funds, which was then worth £5 billion a year. The rather obvious long-term effect of this was to slash the value of private pensions, according to one estimate by £100 billion by 2006. The move subsequently outraged members of the pension schemes affected.

In fact Brown inherited a very favorable financial position from the Tories, as the British economy had begun its long climb out of the recession of 1990-5. Tax revenues increased and debt could be paid off. Capital expenditure on new schools, hospitals, bridges and other infrastructure was simply transferred to the private sector by the Public Finance Initiative (PFI). The commercial sector would pay for the projects and the government would then lease or rent them back, sometimes over a very long period (fifty years). This bright idea meant that new hospitals and schools eventually appeared everywhere, but the cost of them would be borne by future generations.

However, Brown did run a very tight ship in the first Blair government, and this is one reason it achieved so little. Reforms of the type promised by Blair ("Education, Education and Education!") cost money, and Brown made very little of it available. Also, though avoiding headline-grabbing tax increases, Brown became adept at increasing revenue by "stealth taxes". These included freezing the income tax thresholds, so that 1.5 million people found themselves paying the top rate; freezing personal allowances instead of increasing them in line with inflation; increasing national insurance rather than income tax; and increasing the stamp duty on property sales. An election pledge was honoured with the introduction of a national minimum wage from 1 April 1999. As this was set at rather a low level, £3.60 an hour for adults, it caused less trouble than anticipated and has generally come to be regarded as a good thing.

Devolution finally became a reality in 1999 when after referenda in each country, Scotland and Wales got their own Parliaments. The Scottish version had much the greater powers, controlling education, health, welfare, local government, transport and housing, with some power to vary income tax. It did not control defence, foreign policy or the bulk of taxation. Within Scotland, the Tories were very largely replaced by Scottish Nationalists and have not figured significantly in the new Parliament. The new leader was Donald Dewar, once described as resembling a dyspeptic heron, styled first minister, but who died in 2000. Both Parliaments were located in brand-new buildings. The Scottish Parliament was housed in a modernist edifice designed by the Catalan architect Enrico Miralles, a most un-Scottish construction. Budgeted to cost £55 million, the final bill was £470 million. This overspend dominated the early years of the Scottish Parliament. Amongst its first acts, the Scottish Parliament provided much more generous treatment for both old people and students than was available in England, and created new property laws to allow Highland communities to purchase compulsorily the land they occupied. Scotland had always had its own education and legal systems, and to some extent its own newspapers, and now it had its own politics as well.

The euro came into being first as an accounting currency at the beginning of 1999. Banknotes and coins denominated in euros came into use on 1 January 2002, when deutschmarks, francs, lire and other national currencies disappeared. Hence the decision on whether or not to join the new currency fell to Blair and Brown. Blair, a keen

European, would have joined on his own initiative, but found himself outwitted and overruled by Gordon Brown and the mandarins at the Treasury, who had never forgotten Black Wednesday, and who kept Britain out. The Schengen Agreement, removing border controls within the European Union, started life as early as 1985 but was not fully implemented until 1997. Britain also kept out of this, wishing to retain checks at all its own frontiers. Thus the British public was excluded from the two most important aspects of the European Union which actually affect travellers.

Tony Blair himself became very heavily involved in efforts to stop the war in Kosovo, a province of Serbia largely inhabited by ethnic Albanians, during 1998-9. Serbian forces at one point displaced a million fleeing Kosovars. NATO air strikes against the Serbs, coordinated by President Bill Clinton of the USA in association with Blair, failed to have much effect. It was only when firm plans to involve NATO ground troops started to be implemented that the Serbs backed down, paving the way for the effective independence of Kosovo.

After much dispute and enormous expense, a great Dome was erected at Greenwich in which to celebrate the Millennium on 1 January, 2000. The building itself was imaginatively designed but the exhibits inside it on the day proved a damp squib. It all had a "New Labour" feel about it, an impressive construction with very little inside it. The Dome then faced an uncertain future, but it eventually became a successful venue for pop concerts.

Brown finally began to release the purse strings from the middle of 2000 onwards as the next election loomed. The main thrust at first was the National Health Service. It had become obvious that by international standards this was badly underfunded. There was a dramatic increase in expenditure in all areas of it – hospitals, surgeries, health centres, doctors and their salaries, nurses, administrators, drugs and treatments. Waiting lists fell rapidly, but it was Brown's goodbye to Prudence. Meanwhile the general economy was buzzing after the long climb out of the 1990s recession, spurred on by new technology. The personal computer and all its many ramifications – broadband communications, the internet, email, electronic games, office applications – and the mobile phone and multi-channel TV were at the forefront of a whole new electronic world. Low-cost airlines blossomed in the deregulated climate and suddenly dozens of cheap flight destinations became available from previously neglected airports. The public gleefully got on board and one holiday abroad a year rapidly became three, four or five holidays for the middle classes.

All this played well with the electorate. The attempts by William Hague, the Yorkshire-born leader of the Conservatives, to nail Blair as a slimy liar simply bounced off. Blair called an election in June, 2001 and retained virtually the same majority as in 1997, a massive 166 seats, albeit on a very low turnout – just under 60%. The Conservative voters had stayed at home once more.

The world changed suddenly and dramatically on 11 September 2001 when the Arab terrorist organization Al Qaeda, led by the shadowy Saudi Arabian Muslim fanatic Osama Bin Laden, attacked the United States using hijacked airliners. Two of these were flown into the twin towers of the iconic World Trade Centre in New York; the towers both collapsed and 2606 civilians were killed. Another airliner was flown into the Pentagon building in Washington, headquarters of the US military, but did less damage. The new US President, George W Bush, immediately set out to destroy his fanatical Muslim enemies, with the support of Tony Blair. The first to suffer were the Al Qaeda allies, the Taliban of Afghanistan, within a month of "9/11". US aircraft bombed al Qaeda training camps and Taliban defensive positions in Afghanistan; cruise missiles were also fired from British submarines. With the recruitment of the northern warlords of Afghanistan to take Kabul, this short war was over in five weeks. The Al Qaeda fighters and their Taliban hosts were driven into caves at Tora Bora, near the border with Pakistan. However, they would soon be back, and now able to assume the role of Afghan nationalists against foreign imperialist adventurers, would be the cause of much hand-wringing in the west for years to come.

Next in line was the Iraqi dictator Saddam Hussein, in the sights of the US military hawks ever since his invasion of Kuwait in the First Gulf War. He was known to have plans to develop "weapons of mass destruction" and had repeatedly attempted to foil weapons inspectors from the United Nations. No one really knew how much he had actually achieved in developing his own nuclear weapons. In order to convince the sceptical British media and public, Tony Blair assembled a dossier of evidence indicating that weapons development in Iraq had reached a critical level. However there were no reliable sources of information within Iraq and the dossier was criticised as merely speculative. Blair had no mandate for a second Iraq war from the British public, a large proportion of which saw this as an unwarrantable interference in the internal affairs of an independent country. Also no mandate could be obtained from the United Nations for a new war.

Moreover, there seemed to be no real link between Saddam and Al Qaeda.

Nevertheless after all the fruitless diplomatic wrangling, and a great deal of military planning, Bush and Blair went ahead and invaded Iraq on 20 March 2003. This turned out to be another turkey-shoot as local forces were no match for the stealth bombers and other high-tech weaponry available to the USA. Saddam fled into hiding, eventually to be captured and hung by Iraqi opponents. Attempts were then made to install a pro-western government in Baghdad, but years of anti-terrorist fighting were to follow before the situation settled down. Meanwhile, American, British and other allied troops found no trace whatsoever of weapons of mass destruction within Iraq. Blair's reputation as a "pretty straight kind of guy" (as he called himself) was in ruins, but victory – of a sort – had been achieved on the ground in Iraq.

One side-effect of the Second Gulf War was the arrival of large numbers of refugees from Iraq in Britain, to join an ever-increasing flow of migrants mainly from Asia and Africa. Then in 2004 ten countries from eastern Europe joined the European Union. Britain was one of the few existing member countries to allow immediate unrestricted immigration from these new member states. A mass movement of population followed, especially from Poland - probably over 600,000 people in the first two years. This simply dwarfed the 28,000 Asians who arrived from Uganda in 1971. Drawn by the prosperity of the UK, this immigration has shown little sign of abating even during the recession which began in 2007. In the meanwhile, going in the opposite direction has been a flood of older Britons retiring to the sun in Spain and southern France.

Tony Blair called his second election in May, 2005. This time he won an overall majority of 67 seats, a hundred less than in 2001, but with 355 MPs, Labour was still far ahead of the Conservatives on 198. After a period of revival the Liberal Democrats took 62 seats.

Blair continued in office for two more years before finally handing over to the ever-impatient Gordon Brown in June, 2007. He had been Labour's longest-ever serving Prime Minister, and the only one ever to win three consecutive general elections. The timing of his departure, if coincidental, was impeccable. During the previous seven years, ever since Gordon Brown had waved farewell to Prudence, the country had indulged itself in an orgy of borrowing, affecting all credit purchases but, more than anything, mortgages for property. In an uncanny rerun of the eighties, all lending restrictions had been lifted by the lenders themselves. Mortgage applicants found themselves able to raise loans to five or six times their annual salary (instead of the two-and-a-half of traditional borrowing). In many cases no proof of earnings was requested. House prices responded accordingly, doubling in four years from the year 2000, then continuing to rise until houses were worth three times their pre-2000 values. The Bank of England looked on benignly as it did not include house price inflation in its main statistics, the Retail Price and Consumer Price Indices. Headline inflation figures remained low. Those who had watched the 1990s house price crash – and memories seemed extremely short amongst media commentators – shook their heads in disbelief.

However by the autumn of 2007, the chickens had started to come home to roost. The lending banks – for the most part, demutualised former building societies – no longer relied on their depositors to fund lending, instead tapping the international money markets to vastly increase their lending power. The problem of unsuitable mortgages was most severe in the United States, where millions of so-called "sub-prime loans" had been issued to borrowers who had little hope even of financing the first few monthly repayments. As the nature and scale of sub-prime lending began to become clear, fear entered the financial markets and international credit dried up. Suddenly the big British lenders were unable to roll over their loans.

One of the first institutions to fail was Northern Rock, a former building society based in Newcastle. It became the first British bank to suffer a bank run in 150 years as queues of customers formed outside its doors, desperate to get their money out, in September 2007. It had to be taken over by the Bank of England. However it was not alone – the other main mortgage banks had followed the same business model, and they in their turn also failed – the Halifax, largest of them all (called HBOS since its merger with Bank of Scotland); the Bradford and Bingley; the Alliance and Leicester. Then came the turn of the retail banks, led by the Royal Bank of Scotland under Sir Fred ("the Shred") Goodwin. This bank had expanded enormously and had agreed the takeover of the Dutch bank ABN Amro, fifteenth-largest bank in the world, in the biggest banking takeover in history. RBS collapsed and the government had to step in to save it. One of Britain's other big banks, Lloyds TSB, was then urged by Gordon Brown to take over the collapsing HBOS; this it did, only to discover that its due diligence had not been good enough. It did not realise what it had bought, and in its turn it had to be rescued by a partial government takeover. So banks and former building societies which had been household names for generations collapsed, one after another. The stock market followed, the Footsie index falling from a peak of over 6700 in 2007 to 3500 two years later. The large American investment banks Bear Stearns and Lehman Brothers went under, and the major American home lenders and even insurance companies suffered the same fate as their British equivalents.

The subsequent recession caused unemployment to rise sharply, though the peak of 2.5 million was well below the 1990s level, despite silly press talk of "the worst recession since the Great Depression". House prices fell nationally by 20% even though the Bank of England held interest rates at near-zero levels.

It was certainly a very bad time to take over as Prime Minister, as Gordon Brown discovered. He took a lead internationally in organizing emergency measures to prevent a systemic international economic failure, but the electorate regarded him as the man who was responsible for the boom in the first place. After three years in office, Brown was obliged to call a general election in May 2010. The result was a win for the Conservatives under their new leader, David Cameron. They took 306 seats to 258 for Labour, 57 for the Liberal Democrats and 29 for the minor parties. The Conservatives therefore had no overall majority and needed a coalition partner. The Liberals, again with a new young leader, Nick Clegg, were in a position to select either main party in a beauty contest. Traditionally closer to Labour, this time they realised that only a minority wanted Labour and especially Brown to continue in office. Unwilling to be chained to a corpse, they made an agreement with the Conservatives. David Cameron became the first old Etonian Prime Minister since Douglas-Home, and Nick Clegg his deputy.

The new team had many similarities. Cameron was educated at Eton and Brasenose College, Oxford, and was 43 years old. Nick Clegg, the same age, was educated at another top public school, Westminster, then at Robinson College, Cambridge. The new Chancellor, George Osborne, slightly younger at 39, could look back on an education at St Paul's, another top London public school, and Magdalen College, Oxford. The new administration was not expecting an easy ride, as it was widely recognised that a dose of austerity and retrenchment was required after the mad binge of the "noughties", and that this would mean higher taxes and a long, painful pull away from recession; but none of this seemed to worry Cameron. Osborne quickly introduced a budget designed to start paying off the vast increase in government debt which had built up in the financial crisis. The standard rate of VAT, which had stood at 17.5% since 1991 and had then been reduced to 15% as an emergency measure to stimulate the economy in late 2008, was increased to 20%. Plans were put in hand to cut back public sector employment and pensions, both of which had become inflated during the boom years.

*   *   *   *

Looking back over the period since the end of the Second World War, it is clear that Britain had overall done well. It had been one of the great slices of luck internationally to have been born and brought up in the UK in this period. Contrast the lot of the typical full-time male worker in the United States, where the distribution of wealth is very uneven. Over the forty years to 2011, adjusted for inflation, he had seen no increase in his earnings. This catching-up process is still going on, in Britain and the rest of western Europe, and is one of the great stories of these 65 years. American per capita gross domestic product is still significantly higher than in the UK – as much as a third higher on some figures, but this is nothing like the golden era of the fifties in the USA. Contrast also two of the so-called great successes of recent years - China, where average GDP per capita is still only one-tenth of the US figure, and India, one-twentieth. Despite the angst which it caused at the time, the loss of the Indian part of the British empire was a problem for the Indians, not for the British. The same can be said for the African countries which demanded their own independence in turn. Of the colonies given their independence by Britain after the war, the only ones to make real progress the modern world have been Malaysia, Singapore and Hong Kong.

Appendix 1 – The French Wars – a Summary

Particularly if you happen to be French, it sometimes seems that the English have been almost perpetually at war with France, their traditional enemy, but only a casual inspection of the facts shows that these wars fell into distinct phases, and there have been long periods when there were no wars. From the accession of William the Conqueror in 1066 until the death of King John in 1216, the English monarchy was in any case very much an Anglo-French enterprise, based first on the Duchy of Normandy, then later on the French territories inherited by Henry II and his wife Eleanor of Aquitaine. French was spoken at court, and French wars were based largely on the French territories. King John lost all his provinces in northern and central France, remaining in possession of only Calais and Gascony. After his time, there was simply less to fight about, as the King of France controlled most of the territory which was easily accessible to him.

In 1242-3, Henry III fought a campaign in Gascony, and this was followed in 1295 by a war of four years under Edward I following disputes which arose in this same region of France. Apart from these two small wars, there was no major fighting between England and France during all the time from 1216 until the outbreak of the Hundred Years War in 1336, which started when Philip VI of France invaded Gascony. Once started, this war assumed a different character from previous wars. The English kings regarded themselves not as (rebellious) vassals of the French king, but as legal claimants to the French throne. The Hundred Years War lasted intermittently until 1453, when all English possessions in France, apart from Calais, had been lost to the French.

From 1453 until 1689 – 236 years – there were no major wars with France. The simple reason for this is that, having given up claims to French provinces permanently, the English had no reason to fight the French. Two monarchs, Henry VII (1485-1509) and James I (1603-1625), founders of the Tudor and Stuart dynasties respectively, deliberately eschewed foreign wars. There were short wars against the combined French and Scots towards the beginning and end of the reign of Henry VIII (1509-1547) in which the Scots were the chief sufferers. Under the reign of Mary I (1553-1558), Calais was finally lost (1558), a terrible blow to the English. Mary's successor Elizabeth I (1558-1603) was never able to regain it as she had problems enough of her own with the Spanish (including the Armada) and the Irish.

Formally declared wars on land may have been few, but informal wars at sea were another matter. Throughout the sixteenth and seventeenth century, English seamen would regularly attack a foreign vessel or even fleet if they thought it was a fight they could win. The victims were at first mainly the Spanish but there were also many engagements with the French, the Dutch and the Portuguese. Some of the famous English sailors of the Elizabethan period including Sir John Hawkins and Sir Francis Drake were little better than pirates. The Dutch were equally aggressive and indeed there were three full-scale wars with the Dutch navy in the second half of the seventeenth century.

When William III, Stadtholder of the United Provinces, came to the English throne in 1689 by virtue of his marriage to Mary, daughter of the deposed James II (1685-1688), everything changed, because the English king once again had important continental possessions to defend against the French, and the wars between England and France resumed immediately. These were continued into the next reign, that of Queen Anne (1702-14), when the War of the Spanish Succession dominated the entire reign. This war stemmed from an alliance of several European powers against France, in order to stop the French king inheriting the kingdom of Spain. It produced for England one of its most famous generals, John Churchill, created Duke of Marlborough, and is notable as the first important occasion when the English fought not only the French, but the Germans as well, as the Catholic Bavarians had taken the side of the French.

During the eighteenth century, a new consideration was the extension of both English and French colonial possessions in the Caribbean Sea, North America, India and elsewhere which had taken place by this time. This meant that there was new ground to fight over. Hence there was a series of important wars in the eighteenth century both on the traditional battlegrounds of Europe, in the Americas and in India. These included the Seven Years War (1756-1763) which won much of the European-settled area of North America for the English, and the War of American Independence (1775-1783), which lost it again.

The French Revolution of 1789 set off a long war starting in 1793 as the European powers sought to put down the revolutionary ideas emanating from France. With one break these wars lasted until the final defeat of Napoleon in 1815. The French Revolutionary and Napoleonic Wars were very unusual for their length. A normal war of the eighteenth century would run for about seven years. After that time, one or both sides had simply run out of money to pay for the war, so there would be a peace. However, by the 1790s, England – or Britain, as it had become – had undergone its Industrial Revolution, and its new economy boomed. At the same time the British never attempted to maintain a large and expensive army of home troops in Europe, preferring to subsidize the Prussians and others against Napoleon. The longest campaign of the war, the Peninsular War in Spain and Portugal, did involve troops from Britain, but not on the scale of the armies in the field on the eastern front.

The defeat of Napoleon in 1815 marked the final end of the French wars, as there has been no other in the two hundred years which followed. Why did the wars end? Probably because the French had had enough of them. After 1870 there was in any case a much greater threat than England – the newly united Germany.

In fact a state of war was replaced by a series of alliances, notably to fight the Russians in the Crimean War (1853-6) and the Germans in the two world wars of the twentieth century. Nevertheless this apparent harmony was shattered during the Second World War when, after the fall of France in 1940, its Vichy government became the effective allies of the Germans. The British then found themselves fighting the colonial French, notably in Syria and at Dakar in Senegal.

Appendix 2 – List of English Monarchs from Alfred

Saxon and Danish
Alfred 871-899
Edward the Elder 899-925
Athelstan 925-939
Edmund I 939-946
Edred 946-955
Edwy 955-959
Edgar the Peaceable 959-975
Edward 975-979
Ethelred the Unready 978-1013-1016
Sweyn Forkbeard 1013-14
Canute 1016-1035
Harold I 1035-1042
Hardicanute 1042
Edward the Confessor 1042-1066
Harold II 1066

Norman
William the Conqueror 1066-1087
William Rufus 1087-1100
Henry I 1100-1135
Stephen 1135-1154

Angevins (Plantagenets)
Henry II 1154-1189
Richard I the Lionheart 1189-1199
John 1199-1216
Henry III 1216-1272
Edward I 1272-1307
Edward II 1307-1327
Edward III 1327-1377
Richard II 1377-1399

Lancaster and York
Henry IV (Bolingbroke) 1399-1413
Henry V 1413-1422
Henry VI 1422-1461
Edward IV 1461-1483
Edward V 1483
Richard III 1483-1485

Tudors
Henry VII 1485-1509
Henry VIII 1509-1547
Edward VI 1547-1553
Mary I 1553-1558
Elizabeth I 1558-1603

Stuarts
James I 1603-1625
Charles I 1625-1649
Commonwealth and Protectorate 1649-1660
Charles II 1660-1685
James II 1685-1689
William III 1689-1702 and Mary II 1689-1694
Anne 1702-1714

Hanoverians
George I 1715-27
George II 1727-60
George III 1760-1820
George IV 1820-30
William IV 1830-1837
Victoria 1837-1901

Saxe Coburg, Windsor
Edward VII 1901-1910
George V 1910-36
Edward VIII 1936
George VI 1936-52
Elizabeth II 1952-

Appendix 3 – Prime Ministers

1721 Robert Walpole	Whig
1742 Spencer Compton (Lord Wilmington)	Whig
1743 Henry Pelham	Whig
1754 Duke of Newcastle	Whig
1756 Duke of Devonshire (Wm Cavendish) Aka Marquess of Hartington	Whig
1757 Duke of Newcastle	Whig
1762 Earl of Bute	Tory
1763 George Grenville	Whig
1765 Marquess of Rockingham	Whig
1766 William Pitt the Elder (Earl of Chatham)	Whig
1768 Duke of Grafton	Whig
1770 Frederick Lord North	Tory
1782 Marquess of Rockingham	Whig
1782 William Petty FitzMaurice, Earl of Shelburne	Whig
1783 Duke of Portland	Whig
1783 William Pitt the Younger	Tory
1801 Henry Addington	Tory
1804 William Pitt the Younger	Tory
1806 Lord William Grenville	Whig
1807 Duke of Portland	Tory
1809 Spencer Perceval	Tory
1812 Robert Jenkinson, Lord Liverpool	Tory
1827 George Canning	Tory
1827 Frederick Robinson, Viscount Goderich	Tory
1828 Duke of Wellington	Tory
1830 Charles, Earl Grey	Whig
1834 William Lamb, Viscount Melbourne	Whig
1834 Duke of Wellington	Tory
1834 Robert Peel	Cons
1835 Viscount Melbourne	Whig
1841 Robert Peel	Cons
1846 Lord John Russell	Whig
1852 Edward Stanley, Earl of Derby	Cons
1852 Earl of Aberdeen	Cons
1855 Viscount Palmerston	Whig
1858 Edward Stanley, Earl of Derby	Cons
1858 Viscount Palmerston	Lib

1865 Lord John Russell	Lib
1866 Edward Stanley, Earl of Derby	Cons
1868 Benjamin Disraeli	Cons
1868 William Gladstone	Lib
1874 Benjamin Disraeli	Cons
1880 William Gladstone	Lib
1885 Marquess of Salisbury	Cons
1886 William Gladstone	Lib
1886 Marquess of Salisbury	Cons
1892 William Gladstone	Lib
1894 Earl of Roseberry	Lib
1895 Marquess of Salisbury	Cons
1902 Arthur Balfour	Cons
1905 Sir Henry Campbell-Bannerman	Lib
1908 Herbert Asquith	Lib
1916 David Lloyd George	Lib
1922 Andrew Bonar Law	Cons
1923 Stanley Baldwin	Cons
1924 Ramsay MacDonald	Lab
1924 Stanley Baldwin	Cons
1929 Ramsey MacDonald	Lab then Nat
1935 Stanley Baldwin	Cons
1937 Neville Chamberlain	Cons
1940 Winston Churchill	Cons
1945 Clement Attlee	Lab
1951 Winston Churchill	Cons
1955 Anthony Eden	Cons
1957 Harold Macmillan	Cons
1963 Sir Alec Douglas-Home	Cons
1964 Harold Wilson	Lab
1970 Edward Heath	Cons
1974 Harold Wilson	Lab
1976 James Callaghan	Lab
1979 Margaret Thatcher	Con
1990 John Major	Con
1997 Tony Blair	Lab
2007 Gordon Brown	Lab
2010 David Cameron	Con

Appendix 4 – Genealogies

I - The Kings of the House of Egbert

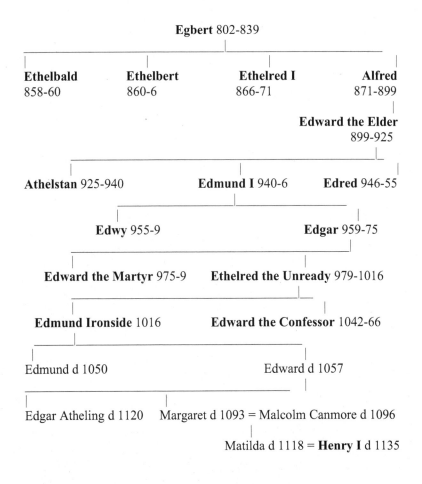

Egbert 802-839

Ethelbald 858-60 **Ethelbert** 860-6 **Ethelred I** 866-71 **Alfred** 871-899

Edward the Elder 899-925

Athelstan 925-940 **Edmund I** 940-6 **Edred** 946-55

Edwy 955-9 **Edgar** 959-75

Edward the Martyr 975-9 **Ethelred the Unready** 979-1016

Edmund Ironside 1016 **Edward the Confessor** 1042-66

Edmund d 1050 Edward d 1057

Edgar Atheling d 1120 Margaret d 1093 = Malcolm Canmore d 1096

Matilda d 1118 = **Henry I** d 1135

II - Danes

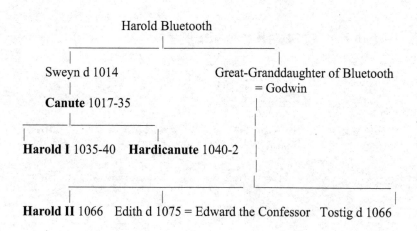

III - The Norman Kings of England

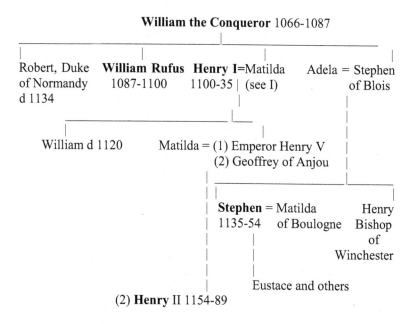

William the Conqueror 1066-1087

Robert, Duke   **William Rufus**   **Henry I**=Matilda   Adela = Stephen
of Normandy   1087-1100   1100-35 | (see I)   of Blois
d 1134

    William d 1120   Matilda = (1) Emperor Henry V
                              (2) Geoffrey of Anjou

                    Stephen = Matilda   Henry
                    1135-54   of Boulogne Bishop
                                         of
                                    Winchester

                            Eustace and others
      (2) **Henry** II 1154-89

IV - The Kings of Scotland 1034-1214

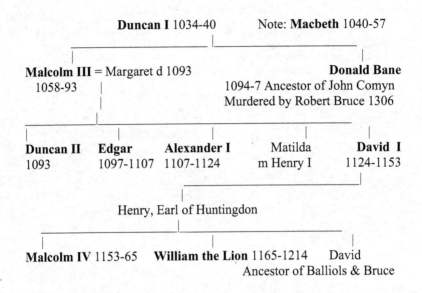

Duncan I 1034-40   Note: **Macbeth** 1040-57

Malcolm III = Margaret d 1093   **Donald Bane**
   1058-93   1094-7 Ancestor of John Comyn
                                  Murdered by Robert Bruce 1306

Duncan II   **Edgar**   **Alexander I**   Matilda   **David I**
1093   1097-1107 1107-1124   m Henry I   1124-1153

Henry, Earl of Huntingdon

Malcolm IV 1153-65   **William the Lion** 1165-1214   David
                                   Ancestor of Balliols & Bruce

V - Earlier Angevin Kings 1154-1272

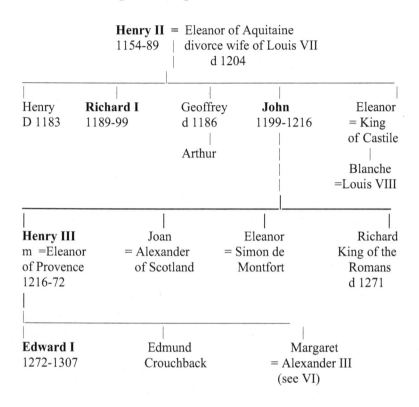

Henry II = Eleanor of Aquitaine
1154-89 | divorce wife of Louis VII
| d 1204

Henry	**Richard I**	Geoffrey	**John**	Eleanor
D 1183	1189-99	d 1186	1199-1216	= King
				of Castile
		Arthur		
				Blanche
				=Louis VIII

Henry III	Joan	Eleanor	Richard
m =Eleanor	= Alexander	= Simon de	King of the
of Provence	of Scotland	Montfort	Romans
1216-72			d 1271

Edward I	Edmund	Margaret
1272-1307	Crouchback	= Alexander III
		(see VI)

VI - Kings of Scotland 1153-1286

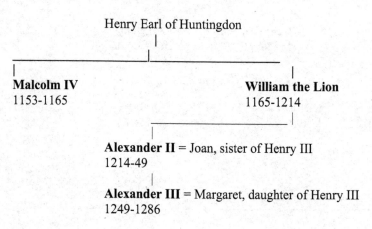

Henry Earl of Huntingdon

Malcolm IV
1153-1165

William the Lion
1165-1214

Alexander II = Joan, sister of Henry III
1214-49

Alexander III = Margaret, daughter of Henry III
1249-1286

VII - Kings of France 987-1285

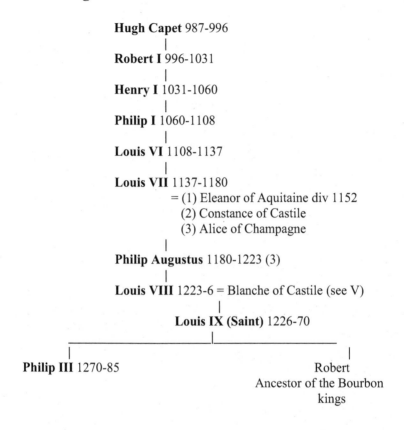

Hugh Capet 987-996
|
Robert I 996-1031
|
Henry I 1031-1060
|
Philip I 1060-1108
|
Louis VI 1108-1137
|
Louis VII 1137-1180
      = (1) Eleanor of Aquitaine div 1152
         (2) Constance of Castile
         (3) Alice of Champagne
|
Philip Augustus 1180-1223 (3)
|
Louis VIII 1223-6 = Blanche of Castile (see V)
|
Louis IX (Saint) 1226-70

Philip III 1270-85   Robert
                    Ancestor of the Bourbon
                          kings

VIII - Kings of France 1270-1422 and the claim of Edward III

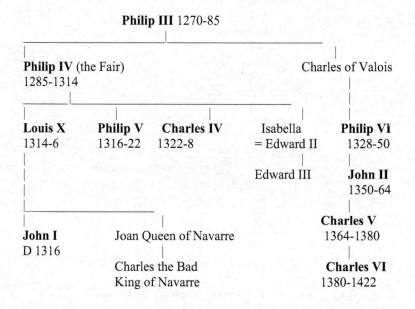

Philip III 1270-85

Philip IV (the Fair)
1285-1314

Charles of Valois

Louis X
1314-6

Philip V
1316-22

Charles IV
1322-8

Isabella
= Edward II

Edward III

Philip VI
1328-50

John II
1350-64

John I
D 1316

Joan Queen of Navarre

Charles the Bad
King of Navarre

Charles V
1364-1380

Charles VI
1380-1422

IX - The Houses of Lancaster and York

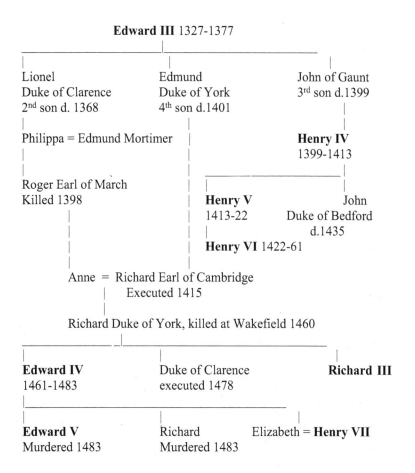

Edward III 1327-1377

Lionel	Edmund	John of Gaunt
Duke of Clarence	Duke of York	3rd son d.1399
2nd son d. 1368	4th son d.1401	

Philippa = Edmund Mortimer

Roger Earl of March
Killed 1398

Henry IV
1399-1413

Henry V
1413-22

John
Duke of Bedford
d.1435

Henry VI 1422-61

Anne = Richard Earl of Cambridge
Executed 1415

Richard Duke of York, killed at Wakefield 1460

Edward IV
1461-1483

Duke of Clarence
executed 1478

Richard III

Edward V
Murdered 1483

Richard
Murdered 1483

Elizabeth = **Henry VII**

Note: the first son of Edward III was Edward, the Black Prince, father of **Richard II** 1377-99

Appendix 5 – Main Wars from 1337 to 1953

Hundred Years War 1337-1453, divided into: Edwardian War 1337-1360; Caroline War 1369-1389; Lancastrian War 1414-1429

War of the Roses 1455-1485

French/Scottish War 1513-4

French/Scottish War 1542-7

Spanish War 1587-96

Civil War 1642-9

First Dutch War 1652-4

Second Dutch War 1665-7

Third Dutch War 1672-4

War of the Grand Alliance/League of Augsburg 1689-97

War of the Spanish Succession 1702-1714

War of Jenkins' Ear 1739-42

War of the Austrian Succession 1742-8

Seven Years War 1756-63

War of American Independence 1775-83

French Revolutionary War 1793-1802

Napoleonic War 1803-1815

First Afghan War 1838-42

First Opium War 1839-42

Crimean War 1853-6

Second Opium War 1856-60

Second Afghan War 1878-80

Zulu War 1879

First Boer War 1880-1

Second Boer War 1899-1902

First World War 1914-18

Second World War 1939-45

Korean War 1950-3

Appendix 6 – United States Presidents

1789	George Washington	No party
1797	John Adams	Federalist
1801	Thomas Jefferson	Dem/Rep
1809	James Madison	Dem/Rep
1817	James Monroe	Dem/Rep
1825	John Quincy Adams	Dem/Rep
1829	Andrew Jackson	Dem
1837	Martin Van Buren	Dem
1841	William Harrison	Whig
	Died after 32 days in office	
1841	John Tyler	Whig
1845	James Polk	Dem
1849	Zachary Taylor	Whig
	Died after 16 months in office	
1850	Millard Fillmore	Whig
1853	Franklin Pierce	Dem
1857	James Buchanan	Dem
1861	Abraham Lincoln	Rep
	Assassinated by John Wilkes Booth	
1865	Andrew Johnson	Dem
1869	Ulysses Grant	Rep
1877	Rutherford Hayes	Rep
1881	James Garfield	Rep
	Assassinated by Charles Guiteau	
1881	Chester Arthur	Rep
1885	Grover Cleveland	Dem
1889	Benjamin Harrison	Rep
1893	Grover Cleveland	Dem
1897	William McKinley	Rep
	Assassinated by Leon Czolgosz	
1901	Theodore Roosevelt	Rep
1909	William Taft	Rep
1913	Woodrow Wilson	Dem
1921	Warren Harding	Rep
	Died in office	
1923	Calvin Coolidge	Rep
1929	Herbert Hoover	Rep

1933	Franklin Roosevelt	Dem
	Died in office	
1945	Harry Truman	Dem
1953	Dwight Eisenhower	Rep
1961	John Kennedy	Dem
	Assassinated by Lee Harvey Oswald	
1963	Lyndon Johnson	Dem
1969	Richard Nixon	Rep
	Resigned	
1974	Gerald Ford	Rep
1977	Jimmy Carter	Dem
1981	Ronald Reagan	Rep
1989	George Bush Snr	Rep
1993	Bill Clinton	Dem
2001	George W Bush	Rep
2009	Barrack Obama	Dem

BIBLIOGRAPHY

Archaeology of the British Isles, Andrew Hayes, Batsford 1993

Iron Age Britain, Barry Cunliffe, Batsford 2003

Prehistoric Europe, ed. Barry Cunliffe, Oxford University Press 1997

I Claudius, Robert Graves, Penguin 1953

Claudius the God, Robert Graves, Pengiun 1954

Roman Britain, Peter Salway, Oxford History of England 1a 1981

Britain AD, Francis Pryor, Harper 2004

Barbarians, Terry Jones, BBC Books 2007

The Ecclesiastical History of the English People, Venerable Bede, Penguin Classics 1990

The Age of Arthur, John Morris, Phoenix Giant 1973

Celt and Saxon, Peter Berresford Ellis, Constable 1995

The Origins of the British, Stephen Oppenheimer, Robinson 2006

Blood of the Isles, Brian Sykes, Bantam Press 2006

Catastrophe, David Keys, Arrow 1999

1066 and all that, W C Sellar & R J Yeatman, Methuen 1991

The English Language, David Crystal, Penguin 2002

Keith Feiling, History of England, Macmillan 1950

Eleanor of Aquitaine, Alison Weir, Jonathan Cape 1999

The English Settlements, J N L Myres, Oxford University Press 1989

In the Footsteps of Robert the Bruce, A Young and M Stead, Sutton 1999

Arthur's Britain, Leslie Alcock, Classic Penguin 2001

The Tribes of Britain, David Miles, Phoenix 2005.

Scotland, the History of a Nation, Magnus Magnusson, Harper Collins 2001

Medieval England, Edmund King, Tempus 2001

Francis Drake, John Cummings, Phoenix 1995

A Brief History of the Normans, Francois Neveux, Robinson 2008

Marlborough, John Hussey, Weidenfeld & Nicholson 2004

Maritime Supremacy 1588-1782, Peter Padfield, John Murray 1999

Maritime Power 1788-1857, Peter Padfield, John Murray 2003

Maritime Dominion 1852-2001, Peter Padfield, John Murray 2009

A Short History of England, Cyril Ransome, Longmans Green 1903

Wellington, Elizabeth Longford, Abacus 1972

Napoleon and Wellington, Andrew Roberts, Weidenfield and Nicholson 2001

Napoleon, Paul Johnson, Phoenix 2002

William Pitt the Younger, William Hague, Harper Perennial 2006

The Dynasties of China, Bamber Gascoigne, Robinson 2003

English History in the Nineteenth Century, David Thomson, Penguin 1950

English History in the Twentieth Century, David Thomson, Penguin 1981

Robert Peel, Douglas Hurd, Phoenix 2007

The Making of Modern Britain, Andrew Marr, Pan 2009

The Western Front, Richard Holmes, BBC, 1999

The Second World War, Winston Churchill, volumes 1-6, Cassell 1948

The Second World War, RAC Parker, Oxford 1989

Winston Churchill, Martin Gilbert, Mandarin 1993

A History of Modern Britain, Andrew Marr, Pan 2009

The Course of my Life, Edward Heath, Coronet 1998

The Time of my Life, Denis Healey, Penguin 1990

The Path to Power, Margaret Thatcher, Harper Collins 1995

The Downing Street Years, Margaret Thatcher, Harper Collins 1993

The Autobiography, John Major, Harper Collins 2000

Blair, Anthony Seldon, Simon & Schuster 2005

INDEX

Ashley-Cooper, Anthony (William IV) see Shaftesbury

Bucharest 325

Buchenwald 368

Buckingham, Edward Duke of (Henry VIII) 160

Buckingham, George Villiers, Duke of 190, 192-4, 214

Buckingham, George Villiers, second Duke of 214, 216

Bulge, battle of the 364

Bunker's Hill 257

Burgoyne 257

Burgundy, Charles (the Bold), Duke of 149

Burgundy, Duke John of (Henry IV) 145

Burgundy, Philip Duke of (Henry V) 146, 148

Burke, Edmund 256-7, 259, 266

Burleigh, William Cecil Lord 174, 177, 182-3

Burma 289, 304

Burns, Robert 262

Burton, Richard 302

Busaco, battle of 274

Bush, President George W 411

Bute, Lord 254-5

Butler RA 375, 381

Bye Plot 187

Byng, Admiral 243, 252

Byrhtnoth 63

Byron, Lord 3277, 283

Cabal 214-6

Cabot, John 156

Cade, Jack 147, 258

Cadwallon 50

Caedwalla 51

Caesar, Julius 20-1, 25-27, 98

Calcutta, Black Hole of 252

Cavendish, Lord Frederick 301

Cawnpore 295

Caxton, William 155

Ceawlin 44-5, 51

Cecil, Robert 183, 187, 189, 190

Cenwahl of Wessex 51

Cerdic 39, 40

Cerdic of Elmet 49

Cetswayo 301

Chaim, Ernst 370

Chalgrove Field, battle of 201

Chamberlain Joseph 310

Chamberlain, Neville 341, 345-6, 349-50

Chanak Crisis 338

Charge of the Light Brigade 293

Charlemagne 52, 84, 130, 287

Charles 1 187, 192-204

Charles II 81, 211-221, 233

Charles II of Spain 234

Charles V of France 133

Charles V of Spain 157, 159, 160, 164, 167, 171, 173

Charles VI of Austria 248

Charles VI of France 143, 145-6

Charles VII of France 146

Charles, Archduke and Emperor 235, 240

Charlotte, Princess 282

Charter of Henry I, 80

Chartists 288, 293

Chaucer, Geoffrey 133, 137

Chelmsford, Lord 301

Chesapeake Bay, battle of 258

Dunkirk 350

Dunning 257

Dupleix, Joseph 251-2

Durham Report 2989

Durham, Lord 287

Dutch War (1652-3) 206-7

Dutch War (1664-6) 213-4

Dutch War (1672-4) 215-7

Dyer, Brigadier-General 338

Dyrham 44

East India Company 188, 251, 256, 259-60, 269, 289, 296

Easter Rebellion 323

Ecclesiastical Commission 223, 225

Eden, Anthony 343, 346, 349, 375-7, 380

Edgar Atheling 66, 68, 71

Edgar the Elder 61

Edgar, King of Wessex 62

Edgehill, battle of 200

Edington, battle of 58

Edith Swan-Neck 67

Edmund, Earl of March 142

Edmund, Saint, King of East Anglia 57

Edmund, son of Ethelred 63

Edmund, son of Henry III 110

Edric Streona 55, 63

Education Act (1870) 299

Education Act (1891) 303

Education Act (1902) 311

Education Act, Butler's 369

Edward I 110, 112, 114-22

Edward II 123-8, 134, 139

National Debt 231-2, 244, 265

National Economic Development Council 380

National Health Service 369, 373, 410

National Incomes Commission 380

National Insurance Act 310

National Socialists (Nazis) 339, 342, 347, 367-8

NATO 372

Navarino, battle of 283

Navigation Act (1652) 207, 214, 238

Nazi-Soviet Non-Aggression Pact 346

Nelson 267-70

Nennius 33, 40

Nepal 289

Nero 26

Neuve Chapelle, battle of 320

Neville, Cecily 150

Neville, Richard see Warwick king-maker

Neville's Cross, battle of 130

New Deal 342

New Guinea 304

New Orleans, battle of 276

New York 213, 217, 257-8

New Zealand 289

Newbury, first battle of 201

Newbury, second battle of 202

Newcastle, Duke of 245, 248, 251-2, 254

Newcastle, Marquess of 201-2

Newgrange 12

Newton, Isaac 214, 225-6, 232

Ney, General 272

Nicholas I, Tsar of Russia 294

Parker, Matthew, Archbishop of Canterbury 175
Parliament Act (1911) 311
Parliament, Addled 190
Parliament, Bad 133
Parliament, Barebones 207
Parliament, Good 133, 139
Parliament, Houses of 296
Parliament, Short 197
Parma, Duke of 179-81
Parnell, Charles 301
Parr, Katherine 164, 168
Pasha, Enver 321
Passaro, battle of Cape 243
Passchendaele 327
Paterson, William 232, 238
Patrick, Saint 45-6
Patton, General 363, 365
Paul I, Tsar 268
Paulinus 49
Paulus, General von 359
Peace Pledge Union 344
Pearl Harbour 356
Peasants Revolt 128, 139
Pedro, King of Spain 132
Peel, Robert 281-2, 284, 286, 288, 291-2
Peking 295, 305
Pelagius 35
Pelham, Henry 245, 248, 250-1
Penda King of Mercia 50-2
Penicillin 369
Penn, William 213